T◉TAL
AIRGUNS

TOTAL AIRGUNS

The complete guide to hunting with air rifles

PETE WADESON

SWAN·HILL
PRESS

First published in the UK in 2005
by Swan Hill Press, an imprint of Quiller Publishing Ltd
Reprinted 2006, 2007

British Library Cataloguing-in-Publication Data
  A catalogue record for this book
  is available from the British Library

ISBN 978 1904057 38 3

The information in this book is true and complete to the best of our knowledge.
All recommendations are made without any guarantee on the part of the Publisher,
who also disclaims any liability incurred in connection with the use of this data or
specific details.

Printed in China

Swan Hill Press

An imprint of Quiller Publishing Ltd
Wykey House, Wykey, Shrewsbury, SY4 1JA
Tel: 01939 261616 Fax: 01939 261606
E-mail: info@quillerbooks.com
Website: www.countrybooksdirect.com

Contents

Pete Wadeson is one of Britain's most highly regarded airgun hunters, and is also an established shooting correspondent and photo-journalist. As a lifelong shooter and outdoorsman with over twenty years' experience of hunting with all manner of sporting air rifles and firearms, Pete has amassed a wealth of practical and technical experience. He has emerged as the foremost contemporary authority on hunting with air rifles.

He regularly contributes to sporting magazines such as *GunMart*, *Shooting Sports*, *Shooting Times*, *Sporting Gun*, *Airgunner*, *Airgun World* and others, including several angling publications.

In the writing of *Total Airguns*, his first full-length book on the subject, Pete has combined all his practical field experience and shooting know-how to produce the most comprehensive reference work ever written on the hunting of live quarry with air rifles.

Foreword

I didn't by any stretch of the imagination grow up in what you could term a rural area. Even so, it was considered the norm, when you reached your teenage years that you'd be given your very own air rifle as a birthday or Christmas present. It was in a sense a rite of passage, an acceptance by your parents and elders that you were growing up. In today's climate of rising crime and widespread anti-gun hysteria fuelled by confused news media, it seems difficult to believe that those days ever existed. I'm sure many hunters of all shooting disciplines can identify with that.

Looking back to carefree times 'blatting rats' with a break-barrel air rifle at the side of the canal with my mates, I would never have envisaged the day would come when I'd be writing a comprehensive book on the now-serious discipline of hunting with an air rifle.

As I've now been given this opportunity I hope that what follows in these pages will be seen by the sensible non-shooting public – as well as my friends, associates and peers in the shooting fraternity – as a considered and well-informed book on the sport. Because that's what it is – a sport. Additionally, there are many occasions when an air rifle of suitable power is a very effective tool for pest control, being widely used by professionals worldwide.

In this book I hope to dispel a few half-truths and wrongheaded ideas, and clear up what is often nonsensical rubbish written as little more than fanciful hunters' tales. Truth to tell, even so called airgun-hunting 'experts' like myself return empty handed, or only get the chance of one shot in exchange for a lot of effort. That's the way it goes.

But even though there is a certain element of luck in being successful, there are many ways to help put luck on your side. Put in the practice, time and preparation and it will put the odds in your favour. In the following pages I hope that I'll help others to achieve just that.

Air rifle hunting is amongst the most challenging and demanding of the shooting sports

Introduction

In over two decades of sporting shooting I've used a great variety of sporting guns and calibres. Although I enjoy the challenge of taking wood pigeon on the wing with a shotgun, long-range rimfire work on rabbits, or fullbore foxing, rarely is the feeling of achievement greater than when I've taken a precision shot with a 12ft lb air rifle.

As it's such a demanding but rewarding form of shooting, it's hardly surprising that many who are newcomers, and even those not so new to airgunning, eventually try their shooting skills against live quarry. But you need to know the law, not only pertaining to hunting with airguns but governing their ownership and general use. A Chapter devoted to The Law as it currently stands can be found at the end of this book; but as legislation can change it's advisable to keep yourself up to date by checking regularly with the relevant government departments – primarily the Home Office and DEFRA – and of course the latest literature on the subject. Books are few and can date quickly as regards the law, but the shooting magazines keep their readers constantly briefed on legal changes.

I must emphasise that it's the responsibility of every individual to know the law pertaining to hunting with airguns. It's no use having the appropriate kit, even if you have somewhere suitable to hunt over, if you don't know the can do's and can't do's. Ignorance of the law is never accepted as a defence by the police or the courts. All reputable shooting organisations have the appropriate legal guidelines available on request, so do make a point of requesting them and – most importantly – reading, memorising and adhering to them.

It is also the responsibility of those wanting to hunt to be able to recognise the quarry species that are deemed suitable for control with air rifles. All the legitimate pest species that airgun hunters are allowed to shoot are listed in the 1981 Wildlife & Countryside Act. Amongst these listed and appropriate to control with an air rifle with a power of 12ft lbs are rabbits, squirrels, brown rats, magpies, crows, rooks, jackdaws, jays, wood pigeons, feral pigeons and collared doves. There are some others you can add to that list, such as house sparrows and starlings, though at present it looks a certainty that these two species will become exempt from the list. So though I do make occasional mention of the birds in other areas of the book, I'd wager the cocky little sparrow will earn a deserved reprieve because it isn't nearly as common as it once was. The culling of the starling I feel has been in a 'grey area' for a long while in relation to the 'general licence' and therefore only pest controllers with the correct legal paperwork will be allowed to curtail their numbers. Then again, they are 'geared up' to do the job far more effectively than any airgun hunter.

Other species of birds that stay on the list at the time of writing this book are herring gulls, greater and lesser black-backed gulls and even waterfowl such as moorhens and coots – the last two being a genre of duck so only when in season.

The major quarry species will be dealt with in due course, but the main aim here is to illustrate and introduce when and why the precision accuracy of a good-quality air rifle is more suitable than the out-and-out stopping power produced by a live-round sporting rifle. First, we need to take into consideration that the kill-zone of smaller vermin deemed appropriate for control with an air rifle is relatively small. In many cases the hunter needs to place a pellet into a target area not much larger than a 10p piece, and in some cases such as when taking a head shot this kill-zone is even smaller. An obvious scenario where an air rifle is the optimum tool, and preferable to a more powerful firearm, is when shooting inside buildings such as barns, or around outbuildings. A more high-powered rifle could cause major damage and the possibility of dangerous ricochets.

The airgun hunter using a 12ft lb air rifle can often operate safely and legally in locations where a live-round firearm user can't. Many areas of open land just aren't deemed suitable by the police for a rimfire rifle to be used, but that doesn't mean that the area will be devoid of vermin. Often it's quite the opposite, as these places become havens for all manner of unwanted pests. Another example is in dense woodland, when squirrels or corvids such as magpies and jackdaws are the quarry. In many such situations you can't use a shotgun due to the damage that many shot pellets can do to the trees. A rim-fire is totally out of the question due to the high power of the bullet, but a pellet fired from a 12ft lb air rifle has more than enough stopping power for tree rats and egg-thieving corvids. Some of the most challenging shots I've taken have been against these species. To be able to 'thread' a pellet through a maze of branches and twigs to hit a kill zone on quarry such as these takes precision – precision accuracy from the hunter and precision performance from the air rifle. And there's the rub! We're already at the stage where you'll have realised that not only must the equipment you're using be up to the job, but also your shooting skills. These include accuracy with the rifle, and fieldcraft in your approach to the quarry. Accuracy comes with practice – an absolutely essential part of the airgun hunter's learning curve. This and fieldcraft will both be dealt with in detail later on.

If your rifle and marksmanship aren't up to the job, then you simply won't be successful. Fortunately, as regards rifles, modern air rifle engineering technology has come along in leaps and bounds in very recent years. Indeed, a newcomer to the sport can almost be spoilt by the fact that today's best air rifles, particular the precharged pneumatic (PCP) types, almost shoot themselves, needing only a helping hand or two to place the pellet exactly where it needs to go – the all important kill-zone. The air rifle is a precision tool that can do what many other sporting guns are just incapable of doing, which is to afford the shooter pinpoint accuracy without the 'overkill' factor that can be produced when using live-round sporting rifles. It's worth bearing in mind that quarry such as rabbits – a species obviously suited to the hunter using a rimfire or an air rifle – can often be encountered well within 50yds. Within that range only 4ft lbs of energy at the target is necessary to dispatch it cleanly, so long as the pellet strikes with precision within the kill-zone. Precise, low-power pellet placement is often better than greater power with poorer accuracy. But I must emphasise that using an air pistol for hunting is a definite no-no. The legal power limit for a non-licensable air pistol in the UK is 6ft lbs at the muzzle, and at typical quarry ranges that is simply not powerful enough. The only exception is at extremely close quarters, when you need to dispatch small vermin in a live-catch trap or administer a coup de grace.

But why even carry an air pistol when the first shot from the rifle should have made a clean kill? Follow-up shots, if needed, are easy and quick to fire from the rifle, too – especially one with multi-shot capability.

Choosing an air rifle from the vast selection of those available and suitable for hunting can be a daunting prospect. Assuming you're already familiar with shooting air rifles, then beginning hunting can be a simple matter of transition, but even before choosing a gun we've not only got to decide upon the calibre – a topic which will be dealt with in the Ammo section and individually in Quarry Files – but the power source the air rifle uses to propel the pellet. Essentially you have a choice of three types – either a traditional spring-powered rifle, one that's gas ram powered, or a precharged pneumatic powered (PCP) rifle. Whichever you choose, as you're going to be hunting you will need a rifle that's capable of a muzzle energy of at least 11ft lbs – i.e. as close as possible to, but still comfortably within, the 12ft lb legal limit. Anything more powerful requires a Firearm Certificate.

Choosing an air rifle from the vast selection available and suitable for hunting can be a very daunting prospect

As regards choosing an air rifle I'm deliberately not naming too many specific models, with the exception of certain landmark rifles and those that I feel are particularly suitable for hunters. Some models have already been consigned to the history books, and a few may not still be available by the time you come to read this. But I do mention certain rifles because of the classic status they've achieved, which deserves credit and recognition. I also mention those established airgun manufacturers who have rifles in their stable that are particularly well worth considering, because with so many different models being launched each year, I don't want what I've written to be out of date before it's even published. So, when I refer to particular air rifle features, you'll be able to look for those in the market place at any time and choose a rifle from among those in production, which suit your needs and your budget.

I've taken the same approach when I mention optics manufacturers and suppliers of any shooting related accessories and products.

Here I must mention the fact no book concerning itself with hunting with an air rifle would be complete without giving credit to the late John Darling. His book *Air Rifle Hunting* is the seminal work on the subject, and one that certainly help pave the way for our sport to be more widely accepted. It's packed with solid information that is as relevant today as it was when it was first published in the late 80's. A book now of 'classic' status that has stood the test of time. The air rifle hunter with a thirst for knowledge would be well advised to read it at their earliest opportunity.

Now – time to look at air rifles, their power sources and workings, the pro's and con's of each type, and the necessary skills of the hunter who uses them successfully. Read on – and welcome to the wonderful world of airgun hunting!

A basic but good quality 'springer' is easily capable of kill-zone accuracy out to 30yds

Chapter 1
Power Sources, Actions and Options

You can't see it, but boy can your quarry feel it. Of course I'm referring to the 'ghost in the machine', the unseen, untouchable force that sends the pellet towards the target – Air!

Yes, that's all it is, the air we breathe, albeit compressed to a pressure level that can project a small piece of lead effectively out towards a given target. How it's compressed is a matter of mechanics and the way we produce that to use in airguns is by compressing a metal spring in a cylinder or pre-charging an air reservoir that in turn lets out a measured (regulated) amount of the compressed air for each and every shot. Of course there is the gas-ram, but this again is a version of the compressed power source, but this time using a gas filled strut instead of air compressed by other mechanical means. All of these 'systems' will be explained in detail as we come to them.

As it currently stands by law, the muzzle energy a legal limit air rifle can produce is 12ft lbs, but go 'on ticket' by obtaining a Firearms Certificate (FAC) and you can go all the way up to 30, 50, 80ft lbs and beyond.

However, most UK airgun hunters are content – and rightly so – with 'off ticket' rifles that are capable (in the right hands), of effectively and humanely dispatching quarry comfortably right out to 50yds, but more sensibly and generally, hunting ranges should be kept down to within 30-35yds. So that's what we can do with the power that's available and attainable, but how in the first place do we get that 'charge' into the gun?

Incidentally, an air pistol should never be used for hunting as it is too low powered. Also, when CO_2 (Carbon Dioxide)powered air pistols and rifles came 'off-ticket', meaning you no longer needed an FAC to own and use one, a whole industry devoted to their manufacture seemingly sprang up overnight. A glut of low powered plinking pistols were launched, virtually all chambered to fire standard .177 airgun pellets or steel BBs. Some even have the ability to shoot both. However, the CO_2 power source was always capable of producing power up to the 12ft lb legal limit in rifle format. You guessed it. A few companies actually specialise in producing rifles that use the power source suitable for hunting. Using CO_2 as a propellant results in the rifle having recoilless attributes similar to the precharged pneumatic powered (PCP) air rifles without the need for a cumbersome divers bottle or manually operated stirrup-type pump to refill. But, fact of the matter is, that although CO_2 has come a long way there are still only a very few notable rifles that use this propellant to produce the required power for hunting. Whether they'll increase or decrease in popularity as time progresses is anybody's guess, but personally I feel these rifles and their 'powerplant' will always be on the fringes of the hunting scene.

Now to the most traditional and arguably most popular of power sources – the spring and piston.

Spring Powered

Basic spring air rifle design hasn't really changed much in well over a century, although there have been huge advances in materials, technology and production methods. To get power from the spring, it first needs to have power put into it by manual compression – and that means you. There are three types of mechanisms (or 'actions', as they're known), for compressing the rifle mainspring. The most common is where the barrel itself 'breaks' at the breech (break-barrel) and is used as a lever to compress the spring, or with fixed barrel rifles a separate pivoting lever is used, either under the barrel (under-lever), or on the side of the rifle (side-lever).

By far the most popular action for a spring powered air rifle, or 'springer' as it's often affectionately termed, is the break-barrel. And as manufacturing processes are now much more advanced, a good quality break-barrel's accuracy potential is equal to most comparably priced fixed barrel rifles operated by under-lever or side-lever action. The mainspring – irrespective of action type – sits inside the piston, which is dragged back and locked in place by the trigger sear when the rifle is cocked. This in itself is just one of the reasons a trigger mechanism is a high-stress component in a spring gun and the mainspring will, with time and use, eventually wear. This is because the spring can weaken resulting in the rifle having a drop in power. Incidentally it's worth explaining a few trigger terms as you'll come across them in magazine articles that may help you decide which rifle to buy. Firstly the sear or sears are internal trigger components that fit together when engaged, to hold back the rifle piston or hammer, depending on the power source. The term 'creep' refers to the drag felt when pulling the

trigger, usually due to ill-fitting or shoddily made internals. A 'two-stage' trigger has two movements before firing. The first stage takes up the pressure from the blade to the first engagement of the unit, whilst the second stage 'trips' the sear and the rifle fires. A 'single-stage' trigger has only one movement and that's the one that fires the gun. But virtually all-hunting rifles are now graced with top quality two-stage units with plenty of facility for adjustment to suit the shooter's requirement. And these terms apply to triggers on all air rifles, regardless of power source.

Now we go back to the mechanics of the spring piston power source. When the trigger is released (i.e. pulled) the spring uncoils, driving the piston forward in the compression cylinder, which forces accumulated air in the cylinder through a transfer port, which in turn propels the pellet along the barrel. The size and strength of the spring, together with the air volume in the compression cylinder or chamber, are the major contributing factors to the power of the rifle. The main drawback of the spring-powered airgun is recoil and piston bounce on firing, created by the piston rebounding as it comes to the end of its travel. This can manifest itself as muzzle flip, which is the main 'mechanical' reason for pellets going off target.

The break-barrel – still the most popular action for a spring powered air rifle

Virtually all hunting air rifles have two-stage adjustable trigger units

A muzzle weight can be fitted and to a certain extent the addition of a silencer also helps, but more importantly, accurate shooting with a spring-powered air rifle needs the shooter to adhere to a few basic set rules of good gun handling. Shooting stances and styles will be outlined as we come to the relevant section.

Although the spring piston powered air rifle has its downsides it certainly has its plus points. Firstly, it's completely self-contained and therefore a highly portable power source. As the rifle is cocked for each and every shot, this removes the possibility that the rifle will fail to operate due to the lack of propellant, because the compressed air is created manually. However, this means one shot is often your lot, as mechanical multi-shot rifles become fewer by the year. The famous British gun manufacturer BSA gave us the Goldstar while Theoben – whom you'll hear much more of later – gave us their own uniquely 'power sourced' SLR88, another rifle which was eventually and very sadly discontinued. However, it was upgraded and brought back into production to become known as the SLR98.

Even though the springer is so popular, it must be appreciated that piston bounce and resultant recoil are its biggest drawbacks. These combine to affect accuracy but thankfully can to a large extent be managed by proper gun handling. Also, these mechanical reactions resulting from the spring piston action can be reduced further by having the rifle tuned by a specialist gunsmith. Amongst other things, this entails piston heads being correctly sized, the mainspring being replaced with a special one, spring guides being fitted – that is if they aren't already in the rifle – and all internals being polished to reduce friction, with all metal to metal parts being suitably lubricated upon reassembly. Although the firing cycle can be smoothed out with tuning, recoil will still to some extent always be a by-product of the spring powered airgun.

An ingenious gun designer, John Whiscombe, actually designed a springer that uses opposing springs and pistons so that when one travels forwards, the other travels back to cancel out the effects of the first piston's forward motion. Whilst it doesn't completely negate recoil, the Whiscombe Rifle, first seen in the mid 1980s is probably the lowest recoiling springer ever produced, and it deserves to be mentioned for its sheer ingenuity of design. Similarly the Ken Turner-designed Air Arms TX200SR ('SR' denoting Semi Recoil-less) had a radical action that moved and locked forward on cocking the under-lever. When fired the action actually slid backwards in the stock, drastically reducing recoil. It worked on what was fittingly termed a 'sliding sledge' system. Its success as a Field Target rifle surely proved that it was a very effective design, and as I hunted with one very successfully for many years, it's one I have fond memories of.

Even a basic, but good quality 'single' spring powered rifle is still easily capable of kill-zone accuracy out to 30yds, and dealing with most scenarios the airgun hunter will encounter. Incidentally, it's worth mentioning here that a side effect of recoil can be scope damage. The recoil from a spring powered rifle can be more vicious in jarring the scope than a sporting firearm firing powder-loaded cartridges. Some early models of air rifle became notorious as reticle (or 'reticule') breakers. Whatever the term, these are the cross hairs in a scope and they would actually break and be seen to split into

The Theoben Rapid 7 – this rifle single-handedly began the popularity of multi-shot PCP air rifles in hunting

two, or actually fall down into the eye bell. Of course a lot of this is now history, not only due to the fact that reticles are now often etched onto glass rather than actually being fine, hair-size metal wires; but the firing cycle of virtually all modern day production springers is far less harsh than in the early days of the sport. More likely, the annoying trait known as 'scope creep' can occur. This involves the scope moving slightly in its rings or on its mounts each time the rifle is fired. But scope creep can easily be overcome by using good-quality scope mounts, a special dampened mount such as the DampaMount™ designed by British gun manufacturers Theoben, or by using scope mounts with an arrestor peg or arrestor block. But as I said previously, springers aren't the 'clangy' unruly beasts they once were, and scope creep should be – and to a large extent is – a thing of the past. That is assuming that scopes have been correctly fitted in quality scope mounts. Correct scope mounting is a subject that will be dealt with in a later section.

The other factor of a spring powered air rifle that needs to be considered is internal spring noise on firing. This is usually caused by the spring uncoiling, and can usually be remedied by a spring guide. Most established airgun manufacturers combat internal mechanical noise in their own ways. Special synthetic bearings and spring guides have all been used, but it was the British manufacturers Webley & Scott who were the first to develop what they termed 'Silent Spring Technology' to help combat the problem. Basically, a sleeve for the mainspring was fitted inside the compression cylinder, and various bushes and synthetic parts were fitted to the piston head. The result is that the metal-to-metal contact is kept to a minimum, and all areas are lubricated to ensure a smooth firing cycle. Indeed, this is one of the reasons why, if you're serious about hunting and still want to use a springer, I'd have no hesitation in advising you to have your rifle specially tuned.

By far the most famous custom house for tuning is the now legendary Venom Arms. Originally founded and once led by the individualistic gunsmith Ivan Hancock, his team are responsible for inventing the now legendary Lazaglide tune – first seen and given to the classic powerhouse, the German manufactured Weihrauch HW80 and its under-lever cousin the HW77. At the time of writing (2004) Venom are allied with Webley and ensconced within the Webley & Scott factory environs as the Venom Custom Shop. The 'top tune' for a springer is now known as the Lazahunter. Again, it comes down to internals being specially worked upon or completely changed, but no matter what is done, it's all with the objective of smoothing out the firing cycle. Another highly reputable gunsmith is Tony Wall, a man who stamped his signature seal of worthy 'tune ups' and custom wizardry working from Sandwell Field Sports in the West Midlands. In fact, I'm sure that his rifles will eventually gain the same recognition as many Venom creations. Mr Wall kindly proffers sound advice on looking after your rifle, and this can be found in the chapter on General Maintenance. And as a 'springer fan' himself, it's no surprise that his words lean heavily towards how best to keep the humble springer working as it should.

While on the subject of 'springers' it's worth noting that if you require open sights (or 'irons' as they're affectionately known) then you'll undoubtedly be buying a spring powered air rifle. Open sights are extremely useful if your shooting involves close range work or indoor shooting on targets such as rats and feral pigeons, where in many cases they will be too close for accurate aiming with a scope. Wherever possible I champion the use of open sights; and for specialist shooting scenarios you can even use a pair of see-thru scope mounts, which allow you to fit a scope to the rifle but also take aim by sighting under the scope and through the mounts, which have a cut-out for open sights when required – in effect, offering the shooter the best of both worlds. But don't worry, because these will be fully detailed in due course.

If you're wondering why I haven't yet addressed muzzle report (the sound the air makes on firing, as it exits the barrel's muzzle behind the pellet) as a downside of the springer, it's because all rifles, regardless of their power source, produce muzzle report. Obviously some produce less than others and the only way to overcome this is to choose a rifle with a silencer, or one that can be fitted with a suitable sound moderator. Again, this is a subject we'll deal with later. So, with the spring and piston power source explained, we move on to the next alternative.

The Gas-Ram

While there are many companies which manufacture spring powered air rifles and indeed PCPs, there is only one that manufactures rifles that use the gas-ram power source. This is Theoben Engineering (or, as they're now known, Theoben Limited) and they're able to do this chiefly because they invented the system, which is heavily protected by patents. The gas-ram gives the shooter the benefits of a faster lock time (i.e. the time it takes for the pellet to leave the muzzle after the trigger is 'squeezed') and, due to its design, the rifle has far less recoil on firing. So how does it work?

When Theoben decided to throw away the spring and develop the gas-ram system they revolutionised manually operated air rifle technology. Over the years they've refined the system and used it in under-lever and also the more traditional break-barrel action rifles. The gas-ram, as the name implies, uses gas pressure to drive the piston. Specifically, this is a 'slug' of compressed nitrogen in a unit similar to the shock absorber of a car, and it replaces the traditional spring and piston compression cylinder. Recoil is reduced to an absolute minimum by means of a floating inertia piston, which is fitted to the gas-ram. This slides independently behind the main piston, travelling fractionally to the rear after the main piston has been propelled forward. Thus, when the main piston reaches the end of its stroke on firing and starts to 'rebound' from the wall of compressed air it has created after firing, the floating inertia piston behind it catches up. As it meets the main piston a split second later in the firing cycle, it reduces piston bounce and thereby radically reduces recoil.

On most Theoben gas-ram rifles you'll notice the letters HE. This stands for High Efficiency, and a very fitting term it is, too. However, the rifle doesn't stop there, with just using nitrogen gas and 'secondary pistons', because the company later developed a special piston crown to complement the design. This is the Zephyr piston crown, which has air channels cut in it so that air can escape and isn't trapped where it could cause the unwanted piston bounce.

The first production rifle to use the early form of this system was the Theoben Sirocco, produced in 1982. By the mid 1980s Theoben were going full tilt on the gas-ram system and releasing the first higher-powered, FAC rated version of the Sirocco, and, more importantly, they'd also redesigned the system. This process of development continues, as Theoben have made further advances in the design, all intended to help reduce recoil and smooth out the firing cycle. All in all, the gas-ram is a very credible alternative to the springer, and useful in the sense that the rifle can actually be 'de-tuned' to suit your shooting requirements. Generally, I'd advise you don't meddle with the gas-ram; but if you're shooting rats or feral pigeon indoors at close range, it's handy to have a rifle that can be slightly 'de-powered'. The company can do this for you, and it's a matter of unscrewing the valve at the back to let out a proportion of the gas in the internal strut. Obviously, a few irresponsible shooters have been tempted to go the other way and try to pump in more power. All this will do, if you're not specially qualified and the components changed to cope with FAC power levels, is render your gun illegal if you don't have the required certificate, and in addition the valve will quite literally blow out the back of the mechanism.

While the level of accuracy that can be achieved with a 'gas-ram' rifle is very impressive, there certainly is a knack to firing one, just as there is for a spring powered rifle. Granted, the gas-ram doesn't have the recoil of a springer, but it does have a definite movement on firing. Rather than feeling the shudder that certain full-power springers can deliver, it has some slight muzzle flip which is felt as a nudge in the shoulder. This could never be termed unruly or unmanageable, but it is a side-effect of the power source that needs to be taken into consideration when shooting.

As we've seen, the major benefits of the gas-ram powered air rifle are radically reduced recoil and faster lock time, and, like the springer, the rifle is self-contained so that you cock it for each and every shot. Little wonder, therefore, that the company's compact carbine, the Fenman, has been a long-standing favourite with hunters since its introduction back in 1993, and it is yet another high-quality rifle I've hunted extensively with over the years. The company has now slimmed down its range of rifles, but the 'rammers' still feature heavily among their hunting rifles. Some, like the break-barrel action Eliminator, are being produced specifically to give FAC-liable power levels of 22ft lbs.

We now come to the most talked-about power source of recent times, the precharged pneumatic system.

The Precharged Pneumatic

Before going any further it's worth mentioning that the technology of the precharged pneumatic (PCP) air rifle, or more precisely the basic concept of the system, dates back to the eighteenth century when some rifles used a large ball-shaped reservoir as a vessel for storing powerfully compressed air. Apparently this is one of the reasons why acquiring and enforcing exclusive patents on PCP technology is so difficult.

Lets examine the workings of the PCP air rifle and outline what happens when you charge and fire one. The fact that you need to pre-charge, or 'fill' the rifle with compressed air is what deters many shooters from acquiring their first PCP. Many just don't want the hassle of storing compressed air

Selection of magazine systems – virtually all multi-shot PCP air rifles use a removable rotary-feed magazine

bottles, but it's far easier now to own and run a PCP than ever before. You can fill them with a manually operated pump, but I'd only advise using these for small top-ups. Filling a reservoir from empty would leave you with arms like Pop-Eye's. Alternatively, a small charging unit with a compressed air bottle, gauge and hose doesn't cost the earth, and will only need re-filling dependant on the amount of shooting you actually do.

For obvious safety reasons, I must mention that using compressed air does require the shooter to adhere to a few basic rules:

• Always ensure the connector and filler point are clean, dry and free from grit or dirt.
• Only use diver's-quality compressed air, and never under any circumstances use anything else.
• Once connected to a diver's bottle, open the valve slowly to allow the air to flow smoothly into the rifle's reservoir. If using a pump, start the pumping slowly.
• You should never over charge a rifle above the manufacturer's specified fill pressure. Once this is achieved, close the air valve on the bottle and open the bleed screw to let excess air discharge from the connecting hose. Then disconnect the probe or bayonet snap connector from the rifle's filler point.
• Where applicable, always refit the front cover cap to keep the inlet valve protected from dirt and grime.

Next, a word on the fill pressure of PCP air rifles. Each gun's manual will clearly state a maximum fill pressure and also a recommended but lower fill pressure. Obviously the former should never be exceeded, and if you do so, don't think that this will give more power. It won't, but will merely create a potentially dangerous situation. Also, the rifle will function, if it functions at all, much less efficiently. The recommended fill pressure is often given as the optimum charge for what is known as a 'flat power curve' of the charge and one that gives an optimum number of shots. It's worth noting that quite a few PCPs run that little bit sweeter on a lower fill pressure than on the one recommended.

You do get a few less shots, but usually you gain the benefit of a smoother, flatter power curve throughout the charge.

As regards the charging equipment itself, if your budget stretches you could treat yourself and purchase an electric compressor, which will pay for itself in the long run. However, a very handy feature of some PCPs is the fact that they use a detachable air reservoir or, as it's more commonly known, the 'buddy bottle'. Two examples of this are BSA's Superten and Theoben's 'classic' rifle, the Rapid 7. No matter what the make of rifle may be, if it uses a buddy bottle, this stores the compressed air, and when filled and screwed onto the rifle it becomes the on-board air reservoir. These bottles, when empty, can be taken to any good gun shop and re-filled, so you could in effect run this type of PCP without needing any charging gear. With a few spare pre-filled buddy bottles you'd never have an excuse for running short of air.

PCPs are split into two categories – unregulated and regulated. This refers to the fact that some rifles use a knock-open valve to dispense air to the pellet on firing, whilst others have an internal air regulator. Simply put, the knock-open valve literally 'knocks open' when the trigger is pulled, allowing a certain amount of air to pass through the transfer valve to act on the pellet. Alternatively, a PCP air rifle fitted with an air regulator 'meters' a measured amount of air to the pellet on firing. I'm sure you can realise that the latter results in a very consistent level of performance, and therefore these rifles are known for having better accuracy throughout the fill charge. However, regulated rifles can be more costly, and even so it's now argued that unregulated rifles, and even some classed as 'self regulating', are so well developed and designed that their inherent accuracy potential is far superior to the shooter's ability. So it follows that the benefit of the PCP is that you get a very high level of accuracy due to the rifle having no recoil.

Has it struck you yet what's been taken out of the mechanical equation? Yes, it's that dreaded phenomenon known as piston bounce. Simply put, that means there's no mainspring, no piston, and therefore no recoil!

When it comes to the PCP as a hunting tool, in many cases it's capable of being fitted with a magazine so you don't need to load a pellet manually for each and every shot. There are many single-shot PCP air rifles on the market, but if there's one area that has seen an unbridled upsurge of interest from both manufacturers and consumers it's the multi-shot precharged pneumatic hunting rifle. The ease of the 'cocking and cycling' operation means that at the 'throw of a bolt' another pellet can be ready to go, maximising the hunter's chances should the first shot miss. This bolt can be a short-throw bolt, a lever sited on the side of the rifle's action, or a cocking bolt positioned at the rear of the action block.

Another bonus of the PCP is that the rifle can be rested on a bipod, fencepost or similar static object to steady your aim. Try that with one of the other power sources and shots would fly wide and inaccurately.

Now to the disadvantages. Obviously the main one, which we've already dealt with, is the need for charging gear or access to a gunshop that provides a re-fill service. You also need to keep a check on the rifle so you don't run out of air while shooting. Many PCP rifles now have on-board, integrally fitted air pressure gauges. Whilst I personally feel these are quite handy, they should only be used as a guide. Before any hunting trip, top up the rifle to its required fill pressure so you're running your rifle at its optimum level of performance.

Pneumania – A Brief History

Few would argue that it's largely due to Daystate Ltd that PCPs have become so widely accepted, as they were the company that first began producing them in any number. Due to this, it's worth taking a brief look at the company's origins, and because of the importance and impact that precharged pneumatics have made on the hunting scene, I'll outline others when applicable who have helped popularise this power source in the UK.

Founded in 1978 by Don Lowndes, Jim Phillips, Ken Gibbon and Mike Seddon, Daystate first used the concept of a rifle with a precharged air reservoir to fire tranquilliser darts into animals for veterinary and game reserve purposes. Originally this was the sole reason they produced PCPs. As the company's reputation grew they received various enquiries from pest control operatives looking for a more efficient tool for vermin control than was generally available at the time. It soon became obvious there was a market for producing a precharged air rifle that would fire the more traditional lead pellet projectile. The major attraction was that a PCP air rifle would afford the shooter better accuracy due to the lack of recoil.

This resulted in the company producing the original Huntsman Midas, a landmark rifle which sowed the seeds for the power source to become more widely accepted. Daystate rifles quickly attracted the attention of target shooters and due to their accuracy these air rifles radically changed the face of Field Target (FT) shooting. Even so, the general public, and particularly specialist airgun hunters, are wary of change, and for almost ten years Daystate stood alone in trying to convince the shooters of the world of the potential of this new power source. However, there are other independent designers to be credited with popularising the power source, and one ingenious designer in particular – John Bowkett. Indeed, Mr Bowkett is a giant amongst airgun designers, and some of his designs are landmarks in airgunning history. His first mainstream creation was the Titan Manitou, now unfortunately

In the right hands, a silenced air rifle is a deadly, effective tool

defunct but still highly sought after on the used airgun market. More recently John has created award-winning rifles for BSA, the multi-shot Superten being one of the most notable. Prior to that he was 'pushing the envelope' of design and performance right from the beginning of his career as a gunsmith, and his involvement with this power source ran somewhat alongside Daystate's.

However, in the late 1970s, while Daystate were still developing a production PCP, John independently produced a rifle that used a side-lever to manually pump in enough compressed air to produce 12ft lbs of power for one single shot. In fact this was actually advertised in *Airgun World* as 'The World's First Single-Stroke 12ft/lb Pneumatic'.

By the late '80s, the airgun scene was fast becoming caught up in 'Pneu-Mania', with more and more gun companies producing pneumatic powered rifles. For the average airgunner, however, most were just too expensive.

There's no denying that this era was a very exciting time in the development of new precharged designs. As well as John Bowkett – whom you'll hear even more of soon – a man named Richard Spenser designed and produced the Air Logic Genesis, a rifle also capable of nearly 12ft lbs, but required a mechanical action for the air to be pumped in using a side-lever system.

Similarly, taking its charge from a single-stroke and again utilising a side-lever Graham Bluck invented the Dragon, to be marketed by Parker Hale, and this was the first mass-produced single-stroke pneumatic air rifle to hit the streets. But we're straying into mechanically operated pneumatics, which you'll hear a little more of later. In relation to the more familiar precharged guns, you can't even touch on this subject without paying tribute to Gerald Cardew. In particular no-one can ignore his development with John Ford of the company Sportsmatch, and what was to become the 'Rolls-Royce' of airguns, the Sportsmatch GC2. To this day many believe that this air rifle took the 'humble' airgun into a whole new era in construction, quality and accuracy. Even in the early '80s the gun cost £1000! Nor can we dismiss the genius of Mick Dawes, working in the West Midlands, who made the Brocock MDS. Although this is a rifle used purely for Field Target work, I mention it because it was Mick Dawes who, at the same time as a man named Barry McGraw (a nuclear physicist no less), was at the forefront of regulator design. For their work all manufacturers should be eternally grateful. Other names such as Joe Wilkins and his son Steve of Ripley Rifles, Steve Harper and Ken Turner, have all had a hand in some very innovative designs, many of which are still being produced. To this day rifles based on their designs are still considered amongst the finest of their kind. I could go on naming names, but as this isn't a detailed in-depth look at the history of the PCP I'll leave the thread here, apart from saying that many of those mentioned above also have worked on and helped develop spring powered rifles.

As for John Bowkett, it was around the early 1980s that he became involved with a company that was to become one of the most successful and prolific airgun makers of the 1990s, Titan Developments. At first, he carried on with a side-lever action design that was named the 'JB1' but eventually dropped this and concentrated on his first production 'pre-filled' pneumatic designs, which led to the development of the Manitou. This nifty air rifle virtually revolutionised the airgun industry, as it had a small lightweight action which was capable of giving a large amount of shots from a small amount of air, thanks to the clever internal valving set-up. In fact, the Manitou's valve design meant it was a unit that could be fitted with different sizes of barrels and air reservoirs. So solid a design is this that it carried through into the rifles produced since 2000 by Falcon Pneumatics.

It was in 1990 that the first multi-shot rifle appeared – the now legendary Theoben Rapid 7. This rifle slowly but surely heralded the start of a trend that was to change the face of airgun hunting. Indeed the Theoben Rapid 7 multi-shot was at one time the undisputed champion for hunters preferring not to have to reload for each and every shot. Such is the importance of multi-shot rifles in hunting that you'll see much more of them later on. Since the mid 1990s, with the onset of 'multi-shot mania', a whole new breed of magazine-fed rifles not only became available but also affordable.

This account of the development of the precharged pneumatic air rifle is, I believe, fully warranted, and much more detail could be added. But since this book is for the airgun hunter who is keen to go hunting live quarry, enough has probably been said to illustrate the importance of the 1980s–1990s period in relation to the development of the precharged pneumatic power source for hunting rifles. Over the years many other models of air rifles were produced, and just as many were discontinued. Most made way for better rifles to take pride of place on hunter's gun racks, and new developments still continue.

Now let's check out the particular reasons why the multi-shot PCPs have largely taken the lion's share of the airguns market – and devoured thousands of column inches in the specialist periodicals that are devoted to airgun shooting.

Benefits of the Multi-shot

The benefits of a multi-shot are obvious. No need to place a pellet onto a loading channel or in a barrel for each and every shot, because another shot is ready in an instant at the throw of a bolt. If you miss, this means you can often get a second chance before the quarry does a bunk. Some multi-shot rifles are in fact 'double-shot' models, and therefore not strictly what can be classed as multi-shots, as they only have a two-shot capacity. The first production rifle was the Webley Raider and this rifle, though not as popular, did at the time fill a market need.

So you can see that what was once mainly the chosen tool of the FT shooter made an easy transition from the target to the hunting field, as just as many hunters now choose a PCP. The obvious reason for this is the benefit of the power source, with its lack of recoil on firing, and consequently greater inherent accuracy potential. Couple this with the multi-shot facility and you have a very formidable combination.

The inherent advantages of a recoilless, consistent and accurate system was primarily recognised by Field Target shooters, whilst multi-shot options and lightweight carbines have latterly made PCP air rifles more popular with hunters. The main disadvantage of PCPs – the fact that they had a fixed air reservoir which had to be charged up fairly frequently from a compressed air power source, usually a diver's bottle – has more or less been overcome. Rifles fitted with regulators (air meters) can easily give a full day's shooting – from 100 to 200 shots – on just one charge of air, while hunting rifles have benefited from the introduction of small-ish, replaceable 'on-the-gun' buddy-bottle air reservoirs, which can quickly be replaced in the field for a full one, with the empty one to be refilled later.

The availability of a manual pump, capable of charging rifles without the need for a diving bottle, has also helped popularise PCPs in areas that had a few, if any, commercial compressed air sources. I recap this here as a reminder of how the PCP has become so widely accepted.

It's worth noting that apart from PCPs there are also a few pneumatic air rifles that use an inbuilt pump, operated by an under-lever, that allows the shooter to manually 'pump in' the air to the required compressed level for each shot. These have been with us a long time, the most famous being the American brands of Crosman and Sheridan. Whilst they have their uses, it's obvious why they'll never be able to compete with a dedicated PCP multi-shot hunting rifle. The exertion it takes to pump in the air makes the hunter a tad shaky. If you miss, you've no chance of getting a second shot ready. Need I say more?

I'm sure many airgunners never envisaged a time when we could class any PCP as a budget rifle. Well, that's certainly not the case today. Granted, they'll always be the more expensive option, but in terms of value for money, most single-shot PCPs offer an incredible amount of performance for your investment. If you can live without multi-shot luxury, there are many on the market that don't cost the earth. But, as mentioned earlier, you need to budget from the outset not only for charging equipment but also a set of optics, as no PCP has open sights. Unfortunately there's no avoiding this, and it's here that the price mounts up.

With airguns' power sources explained, you're now armed with enough information to be in a position to start making a considered choice. But before we do, what's the real situation as regards multi-shots, magazine systems and the landmark rifles they're used on?

Multiple Choice

All multi-shot rifles share a common factor – i.e. pellets are held in a magazine before the action cycles them into the barrel for individual firing. While the action is usually a bolt system, what differs is the type of magazine feed employed. This is most commonly a removable rotary magazine, but there are notable exceptions such as the Logun Rifle that popularised the straight-line or linear feed mechanism, and we mustn't forget the two-shot rifles that offer one quick back up shot. It's worth noting that although we're continuously reminded that hunting is a one-shot deal – and in part I'd tend to agree with that – in reality it is never that simple. In fact, I feel the majority of hunters who choose a PCP will choose a multi-shot option straight off. But how many shots do you want? Are two shots enough, or do you want as many 'back up' shots as you can get? As mentioned, it was Webley who first brought the two-shot to the public attention with the innovative Raider. Although this was the first of its type, all air rifles that have a double shot facility use a 'shuttle-type' mechanism. This is a straight or cylindrically shaped bar that holds both pellets. Once the first pellet is fired, and the bolt action cycled, the 'shuttle' magazine flicks over to one side to align the next pellet with the breech to be chambered for the next shot. It's as simple as that, and thus many hunters have found these rifles an attractive option to the more conventional, higher capacity magazine-fed guns.

If you want to 'do the double', several other manufacturers have pitched rifles into this arena. Whichever you choose, you'll immediately appreciate the benefits of that quick back-up shot, and many hunters agree they find it hard to go back to a one-shot rifle once they've experienced the ease of 'next shot' access – so you have been warned!

But by far the most popular are the multi-shots of higher capacity. The rotary magazines in the majority of rifles are either spring loaded to rotate, or are indexed around mechanically by the action once the magazine has been inserted into the rifle's action block and shots are fired. It's hardly surprising that the Theoben Rapid series of rifles utilises a rotary 'sprung' magazine, which we'll return to soon; but you can't mention rotary magazine systems without immediately thinking of the Swedish airgun guru, Fredrik Axelsson.

The Rotary Club

Virtually all multi-shot rifles use a removable rotary-feed magazine. This can either be the classic eight-shot drum magazine as first seen on the Webley Axsor model, the enclosed Perspex-fronted type as used by Theoben and Air Arms, or the metal Superten magazine and the ten-shot version that has been developed from it, and used on Daystate multi-shots.

Airgun hunters have a lot to thank Swedish gun designer Fredrik Axelsson for, because without his eight-shot 'Axsor' action there would probably have been far fewer rifles to choose from. For many established hunters their first move into using a multi-shot was due to the introduction of the Webley Axsor, the first UK creation to use this eight-shot drum. The rifle was launched in August 1997, and a carbine format model followed in 1999. Deluxe versions with high-grade walnut stocks and brass fittings were also available until production ceased early in 2000. All in all, it was a very effective and keenly priced rifle.

Some very well-established manufacturers have models in their range of high quality pre-charged rifles that use this magazine. It's quite a simple design, being little more than a removable circular drum-shaped eight-shot magazine that is loaded with pellets and clicks into the action, where it is held in place by a retaining pin. To load for a shot you simply cycle the action with a side- or rear-mounted cocking bolt for each shot until the magazine is empty. Then just remove the magazine, re-fill it or exchange it for a spare, pre-filled one, and you're good to go for another eight shots. It is a beautifully simple unit, and pretty well foolproof so long as it is kept clean and free from obstructions or fouling.

So which to choose? We could examine almost every one, but that's not my intention here. The mainstream specialist airgun shooting magazines are there for that. Suffice to say that it's very much up to the individual's choice, taste and budget.

There is another design of eight-shot magazine that must be mentioned. Although outwardly square in appearance it is still a rotary, removable unit, and is used on the Falcon multi-shot Raptor and Hawk options. Basically, everything essential that applies to the single-shot Falcon rifles still applies, but the 'multi-bird' Raptors have a single cocking lever that cocks, indexes the magazine around, and presses a pellet into position.

Rapid Fire

No in-depth book on air rifle hunting would be complete without giving due praise to the Theoben Rapid 7 and its variants. The 'Rapid' range of multi-shots is now legendary, and so entrenched in the development of hunting air rifles that it deserves to be looked at thoroughly. It may be named the '7' but it can run a 7, 12, or 17 shot magazine depending on the individual rifle's calibre. It deserves great credit, as this rifle single-handedly began the popularity of multi-shot rifles for hunting. Now available as an upgraded 'Rapid' it's still a very popular choice for hunters. Theoben have many admirers, and it's hardly surprising that the company seem set on continuing the theme. Another rifle that has seen them gain even more fans is the MFR – Multi Function Rifle. This is because it's designed to be used as a multi-shot, but can be converted to run as a single shot too. It's light, compact and goes back to using the company's original smaller 280cc air bottle. With a new slimline stock design and full bull-barrel silencer this rifle could well be seen as a new approach to the Rapid style. Even the company refer to this as the Rapid Mk3.

There's also a multi-shot, 'big wheel' magazine used on German gun manufacturing giants Weihrauch's first ever PCP air rifle. The HW100 model was launched in 2003 to much media praise, and caused quite a stir at the time. One feature of note was it dispenses with a traditional cocking bolt to use a cocking side-lever. Similarly actioned PCPs are available, and, once again, their level of popularity will be largely up to personal taste.

When we get to air rifles offering 10 or more shots per magazine, there are many others besides those in the Rapid stable. These include the BSA Superten and the Air Arms S410, both extremely popular rifles. This is not surprising, as they're affordable multi-shots and excellent, accurate hunting rifles. The 'Beeza' is a very workmanlike, sturdy workhorse; and although it's been around for some time, it's still hard to beat the Superten MkII for quality, efficiency, performance and value for money. Standard rifle, carbine and bull-barrel variants are available, and I'm sure there's more to come; but the base chassis around which it's built is a winner and will surely earn itself classic rifle status.

The Air Arms S410 arrived on the scene in June 2000 and quickly became one of the most 'punter popular' multi-shots. Spawned from the company's less successful S300/310 series, the rifle's slick alloy bolt action runs a conventional, removable rotary index-fed 10-shot magazine. It is certainly one of the more attractive rifles, and the well thought-out design makes the rifle a fast handling, very accurate performer, especially in the 'K' carbine version. It seems that even more variants will emerge in time.

As regards the 'tenners' from Daystate, I think many will agree that they'd stuck it out for long enough with the now-discontinued PH6 multi-shot model, and now they have gracefully conceded and produced a damn fine ten-shot. In fact not just one, but two very different rifles that utilise the same magazine. One is the more conventional, mechanical action X2 or 'X' series as there are variants of this rifle (more surely to come) and the other is the electronic Mk3. The fundamental difference is the fact that one runs mechanically while the other is electronically controlled for trigger and regulator. However, the magazine system is exactly the same for both, as is the cocking mechanism that runs it. Interestingly, these rifles can also be used as single-shots; but, as a hunter, I'd say why not take advantage of the firepower the multi-shot magazine feed gives you? At present Daystate look set to create several more, equally interesting designs in conjunction with other movers and shakers in the airgun trade.

Another rifle of note that uses the fixed rotary magazine system is the Ripley XL9, and what a very fine rifle this is, too. Where to start, except to say for many shooters this is the dream hunter, the rifle they aspire to own. Hand built by Ripley Rifles, the craftsmanship and engineering of the action alone is worth high praise. The stainless steel rotary magazine and cocking bolt are as close to perfection as you'll get, but as we're stepping over the £1000 barrier you'd expect nothing less. Fully regulated internals and the ability to reach FAC power levels of 40ft lbs and beyond comfortably mean that this rifle is a serious hunting tool. You can pretty much request whatever you want from the lads at Ripley, and it will be custom built and fine-tuned accordingly.

Before leaving the multi-shot options we must note that linear-feed magazine rifles are pretty thin on the ground. This is probably due to the fact that in-line magazine mechanisms were once notorious for jamming. However, a few companies have got it right, and the finest is Logun, particularly with the stylish Logun MkII Professional, which is an upgraded version of the original Logun Rifle as designed by Jim Hogan. It should come as no surprise that these fine rifles are also in the luxury price bracket.

So there we have it. The power sources, the actions, the magazines and the multi-shot options available, and most mentioned here are rifles I highly recommend. I'm sure many other new models and makes will come along, and we'll be just as impressed again. Perhaps, in time, many we now think unsurpassable will eventually disappear from the scene.

What to choose is largely an individual matter, but there's no denying that a multi-shot gives you many benefits and the ability to capitalise on hunting opportunities like never before. But just because you have those extra shots in hand at the throw of a bolt, remember that it's no excuse for letting standards slip, resulting in sloppy or bad shooting practice. Each shot fired should be taken with steady care and a good aim.

Chapter 2
Sighting Systems – Scopes, Scope Mounts, Scope Mounting and Alternative Hunting Sights

The vast majority of airgun hunters use telescopic sights – or 'scopes' as they're commonly known – for virtually all hunting applications. So it follows that almost all newcomers to the sport will opt to fit a set of optics to their very first air rifle. In fact, many air rifles, especially PCPs, have no 'iron sights' fitted as standard, so in these cases fitting a scope is a necessity.

Within this chapter you should find all the information you'll need to choose a scope that best suits your needs as a hunter. But remember that, like any consumer market, choosing a scope can be like stepping into a minefield. With such a huge selection available, and every company claiming their products to be better than their competitors', the decision is bound to be difficult. Even the experienced airgunner could well do with taking a little more time in choosing a new scope, and not just falling for the marketing strategies employed by all manufacturers. Scope mounts must also be considered, but this will be dealt with after we've waded through the quagmire of scope choice. First, however, a word or two about open sights.

Any Old Iron?

Open sights, or 'irons' as they're affectionately known, have been the standard and most basic form of sighting system on any gun for as long as they have been made. The basic idea is to align the target with your eye via a sight element towards the rear of the rifle and another near the end of the barrel. This should line up the bore of the rifle with the target, ensuring that you are sighting as close to the path of the fired projectile as possible – always assuming that the sights are set up correctly in the first place.

The benefits of open sights include quick target acquisition, because you have a very wide field of view, unlike a telescopic sight that 'tunnels' a more limited, narrowly angled field of view onto the target. Also, because 'irons' do not magnify the target, rangefinding isn't 'confused' by image-enlarging optics.

There are still many models of air rifle – all spring powered – that are fitted with open sights. These either consist of a post, bead or blade foresight positioned at the front end of the barrel, which is lined up in a U or V shaped notch or a target-style aperture (hole) in the rear sight assembly. (The rear sight unit is usually fitted onto the breech end of the barrel, or on the action body itself.)

See-thru mounts offer the shooter the best of both worlds

The rear sight will always be adjustable for height (elevation) and usually for windage too (i.e. from side to side), so they can be set for the range (zero distance) you require. Elevation and windage adjustments are catered for either by a set of thumbwheels – often numbered – or the adjusters can simply be just a simple screw and plate.

Setting Your Zero

A matter that needs tackling before we go any further is one that relates to all sighting setups and systems, and that is the setting of 'zero' or 'zeroing'. Zero is the term used to refer to a pre-set point (or distance) to which the sights have been adjusted so the pellet strikes the target to coincide with the centre of the scope's crosshairs – or, in relation to an open sight set-up, the point where eye, sights and 'strike point' on the target all line up. On a 'red dot' sight or the projected 'dot' of a laser sight, zero can also be adjusted, but there will be more on such specialised sighting systems later.

With open sights, a maximum zero and hunting range of 15yds is more often than not the accepted and recommended norm. This can be extended to 18-20yds if the open sights are good enough and your 'iron-clad' shooting is of a high enough standard. Because this sighting system is so forgiving at close to medium ranges (because pellet trajectory is flattest for the first 20 yds or so), you can set your sights at a zero of 12yds and then, providing you do not exceed a range of 20yds, you can literally aim 'bang-on' for all ranges in between – except perhaps for the very tiniest quarry targets.

Setting your zero with open sights is simple. Line the foreblade into the centre of the notch of the rear sight, place it over the target and have the top of the foresight element (blade, post or bead) level with the top of the rear sight. The object of accurate target shooting is to produce what is known as good groupings. A group or string of shots – usually five – is fired into a paper target and the grouping is determined by the distance measured on the target between the impact points of the most widely separated pellets in the pattern made by the shot string. For example, if this measured distance is 1½ inches between the two furthest pellets, then you have a 1½ inch group. These measurements are often taken from the outer edge of the pellet holes (because they are easier to measure) and are therefore called 'edge-to-edge' measurements, but for competition purposes they should really be taken from the centre of the pellet hole (often termed 'centre to centre' or 'c-to-c'). For hunting purposes it doesn't much matter how you take the measurements, as long as you always stick to the same method – 'edge-to-edge' or 'c-to-c'. And, of course, be consistent in getting good, tight groups.

To find out what maximum distance you can humanely hunt at, try shooting at paper targets set out at 5 yard intervals. The furthest target on which you can comfortably put a five shot group of approximately 1 inch or so should be your maximum hunting distance – and that applies to all sighting systems. Don't worry about measuring groups, but just draw a series of circles using a 2p piece as a template and aiming point. If your five pellets are within the 2p circle, you're on target.

Incidentally, the main problem you'll encounter with open sights for air rifle hunting is that the sights may actually obscure the target at longer ranges. This is the main reason why open-sight shooting should only be seriously considered for close range work. Whilst this makes open sights ideal for indoor shooting at rats and roosting feral pigeons, this range limitation immediately makes it apparent why a scope is such a necessary addition for the airgun hunter wanting to get the most from his rifle as regards maximum range – which nicely brings us to the subject of scopes.

Open sights are very useful for close range rat and feral pigeon shooting

Choosing a Hunting Scope

Scopes come in all shapes and sizes – small scopes, big scopes, thin scopes, 'fat' scopes, short scopes, long scopes – and that's before you add on the various different features that are offered. But considering there aren't an excessive number of individual component parts used in the construction of a scope, it's still a relatively complex piece of optical equipment.

THE ANATOMY OF A SCOPE

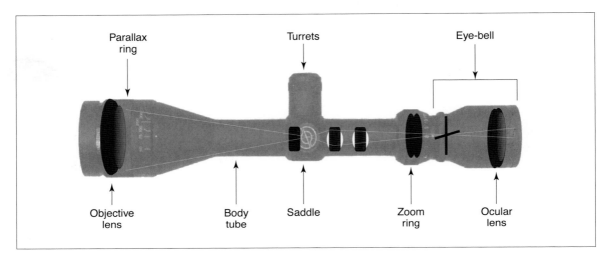

The main external features of a scope are the eye-bell (or ocular lens housing), the zoom magnification ring (if fitted), the main body or tube, the central 'saddle' or turret adjuster housing, the elevation and windage adjuster knobs, the parallax-adjusting ring (if fitted), the objective (frontal) lens bell, and, of course, the lenses and their coatings. It is logical that lens quality is of great importance, as lenses are responsible for gathering light and transmitting the sight image to your eye. Modern scope optics are coated for protection against the elements, and the scratches that can be caused by grit and dirt. They're often also specially treated with other coatings to achieve better light-gathering, more clarity, and a generally improved optical performance.

General Guidelines For All Scopes

Even relatively inexpensive scopes can be packed with eye-catching features, but the most important factors for any optic are lens quality and coatings. Good quality lenses and coatings will not give a distorted image, will maintain edge to edge clarity, and will be less affected by 'flare' (bright spots). They will also last a lot longer. A quality scope can last a lifetime, while poorer offerings can often be rendered useless in a relatively short time. Good glass will always be expensive, and with scopes you normally get what you pay for.

Apart from lens quality, other important things to look for are smooth operation of rings if fitted (front focusing or parallax ring, and rear focusing and 'zoom' or variable magnification rings), and a positive 'click-stop' movement for each increment of adjustment on the elevation and windage turrets. This is so that they only shift the reticle an equal and measured distance for each 'click' of the adjuster turret. They also need to 'hold zero', so they must not move once set.

Overall build quality is also important, especially when fitting to a spring/piston air rifle. The distinctive 'three way recoil' of a springer, already explained, has been known to wreck poorly constructed scopes. The internal mechanisms of all today's quality brand scopes are built to withstand a lot of use. If your scope sits on a recoilless PCP then it won't be subjected to the recoil that can be delivered to it by a spring or gas-ram powered air rifle.

When choosing a scope, have a clear idea of your own intended uses: check these particular points.

- How often will you be shooting? A hard-used scope will need to be well made and robust.
- Will you be shooting in many different locations at varying distances? If so, you may be better off with an adjustable magnification (zoom) scope.
- Do you do most of your shooting at a fixed range? If so, you may prefer a fixed magnification scope.
- Will your scope be mounted to an expensive precharged pneumatic or a springer at the cheaper end of the market? Obviously your scope should be priced to suit.
- Do you intend to do a lot of low-light shooting? You'll need a scope with good light-gathering capabilities, usually with a large objective lens.

All these questions and others will influence your choice, but once you've made up your mind what features you need, buy the best scope and mounts you can afford.

It's worth mentioning that one feature of a scope that many people overlook is its 'closest focus' distance. As the scope is being used on an air rifle and quarry can often be as close as 12yds or less, you need a scope that will focus down to that distance. Many scopes actually don't; but with the popularity of airgun shooting, and in particular of airgun hunting, on the increase, most quality scopes for airgun use will focus down to sight in on targets at fairly close range. If you intend to hunt regularly we now come to the two variables that you should consider. These are the light conditions, and the furthest range limit at which you expect to engage quarry.

The most popular scope specification for all-round hunting is the 3 – 9 × 40. Scope specifications are always written like this. The first two numbers relate to the range of magnifications the scope is capable of, and in this case it means the scope is a variable power scope from a low of 3 times magnification up to a maximum of 9 times magnification of the object you will be looking at. The last figure relates to the diameter (in millimetres) of the front (objective) lens. The importance of the size of the front lens will be dealt with later when we come to low-light or, as they're sometimes known, dawn-dusk scopes. As a general rule of thumb, the larger the front (objective) lens the more efficient at gathering light it will be. Therefore large objective lens scopes are the best choice for low-light conditions. It's worth noting here that the airgun hunter also has the choice of a fixed-magnification scope. At one time the little fixed-magnification 4 × 32 reigned supreme (even for FT) and was very popular. Look around and you'll still find these little scopes for sale, and if a basic model such as this appeals then – although it's a no-frills optic – it will suffice for a good deal of hunting work. In fact there are some fine 6 × and 10 × fixed magnification scopes around, but by and large they're manufactured for use on bullet-firing sporting rifles. There are a few that suit air rifles, and some of the finest fixed-magnification scopes also have large 30mm diameter body tubes (one-inch tubes are the norm) and side-wheel parallax adjustment – both very tempting for the newcomer, who might like the looks and macho appeal of these types of sights.

But before we get into more specialised areas of the market let's take a look at what the general airgun hunter will require. These are: a good sight picture; reasonable and practical magnification range; and a suitably-sized objective lens to give a good balance between field of view and light gathering. A fairly wide field of view (or width of view) is vital for target 'acquisition', which simply means the ability to find the target quickly in the area you are looking at through the scope. I know this may seem just plain common sense, but using a scope with a relatively narrow field of view, and trying to find the quarry in

There's a very varied selection of scope mounts to suit all rifles and fitting configurations

your sights quickly can be a nightmare, costing you time and missed shooting opportunities. A field of view 'angle' or measurement is often given in the scope's 'Tech Spec' sheet or on the box it was supplied in. If given as an angle, the higher the number means the wider the field of view. If given as a figure – say 30ft – this means the distance that can be seen from one side of the scope's image to the other at a range of 100yds. With variable magnification or 'zoom' scopes there will be two figures, corresponding to the fields of view at the lowest and highest magnification (for example, 30ft and 12ft). The higher the magnification of the scope, the narrower the field of view will be.

Build construction is another major feature you need to consider when buying a hunting scope. For most if not all of its active working life it will be exposed to the elements. Even on dry days it's surprising just how much the weather can throw at your equipment. Dampness, early morning dew and humid conditions can cause condensation build-up that can occur when shooting from dawn into daylight and vice versa. You'll notice the times you need to wipe both your lenses due to early morning dew, or the rear lens catching the moisture from your breathing. It's handy to carry a lint-free cloth or better still a few pads of soft tissue for cleaning the lenses.

Scopes are sealed from the elements, and you'll often see that they are termed 'nitrogen purged' to expel all moisture and air before the internals are nitrogen filled and sealed. The main areas where water or air could leak into the scope are around the front and rear lenses, any moveable adjustment rings such as zoom and parallax rings, and of course the turret adjusters. The first barrier to the elements for the turrets is the turret cover caps or dust covers. Not only are they there to prevent turret adjusters being accidentally knocked and therefore your zero being lost, but also just as importantly they offer a first line of defence against the elements. Their main duty is to offer resistance to dirt and grime, so always screw them snugly into place once you've set your chosen zero.

Personally, I wouldn't consider using a scope for hunting that didn't have turret cover caps. Certain models on the market that don't have cover caps use the so-called 'quick access' excuse, as if this was a bonus. Granted, there are some fine optics with side-wheel parallax adjustment that could well be used by a hunter who really knows his scope, but the possibility of a dial being inadvertently shifted is too great a risk to take when you're dealing in fractions of an inch, which mean the difference between a cleanly dispatched animal and an injured one. Target shooters can use these scopes, and certainly use them well, but once you've set your zero on your hunting scope you don't want to have anything that can in the slightest way affect this, or accidentally alter the precisely-set pellet impact point – i.e. the zero. Uncovered adjusters that can be rotated by hand, no matter how positive and secure they seem, will eventually get moved – either by being caught or brushing against clothing as you move, or even when the rifle is being put into and taken out of a gun bag. So be warned against the possible disadvantages of using this type of scope for hunting. But the good news is that specialist scopes with side-wheel adjustment and cover caps can be obtained, and they are worth looking out for when your shooting reaches a standard where you'd benefit from such a sophisticated optic.

As for the turrets themselves, those on scopes of good quality will undoubtedly have sealing 'O' rings that prevent moisture leaking into the scope past the threads of the turret caps and the adjusters. With scope build structure, a feature I particularly favour is for the optics to have a 'monocoque build', whereby the body, including the turret saddle, is made out of one piece of material, preferably aircraft-grade aluminium alloy. Having no joins around the turret saddle means one less area to worry about for potential leakage. In any scope's specification list, look for classifications such as 'fogproof', 'water-proof' and 'shockproof'. These important three qualities, if mentioned in a scope's technical marketing blurb, mean that you're heading in the right direction in relation to build characteristics. I'm often asked if a 30mm body tube is better than the standard, more common 1 inch. Basically it doesn't have any bearing on practical performance that should concern the airgun hunter. Thicker body tubes are likely to be stronger but this is usually due to the fact that they are intended to sit mounted on powerful centrefire sporting and target rifles.

In respect of visual inspection and careful reading of the information slip or pamphlet that may come with the scope, that's about all you can achieve. Any reasonable gunshop owner will – to a certain extent – allow you to handle the goods, and you really should look through the lenses yourself. Even though you can't fit the scope to a rifle, there are still a few basic features to check 'hands on' without appearing to be overly fussy or fiddly.

First try the magnification zoom ring. It should glide easily up from low to full magnification and back again. Then, if present, check the front parallax adjustment (PA) or adjustable objective (AO) ring, which are the same thing. This won't be fitted to all scopes, but if it's present try it for operation. You'll probably find this quite stiff to turn, but once the scope is on a rifle they usually operate far more easily and smoothly. Those who say they work loose with use aren't talking sense, because they don't, and you certainly don't want things to work loose. What you might notice is that a parallax ring may stiffen up as you move it to the end of its travel towards the higher settings, which will be the longer-range marks. This is quite common so don't worry yourself unduly over it, as it'll be fine if it runs smoothly from low up to the 50 and 55 yard marks.

Now, we come to the features of most contention, the turret adjusters. Whether these are finger-adjustable, target-style or 'coin slot' operated, give them a good work-through. Listen and feel for the adjusters as they click around to the next setting. Feel for any slack or stiff spots, and give a scope a wide berth if you feel the turrets miss a click to the next station on rotation. Don't go dialling around wildly, but count the clicks left and count the clicks back again, as the scope is probably already centralised, and if you buy the scope you don't want to start off with a unit that is too far off centre. Similarly, if you don't choose to buy, leave it as you found it for the next potential customer. In passing, I'll mention something almost all hunters I've come across don't check before fitting a scope, but FT shooters take for granted as part of their scope fitting procedure. This is what is termed setting or checking the scope's 'optical zero', and it will be dealt with in more detail shortly.

For the general specification of a hunting scope, I'd have no hesitation in saying that the 3 – 9 x 40 is the best option for most situations, and a good quality optic with this specification will serve you well for many years. Buy a good quality scope and it will be more than capable of handling most hunting scenarios you'll encounter. But what if you want that little bit extra?

Features, Features, Features

Before we look at the main attributes that you should consider on a scope, think about this. Are you choosing a scope with lots of extra, dubiously-useful features, rather than the basic specifications you really need? I've met many people who do. They've read the advertisements, and they've been convinced that their shooting won't be as productive if they don't buy an all-singing all-dancing mega-scope. The trouble is that such a scope usually has so many features that they'll probably only use a fraction of what the scope is actually capable of and designed to do. So here are the main features that you'll see mentioned in a scope specification, and one by one I'll explain in simple terms what they refer to.

Reticle Types

Reticle or reticule is the term for the two centrally crossed lines (or other pattern of lines, sometimes called 'stadia', or even 'graticule') that are used for aiming – the most common simply being called a 'cross-hair'. Don't get confused, as all the terms used are recognised words for cross-hairs. I prefer to use the term reticle.

There are many different types of reticle, and their design and methods of use could take a whole chapter in itself; but on the whole most airgun hunters are happy enough with standard cross-hairs, usually in a 30/30 'thick-'n-thin post' style format (sometimes called a 'Duplex'). This is more than capable of fulfilling all the criteria needed of it from the general airgun hunter's perspective. However, certain other reticle types are worth considering. These include cross-hairs that have a central diamond 'bracketed' shape, scopes with illuminated reticles, and the latest favourite, the much misunderstood Mil-Dot reticle. All have certain attributes that different shooters may or may not feel will help them shoot better. However, in keeping with my view on specifications, I feel many are swayed towards the very latest 'have to have' feature. Remember, shooters of all disciplines have hunted successfully with both open sights and standard 30/30 thick-'n-thin cross-hair scopes for a great many years. (FT shooters have used scopes with specialist reticles for many a moon. An example is Tasco's TR Ranging reticle that was designed to 'range' on 40mm target discs; and you can even go as far as to have a custom reticle manufactured for your scope. These can be adapted for hunting use, but by and large we're stepping into the specialist FT arena.)

Other specialist scopes with 'ladder' or 'grid' reticle types, mil-dots and even a diamond shaped reticle (Simmons Diamond Mag and Pro Diamond) have been introduced for the benefits they give a shooter for long range shots. Most of these are only of real use for rimfire or centrefire cartridge rifles, and the mil-dot system isn't of any major use for an airgun hunter shooting out to 40yds with a 12ft lbs air rifle. However, for the specialised 'long ranger' who has really done his homework, then the extra aim-points that ladder, Mil-Dot or Diamond reticles offer may be beneficial. I use a scope with either a ladder reticle or Mil-Dot for my FAC power rated hunting air rifles, but only because I sometimes push these rifles to the limits of effective killing ranges. You'll find more on this in the section on FAC-specification rifles.

Here, however, I'll outline all the types of scope reticle available that I personally feel are worth considering for the 12ft lb hunter using a standard-power airgun. First comes the diamond reticle from Simmons, mentioned above. This is sometimes called a SMART reticle, and provides a diamond shaped centre to help the shooter 'frame' the target for speedy range estimation, plus 13 aiming points for windage and different distances. The reticle is etched on the first focal plane (in front of the internal

A compact wide-angle scope is the optimum choice for quick target acquisition – ideal for squirrel shooting

zoom tube rather than behind it), so the 'size' of the diamond will vary (i.e. get larger or smaller) in direct proportion to the magnification setting. This means that zero and holdover aiming points will stay constant, no matter what magnification is used.

Scopes fitted with illuminated reticles have their admirers, but are only of use in low light situations where you might lose thin cross-hairs in your sight picture against a dark background. They also have a place when shooting at night with an artificial light source (or lamping, as it's known). I've never really found an illuminated reticle especially useful, but 'each to their own'. My advice, should you choose such an optic, is to ensure that the reticle brightness control (rheostat) gives good variation from low intensity to bright without overly thickening or blurring the cross-hairs on the higher (i.e. brightest) settings. While on the subject of low light shooting, some prefer the vertical post and horizontal cross-hair design or, as it is sometimes know, the German Post reticle. Personally, I find the posts too heavy and of little benefit; but that's only my opinion, and as they're available and usable for airgun hunting they are worth a mention.

Now to the Mil-Dot or multi-dot scope. You could write another whole chapter on this type of scope reticle alone, but I'll concentrate solely on the benefits it specifically affords the airgun hunter. 'Mil' in the term Mil-Dot doesn't derive from its military usage but is in fact an abbreviation of the word milradian. Without getting too complicated, it is the term the military gave to the system they devised to make an accurate way of measuring angles and therefore distances in optical instruments. When used correctly this reticle can be used to establish the milradian angle from the top to the bottom of an object (quarry or target) of a known size. This then allows the distance to the object to be calculated using that pre-determined size. The correct dot in the reticle grid can then be used as an aiming point to sight onto the target.

Two of the Most Popular Reticles for a Hunting Scope

I'm not going to get into the physics and logistics of all this 'dottiness', as an in-depth article on mil-dot systems could quite frankly send you dotty! But these systems are very accurate when used with firearms that have very long-range shooting capabilities. For airgun use, however, the Mil-Dot is pretty much used as a standard cross-hair but with a far greater range of aiming points. So if you feel this reticle will be of use to you, then it's an option that's available. Granted, you get multi-aim-points for different ranges and side dots for wind allowance, but they're

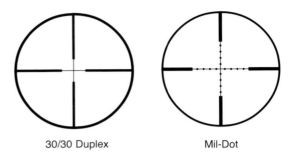

30/30 Duplex   Mil-Dot

only of use if you've done your homework very carefully on the target range to familiarise yourself with the trajectory of the pellet's flight. Once you can correspond specific distances with each 'dot' on the vertical post, you'll effectively have a 'zero' point for a whole range of distances.

A final factor to consider when choosing a reticle is how it appears to your eye in different lighting conditions. By far the most versatile is the reticle that appears black against a light background, but a reflective 'gold' colour against a dark background. This small feature can be found on some relatively low-priced scopes, yet may be absent on some quite expensive models (especially high-magnification target models). Nevertheless, this one feature can make all the difference when it comes to being able to place a cross-hair on the target, or, if targeting on a dark background, not being able to see the cross-hair at all.

Magnification and Range Estimation

A major factor you should consider when buying a scope is how much you want to magnify the target. That sounds a strange question, as a telescopic sight is, as the name suggests, capable of making a target look bigger. However, the downside is that the higher the magnification setting the more it will appear to exaggerate the dreaded 'wobble' we can all experience when shooting from an unsupported position. But a good point about high magnification is that it can be used in conjunction with the scope's parallax adjustment (or forward-placed focusing ring) to determine range. Not all scopes have a parallax adjustment facility, but those that do usually have the adjustment ring at the front of the scope, around the objective lens hood. On certain other scopes the PA may be positioned as a focusing wheel set on the opposite side of the windage turret. Whatever the design, this 'focus' ring is marked for distance, and with the magnification ring turned up full, it is turned until the object targeted comes into pin-sharp focus. You then read the range off the PA ring – simple! Sometimes the distance that you are actually focusing at is slightly different to that indicated on the side of the parallax ring, but you can easily put masking tape around the parallax ring and then mark each distance from 10yds to 60yds in 5-yard increments to suit your particular vision.

I'm sorry to blow away a popular misconception, but all this is fine in theory and, to the experienced trained FT shooter's eye, it's the tool for the job. But how many times in a practical hunting situation is old 'big-ears' going to hang around while you fiddle around with the focus ring, then look over the top to read the distance off a dial, and then make even more movements if you decide to dial in the range from the BDC (Bullet Drop Compensation) facility on the elevation turret? You may get away with it from a totally hidden ambush shooting position, but if not you'll have to use some other method of range estimation.

This brings us to bracketing, a more useful method of calculating the range quickly for the hunter. As the name suggests, this is where the reticle is used to bracket the target and therefore calculate range in relation to the size of quarry. Military snipers have long used this term, but they have their own way of using it. Basically they estimate the furthest a target can be and the closest it could be. The difference between the two is known as the 'bracket' and they then use the average of that as an estimation of the range. But to airgun shooters, both FT and hunter, the term bracketing applies to using fixed marks on the scope's reticle in relation to the size of the quarry or target, in order to estimate distance to the target. This can have major drawbacks for hunters, however. FT shooters know that they are bracketing on a standardised 40mm circular hit-zone on a static target, so they can be fairly confident of consistent results, yet even they rarely use the method any more because it is not precise enough for their needs. (But it does work well in conjunction with the focus method, just to confirm a parallaxed range estimate.)

Unfortunately, live quarry doesn't come in standard sizes, and they also move – both factors that make things far more difficult for the hunter to bracket a range accurately. Also, in the case of rabbits, although it's fairly easy to establish that you're looking at a young rabbit due to the size of its ears in relation to its head, it can be very difficult to assess if a rabbit is three-quarters or fully grown. All bracketing methods should be treated as guidelines only, and not set in stone; so once you've worked out the distances these targets appear to be, it's still only an approximation.

Obviously, different reticle types offer various bracketing capabilities. What suits one shooter won't necessarily suit the next, but many find the standard 30/30 or Duplex cross-hair more than useful. Here it's worth noting that the reticle got the 30/30 designation as this scope, when set on 4 x magnification, is designed to measure 30 inches from point to point of the thick, outer posts at 100yds, which is the approximate chest depth of an average North American deer. This predetermined size can be scaled down on more appropriate airgun quarry, and then used quite effectively for range-finding by the shooter who's done his homework on the target range. On this style of reticle you also have three set aim points on the vertical 'line' for range – the central cross and the two points where the thin 'hair' meets the thick posts at the top and bottom. You can even add the midway point between dead centre and thick post of the upper and lower horizontal as a 'floating', semi-fixed aim point. Using the cross-hair I like to set my scope zero, then find the optimum magnification where the tip of the bottom thick post gives an aim point to hit the target cleanly at 60yds. This gives a very good reference for adjusting and 'guesstimating' holdover above my original initial zero for longer-range shots. If using the scope in this manner, always remember to change up to or stay on that set magnification, otherwise it can become confusing due to variables. In fact, only dedicated practice and field hunting experience will eventually give you the required rangefinding skills.

Armed with all this general background information you should look to the established names in optics. All have scopes that suit every shooter's pocket. Optical giants Simmons especially have a long and fine track record in the manufacture of scopes. I've used virtually all their models extensively, particularly the Whitetail Classic Nightviews. Another brand I rate highly is Weaver, while a company continually impressing with the quality of their scopes are Deben Group Industries Ltd with their Hawke range of sights. Various reticle types, illuminated reticles and all manner of tempting features abound in the range they now offer. Of course there are many other quality brands such as AGS, Bushnell and Tasco – if your budget stretches and you feel you want to spend more then there are plenty of top class optics available from such hallowed names as Leupold, Schmidt & Bender, and Zeiss, and many are suited to airgun use.

To recap on scope choice, here are a few key guidelines on optics, giving general specifications and the hunting techniques and situations they're best suited to.

Scope – Minimum 1.5 × or 2 × up to 5, or 6 × magnification with min 20mm or 32mm objective lens.

These scopes are ideal for carbine-sized rifles due to their compact dimensions. They're also the ideal choice for close range shooting and when the target needs to be quickly found in your sights. The latter is allowed for due to the low magnification giving a wider field of view. The drawbacks of low-magnification, small-objective lens scopes are limited range for precise pellet placement, and lower light-gathering capabilities. However, some models of these scopes are worth a look for hunting at mainly close to medium range, no matter what the light conditions. They're ideal for close range rat and feral pigeon shooting, indoor work, and certain night-shooting applications with a lamp.

Scope – Minimum of 3 × or 4 × up to 9, 10, or 12 × magnification with minimum 40mm objective lens.

Here we fall firmly into the general purpose category and these scopes suit both carbine and full-length rifles. As I've said before, there's not much a 3 – 9 × 40 scope can't cope with. It can be mounted in medium-height mounts, and mounting shouldn't be a problem on any air rifle. They'll suit the hunter looking to try his hand at everything and anything, from stalking to roost shooting. They give a good compromise of reasonable magnification range, reasonable field of view on the lowest magnification setting, and have very acceptable light-gathering properties.

Scope – Minimum 3 × or 4 × variable up to12 ×, 16 × or 24 × magnification with minimum 40mm objective lens with parallax adjustment.

The higher magnification range means longer-range work is feasible, and the PA – if used with a high magnification facility – can be useful for estimating range. Still of use for general hunting, you may find these scopes are generally longer in the body, and mounting therefore has to be suitably catered for. These are scopes for the hunter who wants to gain optimum accuracy at long range, and they're especially handy for roost shooting and longer range, sniper-style ambush shooting on bunnies.

Scope – Minimum 3 × or 4 × variable up to 12 × magnification with minimum 50mm objective lens.

This is the classic specification for low-light dawn/dusk hunting. Some prefer an even larger objective lens, but despite the slight benefit that may offer many feel the 'Five-O' to be more than adequate. That big objective lens will suck in all available, useable light, and you can still wind the magnification down to take advantage of a wider field of view. The lower magnification should give better picture quality, and will certainly be more efficient at light gathering.

There are more options but of those mentioned, there is one that will suit every hunter. Of course, there are scopes with objective lenses up to 56mm, and also a few specialist optics that can drop down a touch from 3 × in an otherwise 'general-purpose' specification scope. But by and large, the scopes discussed above are the ones to concentrate on.

Scope Accessories

Some optics can be fitted with sun shades. These are plain black tubes that screw into the front lens housing to stop the sun causing glare across the scope's lenses. Lens covers can also be bought that simply slip over the front lens to protect the glass elements when not in use. Some are see-through with a tinted shade, which allow the scope to be used while still in place – a useful feature in bright sunlight. Rubber eye-shades are available that can be slipped over the eye-piece, and the intention is to block out light that could potentially cause glare in the rear lens, again affecting the performance of the scope.

Scope Mounts and Rings

It's strange how many shooters pay scant regard to scope mounts, especially as they play a vital role, being the only attachment points for the two major components of your hunting combo – the rifle and the scope. All modern air rifles have machined grooves or raised rails to take a standard dove-tailed scope mount – the width of the grooves usually being between 11mm and 13mm.

Mounts come either in two pieces, logically known as two-piece mounts, or as a one-piece mounting unit. Usually they're designed for scopes with 1 inch diameter body tubes but as scopes of 30mm are available it follows that suitable mounts are readily obtained for those, too. Good quality scope mounts are manufactured from either aluminium alloy or steel. Obviously steel ones are the stronger, but over-tightening the rings can easily damage an alloy scope body tube. Alternatively, alloy mounts can easily be damaged by the steel screws used to fasten the mounts to the top of the dovetails and around the scope body tube. So be careful not to over-tighten the screws when mounting your scope.

Mounts are available in low, medium and high sizes. These are to accommodate the fitting of the scope as close to the bore line of the barrel without the objective lens fouling the top of the rifle. Low mounts will usually suffice for scopes with objective lenses up to 32mm, medium ones will accept up to 42mm, while high mounts will be necessary for scopes with big front lenses of up to 56mm. It is worth noting that if low mounts can be used, then this is the better option for close-range hunting. Higher mounts are the optimum choice not only for scopes with large objective lenses but also if most hunting is done at longer ranges. Thus, medium-height mounts are the optimum choice for general-purpose work at medium range, and will suit most airgun hunting needs. Scope mounting height is particularly relevant to pellet trajectory, and this will be dealt with in detail in a later section.

A mount comprises three main components, the rings (the lower cradle where the scope sits, and upper part that clamps it down into place), the base or bases (the attachment points to the rifle) and the bolts (usually Allen head screws) that hold everything securely together. The top halves of the rings are removable, while the bottom section (cradle) is either bolted or otherwise permanently fixed to the base. Some mounts are designed with the upper rings being almost two-thirds the diameter of the scope body tube, often referred to as having a wrap-around design. Some prefer these, as they reputedly offer a more stable mount due to the fact the upper ring pulls down and around the scope, providing more clamping area than a conventional mount involving two hemispheres. In reality, both are very well suited to airgun use.

Opting to use either one-piece or two-piece mounts is largely a personal choice. However, a one-piece mount was formerly recommended for use with a recoiling air rifle, because you had a greater length of scope mount base and therefore additional grip due to the extra metal-to-metal contact. However, if you mount your scope sensibly, two-piece mounts are just as efficient. Generally speaking, one-piece mounts are unsuitable for PCP air rifles. Unless the one-piece mount fits behind

Correct alignment of the scope's cross-hairs to the rifle is very important in making your combo perform to its maximum accuracy potential

the breech loading area (for a single-shot rifle) or behind the magazine housing (of a multi-shot rifle) then you can't use it, because it covers the breech, making it difficult or impossible to load a pellet, or else it fouls the magazine. Two-piece mounts are much more versatile as they can be positioned almost anywhere along the scope body and on the rifle's grooves or rail.

That brings us to the mounting point itself – the grooved channel cut into the top of the rifle's compression chamber or the machined rail on top of a PCP's action block. The former is found on most springers, and, as we mentioned 'scope creep' earlier, this is where certain manufacturers machine in special features to stop mounts moving on recoil. These can be cross-slots or shallow holes drilled between the dovetails, which engage small lugs or studs found on the base of some scope mounts. Once a mount with a stud on the base is located at this position, it isn't going anywhere. Similarly if a recoil lug or arrestor block is fitted, with the scope mount butted up to it, this shouldn't move. Both act as a physical stop to anchor the rear scope mount in place, thus resisting movement on recoil.

If you're using a rifle with hefty recoil – say an FAC-rated springer – then anti-slip studs on the mount or an arrestor block is a very sensible precaution. Alternatively, use the Theoben DampaMount™ mentioned earlier, as it's a handy solution to stop the effects of recoil being transmitted to the scope on firing. Many rifles in the Theoben range have integrally fitted scope mounts which are bolted in place through the base, so they'll never move. Theoben also market special raiser blocks which are needed for scopes with big objective lenses, and special 'set back' mounts that may be required to obtain the correct eye-relief (i.e. the optimum distance between the shooter's eye and the rear lens). For those choosing a PCP, mounting can be a very simple affair, so long as you remember not to foul the breech or magazine system with the mounts or any part of the scope itself.

Before leaving mount design, it's worth glancing at the 'specials' that are available, such as adjustable mounts and risers. You can find that even though you have correctly fitted and set up the scope, you run out of movement on the elevation turret to set your zero at the required range. This usually happens when fitting a scope more suited to firearms use, and therefore calibrated for much greater distances. Even so, if you want to fit such a scope you can pack the rear mount with shims made from small strips of film negative. These go between the cradle and the scope body until the rear section is raised sufficiently to allow adjustment to be made. However, if you overdo it and try to raise the rear of the scope too much, there's a danger of exerting undue leverage on the scope body, with the potential for damage by bending forces. In this case it is much better to use a special mount raiser. These are usually one-piece mounts with the rear mount made slightly higher than the front one. Some can actually be adjusted to sit higher or lower, and even to move from side to side. However, we're really getting into rather specialised kit here, and I feel that 99.9 per cent of airgun hunters will never need to go this far. So we'll move on to other mounts that will be more generally useful. These are 'set-backs' and 'see-thrus'.

Set-back mounts are always of the two-piece type, and can also be known as 'reach' or cantilever mounts. This is because they can be used either for mounting a scope further back on the rifle or further forward, in both cases to give optimum eye relief. This is done by one mount having the rings positioned away from the base of the mount – from the side, looking rather like an L-bracket. These mounts also allow scope mounting on PCPs that may have an awkwardly located breech, or the rails machined in such a way as to restrict positional adjustment of the scope. These mounts are also handy for avoiding any fouling of the scope's eyebell, saddle or front lens assembly against any part of the rifle. 'See-thru' mounts have already been mentioned for spring-powered rifles, where the shooter uses a scope but also wishes to take advantage of using the fitted open sights. These can be advantageous if your shooting takes you from normal ranges to close up work.

So those are your mounting options. Now we look to setting up the scope.

Mounting and Setting

Even some quite experienced airgun shooters will just plonk a scope in mounts, set the middle cross hair as horizontal as possible, clamp up and then set zero. In theory that's pretty much all you need to do, but it really needs to be done correctly. Here are some important dos and don'ts.

With suitable mounts chosen, fit them loosely but firmly onto the dovetails or rails, taking care not to obstruct the barrel's loading area or magazine housing. Then remove the top ring sections from the mounts and you're left with the cradles for the scope to sit in. This brings us to a feature mentioned earlier, and that's optical zero. On a new shop-bought scope the optical zero should be pre-centred, but to save time and get the best performance from your optics it's well worth taking the trouble to check.

Basically, all you're doing is ensuring the reticle is central in the scope body and therefore making the best use of available leeway for elevation and windage adjustments. First, dial the elevation turret all the way to the top of its travel (i.e. in the arrow direction up), then wind it fully down again, while carefully counting the number of full turns the turret takes until it 'bottoms out'. This will usually be around five full turns, so if the total is five, you should wind back two and a half turns, and then it's approximately centred vertically. Go through the same procedure with the windage turret and that will set the optical zero in both the vertical and lateral planes.

Eye-relief and cross-hair alignment

Having done the 'centralising check', carefully tighten the base of the mounts to the dovetails or rail, and loosely fit the top sections of the rings so that the scope can't fall off the rifle, but loose enough for it to be moved backwards and forwards, and rotated. If using a break-barrel rifle, check that the front of the scope doesn't overhang the breech, which would foul the barrel and prevent it from opening fully. That's commonsense stuff, but easily overlooked.

Next you have to set eye-relief as follows. Lift the rifle/scope combo to your shoulder, get into a comfortable shooting position, slide the scope gently within the mounts until you can clearly see a perfectly circular 'sight picture' through the scope with a minimum amount of black border around it. This should be around 2½–3½ inches between your eye and the scope's ocular bell. You may find that this procedure is easier to do while sitting down with the rifle in a bench-rest shooting position, but take care to check that you still have approximately the same sight picture when standing, kneeling or lying prone with the rifle unsupported. If not, make the final adjustments to eye-relief while holding the rifle in your most frequently used shooting position.

Once you've attained the eye-relief that's suited to you, you need to align the cross-hairs square to the rifle itself. I advise hanging a vertical plumb line (a thread or string with a weight at one end) at approximately 10 to 20yds distance from the scope. I have an old door to the side of my target range backstop set up with a plumb line just for this purpose. Look through the scope and make sure that the vertical wire of the cross hair lines up with the plumb line when you are holding the rifle in your usual shooting position. If it doesn't, gently rotate the scope within the mount rings until it does. Once you are certain that the scope is square to the rifle, carefully tighten the mount top rings on to the scope by nipping up the Allen screws in rotation. If using mounts with four top screws per mount, tighten those which are diagonally opposite each other. Tighten firmly, but don't over-tighten. If you're using a PCP, recoil won't be a problem in causing scope shift, so over-tightening shouldn't even be an issue. Once the scope is secured, re-check that the cross hairs are still set correctly. If not, loosen the screws and repeat the procedure until you are satisfied with the result.

A scope set slightly off the horizontal won't perform to its optimum level when using the turret adjusters. This is because of ' rifle cant', which I'll explain. For instance, if the horizontal line of the cross-hair is only slightly askew to the rifle, then when you adjust the elevation turret of the scope – say to alter the impact higher – you could also unintentionally shift the pellet impact point to the left or right, depending on which way the scoped rifle is canted. This is because your brain will automatically make you twist (or cant) the rifle to one side or the other to make the cross-hair appear 'square on'. If you're not shooting at long ranges the lateral variation of the aim point caused by cant may not be very noticeable, but at longer distances the deviation to right or left gets progressively greater. So as you can see, correct alignment of the scope's cross-hairs to the rifle is very important in making your rifle-and-scope perform to its maximum accuracy potential. A scope set perfectly in line with the rifle is also important for using the BDC (Bullet Drop Compensation) facility that is a feature on many rangefinding scopes.

Now we move on to the next adjustment you should take time over – the fast-focus or reticle focus ring. Strange though it seems this is a feature many don't bother with, but if your scope has this adjustment you should definitely take advantage of it. This feature allows you to set the scope reticle to 'focus' for your individual eyesight. It's a simple procedure, but one that needs doing correctly. First, look through the scope at a light-coloured blank wall, or up into an overcast sky (never a sunny one). Look into the middle distance but take notice if the cross hairs are blurred or sharp. The reticle must suit your eyesight, so adjust the eyepiece until the cross-hairs appear crisp and sharp to you. Many scopes have fast-focus rings and very handy they are too, but if not you may have to loosen the locking ring on the eyebell and rotate the bell itself until focus is achieved, and then re-tighten the locking ring. Once this is achieved, you're ready to set the rifle to shoot to a chosen zero point. (In addition to these manual instructions, there are commercially available devices that help you visually align the cross hairs with the bore axis, and even for the scope cross hair to be set perfectly vertical in relation to action of the rifle. If you feel you need it, they can help.)

Setting Scope Zero

Setting the zero on the rifle/scope combo is also a relatively simple procedure, but one that needs to be done correctly so that you'll always hit your mark. Note that the rifle's zero, even when set, will shift depending on your shooting position. This applies more to a recoiling spring rifle than a recoilless PCP, but if you set the zero for a standing shooting position, it will still alter slightly for a shot taken in a kneeling or prone position.

To start by getting roughly on target, first set up a large piece of paper at 12 to 15yds range on a suitable backstop. This target needs an aiming point, and a 2 inch black circle marked in the centre with a marker pen is ideal. Fire a string of four or five pellets, with your cross hairs trained precisely on this point. Make a note where the pellets group and then dial the turret adjusters accordingly, to move the group closer to your black dot aiming point. Repeat this until you're hitting the point you're aiming at. Next, put up another target with a 1½ inch circle on a suitable backstop and pull back so that you are shooting from the distance at which you want to zero your combo for hunting. Shoot and adjust until you're grouping your shots inside the circle on the target.

The turret adjusters on most hunting scopes alter impact by what is known as ¼ MOA (Minute Of Angle) increments. This means that the impact point is shifted a quarter of an inch per click at one hundred yards. At airgun distances this has to be compensated for, so at 25yds this equates to four 'clicks' moving the impact point of the pellet by a quarter of an inch. (Specialist target scopes often have ⅛ MOA adjustment, moving the aim point ⅛ inch at 100yds.) Which distance to choose for your zero can be debatable. Newcomers, and airgun hunters looking to undertake some 'general' hunting, would be advised to use this as a loose guide. For a .22 calibre recoiling spring or gas-ram powered rifle set your zero at 25 yds. For a .177 recoilless PCP air rifle set the zero point for 30yds. These zeros

Under a heavy canopy of foliage light can be very low, that's when a scope with a large objective lens can be beneficial

give you a good aim point for longer-range effectiveness, yet with a closer range reference point. With a .22 set to 25 yards zero you can also aim 'bang on' for 10-12yds, then slightly lower for 18yds. Then raise your aim appropriately to put the cross hairs bang on target for 25yds. After that only practice on target cards will show you how much to allow for aiming holdover at longer range. This is something we will deal with more fully in the relevant section. As you can see, the set zero is there to give you a definite aim point at your set zero range, and also a reference for closer range shots.

Precharged pneumatics (PCPs) are recoilless, and the .177 calibre has a much flatter trajectory than a .22, so the whole package is much more forgiving in range estimation and assessment. You'll find on larger target kill-zones, such as a rabbit's head, with a zero of 30yds you can actually aim bang on for ranges of approximately 20yds to 40yds and still be within the kill-zone. Incidentally, an important factor in zeroing that should always be adhered to is using the same ammo as you set your zero with. Change ammo and the zero will change. It may only be slight in relation to pellets of a similar weight and profile, but often it is enough to upset your accuracy, and therefore your efficiency as a hunter.

Although I've fully detailed how to manually – i.e. by eye – set the zero, you can purchase a gadget which is known as a 'Bore Sighter' or 'Shot Saver' that will aid the process. These can be in the form of a collimator gauge or a more hi-tech laser bore sighter. The latter fits into the barrel and actually projects a laser dot out from the barrel bore. This is all good kit, but setting up in the 'old school' way is by far the most commonly used method for airgun use.

Alternative Sighting Systems

With the exception of specialised nightvision riflescopes, there are few alternative sighting systems for use in hunting, and none that offer a better option for all-round, precision shooting than the telescopic sight. However, for close to medium range work, you do have a choice of sights that offer a reasonable (and in some cases better) option to obtain quick target acquisition. These are red-dot or 'holo' sights. I'd recommend a few of the red-dots that are available, but then only for rat and feral pigeon shooting, or possibly rabbit shooting when I'm sure the range will not exceed 25yds. And even then, if the quarry is further out I keep disciplined by using the sight at its optimum level of accuracy. The main reasons I'll use a red-dot are when using a PCP air rifle for close to medium range shooting. The sight then virtually offers all the simplicity and benefits of an open sight coupled with the obvious benefits of a multi-shot PCP.

The red-dot sight that made the biggest impact on my own hunting was the Russian-manufactured Cobra, a sight originally designed for the Russian military for use on the AK47 assault rifle. Obviously, reliability and build construction aren't an issue. Swedish manufacturer Aimpoint have red-dots suited to hunting, as also is the Bushnell Holo-Sight. If a red-dot appeals to you and will be the suitable sighting option for the hunting you are doing, they're all worth checking out. However, I'd like to dispel the popular misconception that they're useful for night shooting. Where this myth has arisen from is any-body's guess, as they're of little use without some light. In gloomy conditions they do give you a sight point, but as for being a true night sight – they're not.

Electric Eye

Laser sights project a laser 'dot' onto the target, but rather than being a primary sighting system they are more useful in helping the shooter estimate range in low light conditions.

I first took an interest in lasers in the mid 1990s when the American Beamshot lasers came onto the UK hunting scene. I must say my flirtations with them have been somewhat sporadic, sometimes favouring them and at others having little use for them. Though specialised, in the right situations, they're handy to have.

How the laser sight is mounted dictates how you use it to assess if a target is closer or further from your set zero. But the rules are simple to remember once the laser is mounted securely and has been set to coincide exactly with your cross hairs at the rifle's set zero point. If the laser is mounted below the rifle barrel, and therefore below the bore line and scope line of sight, then when the laser dot shows on the target lower than the cross hairs, the target is closer than your set zero. If the laser dot appears above it, the target is further than your set zero. Of course, the opposite applies to a laser mounted above the scope – laser dot lower = target further; laser dot higher = target closer.

A radical move in the development of lasers is the fact there are now models available that project an infrared dot which can only be seen when viewed through a Nightvision device. For instance when wearing night-vision goggles or, more commonly, when used in conjunction with a night-vision (NV) riflescope. Their uses are one and the same – to help in rangefinding under difficult shooting conditions. Infrared (IR) lasers and NV Sighting systems and other relevant NV equipment are very specialised, but make exciting and worthy additions to the airgun hunting scene. All these 'after hours' sighting devices and their use will be fully detailed later, in the applicable sections on hunting methods, and there'll be more pertaining to the use of both types of lasers and their benefits and usage in the chapter on Shooting At Night.

Finally, one very important factor should be remembered. Even with all this hi-tech help, it's the hunter who has fully familiarised himself with his kit who will be really successful.

Chapter 3
Choosing a Rifle –
Combinations and Usage

On first inspection of my gun rack and gun cabinet you'd be forgiven for thinking one (or perhaps two) of two things. **A:** I've far too many air rifles or **B:** I'm a collector. In fact, neither is correct, because each rifle and scope combination – or, to use the shortened term, 'combo' – is in my armoury because it serves a specific purpose.

As well as being a very keen sporting shooter, I do a lot of pest control shooting in every conceivable situation where the air rifle is useful. It's largely for that reason I have so many different combos. But if I was only using air rifles for sport shooting, I admit I'd certainly own and use fewer. I also fully realise that not everybody wants, needs or indeed can afford to have a gun rack full of different rifles. Many manage with just the one combo, do well with two and certainly are very well equipped with three at the most. I recommend you opt for three, as in my opinion all hunters should have a selection of rifles at their disposal to help them hunt more efficiently under differing conditions. I'd certainly not stipulate the need for a high-powered FAC-rated air rifle, as that's very much down to personal choice. One thing's certain, however, and that's the fact that all airgunners should have an air rifle with specifications that allow the rifle to be used for what can be termed 'general purpose' shooting. But what are the specifications and features to look for? First, I'll break the selection and choices down into what I see as the three main categories of combo most useful for hunting.

1. **General Purpose Hunting Combo:** Either spring powered or gas-ram with iron sights or, preferably and more commonly, a general specification scope.
2. **Precision Hunter:** Single or multi-shot PCP with a higher specification scope.
3. **Dedicated Night Hunting Rig:** A multi-shot PCP with a nightvision riflescope onboard; or, if a traditionalist, a springer, gas-ram or PCP with a suitable optic and scope-mounted lamping kit.

As you'll immediately notice, if you don't intend to hunt regularly at night, then you can forget number three; so now we're down to just two combos. You're probably already aware, even if you've chosen all three, that there can be many permutations of mixing and matching. A rifle classed as a precision hunter could easily handle anything asked of a general-purpose rifle. Also, if you are going to hunt at night, but only infrequently, a scope-mounted lamping kit will fit on any scoped air rifle. In fact, it would be all too easy just to say, 'Buy the best springer and best PCP multi-shot air rifles you can afford, get a gun-mounted lamping kit and leave it at that'. If I did, this would be a very short chapter and you'd not be given a reasonable number of useful guidelines.

To have a spring or gas-ram powered air rifle as a back-up to a precharged pneumatic is, in my opinion, the least expensive option, and a very sensible and practical route to take. If you have a .22 calibre springer or gas-ram, then seriously consider a .177 PCP for your main hunting rifle. You'll notice as you progress through this book that I lean heavily towards the .177 calibre. I use it extensively and rate the smaller slug very highly. But before I begin my list of things to look for in a rifle, consider this. Under current (2004) legislation you're not restricted as to the number or type of 12ft lb air rifles you can possess, unlike the stipulations on FACs as regards exactly which high-powered

The author reckons he doesn't have too many combos but recommends most hunters have a choice of three

airguns you may own. This absence of tight regulation means you can easily chop and change as your shooting dictates or (relevant to most shooters) as your budget allows. In other words, making a costly mistake isn't the biggest risk facing you in your purchase, as you can easily trade-in a good quality 12ft lb air rifle for a different model. Before outlining what I feel all shooters should look for in the choosing of a good all-round 'general-purpose' hunting rifle, a bit of treading back down memory lane is useful.

Suits You

When many shooters like myself started hunting, we only had the choice of a few lower-price rifles, but of course there were many 'big name', established, adult size hunting rifles that we aspired to, and vowed to own one day. Most of us started with humble springers, usually Webley Excels or BSA Airsporters and Supersports. The older lads had bigger rifles, and when I mention the Weihrauch HW80 I'm sure many readers will smile as they remember it, as this is the rifle that fits this category perfectly. It was certainly a rifle that many airgun hunters like myself eventually acquired, not only to cut our hunting teeth on it, but also to sharpen them well and truly. There was also the Webley Eclipse, an under-lever rifle that has been discontinued, but, along with the Omega model, it's a rifle that many still believe was one of Webley's finest production spring-powered creations. I must also mention a personal favourite from the 'old days,' the now sadly discontinued Air Arms Khamsin. This was a side-lever springer that I hold largely responsible for my penchant for thumbhole-style stocks – but more on stock designs later.

So, why this reminiscing? Obviously we had to use what was available, and the selection within our meagre budgets wasn't anything like as varied as it is today. Also, we usually went for the rifle that we thought was the most powerful. The HW80 was even nicknamed 'The Powerhouse' in the advertisements, so it's little wonder that it drew us impressionable kids to it. This brings us to the first consideration because, depending on your stature and physique, you should choose a rifle accordingly. The bonus for today's shooter is that many more carbines and lightweight rifles are available that are capable, full-power hunters. These are not only handy for younger or small-stature shooters, but are the optimum choice for stalking, hide shooting and even for use from an off-road vehicle. But the primary factor concerning your first choice is – does the rifle fit you? That is the way to look at it, because although you needn't go as far as the custom-made stock tailored to suit you for FT perfectionism, finding a 'nice stick to hold' is a vital step towards becoming a proficient shot.

Stock-taking

There are three specifics of a rifle stock that need examination in relation to your personal build. The weight (including action), the reach to the trigger pull and the height of the cheekpiece or comb. The latter feature can be altered (raised or lowered) by fitting an adjustable butt pad, but let's assume that most of us will be happy enough with the stock in standard form. Never be fooled into thinking that a nice-looking gun equals a good-handling gun. Aesthetics help sell rifles, but they don't make for better shooting. In that respect I'd advise you to devote some careful handling to the rifle you've 'short-listed' in the gun shop, and see if it really suits you. Or, to put it another way, to see if it feels right. What is right for one individual isn't right for everyone. This includes what is known as the 'reach to pull', which is the distance from the middle of the butt pad to the forward surface of the trigger blade – i.e. the reach to 'squeezing' the trigger. Most traditional style sporters hover around a length of 13 to 14 inches. If it's more, you could find it rather a stretch to reach the trigger, and nothing's more infuriating than a rifle that feels uncomfortable to hold and use like that.

Some prefer to have chequering or stippling on the pistol grip and the fore-end, which supposedly affords the shooter a surer hold. Unfortunately, the fore-end chequering or stippling on many rifles is not always in the ideal position, so in many cases this can be purely cosmetic. Granted, it is very handy if you want to carry your rifle in one hand. The method for using the fore-end for this is to grip the rifle under the stock and along the fore-end with your right hand at the chequering, allowing the unloaded rifle to point downwards at the ground when carried alongside your right leg (assuming you shoot from your right shoulder). It is a safe, comfortable hold when you have to move across ground where you may need to use your other hand to steady yourself. And it is a very much better proposition than using the scope as a carry-handle! Alternatively, of course, if you've got quick-detachable (QD) swivel studs fitted, you can quickly and easily attach a rifle sling and shoulder the gun while you negotiate the terrain.

Chequering or stippling can be useful at the pistol grip, especially if the hunter becomes a devotee of full camo, and wears gloves. Personally, I don't worry unduly about these stock characteristics, but I do prefer the stock to be of a thumbhole design and/or to have an adjustable butt pad. Some think that's strange for a dedicated hunter such as myself, but I've taken these preferences from the stocks fitted to FT rifles. These features allow me to tailor the height of the cheekpiece or comb for optimum eye-relief on the scope, and the thumbhole gives me a very assured handling feel. The latter I can live without, but the majority of my hunting rifles have adjustable butt pads. These are often fitted after purchase, but some rifles do come ready fitted with them. If the rifle you're thinking of buying hasn't got one – and if it's a basic springer it probably won't – fitting one afterwards isn't difficult for the average DIY-er.

Next on the checklist is whether you opt for a walnut stock, or the less expensive beech or hardwood. We constantly hear prophets of doom warning that there'll come a time when good stock wood will be too expensive, and all stocks will be synthetic, made from ABS or toughened plastics. Even though my rifles are tools for hunting, how I'd hate to see or 'feel' that happen! Some manufacturers have already started down that road which, in certain respects, isn't such a bad thing. I even own and use rifles like that myself, and for the situations I use them in, synthetic stocks can often be more practical. However, if you are worried about the disappearance of wooden stocks (as some have foretold) or them becoming prohibitively costly – don't worry! With the existence of many different hardwoods worldwide, most actually being the wood of fruit trees, I believe that new types of wood will eventually enter the scene. But the old 'traditional' woods will still be with us for a good deal longer. So, is it to be beech or walnut? I'm certainly no 'mantle-piece' gun collector, but I do like a nice-looking grain on my walnut stocks. I have rifles in very figured walnut stocks, rich dark brown stained beech, laminated specials and even some bland-looking woods of unknown origin. And of course there are the synthetics, and even some that are metal-based! I believe it really comes down to design, and if the stock is well designed the rifle will handle well. But do remember that a hunting rifle will be subjected to its fair share of knocks and scrapes. If you can't bear the thought of that lovely wood getting scratched, don't buy that type of stock. As for weight difference between wood types, it's usually so minimal that I feel it has little relevance. If there is one thing to consider it's this: a walnut stock that is kept dry after use and regularly oiled does last longer than beech. If weight-saving is a major consideration then look to the rifles that have what are known as 'skeleton' or 'profile' stocks. These are paired down to the barest minimum to save weight, but without sacrificing strength.

As you progress as a hunter you might decide to have a stock specially made for your particular style of hunting, a stock that your favoured hunting rifle would slip into and which would fit you like a glove. Interestingly, of all shooting disciplines, airgunners are some of the most likely to have a custom stock built and fitted to their rifle. And that's not only FT shooters, because more and more airgun hunters choose this route as well. So maybe I wasn't so strange in my yearnings to have thumbhole stocks and adjustable butt pads all those years ago.

All Important

This may sound obvious, but a general purpose hunting air rifle needs to be capable of cleanly dispatching vermin out to 30yds. That's not a great distance, and virtually all good quality spring powered and gas-ram powered air rifles will be up to the job. So in that sense you don't need the all-singing, all-dancing, recoil-free PCP multi-shot to be successful in the field. But consider the following: the best racing cars are usually the ones that you regularly see winning races. This might seem a strange analogy, but the fact of the matter is that a better rifle generally means more success. The operator, be he shooter or driver, also has a hand in it, but I'm sure you get my drift. Often the rifle can be capable of achieving more than the hunter who uses it, so if you're only planning the occasional hunting foray then a basic springer or gas-ram powered air rifle will serve you well for many, many years. But I must reiterate an important aspect of the sport. Not that long ago, most experienced shooters would advise you to start off by choosing a spring-powered rifle for hunting; but due to the fact that good-quality precharged pneumatics are now much more affordable, if you're willing to fork out for charging gear, then a PCP can be a better choice for many hunting scenarios, and a multi-shot is even better. Before we look at precharged or multi-shots, it's time to get back to basics and

A basic spring powered hunting combo such as this will suffice for many hunting scenarios

see what the hunter should be looking for in a 'mechanically charged and primed' single-shot air rifle.

For spring-powered air rifles, there are high quality models with all the requisites from established British manufacturers such as Air Arms, BSA, Webley & Scott Ltd, and of course the German company Weihrauch. If it's a gas-ram then it'll be a Theoben, or another gun manufacturer's 'springer' fitted with a gas-ram strut replacement. Of the companies mentioned, all have rifles suitable for general hunting work. These will be no-nonsense, ruggedly built, reliable, accurate sporters. They'll handle well, and some will even be fitted with a good set of open sights. Immediately this brings us to a feature of certain 'springers' that makes them advantageous over others for certain hunting situations. If you're intending to shoot at close to medium range at quarry such as rats or feral pigeons then you can't beat a basic break-barrel springer with open sights. For what I'd term 'knock-about' work it's still a very useful tool. However, whilst I still have rifles like that, I now only use them for the most basic jobs; and when many like myself began shooting with air rifles, we just couldn't afford a scope!

Shooting with open sights brings its own advantages and merits. Most hunters now skip straight past these rifles and scope up immediately. There's no denying the benefits of using a decent scope, but a whole generation of shooters have missed a very important part of the learning curve associated with the shooting of air rifles, especially if they start with a PCP. The reason is that learning to shoot with a recoiling, spring-powered air rifle instils a definite shooting discipline and, once mastered, you can then fully appreciate the benefits of the recoilless attributes of a PCP. All this will be discussed in the chapter on Gun Handling. But let's return to springers and gas-rams, and in particular to a consideration of the features that should be considered when choosing a rifle of this type.

First, if you don't want open sights, then don't worry. It may seem as if I'm contradicting myself, but if you are going for quarry at 25–30yds, you should be scooping-up straight from the off. Just as importantly, choose a rifle that is threaded at the muzzle to accept a standard ½ inch UNF-threaded silencer. Unless you're sure of the make or you've tried before you buy, be aware of rifles with silencers that come 'bonded' onto the barrel. In most cases these 'perma-fix' moderators are

The author's own design, hand crafted profile stocked HW80K bullpup tuned by Venom – this is about as far as you can go in radical custom chic!

more than adequate for general purpose work. The rifle will also usually be shorter than a similar model that requires you to screw a silencer onto the barrel, thus increasing the rifle's overall length. This is something I'm always critical of, and it does tend to annoy me when I see a company boasting that their new model is 'ultra-short', when the reality is that you need to take the additional length of a silencer into consideration. If it doesn't slip over the end of the barrel it will usually add another 4-6 inches to the overall length of the rifle. On a carbine-size break-barrel springer this can be beneficial, because it will act as a cocking aid for the shortened barrel, but on a standard length rifle it can sometimes make the rifle feel overly long. The worst-case scenario is that it can make the rifle feel unwieldy and unbalanced, but this is thankfully now quite rare. Most are manageable, and you can opt for a carbine or carbine version with a silencer bonded in place, or as an outer sleeve, usually referred to as a bull barrel.

In passing, and on the subject of barrels, it's interesting that British companies such as BSA and Webley & Scott Ltd still produce their own, which is a tradition that I hope will long continue because these tubes are strong, accurate and well manufactured, and bear testimony to the British gun manufacturers' long engineering pedigree. For PCPs, however, virtually all companies now choose to buy barrels from acclaimed German manufacturers such as Anschutz or Lothar Walther.

Silencers, or 'sound moderators' to give them their more accurate term, are of such importance that they'll be dealt with more fully in the chapter on Hunting Accessories. But at this stage it is worth mentioning that most serious hunters, myself included, feel they're essential in attaining optimum results in the field. On a precharged pneumatic they are certainly a necessity, as the muzzle report from an 'untamed' PCP is heard as a loud, sharp crack. On certain springers, the report can be quite acceptable but on the whole I would say that if you want to hunt to the optimum level then give serious consideration to the silencer already fitted to the rifle, or which you will choose to add later. It is sufficient to say that, in the right hands, a silenced air rifle is a deadly, effective tool.

Now to a much discussed aspect of any rifle, its trigger mechanism. The modern air rifle, even a basic model, is generally now fitted with a two-stage adjustable trigger unit. The 'two-stage' term refers to the fact that the length of travel in the first stage can be adjusted, or the length and weight of the second stage – i.e. the 'pull' or point at which the trigger trips the sear – can be altered, or both. Remember back to Chapter 1? As they come from the factory and set by the manufacturer, most triggers will tend to suit the majority of shooters. But as you come to know your gun, you'll probably want to 'tweak' the trigger slightly to adjust its let-off. Be sensible with adjustments, read the manual

Barrel making – a few British manufacturers still produce their own fine tubes

that comes with the rifle thoroughly, and don't set the trigger pressure too light. Hair triggers aren't necessary or useful for a sporting air rifle, and very few hunters would advice or consider using them. Again, as for many alterations that can be done to a rifle, if in doubt get a reputable gunsmith to do the alterations.

The majority of trigger units also have a safety-catch system, either manual or automatic. These are useful because the rifle can be cocked and loaded with a pellet, ready to go, but the trigger is made safe by the safety mechanism blocking its action. However, nothing is safer than an un-cocked, unloaded rifle. If you can hunt in this fashion, all the better, but there are many times when you'll need to be ready to take a shot quickly, which is best done with a cocked and loaded rifle with the safety set to 'on'. Also, many springers can be un-cocked by holding the barrel or under-lever, removing the safety, and tripping the trigger while allowing the barrel or under-lever to return under your manual control to its original position. But remember you've still got a pellet in the breech – assuming you got as far as loading. There is more to a safety catch than using it as an on/off switch, and it's up to the individual to learn to use the safety wisely, as an essential part of good, sensible gun handling.

Compact carbines suit hide shooting, stalking and shooting from the confines of a 4x4 amongst other such duties

For scope mounting, the rifle will have dovetails (and perhaps arrestor stud holes) machined atop the cylinder or action block to help prevent scope creep. This has already been mentioned, so suffice it to say that you should check that the dovetails are well machined and are of a reasonable length to allow for a suitable scope mounting position. Team a rifle such as this with a general specification 3 – 9 × 40 scope and you'll undoubtedly have a very efficient, user-friendly, all-purpose knockabout hunting rifle. If it's a carbine, I'd advise a compact scope of 1.5 – 5 × 20 or 1.5 – 6 × 32. This will handle and balance nicely, and those optics will aid fast target acquisition, so making this combo suitable for snap shooting, as well as stalking with the ability to take shots up to and beyond medium range.

What companies have served this area over the years? As mentioned, our own famous gun manufacturers BSA and Webley & Scott have been doing it for many years. German gun manufacturing giants Weihrauch, as well as producing the legendary HW80 'powerhouse', have downsized some of their models,

What no wood? Metal and synthetic stock rifles are becoming more commonplace

and priced them accordingly. Theoben have the gas-ram market sewn up, and have a few notable models suited to this area. Look to any of these companies and you won't be disappointed.

By now you could well be walking out of the shop with a springer, gas-ram or even a single-shot PCP with a general-type hunting scope onboard. But if you want a bit more versatility, read on.

Precision Hunter

It's here that the sky really is the limit and the options available are innumerable. Do you stay with a single-shot or go for a multi-shot model? Do you stay with the 'mechanical animals' or go pre-charged? It's largely up to personal preference, but personally I'd now not consider hunting without my multi-shot PCP unless it was punishable by law. Admittedly, I do occasionally have a wander around my shoot with a single-shot, but this seems to be getting less frequent by the season. Even so, my first choice would always be a PCP, apart from in the harshest, most grime-ridden conditions where the danger of dirt creeping near or into the precious inlet valve and internals would have me reaching for a spring or gas-ram powered rifle. So what do we look for in your precision hunter rifle?

If you've served your time with the spring gun, moving up to a PCP can be a tad daunting. These days there are both single-shot and multi-shot pneumatics to suit every shooter's requirements and pockets. There are many field proven PCPs specifically designed for the hunter, and I'll try to help you through the quagmire by outlining what a hunting PCP should have in order to warrant its serious consideration.

For airgun hunters new to the PCP, the simplicity of a one-shot capacity rifle is a valid reason to stay with a single. Also, let's not forget that before the multi-shots took over we did very well with single-shot air rifles. In fact, hunting with an air rifle should be a one-shot affair, and there are now a host of top quality very reasonably priced one-shot potters on the market.

Air Arms, BSA and Falcon all have rifles that are very appealing, as do many others. Personally, I'll always have a place in my 'hunter' list of top quality single shot PCPs for the Falcon Lighthunter 12W. In my humble opinion, its action combined with the skeleton stock make it the crème de la crème of single-shot hunting carbines, but the rifle it's derived from is still a recommended buy for those looking to start hunting precharged style, and that is the Falcon FN12, which has been one of the best selling PCPs in the UK since its introduction back in 1994.

We can't talk about single-shot PCPs without immediately thinking of the company mentioned at the outset and often hailed as the founding fathers – Daystate Ltd.

Market demands have dictated that even the one-time kings of the one-shot now mainly produce multi-shot rifles that are capable of being adapted back to shoot in single-shot mode. Indeed, it's interesting to note a definite new trend for rifles to have the facility to be altered to function as single-shot, by conversion from the multi-shot models they're based on. Perhaps this is the way of the future and eventually how most air rifles will be manufactured. Only time will tell, but for the present there's still a good selection of well-priced, dedicated single-shot PCPs available for those who prefer a one-shot hunting rig.

The choice of a single-shot is the simplest to make. Look for ease of operation for loading the pellet into the breech or loading channel. There's nothing worse than trying to load a pellet into a fiddly loading area, especially with cold or gloved fingers. Also take into consideration the number of shots you get per charge or fill. You'll get more from a standard-length rifle than from a carbine-size PCP; but other than that, all the features previously outlined for you to consider when choosing the basic all-round springer also apply here. It's when we get to multi-shot options that you need to weigh up a few major features that will sway you one way or the other, once again depending largely on personal preference.

Bolted

One key area of a multi-shot PCP air rifle is the action that cocks the rifle, indexes the magazine around and then takes a pellet from the magazine to load it into the breech. The other, of course, is the magazine, its type and its pellet capacity. For these two features to function, there are two or three other mechanical aspects to the rifle. Besides the cocking bolt handle there's the magazine indexing lever and also the pellet probe. The cocking bolt always cocks the rifle, but on its rearward travel it can also contact a lever that cams the magazine around to align a pellet with the breech. Often the bolt is also responsible for pushing or 'probing' the pellet forwards from the magazine and into the breech, in position for firing.

The actual layout of the mechanical parts depends largely on the type of magazine – spring-loaded, removable rotary, or of a linear design. These were explained in Chapter 1, so nothing need be added except to recommend choosing the one that you feel will suit you best. Also a matter of personal choice is the bolt position. This will be either what is known as a 'short throw', side-positioned bolt action or else a cocking bolt mounted on the rear of the action block. Generally, a rear-mounted bolt action will have a longer stroke, while side-bolt actions are usually the slickest and quickest to operate, which is one of the reasons they're termed 'short throw'. If you do a lot of shooting in the prone position, either freehand or from a bipod, rifles with side-positioned bolt actions are often easier and more comfortable to use. To be comprehensive I must also mention a few PCP multi-shot air rifles use a pivoting 'side-lever' for cocking and cycling the action. These are fine if you prefer them, but they'll rarely out-perform a 'short throw' bolt action.

Now – are there any other major considerations? Obviously the price will be a deciding factor, as will the choice of a fixed air reservoir design or a buddy bottle. Again, these decisions depend on the individual's circumstances and preferences.

The following is a guide list, to show how combos can be matched and the hunting situations to which they're most suited. Incidentally, it's worth noting that when it comes to matching size of scope to rifle, certain carbine size rifles can easily look and actually be what is known as 'over-scoped'. That being the optic onboard tending to over-power the rifle it sits on in terms of weight, length and in some cases features. At worse, this can affect handling but by and large compact to medium general specification optics suit carbine size rifles whilst general specification to high end scopes suit full length sporters. Even then, choose wisely and you'll get far more from your combo.

Recommended Combos, The Alternatives and Usage

Single-shot spring powered rifle with open sights or single-shot PCP with red-dot.
Rat shooting, feral pigeon shooting. Mostly used for indoor shooting and around the farmyard and feed pens. Good quality makes medium range, general purpose shooting a possibility, but I'd recommend a scoped rifle as follows.

Single-shot spring, gas-ram or PCP air rifle with general specification scope or slightly higher. (See chart in previous chapter for scope choice.)
The true all-rounder. This will or should be a full power one-shot

If you don't intend specialising in night hunting – you won't need a dedicated nightvision rig

potter. Good for most scenarios from bunny-bashing to woodie-whacking.

Multi-shot (including two-shot PCP air rifle option), with a higher specification optic such as a low light scope – possibly even with higher magnification range and parallax adjustment. This is suited to everything, and the hunter with this is spoiled. For closer range shooting you require fast target acquisition, so look to a lower magnification scope. Again, see the scope chart in previous chapter.

A basic gun mounted lamping kit transforms any quality air rifle into a tool for shooting at night

Threesome

At the very beginning of this chapter I suggested that, ideally, airgun hunters should have three combos. As I'm asked so often about what to buy and why, and if you pinned me down and said I could only keep three rifles, I'd most probably choose the following:

1. A springer or gas-ram, preferably with open sights and in .22 calibre. Depending on hunting situation, with either a compact or general spec scope fitted.
2. A multi-shot .177 calibre PCP carbine with a compact scope or similar optic, with the choice of scope dependant on hunting opportunities likely to be encountered.
3. Last but definitely not least, a multi-shot .177 calibre PCP with a nightvision riflescope.

If I'm travelling to another person's shoot as a guest, those three rifles are more often than not exactly what I'd take from the gun rack. Additionally, I'd not forget a selection of camo clothing, charging gear, spare pre-filled buddy bottles, a lamping kit, a plentiful supply of ammo – in fact all my other usual hunting accessories that we'll eventually be looking at.

Chapter 4
Ammo –
Pellet Calibres and General Information

I think it's long overdue that we dispelled the old airgun shooting adage that says .177 for feather and .22 for fur. As a general rule of thumb that was once quite a good guide to choosing which pellet to use, but with the advances in airgun technology and the quality of pellets now on offer an increasing number of hunters now recognise that the choice of hunting calibres isn't so cut and dried.

There are actually four calibres in all, because there are also the .20 and .25 to take into account, with each calibre having its devotees and its specialised uses. I personally feel that the popularity of .22 as a hunting calibre is largely due to the long held misconception that maximum power transfer on impact at the target is the major requisite for successful shooting. This is only partly true and we need to consider other factors – not the least being that the pellet must hit accurately within the kill-zone, no matter what the calibre. I mention this now, because a lot of what follows in this section can be considered quite radical when compared to the beliefs that have long been regarded as written in stone.

Any calibre of pellet hitting a 'kill-zone' on the quarry will do the job of cleanly dispatching it, always assuming that striking energy is adequate. The .177 calibre pellet, because of its faster flight, flatter trajectory and some other characteristics which we'll examine later in this chapter, is usually more forgiving of slight range estimation misjudgements, and therefore more likely to be accurate. Yet it must be acknowledged that if a .177 is slightly off the kill-zone, it could well only wound the animal because it hasn't got the shock effect of the larger, heavier calibres. Be slightly off the mark with a .22 pellet and its heavier weight combined with a larger frontal area will still deliver a lot of energy (i.e. shock power), which means it could still result in a clean kill. This is especially the case with a head shot on a rabbit.

What we learn from this is that accuracy is the prime factor for the clean despatching of any quarry species, but the delivery of lethal energy is still very significant. (Knowledge of the quarry's anatomy and the various all-important lethal areas where one shot will be fatal are fully dealt with elsewhere in this book – along with recommended calibre options – when we look at each quarry species individually.) But first let's look at the airgun pellet, its function and general design, including shapes and types available.

ANATOMY OF AN AIRGUN PELLET

The airgun pellet is quite a simple but clever and practical design, with four main features – the head, waist, skirt and internal profile. Each performs a specific and important function and, along with quality of manufacture, it's the pattern of these in relation to the pellet as a whole that dictates performance and efficiency.

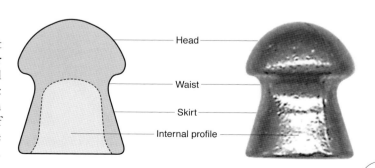

Head

Waist

Skirt

Internal profile

Pellets are manufactured from lead or lead alloy. It's been this way for years because lead is reasonably cheap, easy to work, and heavy enough to supply the weight needed to transfer the energy of 'in flight' velocity (kinetic energy) into weight/mass energy at the target. The softness of lead also helps to deliver energy to the target as the material expands on impact. To be thorough, I must mention that there are also pellets manufactured from zinc alloy, tin alloy and even copper. As to their 'benefits' I'll not comment other than to say that until I'm convinced otherwise – I'm sticking with lead!

Main Pellet Design Features

Head – The head is vitally important, as this is the part of the pellet that transfers the speed (velocity) and weight (mass) of the pellet into what is known as 'shock' or 'shock effect' when it hits the target. The shape of the head also helps (or sometimes hinders) the aerodynamics of the pellet, which should have a straight and accurate flight.

Waist – Pellets are 'waisted' (i.e. pinched in to a smaller diameter roughly midway between the head and the skirt) partly to reduce the weight-to-length ratio, but more importantly to reduce friction in the barrel while separating the head and skirt sections, thereby allowing them to function as they should. The head should stay true aerodynamically in flight to the target, while the skirt expands on catching the first blast of air from the transfer port, and fills the bore. The waist acts as a hinge, so the skirt can expand to meet and engage with the rifling in the bore of the barrel.

Skirt – This is designed to catch the blast of air on firing and to expand, making an airtight seal behind the pellet in the barrel. This is the only part of the pellet that is in full contact with the bore, picking up spin from the rifling to aid accuracy. This is one reason why the skirt should be checked for deformation. It must be perfectly circular and even-edged to

Time we dispelled the old airgun shooting adage of .177 for feather .22 for fur

make a proper seal, and to engage correctly with the rifling along the full length of the bore until the vitally important last millisecond as it exits at the muzzle crown.

Internal Profile – This is the hollowed-out section at the rear of the skirt and inside it, which is designed to catch as much air as possible, thus expanding the skirt. When checking the pellet skirt for deformity it's also worth looking into this hollow section to guard against an irregular profile, which is usually caused by the skirt walls being uneven in thickness. Heavier pellets usually have less 'hollow' in relation to the overall size, due to the fact that more lead is used in their construction, which usually means that there's a thicker skirt and a more solid head. These pellets are usually designed for high-powered FAC-rated air rifles, as they stand up better to the rigours of being blasted along the rifle's bore at much higher velocity.

Pellet Shape and Size

In the distant past, we had a valid excuse for not paying particular attention to our ammo, or 'slugs' as they were and still are affectionately known, as pellet choice was fairly limited.

However, there's now a myriad of different configurations of pellets in all popular calibres, so even when you've chosen your combo and calibre of air rifle you're still faced with which type or shape of pellet to use. Fortunately, top quality ammo is now readily available in all the main pellet designs to suit all shooting disciplines – especially hunting.

Pellet weight is given in what is known as 'grains', denoted by a 'g' or 'gr' after the numerical unit size – e.g. 20g or 20gr – and there are 3000 grains to the pound. The importance of weight in relation to pellet size is more relevant to rifles with FAC power ratings, so it needn't concern us for the moment. More important is choosing the right pellet to suit your particular 12ft lb hunting combo.

Every airgunner should be aware that every now and then a manufacturer might come up with a new pellet type which they 'guarantee' has better flight characteristics or 'power transference' figures. These are intended to impress us into buying and trying them, but they are usually little more than products made for the sake of grabbing your cash. Oddly-shaped pellets invariably perform oddly!

Here are the main pellet shapes, and their principal features.

Round or Domehead

The most popular type of pellet is still the round-shaped or 'domeheaded' pellet, so named because the head has a rounded dome shape! It has all the characteristics a pellet needs and no more. All major pellet manufacturers will have at least one domehead pellet brand in their range. They may have ribbed skirts, long skirts or whatever, but they'll all still have a rounded head. From this design we've had what can be termed 'hybrids', pellets that have pear-drop shaped heads which are slightly pointed but still smoothly rounded rather than finishing with a true 'conical' point. All stem from the good old basic roundhead design. The only true design feature that can be altered on these pellets is the sizing of the head itself, and the length and angle of skirt. To some extent the latter applies to other pellet shapes as well. But whatever the case, so long as the head is uniform and round in profile this will most certainly be the optimum choice for the hunter. The roundhead is the most accurate lead pellet design for any distance, from close range through to long-range shooting. That is why FT shooters use nothing else but these types of pellet. Later on, more will be revealed as to why the roundhead is the optimum shape for an airgun pellet in terms of efficiency.

Hollow-Point

This terminology has been heard many times in cop films. 'The shooter used a hollow-point or dum-dum bullet.' I know I used the term 'bullet', but it's still a projectile, and the term hollow-point fills us with images of a bullet that expands massively on impact, doing maximum damage to the target. In powder-propelled firearms ammunition that's very much the case, mainly because it's travelling so fast. Whether it's a live firearm cartridge or an inert lead projectile, the term 'hollow-point' refers to the fact that the projectile has a hollow or recess in the tip of the head, rather like a dimple. This encourages the head of the projectile (the pellet) to expand on impact. Whilst hollow point pellets will do this to some extent, they're not travelling with enough force to give the hunter using them any marked benefit. Although reasonably efficient at close to medium range, as hunting pellets they can become slightly unstable in flight over longer ranges. If using them, keep the range comfortably within 30yds and then it should only be your quarry that has any cause for concern.

Pointed

There's a long-held belief that a pointed pellet gives maximum penetration and is therefore the best option for hunting. Thankfully, this is now accepted by most thinking airgun hunters as untrue, despite which many pointed pellets are still sold to those who cling to this questionable belief. In fact, penetration as a benefit for hunting ammo is somewhat of a misnomer, because if you fire any pellet into a substance such as plasticine from a 12ft lb rifle at 25yds, penetration won't vary greatly, regardless of the shape of the projectile.

Apart from that, the pointed pellet's design is also quite unsuitable for it to be accurate even over moderate ranges. It has poor flight characteristics, and damages easily on transportation and even on handling whilst loading. To work properly, the point of the pellet would need to be exactly coincidental with the centre line axis of the pellet skirt and the mass of the pellet. To manufacture such a pellet would be either ridiculously expensive or almost impossible.

Wadcutter

Sometimes known as the 'flat-head', it'll come as no surprise that this pellet has a head with a flat profile. The theory behind its being useful to the hunter is that the flat frontal surface should transfer maximum energy on impact with the quarry. It probably does so at close range, but it starts running out of velocity as it pushes against the resistance of the air in flight, and it can become unstable even at medium ranges. This pellet is great for 10-metre match shooters, as it is designed to punch neat holes in paper targets; but for hunting I'd recommend you give it a wide berth.

Does Size Matter?

Despite all the discussion and arguments that have occurred over pellet choice, there are still the 'main two' to be considered – the .177 and .22 calibres. Whilst the world has mostly gone metric, we still know these pellets by their imperial increments (.177 inch and .22 inch), although their metric equivalents are 4.5mm and 5.5mm respectively. However, certain manufacturers supply these calibres in slightly larger width increments. A slightly larger pellet in the same nominal calibre, which may be only 0.1mm larger than the recognised 'standard', could well sit more snugly in the barrel of your particular rifle and be more efficient as it travels down the bore – i.e. shoot more accurately. This is where it really pays to experiment with various pellets to find which best suits your particular rifle. (Shooters using full-blown bullet-firing rifles find the same thing.)

The other, less widely known and used calibres, while they have their followers, do have particular characteristics that give them specific yet limited appeals, and they are therefore worthy of further investigation. The .20 calibre (5mm) pellet is often termed 'the compromise calibre' and because of all the arguments this causes it could be better termed 'the controversial calibre'. In the UK it's by far the

There are many top quality brands of ammo to choose from

least popular, but is much used and respected by our American cousins. It must be noted that the range of pellet choices for the .20 is limited, and therefore in effect it is a self-limiting calibre option. Theoretically, due to its size, you'd think you'd get the 'compromise of benefits' – i.e. that it'd have a flatter trajectory than a .22 calibre, but hit harder than a .177. While on paper this is true, most .20 calibre pellets weigh much the same as their .22 calibre relatives, so by and large you don't gain very much. However, shooters who are seduced by this calibre can be almost fanatical in their devotion to it, especially if shooting at FAC power levels. I can't help but feel that there is some flawed psychology in this devotion. It obviously looks bigger than a .177 and feels heavier, but, as it looks smaller than a .22, then it must be a compromise between the two. You'll note by the trajectory graph that follows that it does have some benefits, not the least of which is a flatter trajectory. But in practical situations facing the hunter shooting at sensible ranges, does wind and gravity have that much less effect on a pellet because it's 0.5mm less in diameter? I'm not convinced that it has these supposed, almost magical ballistic qualities and don't think I ever will be. But they do say 'never say never', don't they? But they also say that having confidence in your rifle/scope/ammo combo has a lot to do with your performance, and I wholeheartedly agree with that.

Now to the 'big slug' – the .25in (6.3mm) calibre. This brute has been around for as long as airguns themselves, but whilst at one time it revelled in a certain amount of infamy for its 'sledge-hammer' hit, it has by and large fallen out of favour with shooters, gun manufacturers and suppliers of good-quality ammo. The trouble is that, like the .20 calibre, it does have its devotees in the specialised uses it supposedly caters for, which are close-range rat and feral pigeon pest control shooting. It does transmit a lot of stopping power with little or no possibility of over-penetration, thus reducing the danger of ricochets and potential damage to buildings, but at the cost of having a very pronounced trajectory curve. This is a most specialised calibre, possibly only worth considering by those who shoot regularly at close ranges with a 12ft lb rifle, or the FAC-power shooter wanting extra clout, and provided you can cope with a trajectory like a horseshoe! I'm half joking, but you'll come to realise

The four basic pellet types – but even these have variations

the validity of that last statement in the section devoted to FAC-rated air rifles.

Ballistics

Let's look now at the physics and facts pertaining to a lead projectile fired at a given muzzle velocity – in this case enough to produce 12ft lbs of pellet muzzle energy – which should be considered by the hunter in relation to the all-important kill-zone on his quarry.

First, it really does come down to physics, or in this case the specific branch of physics known as ballistics, and in particular to the velocity (speed) the pellet is travelling at, in relation to its mass (weight). This in its most basic form is an explanation of how energy is transmitted or delivered to the target. This delivery of energy to the target is often termed shock effect or (a term I tend to use to a lesser extent) trauma. More specifically for a head shot, an animal or bird will die of the equivalent of what is known in human terms as 'blunt force trauma'. 'Heart failure' is a more appropriate term for when a pellet has hit any other vital organ. It's worth looking further into this because, in essence, you have four areas (vital organs are found) that can be termed as kill-zones. In certain species, and due to their position in the body and the quarry's visible profile in relation to your shooting position, these can be so small they're of little use for placing the pellet, but worth mentioning none the less. These are the brain (skull), central nervous system (back or side of neck) heart (chest cavity) and lungs (chest cavity, and found on either side of the breast bone of a bird).

For pellet placement you're now reduced to three major areas on the quarry's body, and then only in relation to how it presents itself to you in your shooting position. These are head, neck and chest. All are dealt with in more detail in the relevant sections on the individual quarry species, but it's worth keeping the headshot at the forefront of your mind, as this is the most important of the aiming points. Deliver your hunting shots with precision into the 'napper' and you're aiming right and killing cleanly.

In considering ballistics, the smaller .177 calibre pellet delivers its shock effect mainly through its speed (velocity). Due to its smaller mass it travels faster than a larger .22 pellet fired at the same muzzle energy (ft lbs). It also retains velocity over a longer range. However, the fact that it travels so fast and is quite small has given rise to criticisms of its tendency to produce over-penetration at the target, and at medium range this can result in the pellet passing right through the target. But a .22 calibre pellet fired at medium range can in fact pretty much duplicate this effect of over-penetration. This is doubly confusing when you consider that a larger pellet delivers more shock value due to its larger mass, but as its velocity is slower there's less likelihood of it over-penetrating at longer distances.

But consider this. While a medium-weight .177 pellet of say 7.9g will fly faster than a heavier-weight pellet of the same calibre, the heavier pellet penetrates further into the target at the same distance. This is due to the pellet's extra weight or, better put, extra mass slamming into the target. And here's a very interesting twist: a faster .177 pellet actually penetrates less than a heavier, larger .22 calibre pellet, and that's with both projectiles fired at the same muzzle energy. This is because a heavier pellet has a better ballistic coefficient, and retains greater downrange energy. Before leaving this topic it's worth noting that, irrespective of calibre, medium-weight domehead pellets – percentage wise –

retain almost the same impact energy and virtually the same velocity at 30yds as their heavyweight counterparts. This further supports the fact that weight or mass of pellet has a strong bearing on penetration at the target at this range, and helps explain why the round-head design is still the 'top dog' for a hunting pellet.

What should we make of all this? Initially it would seem that the .22 calibre pellet is the better choice for hunting, because the facts and figures of penetration, velocity and energy retention all look good on paper. Computer chronograph read-outs of velocities, and ballistic putty or other such media used to illustrate the penetration of pellets, can only give you the base, theoretical guidelines. These are test results in controlled conditions, and not what you can expect to be exactly replicated on flesh and bone in the hunting field, which will be discussed later. Also, as mentioned before, shock or trauma is only part of the 'killing equation.' If you hit the mark with a .177 pellet with sufficient energy, the fact you've hit the vital organ means a cleanly dispatched target. Indeed, anybody who hunts regularly with a .177 can't fail to notice how much 'bloodier' the killing wound often is. The reason for this is that the .177 pellet will sever everything it slices into and cause a lot of internal damage to blood vessels, tissue, organs and arteries. Who says it isn't an efficient hunting calibre? It should therefore now be apparent that getting the pellet accurately to the target has priority over the size of that pellet. This brings us neatly to the facts surrounding trajectory in relation to size of calibre and weight of pellets.

Trajectory

When a pellet is fired from an air rifle, irrespective of calibre, it follows a curved path in flight, known as the trajectory. Incidentally, trajectory applies to the path taken by any object in flight fired under a given pressure. The chart/graph that follows clearly illustrates flight path characteristics of all four pellet sizes.

Trajectory Chart

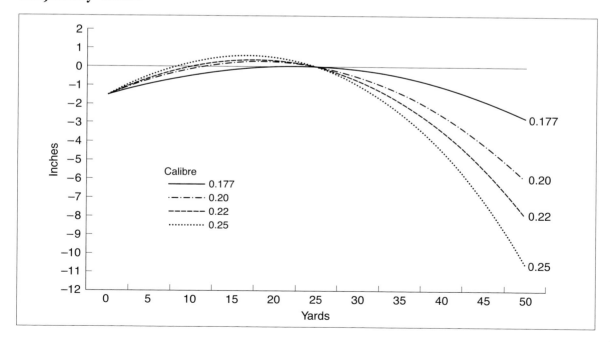

You'll notice the .177 calibre has the flattest trajectory, whilst the large .25 has the most pronounced. Of course, a heavy .177 pellet will have a more pronounced trajectory than a standard or lighter pellet of the same calibre, and this principle obviously applies to all heavier pellets, irrespective of calibre. So why mention it here? If a heavier 'small' calibre pellet is used, more shock effect is created due to its having a larger mass. By and large heavier pellets are designed for higher power-rated rifles, or FAC-rated air rifles as they're known. I don't want to linger unduly on the smaller calibre, but it does give food for thought that a slightly heavier .177 calibre pellet fired at 12ft lbs can be a much better proposition for the hunter, affording more heft on impact, a flatter trajectory, and better stability in flight than a lighter .22 calibre pellet. Heavyweight .22 calibre pellets are very much the choice for FAC rifles, as not only do they transfer much more stopping power but are less likely to lose shape and deform as a result of the higher pressures involved in firing. Interestingly, in general, heavyweight pellets are more suited for all benefits they afford the shooter when fired using a PCP, whereas light to medium weights work more efficiently when fired from a spring or gas-ram powered air rifle.

Earlier I touched on ballistic tests – i.e. pellets being fired into a block of plasticine or ballistic putty. The block is then cut in two to show the path taken as the pellet enters the material and slows to a stop inside it. Whilst these make for interesting study, again note that these results should still be looked upon as guidelines as to what actually happens when a pellet impacts on a live animal. Remember that a layer of fat and an outer protection of feather or fur, depending on the quarry, is added to the flesh and bone surrounding the kill-zone. These aren't uniform substances like the material used in the laboratory tests you often see. If you really want to know how a pellet performs when impacting on the quarry kill-zone, then on retrieving the kill, cut out the pellet. Distasteful as it may seem, it's a good idea to examine the wound externally and internally. Look at how the pellet has distorted on impact. Again – and this is borne out by many years of hunting – if you retrieve a pellet from your quarry, especially a bird, then more often than not the pellet will have changed very little in shape unless it has hit or smashed through bone. Internally the wound will show extensive tissue damage leading to blood loss. But one thing is for certain and that is, whatever calibre and pellet type you choose for your hunting combo, stick with it and learn its trajectory so you are able to make the required adjustments in aim for all distances. This is known as allowing 'holdunder' or 'holdover' at the target, and even though we touch on it here, the practicalities are looked at in much more detail in the following chapter pertaining to range estimation and evaluation.

When considering the physics of pellets in flight, look again at the trajectory chart and notice how the pellets share a common factor, in that they all leave the muzzle well below the set zero before arcing upwards and descending to the zero point – pre-determined by the shooter – and then drop (fall away) the further they get from the zero distance. The pellet exits the muzzle below the horizontal line of the scope due to the simple and obvious fact that the barrel is set below the fixed aiming axis given by the scope mounted above the rifle's barrel. So in effect you have two predetermined zero points for a pellet fired over any distance – one close to the rifle's muzzle and the other at the 'set' zero. These are determined not only by the main zero set by the shooter, but by variables such as scope height, pellet calibre, muzzle velocity and pellet weight.

To simplify this, a medium-weight .22 calibre pellet fired at approximately 12ft lbs and zeroed at 25yds crosses through the horizontal line of aim (the 'first zero') at approximately 10–12 yards, and then drops into the set zero of 25 yards before progressively falling off until it hits the ground due to loss of momentum – or, more correctly, loss of velocity. This very basic explanation serves to illustrate why you need to allow for what is known as holdunder (shooting lower) the closer the target is from the 'set' zero, and allow for holdover (shooting higher) the further from your set zero the target is. As you can see, less 'adjustment' is needed for the smaller, flatter-shooting .177 calibre. This is one of the

Smackdown! Any calibre pellet placed with precision will do its deadly duty

main reasons why the smallest calibre is so popular with FT shooters, and also why it is now becoming increasingly popular with hunters. Indeed, I'll stick my neck out and say that this has only become more accepted by hunters as PCPs have become more accepted and used as hunting tools. The reason is that the recoilless attributes of a PCP air rifle give a much increased accuracy potential. Therefore longer-range shots are taken more often than they were formerly. Once again, it seems we can learn a lot from the target boys.

Unfortunately, if the .177 has a downside it's the fact it can be affected by wind, particularly a 'heavy' crosswind. A larger, heavier pellet does tend to fly more true, but this doesn't mean the .177 pellet gets blown around like confetti. Besides, how often do you hunt at long range in breezy conditions? You shouldn't need or want to, so in that respect I personally find nothing to condemn the smaller calibre.

The trajectory chart only applies to a shot fired along the horizontal plane in ideal conditions. When we come to shooting at upward or downward angles in the field other 'nuances' have to be reckoned with and allowed for. Many hunters find that when shooting at awkward angles, rangefinding and pellet placement can go sorely out of the window. This will be dealt with in the following chapter – because, at times, air rifle hunting ain't easy!

Power Checker

A common misconception is that if the air rifle is more powerful then it will be more efficient at dispatching quarry. Wrong! You're now aware that accuracy at the target is the vital factor. I've often made mention of 12 ft lbs being the legal limit for 'off ticket' (i.e. no FAC required) air rifles, and in the main hunting rifles should be running fairly close to the 12ft lb legal limit. But it's the responsibility of every airgun hunter who does not possess an FAC that his air rifle doesn't exceed that limit. A responsible shooter should actually be thinking of running the rifle at around the 11.4–11.6 ft lb mark with medium weight ammo. This way, if heavier or lighter ammo is used, the power theoretically shouldn't rise above the current 12ft lb legal limit. Remember, should you be stopped by the police and your rifle checked for any reason, then the powers that be are allowed to test the rifle with any ammo they choose.

So – how to stay legal? At this point readers should make a mental note to take their air rifle to the nearest specialist airgun shop and have it checked over their chronograph. This is an electronic gadget that can measure the speed of the pellet, and by using the correct formula it will give you the muzzle energy of the rifle in ft lbs. Muzzle energy can be calculated once you know the speed of the pellet in feet per second (f.p.s) and the pellet's weight. The formula is used like this. First, square the speed of the pellet, then multiply it by the pellet's weight in grains, and then divide by what is known as the 'common factor' or 'gravitational constant' – a figure of 450240. This gives you that pellet's power in ft lbs. There are little chronographs that do the maths for you, and all you need do is punch in the weight and calibre of the pellet, shoot a few to gain an average velocity, and then read the figure off the digital readout. They don't cost the earth, and what's important is that they'll keep you on the right side of the law.

Pellet Preparation and Care

There's no use spending time on pellet preparation if your pellets aren't of a good standard to begin with. Thankfully, most of today's big brand name pellets have got the basics right. These mean good quality lead used in manufacture, a consistent manufacturing quality control, good inspection processes and transportation and supply in suitable protective packaging to prevent pellet deformation.

As the company goes to all this trouble to get pellets in as good condition as possible to the consumer, it seems strange that many of us are still content to just empty a few into the pocket of a shooting jacket and set off for a session. Granted, airgun hunters have done this for aeons, so why shouldn't it continue? Well, it can – if reasonable results are all you desire. But if you want to achieve the finest accuracy and results you and your combo are capable of, then a little time taken preparing pellets can bring surprisingly fewer 'flyers' and save you from those infuriating, 'unexplained' misses.

Don't get me wrong. I'm not suggesting you go to the lengths of the World Class standard FT boys, with washing, grading, weighing, sizing and lubricating. Yes, you can do all that; but just a few simpler procedures will save you much frustration in the field. First, tip your pellets out of the packaging onto a few sheets of clean brown un-waxed wrapping paper or newspaper. Depending on the pellet brand, you'll probably be surprised at the amount of swarf (metal filings and small cuttings) that comes out with them. If the pellets have bits of swarf stuck in the skirts, you have no option than to wash them. A swirl around in a bowl of light soapy water, then rinsing and drying, will suffice. I know, it's hassle, but it's worth the trouble, and if this is a regular occurrence – find another pellet brand.

Hopefully, all you need do is pick the pellets up one at a time, and while checking the skirt for damage blow out the very few bits that may or may not be found. If you find a pellet with a deformed skirt, dispose of it. Also check that the head is undamaged and uniform. While checking this, ensure the waist is central so that the head and skirt are perfectly aligned on the horizontal. You could go as far as to buy a set of special scales, but you're going down a laborious road, and I've not felt the need to weigh top quality pellets individually, so visual inspection is my main criterion for preparation. However, before returning them to the tin or box, a light spray with pellet lube is advisable. Allow them to dry naturally, and then carefully put them back in the box or tin.

At this point I'd like to refer to the fact that some writers say they prefer to use single-shot rifles because they can visually inspect each pellet for every shot. This is a tad misleading. You can visually scrutinise each pellet just as closely while filling a multi-shot magazine as you can when loading one at a time into the breech. The slight damage that may occur when a pellet is probed from a magazine is minimal and soon put to rights when the air blasts the pellet skirt outwards to make contact with the barrel bore. In other words, don't be misled into thinking that a one-shot rifle is the tool for total precision.

After taking all this care, a pellet pouch is a handy aid for carrying extra ammo on your shoot, and much better than just tipping a few into a jacket pocket. If you insist on just pocketing them, then make sure the pocket is clear of dirt and grit, and never put anything else – such as compact binos – into the pocket with them. Also, use a pocket that you're not likely to lean against, so there's no possibility of pellets being crushed and therefore deformed before use.

To sum up all of this, especially pertaining to initial selection of a pellet brand, I'd say choose a 'roundhead' pellet which you find, through careful trial and testing, that really suits your combo and then stick with it. Incidentally, you'll find most roundhead pellets look almost identical in profile, but in actuality they will differ, and you'll find some more suited to precision air rifles with tightly choked barrels. Only by trial and error will you discover which is best suited to your particular rifle. However, as a general rule of thumb, German manufactured pellets are in fact a tad larger than other European ones. The 'best' brands will even have the exact sizing written on the tin in millimetres. In that respect you can see why it really does pay to try a varied selection of quality pellets to really find the brand and type that best suits your rifle. Look for a brand known for its consistency in size and weight. They'll probably be more expensive, but that's because quality pellets are more expensive to produce.

As for buying tin after tin or box upon box of the same batch number, it can be worth your while doing this if you do find a batch that your rifle particularly likes. This is because pellets with the same batch numbers are made from the same die set. Just a little warning though – don't go buying the shop's whole stock of them as, if you don't shoot a hell of a lot pellets, they can oxidise if left for an overly lengthy period of time. No amount of cleaning can sort out badly pitted pellets, and most hunters don't want to buy 10,000 slugs at a time – or will you?

And take heed – don't chop and change ammo, and do regularly check your rifle's zero. While doing that, you also need to get down to some serious target practice to attain hunting accuracy.

The last visual check of a pellet is before loading irrespective of rifle type used

Chapter 5
Gun Handling, Sighting and Firing – Shooting Techniques Explained

Air rifle engineering technology has come along in leaps and bounds in a relatively short space of time. Suffice to say that a newcomer to the sport today can be spoiled, because many modern air rifles, and PCPs in particular, almost shoot themselves! They need only a guiding hand or two and an aiming eye to place the pellet exactly where it needs to go – the all important kill-zone. But no matter how good the gear you might be fortunate enough to use, you still need to have grasped the basics of gun handling to make full, safe and proper use of the technology you're holding.

When hunting with a rifle of any description, the more we shoot the more we tend to take the basics for granted, yet it's the basics that can mean the difference between success and failure in the field. Many like myself probably first began learning to shoot using a spring powered air rifle; but then as we moved up through the ranks, eventually to shoot PCPs, it's all too easy to forget those first tentative shots we fired, and what a basic rifle they were fired with.

Let's get back to basics and look at the various elements of correct gun handling and, in turn, accurate and consistent shooting.

Although airgun hunters are bombarded by stories of successful shots at quarry at 50 yds and beyond, it should always be remembered these are only achieved consistently by very experienced shooters, and only when conditions allow. Every hunter should only shoot within the limits of their personal skills and ability, and always show respect for quarry.

Another important factor the hunter should always remember is that they're taking part in a sport that requires a certain level of physical fitness and that level varies depending on the demands of the hunting techniques you're employing. You shouldn't or wouldn't want to go to the gym or go jogging, for instance, if you had a heavy cold or worse. So why go hunting when you're feeling under the weather. Granted, it may do you good to get out for a spot of fresh air, but it's better to go without your rifle. Take this as a prime opportunity to go out and observe. How you feel physically – and even mentally – will affect your performance in the field. Don't drag yourself out just for the sake of going, as you'll end up missing easy shots, getting frustrated and wishing you hadn't bothered. At worse, you may even have an accident! Instead you could brush up your accuracy at home on targets – which brings me nicely to the subject of where to practise safely, and how to set up your own target range.

Home on the Range

If you're not a member of an established gun club or don't have access to a target range, then there's nothing for it but to build your own. This is known as a 'plinking' range, and as long as you have at least 25 yds of clear, unobstructed, privately-owned space from the shooting position to a secure pellet stopping/catching backstop, then you're in business. The backstop is the most important part of the set-up, as it needs to be strong and secure enough to stop the pellet going through and beyond the property you own. If it isn't, you're not only shooting irresponsibly and illegally, but also inviting an accident to happen. For this reason it should be stressed that a backstop can never be too sturdy. Granted, in relation to a bullet fired from a cartridge-firing firearm, a pellet fired from a 12ft lb air rifle is very low-powered. But when pellets are continuously hitting in the same general area on even the

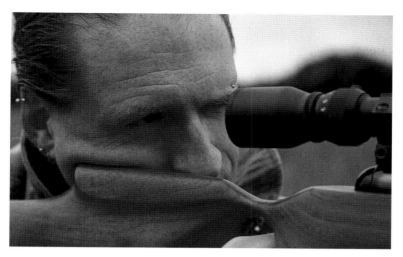

Eye-relief and head position are vital for giving you an accurate full sight picture

thickest piece of wood, they will quickly start to wear a way through. This is why backstops not only need to be of a suitably strong construction but also checked periodically for damage. Many shooters use a couple of old, scrap doors with carpeting thrown over the front to help lessen the penetration of the pellet. The carpet not only helps reduce damage and prevent ricochets but also absorbs the sound the pellet makes if it is allowed to continuously impact on bare wood.

My recommendation for a backstop is at least a double layer of solid wooden doors over which you can put at least two or three layers of carpet. Firedoors are perfect, as they're made from 1½ inch thick solid wood, and like other doors you'll find them on builders' skips when they're demolishing office buildings and the like. Keep your eyes open and don't be afraid to ask if you see doors being thrown out. More often than not the previous owners will be glad to see the back of them, and if you remove them it means less rubbish for them to shift. A word to the wise concerning the carpet used. Although you might think it best to pile umpteen amounts onto the doors it's actually better to use just two or three layers, and when these show signs of too much damage, replace them with fresh layers. This prevents an excessive amount of carpet becoming waterlogged and gungy, and therefore almost impossible to remove come the time to replace them. If you've a garage or large shed you can store old, spare carpet, and never pass up the chance of an unwanted door or two. I use my backstop so often that I've even built a wall of bricks and mortar that the doors lean against. This is approximately 6ft in height by 8ft wide and gives me total peace of mind because the pellets are never going to pass through to the neighbouring garden. Even so, I regularly check the condition of the carpet, the wooden doors and even the wall behind.

With a backstop sorted, what do you shoot at? Well, there are the obvious paper targets, which I mount onto heavy-duty metal bulldog clips hung on metal cup-hooks. A simple idea, but the clips make changing targets very easy. The same goes for 'reactive' targets such as chalk discs. These are simply hung on small nails that I tack onto the backstop itself. Chalk disc targets give a satisfying feeling of achievement as they shatter on pellet impact, and they really do help keep you practising for longer periods. There are many other reactive targets readily available, such as spinners, re-settable fall-flats ('knockovers' or 'knockdowns').

Knockdown targets are nothing new, and have been the norm in FT competitions for almost as long as the sport itself. However, the size of the plate that needs to be hit to knock it over bears no relation in shape or position on the target to the kill-zone of the quarry it mimics. This is because the mechanics of design oblige the makers to position a circular 'hit-zone' in the centre, rather than at the head, for optimum target operation efficiency. Other similar-principle targets, but more realistic to the hunter, are the kill-zone profile fall-flats from AirgunSport. These not only represent a 'true' kill-zone but are in profile as well. The rabbit fall-flat consists of a profile of a rabbit's head, while the rat fall-flat shows the profile of the first third of the body. These are realistic target areas – especially the latter – as hitting the real thing here would result in a clean kill.

Whilst I use both knockdowns and fall-flats, it must be said that while your neighbours might put up with a dull thud of a pellet hitting a sound-deadening backstop, how tolerant would they be to the continuous 'ting' of an airgun pellet on metal? Even now, I prefer to use these targets by taking them along to any reasonable-sized field on one of my shoots, to practice in different shooting positions. This type of 'real-life' practice will also be dealt with further in the chapter on Shooting at Night. Here you'll really appreciate the ability to duplicate a hunting scenario under controlled conditions, but without targeting live quarry. It's much better for the hunter than continuously putting shot after shot down a range from a bench rest. Later in this book there'll be a clear description of setting out a 'field course' to help you hone your range-finding and accuracy. My garden range is mainly used for setting up my hunting rigs, and setting and checking zero. Again, it must be remembered that safety needs to be at the forefront of your mind at all times when preparing or actually shooting. Here are a few safety rules that all shooters should adhere to:

- Never leave a loaded rifle unattended. This applies to the private target range just as much as it does at a club or in the hunting field.
- Never point a gun at anything that you don't regard as a legitimate target – even if you believe the gun to be unloaded.
- When loading a break-barrel, under-lever or side-lever action rifle, always hold onto the barrel or lever while thumbing-in a pellet.
- Never 'dry-fire' a spring or gas-ram powered air rifle – i.e. cocking and firing without a pellet being loaded into the breech. It can cause extensive internal damage as the piston slams forward unbuffered by a pellet, as it should be pushing against one in its effort to propel it from the barrel.

Getting a Grip

Successful air rifle hunting is a combination of many factors, but correct gun handling – thus giving a consistent level of accuracy – is one of the most important. Then there's experience and fieldcraft – and even just good old common sense. Correct gun handling means what the term implies – how you 'handle' or 'hold' the rifle while you take a shot. This is all about consistency – i.e. holding the rifle in the same way for every shot. Correct, consistent handling is even more important when using recoiling rifles such as springers, as they have a definite firing cycle that is mechanically the same for every shot. What the shooter has to do is work with this cycle, rather than against it.

First lets deal with the way you hold the rifle. It shouldn't be held too tightly; rather it should just be snugly supported or cradled by the shooter, allowing it to go through its firing cycle unrestrained. In other words you need to let the rifle 'breathe'. The object is almost to work with the rifle, acting to give it stability while equally 'instructing it' through your actions of steadily aiming it and ultimately guiding the pellet towards the target. 'Follow through' is also important, and this means keeping the gun in aim and on target after it is fired. This is very important because moving the rifle, even slightly, after squeezing off a shot will have pellets flying all over the place. Remember that even after you've slipped the trigger, the pellet is – for milliseconds – still travelling along the barrel, and thus still affected by your actions. Incidentally, follow-through is also needed for a recoilless PCP, as the lock time (the period between 'squeezing' the trigger and the pellet leaving the muzzle) is usually longer than the lock time of a springer or gas-ram rifle.

A problem that can affect any rifle is 'cant' or tilting. Once a rifle/scope combo has been zeroed for a particular range, if you hold the rifle differently, leaning to one side or another, even if the rifle

Practise in the standing position as many times you'll need to take shots such as this

is only slightly 'askew' in your grip, the impact point of the pellet will be off the original set zero. This is called 'cant', and can only be remedied by practice and consistency in your gun handling. You could fit a scope-mounted spirit level or an electronic level aid which visually helps you line up the rifle squarely on the target shot after shot, but it's far better to begin by learning correct gun handling without these aids. Another thing to remember is that you can't rest a spring or gas-ram powered rifle directly on a solid object while taking a shot. The rifle will literally bounce off as it goes through its firing cycle, with accuracy being badly affected as a result. You can, however, rest the rifle 'cushioned' in your hand, which can then be rested on a solid object such as a branch, gate or fencepost.

Because many PCP air rifles use what are known as free-floating barrels, don't make the mistake of resting the front of the barrel or the silencer on any solid object. If you need to, always rest it using the underside of the air reservoir, buddy bottle or preferably the underside of the stock. Resting a rifle on a free-floating barrel will have the weight of the air reservoir or 'buddy bottle' – and of course the stock – 'weighing down' and therefore lifting the barrel upwards, badly affecting accuracy.

Another recommended support is to shoot in a seated position with your left knee pulled up towards your body with your arms forming a brace around you. The left hand should hold your upper right forearm so that the rifle can be rested over your forward arm. Of course for left-handers the opposite applies. This is an established FT shooting style, but one the hunter can adopt when the opportunity arises. Unfortunately it's only of use if you've previously had time to take up an ambush position, but as long as you don't have to stay put for hours it's a surprisingly comfortable position to adopt.

A relaxed grip and steady follow-through are essential to consistent accuracy with a spring or gas-ram powered air rifle, and also major considerations for shooting with any other type of air rifle. Whilst the following applies to most shooting positions, in the main they apply to shooting the rifle 'freehand' or from a standing position.

Shots up at birds in trees are fraught with many variables – one being to ensure the pellet has a clear path to the target

If you're using a spring-powered rifle it should be held firmly enough to keep the rifle on aim, rested in your hold as you sight on the target through the scope or along the open sights. Also, any rifle, irrespective of power source and with or without a scope fitted, has a point of balance. Your leading hand should be positioned approximately 2 to 3 inches in front of this balance point. Adopting this shooting grip while standing is known as the 'offhand' stance, and many opportunist 'snap-shots' will be taken from this position. This is fine if you're using a light- to medium-weight rifle such as a carbine, but if using a hefty full-length sporter it can become a strain and cause you to 'wobble' the longer you hold on aim, due to your arm muscles taking all the weight. If you do have more time to take the shot, pull the elbow of your leading arm round to rest into your hip – another stance favoured by FT shooters - as this affords a much more stable aim.

Even better, if the situation allows, is to adopt the kneeling position. In this position the leading arm can be rested on the left knee with your bottom sitting on your right foot, heel tucked under the body and with the right knee rested on the ground. Of course, the opposite of this applies to 'lefties', which involves resting your leading arm on your right knee, and sitting on your left foot. There's a slight variation of the kneeling position and, if the ground isn't too muddy, it is one that is even more stable. This is to kneel lower with the right shin almost flat to the ground, ensuring you're comfortably sitting on the lower leg with your right foot tucked under your bum. This allows you to rest the upper forearm of your leading arm along your left thigh, rather than only the elbow. A much more relaxed and therefore stable shooting position can be achieved by sitting in this way. More detail for changing shooting positions is outlined later, when we come to combining fieldcraft and shooting techniques in the field.

When on the target range, and whichever shooting position you use, don't pull the rifle butt-pad too tightly into your shoulder, as this will have the same effect as gripping the stock too tightly, because it causes tremors. Another factor that needs to be considered is that the impact point of the pellet shifts off zero when you alter the position you're shooting from. For instance, if you set zero in the kneeling position, don't expect it to be the same when shooting in the standing or prone position. Again, judging these zero shifts is a skill which, like all aspects pertaining to your shooting technique, can only be achieved with dedicated and applied practice.

When shooting prone (i.e. lying down), where possible I prefer to deploy a bipod, especially if waiting in ambush. Often this isn't possible, and if you've decided to go stalking you might not even have the bipod in place. And for most airgun hunters out for a spot of general hunting, the shot taken from the prone position is more often than not at the end of a 'stalk'. You'd think the shot would be the easy part as you are well within range, and taking the shot should be a matter of course. Often it is, but after stalking a twitchy bunny you'll be pumping with adrenalin and this, coupled with the physical and mental exertion, means your nerves will probably be sending tremors around every muscle and fibre, with your breathing being laboured, heavy or both!

The technique of stalking is dealt with in full in the chapter on Hunting Techniques, but the prone shooting style needs further discussion here. For a recoilless PCP then as long as you're comfortable, the main difference you'll notice is that the scope will seem closer to your eye, because lying prone tends to push your head further forward than when you are shooting either kneeling or standing. It doesn't take much to adopt a style that will allow for this, and the optimum way to combat it is to let the rifle out of the crook of the shoulder to rest in the upper arm, pulled slightly back. In this position your shooting (trigger) hand is holding the grip and rifle squarely onto the target, whilst your leading arm should act as a rest for the rifle's fore-end.

Shooting a recoiling rifle such as a springer or gas-ram from the prone position is a different matter altogether. This is because in this position both arms holding the rifle are in direct contact with the ground – i.e. a hard surface. The rifle will therefore tend to jump off zero, either to the left or right. Some find the muzzle is more likely to flip, causing pellets to fly higher than the set zero. There's no way around this but to familiarise yourself with the particular zero shift and keep a mental note of it while you target your quarry and 'aim off' accordingly. Again, only practice will give you the ability to shoot like this and, like the standing position, this is one you need to fully master. I'll reiterate the fact that you can't always get away with using a bipod with a PCP, as many times it won't be practical to have the 'pod' in situ. One aspect of the prone position is that strain is soon felt on the lower back muscles. To combat this you can raise yourself up more on your elbows with your back slightly arched, so you're not 'cricking' the back upwards at the waist. There are some situations that allow the body to fall into a more relaxed position for prone shooting, such as when lying over a slight hillock or from a ditch. These are usually prime areas for ambush shooting, and more information for body positioning can be found in the relevant sections pertaining to shooting using a bipod. Always remember that an unduly uncomfortable shooting position isn't conducive to accuracy.

It's worth noting here that of all shooting positions, the seated position is the one that offers most variations on a theme – almost like a fine-tuning of the body position to achieve the most stable and comfortable hold. You will find which suits you by trial and error, and simply by practising. As examples, you can sit with the left leg half outstretched and your leading arm rested along the thigh, with the left leg raising or lowering to adjust height of shot. Alternatively, you can form a brace for the arms. Sit with your bottom flat on the floor, and half raise both legs at the knee approximately a shoulder-width apart. Then rest the elbows of both arms into the lower inner thighs or alongside the knees of the corresponding leg to arm. It sounds confusing, but is a very comfortable position and one that can be held for quite a lengthy period of time.

Then there is another particularly stable seated position, which is found by keeping the bum flat to the ground but drawing the right leg towards and across you into the half-lotus position (no sniggering!) and drawing the left leg inwards and upwards to form the front support. Rest the elbow of the leading arm on the lower thigh of the left leg, just behind the kneecap. Obvious, for left-handed shooting from all positions, the opposite leading arms to raised legs apply. You don't need to take yoga classes, but do take the trouble to experiment with the seated position because many times it's the body position that will keep a shot steady.

Sight Pictures

For open sights the 'sight picture' relates to the position of the foresight within the rear sight, and those two superimposed on the quarry. For telescopic sights it relates to the clearer view you see as you look through the scope.

Although many hunters will go straight for a set of optics on their hunting rifle, for reasons of thoroughness I've already dealt with open sights. In relation to shooting with a scope I've also explained the distance known as eye relief, but it is worth re-capping here in relation to your shooting technique. Eye relief means the distance your leading (aiming) eye is positioned rearwards from the scope's eyepiece. This varies with individuals (and also depends on the scope being used) but for most shooters it's usually around 3 inches or so, a distance that gives you a full sight picture – i.e. you can see the full circle of the front objective lens through the rear lens. Once you've set your scope in the scope mounts you'll probably feel you've got it just right, and more often than not you will. However, a little trick to fully ensure correct eye relief is to close your eyes for a few seconds, bring the rifle up to your shoulder and hold it in the most comfortable aim position with your head resting on the cheekpiece. Then open your aiming eye to look through the scope. If you need to move your head forward or backwards, even slightly, to attain a full sight picture through the scope, then you've not

Many times during a hunt, it'll be possible to adopt the more stable kneeling position

set the scope eye relief correctly to suit your natural hold. Also check that the scope cross-hairs are still in line with the plumb line on the backstop you originally used to centre the scope. They too could be slightly out. Try it, as you may well be surprised to find that the eye relief and scope setting you've previously been shooting with is incorrect. If so take the time to adjust the scope accordingly. Listen to your body, because while your eyes are closed it will naturally adopt the most comfortable position that is best for you when holding the rifle. Get it right, and you'll soon notice the difference in your accuracy and your success in the field. Do set the eye relief up for the standing shooting position if you are sure most shots will be taken from that stance. It's worth noting that scopes that have a longer

The 'over knee' F.T. position is very stable to use but not always practical

degree of eye relief often prevent the shooter having to waste precious time in adjusting head position for awkwardly angled shots.

When adjusting the power ring for different magnifications on a variable-power scope, you'll find that a scope with a longer eye relief always gives you a full sight picture, as long as you've mounted the scope correctly. Scopes like this are also one solution for a rifle that may otherwise need to have more conventional optics fitted in set-back mounts to obtain correct eye relief.

Allowing For Range and Other Variables

Range finding and estimation have already been discussed in the chapter on Scopes, but a scope can only help you determine the range if you know how to use that particular optic's reticle to do so. Also, most hunters using the 30/30 or Duplex-style reticle will use what is known as 'hold-over' for a target further than the set zero, and 'hold-under' for a closer target.

Now for the nitty-gritty of considerations relating to shooting at live quarry. In a perfect world the target would be perpendicular to your aim and within a yard or so of your set zero. In reality, what is more likely is that after hours of waiting in ambush or careful stalking you either virtually trip over a bunny, or a woodie pitches into the trees at well beyond your set zero. Here you have two obvious range differences and two vastly different angles of fire to the target. So what to do? I'm sorry to harp on, but only practice and familiarisation with your combo will give you the experience to allow the correct amount of hold-under or hold-over. These allowances will also vary depending on whether you're shooting the smaller .177 or larger .22 calibre pellet. Less adjustment – i.e. less aiming-off allowance – is needed for the .177 calibre and that is one of the main reasons why many hunters are now switching to it. It does not allow a sloppy shooting technique or bad range estimation, but by and large it is far more forgiving of slight errors on the part of the shooter.

As I've recommended hunters to have a selection of rifles at their disposal in at least the two main calibres, I must also stress the importance of re-learning those aim points for hold-under and hold-over when you switch rifle combo. Even the occasional flirtation with the smaller calibre will have you feeling over-confident at longer range with the .22. In other words, it's back to the target range before you shoot at live quarry, so that you're back in tune with the trajectory and particular qualities of the rifle/scope/ammo equation that makes up the combo. Yes, it is a combo because all three (indeed four, including yourself) make up the final 'team' you use to cleanly dispatch your chosen quarry. And always, repeat always stick with the same ammo you used to zero your rifle and scope for the hunting trips that follow.

Earlier I touched on the 'angle of fire'. This is the angle at which the barrel is pointed towards the target, whether upwards or downwards. It seems that even experienced hunters disagree on the allowance that needs to be made for awkwardly angled shots. Even now I'm not a great fan of the longer-range shot into the tops of trees, the reason being that there are so many variables to contend with besides gravity. At the top of a tree the wind will be at its strongest, and will therefore affect your pellet in flight. You can of course watch the upper branches and twigs for indications of any wind strength and direction. Those who say they can regularly judge a shot on a swaying bird are usually not giving the full story. It can be done, but should only be the type of shot you make when you have become fully accustomed to virtually every shooting situation and angle, and have experienced what gravity, wind and even your confidence can do to a pellet's flight path. The same airgun hunters who brag about these shots might admit to clean misses, but they're certainly not admitting to the times they've downed the bird but only wounded it. This is worse still if it has flown off to die, rather than to be retrieved at the foot of the tree and swiftly dispatched. So if unsure – don't take the shot. Wait until a shot within your capabilities presents itself – and don't worry, because it will. While on the sensitive subject of wounding, it's a situation that will happen to even the most experienced shooter, and it is wise to be prepared for this eventuality. Should you 'wing' a woodie from the trees then the best way to kill the bird is by a swift, solid blow to the head with a 'priest' or by swinging it around by the head to break the bird's neck. I have seen many fancy methods that allegedly dispatch birds more humanely – but they don't! It's either a pellet in the kill-zone, a sharp 'knock' from a priest, or the 'neck twist'. If you think this barbaric, then don't hunt, because you will at times need to get your hands bloodied.

But we mustn't stray from the main subject of how to shoot accurately and compensate for elevation. First, you need to appreciate the relatively low speed at which a pellet fired from a 12ft lb air rifle travels. For instance, a medium-weight .177 calibre pellet of 7.9g travels at approximately 825 f.p.s and a medium-weight .22 calibre pellet of 14.3g calibre travels at approximately 612 f.p.s. These figures might seem fast, but when you consider that an average .22LR calibre 45g sub-sonic medium-weight rimfire bullet travels at approximately 1050 f.p.s (which equates to approximately 100 ft lb) I think this clearly illustrates why an airgun pellet loses trajectory in flight rather rapidly, due in part to gravity dragging the pellet towards the ground.

A pellet fired horizontally will behave differently from a pellet fired at an angle, simply due to the effects of gravitational pull. For instance, let's say that your rifle is zeroed for 30 yards. If a shot is taken horizontally at this distance the pellet will travel 30 yards under the pull of gravity over all of that distance, but your zero has already been compensated for the expected drop (i.e. the trajectory), so you aim 'dead on'. But if the target is in the top of a tree (or the bottom of a gully) and you judge it to be 30 yards from rifle to target, you will have to aim slightly lower in both cases. The reason is that while the target is 30 yards away, the horizontal distance the pellet will have to cover will be less than 30 yards so the pellet's trajectory will effectively be less, and you have to act as though the target is closer. Hence you aim lower.

I know this might fly in the face of what you've possibly read previously in various publications on the supposed 'fact' that a pellet travelling upwards is affected by gravity pulling more towards the rear of the pellet. That's not strictly true, and it's in the field that you'll realise that steeply-angled shots are awkward to calculate. But by following the simple guide I'll outline, you can counteract the difference in trajectory you will experience. To determine the exact amount of hold-under necessary would take a degree in trigonometry (or at least a calculator), as you would need to know the distance to the target, the exact angle of the shot and the height or depth of the target from the horizontal plane of the shooter, and then how all these and other factors would affect trajectory. Phew! Basically, you just judge the range of the target from the rifle as usual, then aim slightly lower than you normally would for that distance if it were horizontal. Try this out on high and low practice targets before you attempt such shots at live quarry, in order to accurately know your own required point of aim. These can be twigs or leaves high up in trees.

As a starting point, try aiming a ½ inch or so low at the target with a .177 and around ¾ inch low with a .22 calibre rifle. If the angle is particularly steep – say for instance you are at the base of a tree – you will have to use even more hold-under. This is because you will probably be much closer to the target so pellet drop is far less.

To recap, and as a rule of thumb – the steeper the angle to the target then the more allowance is needed as the pellet arches upwards instead of following the more traditional horizontal trajectory line. But this only applies if the angle of fire you're shooting at is 45 degrees or higher and the range to the target is close to your set zero. Should you be lining up for a longer shot, much further than your set zero, and the bird is high in a tree then you'll probably now need to allow for holdover, as the pellet will be affected by gravity over a longer distance. This can get confusing, and only practice will help you master the art of awkwardly angled shots. Usually it's the high ones that will present themselves and be the most difficult to assess. In fact, it's only when the angle gets to around 60 degrees and above that you should have to consider compensating for the change in trajectory. Most upward shots into trees are at roosting birds, or those alighting into 'sitty' trees. It is a skill that needs mastering, should you choose to tackle quarry in those situations. (Incidentally, I'll dispense with vertical shots, as they're nigh-on impossible and virtually never worth taking because the bird is likely to be in a position that offers no clear kill-zone.)

As for downward-angled shots, particularly if taken at a slightly downward angle and either in the standing or kneeling position towards quarry on the ground, most times you won't need to allow for any compensation for the change in trajectory from its horizontal line as the angular distance isn't very great. But if you're shooting from a high seat, a tree position or an upper window of an old building (where the situation is allowed, and opportunity arises) then it certainly does need consideration.

To all this we must add the need at times to compensate for a crosswind so, as you can see, the subject of elevation compensation is fraught with many variables, and only experience using the infor-mation given as guidelines will help you to be consistently successful.

On the subject of shooting in very breezy conditions, I'd always advise the relatively inexperienced shooter to avoid this if possible. But shooting in a light wind can be beneficial, especially if stalking, as to a certain extent the wind carries away your scent and any sounds you might make. However, if it's only a light cross-breeze, a shot taken over a medium range of 25 yards shouldn't be duly affected. If shooting at ground level near hedges, the strength of the breeze will be less than if shooting over an open field or into trees. Even a moderate crosswind will create the need for what is known as 'aiming off' (to one side or the other, depending on wind direction) in order to allow for the wind to 'drift' the pellet back into the kill-zone. Again, only practice and a great deal of experience will help you determine just how much lateral allowance to give for any given wind conditions. The shooter who forgets to allow for these variables is the one who has the smallest game bag.

These variable factors lend more weight to the .177 slug as being a better option for the hunter. The pellet is lighter and flies faster. It zips through the air, and a light crosswind affects its smaller mass less. But remember that the greater the distance your pellet has to travel, or the more disturbed the conditions it has to contend with to get to the target, then the more it is affected and the less 'oomph' it delivers when it gets there. So in inclement weather I'd never chance a longer-range shot, and all will be taken with 30–35 yards at most. You might think this sounds close for an experienced shot, and it may well be; but it's a more responsible attitude than to risk injuring your quarry.

Trigger Control

Consistent trigger control or 'trigger release' is a technique neglected by just as many live-round shooters as airgunners. Many are seemingly quite happy to just hook their finger around the trigger blade and pull. Maybe that's a crude description, but it suits the crude trigger control and hand grip positions I've often seen many so called 'experienced' airgunners adopt. For optimum trigger control your trigger finger should be square to the trigger blade, and the only part of your finger touching the front of the trigger blade should be the pad of your forefinger. When ready to take a shot, you should gently

Practise shooting in the prone position as more often after a long stalk you'll need to take the shot like this

79

'squeeze' the trigger, almost feeling your way through the shot until the trigger mechanism trips the sear to send a pellet 'zinging' along down the bore. Also, at the pistol grip, the stock might have a channel allowing you to adopt a thumb-up hold. Many feel this helps with trigger control, as the hand is in a more relaxed and natural position. Personally I prefer this hold when catered for, especially if the stock has no thumbhole for my big digit!

Before leaving this important aspect of shooting it's worth thinking about the thorny subject of breathing in relation to taking the shot. I know some who take a deep breath, hold it in, and then shoot. Wrong! I know it can be very hard when the adrenalin is pumping, but try to consciously calm your breathing into a slow, easy rhythm. Then breathe out gently and fairly fully, pause and shoot. In most hunting situations you'll probably think you don't have time to do this, but apart from 'snap' shooting, where you don't have time except to aim and fire, you do. Once you get experienced in this breathing technique it will become second nature, and you'll do it subconsciously before every shot is taken. Then just watch the tally of your hunting 'bags' grow. And it doesn't end there as let's not forget that once you've tripped the sear, you need to allow for follow-through. Personally, after squeezing the trigger I hold the sights on aim and watch through the scope, almost willing the pellet to impact where I'd placed the scope's crosshairs before I'd squeezed the trigger.

Incidentally, most of this relates to the basics of shooting with a 'recoiling' rifle, but most also applies to shooting with a PCP. I'm sure you can guess what I'm going to say now. If you're a hunter who's 'spoiled' themselves by recently using a PCP air rifle but still have a springer lurking in the back of the gun cabinet. or in a case at the bottom of the wardrobe, then why not really get back to basics? As you blow off the cobwebs against paper targets, chalk discs or knockdowns, you just might be very surprised to discover just how much you've been taking for granted about your shooting, and maybe even just how much you've forgotten about the essentials of the very art of shooting itself.

Field Technique

Practice is the only way you will achieve a consistent level of accuracy. I can't stress enough the importance of making yourself fully accustomed to the capabilities of your rifle, scope and ammo combination. Everything should become second nature. Bringing the gun up to the shoulder, aligning the eye, and taking care not to 'cant' to left or right before shooting. And, of course, a consistent and smooth trigger release. Before attempting to shoot any live quarry, it's imperative that you achieve an acceptable level of accuracy at inanimate targets. In other words, it's back to the target or plinking range until you can consistently make good groups of approximately an inch out to 25 or 30 yards, depending on your set zero. Practice should ideally involve shooting at different ranges and angles of fire, and from different positions. Remember that in many cases when out hunting, your shots will have to be taken in the standing position. Although it's not the most comfortable of stances, do take time to practice shooting from this position. It may sound obvious, but the way you stand will affect the accuracy of the shot. When we naturally stand, say in a queue, most people lean on one leg more than the other. It's a similar 'comfortable' position that you need to adopt for taking a standing shot. Your feet will be shoulder-width apart, with most of your body weight transferred to the left leg, which should be forward of the body. For lefties, the opposite applies. You should be standing almost side-on to the target with the rifle across the front of your upper torso, and squarely lined up at the target.

The standing shot certainly needs mastering, but in the field you'll often get the chance to adopt the kneeling or even prone position, especially if you're targeting a rabbit. Only experience will tell you when you need to act quickly with a standing 'snap shot' or when the quarry is sufficiently comfortable to let you take a little more time to rest yourself into a more stable position. When the adrenalin is pumping it's all too easy to rush, but experience has taught me that I can more often than not get

The seated position is the most versatile and offers the widest variations

myself into a rested or supported position. Even at your most comfortable, you'll probably become aware of the reason why shooters miss, and that's the simple fact of your body moving with your breathing and your pulse. You'll find you can never actually hold a rifle stock-still in any position except off a bipod or similar rest, and even then natural body movements can affect the shot. The most important art is learning to control that movement as mentioned earlier, with your breathing and basically by calming your nerves. It's not easy when under pressure, but it's this technique, when mastered, that has won many FT competitions and filled the biggest game bags. Learn to take the shot only when your timing is right, the cross-hairs are on the target, and your body is 'under your control'.

With the standing shot there are times when you need to shoot upwards into trees. We've covered the need to allow for the angle of fire, but this is also when you will need to slightly adapt your stance and rifle hold. Your body should be leant slightly back to transfer your weight onto the right (i.e. rearward) foot. The opposite applies for lefties. Whichever the case, avoid leaning back from the waist as this will result in straining the back muscles and accentuating any wobbles. Your leading hand will and should be allowed to naturally slide back along the forend to hold the rifle at the optimum point of balance. Basically, as the rifle is elevated, the combo's point of balance moves back and so should your hand accordingly. Let the rifle fall more onto the upper shoulder, and all other aspects for physically taking the shot remain the same. Where possible – and often it is because I'm shooting in a pre-determined ambush point waiting for birds to come in to roost – I'll stand or sit with my back to a tree trunk as a rest, and to disguise my form on the woodland floor from eyes up above.

As regards changing position when encountering ground level quarry, should you be in a standing position when you encounter it, you can be almost certain that if the quarry isn't overly twitchy, it'll be far more appropriate for you to slowly lower yourself to one knee or even flat out on the ground. Often a rabbit will have spotted you, but by lowering yourself you can fool the animal into a false sense of security because in effect you are adopting an unthreatening posture. Try this and you'll soon discover rabbits will resume feeding, so you have time now to either move slowly forward, or just rest, before gathering yourself and calming your nerves ready for the shot.

Some of the advice I've given may initially seem unfamiliar, but the more you shoot and hunt it will become obvious why you need to hold, stand, sit or lie down on the job like this. Before leaving the subject of the shot, it's imperative before trying your hand against any live quarry that you make yourself fully familiar with the vulnerable aim points of each individual quarry species, or as it's known – the 'kill-zone'. On any species this is the area on its body that when hit with a pellet with sufficient force will cleanly dispatch it. Only when you have the ability and knowledge to achieve this should you embark on your first hunting foray. The aim point is always quite small, usually a headshot, neck-shot or into the heart and lungs. This is why consistent, accurate performance is essential. Never overestimate your ability to shoot accurately at various ranges. In the field with adrenalin pumping even the relatively experienced can make hasty and, to your quarry, painful mistakes. You should always strive to effectively dispatch your quarry as quick and humanely as possible. There are also as many times when you'll need to be disciplined enough not to shoot, for risk of wounding quarry due to the animal not presenting a clear kill-zone. Similarly, there could be foliage or twigs between you and the target. In most cases only patience will solve the problem as, more often than not, rather than move position and risk being spotted it's better to wait until the animal turns so that a kill-zone is clearly visible. Also, although the target may look clear through the scope, look to the side or carefully peek over the optic and you'll often clearly see twigs or plant stems that could possibly cause a pellet deflection. In this case slightly shifting your shooting position to your left or right might just find a pathway for your lead.

As for the kill-zone, different angles presented by your quarry in relation to you give different degrees of size in terms of both surface area and shape. By this I refer specifically to instances when the quarry is facing you, standing sideways on, sitting or standing. All kill-zones are fully explained later as we deal with each quarry species, but as a rule of thumb a full-on shot presents a larger horizontal 'line' for you to drop the pellet into.

As I'm sure you can now appreciate, airgun hunting can be one of the most infuriating of shooting sports but, due to the demands put on the hunter, when you make that successful shot it's also one of the most rewarding. Before leaving the subject of taking shots, I must comment on shooting at a moving target. It may well sound enthralling that you can get to a level of accuracy with an air rifle that affords you the ability to shoot quarry that's running for cover. I've been shooting for many moons, and the only quarry that I regularly shoot 'on the hoof' so to speak is rats. One of the reasons is the rat is a crafty critter that often doesn't keep still long enough for a studied, measured shot; but when it's on a regular run across a beam or along the foot of a wall, then you can (with experience) give the shot enough lead to put the pellet into the front one-third section of the rat's body, which gives a clean kill.

Shooting at running or even moving rabbits is another matter altogether. I'm not being biased, and my advice is born of years of experience. I feel the responsible shooter should never attempt to do this, for a few specific reasons. A moving rabbit rarely runs in a straight line, or with its head (or for that matter enough of any exposed kill-zone on the body) perfectly level. A rabbit can scurry, scamper, hop, zigzag or bound to safety. Loosing off a pellet in its direction serves no purpose other than to educate the rabbit to the danger of the raised rifle, the muted muzzle report and the subsequent whistling sound from the pellet flying past it. If you do fluke it and hit the animal, it's more likely that – through pure adrenalin and momentum – it will get into cover or down a hole to meet a painful, lingering end. Do you want this? No, and your quarry deserves much more respect. Both rats and rabbits are regarded as vermin, and this attitude might seem like a case of double standards, but whilst the rat is little more than a walking disease, the rabbit is quite a noble little creature. If you want to shoot quarry on the move – get the official police paperwork sorted out and buy yourself a nice-handling 20-bore or 410 shotgun.

Chapter 6
Finding a Shoot

Finding a suitable area to shoot over is without doubt the hardest part of getting started as a hunter, and especially as an airgun hunter. From the start I feel I should fully clarify this. Farmers understand the need and use of the shotgun, and are usually grateful for the shotgunner's help in the ongoing battle with the woodpigeon. However, we have to admit that the airgun has had a lot of bad press in various ways, and is perceived by some as not really being a 'proper' gun for general vermin control. So before you even start, the odds are rather stacked against you, as you may have to convince your prospective hosts as to your effectiveness, as well as your responsible nature and attitude.

All land in the UK is privately or publicly owned. You can't shoot over public land, and for private land the permission of the owners is always needed. Without permission to shoot on somebody's land, you are poaching. There's no middle ground or grey areas because the law sees it like this. In law, you can be charged with armed trespass, and in these increasingly gun-sensitive times, the penalty for 'being where you shouldn't be' are quite severe. Pleading ignorance isn't going to do much to get you a reprieve or pardon – so how do you go about obtaining permission to shoot on somebody's land?

If You Don't Ask You Don't Get

That pretty much sums it up. A good way to start is to really get to know your local area. Not just where the farms, fields and woods are, but more importantly who owns them and employs the people

Finding suitable land to shoot over – the most difficult hunt of all

Do your homework – the search begins here

who work there. You can begin by asking at your local gun shop, and they will be more than happy to help you with any queries and questions. They will possibly be able to supply contact numbers of known rough shoots already established in the area. Indeed, it's in their interests to point you in the right direction because the more you go shooting, the more ammo and shooting kit you'll require to buy. Although I don't want to dampen enthusiasm before you get started on searching, they'll have been asked many, many times by others before you. Also, whilst rough shooting often comes available for the shotgun shooter, the airgun is still seen by many as the 'boy's toy'. Of course we know otherwise, so that's one of the factors you should keep in mind when asking and looking for land to shoot over. An area that's unsuitable for a shotgunner or firearm sportsman may still be riddled with vermin, and many areas that are 'un-shot' can get overrun with pests. Finding yourself in the right place at the right time, asking the right questions, can bring surprising results. So even though it may just be a few fields and hedgerows covering little more than a few acres, don't ignore it as a possible place to begin your quest to find a shoot. As they say, 'from small acorns…'

To make the most of your shoot area it's essential to obtain the relevant Ordnance Survey (OS) maps. OS maps show all the roads, footpaths, farm tracks, buildings, features and even the contours of the land, and you need to know the type and lie of the land if you are going to hunt certain species. For instance, if it's rabbits you intend to target, then you will be looking for fields surrounded by hedgerows. If it's woodpigeons, magpies and other corvids, you will be looking for land that contains at least a small wood, at the very least one copse, or better still scattered clumps of trees. As for rats, collared doves and feral pigeons, any farm with a barn or a few run-down outbuildings should fit the bill. Once you've marked the particular farms that meet with your requirements on your O.S. map, you've still got some homework to do before making your initial contact.

First, go along to the farms you have picked out for an initial reconnaissance of the area, but do keep to the public access routes. I know I shouldn't need to say this, but do leave your gun at home. Don't trespass, even if only jumping over a gate to get a better look at a far hedge line or wood, as you could blow your chances of getting a shoot before you start. Keep a record of the farm, its land and any quarry you see during your recce, as this will be useful later when – or indeed if – you get to talk to the owners.

Check out whether the place is still a fully working farm. Look for signs of farming activity, such as farm machinery, livestock or crops in the fields – anything that indicates the land is being worked. If none of these are in evidence, then the farm could have changed hands and may now just be a private dwelling. If that's the case, then this is usually not the place to find your shooting ground. The owners will probably have little interest in the land in terms of land management, and they'll probably enjoy seeing the 'cute fluffy bunnies' in the morning – as long as they tolerate the critters hammering their lawn and garden. In other words, they'll have bought the house and land for its scenic attraction and the privacy it affords them. Unless they realise the benefits of controlling certain vermin, an airgun hunter won't be high on their list of priorities.

However, always keep that in mind about 'smaller bits' of land that are unsuitable for shotguns or firearms. Market gardens, plant nurseries and the like can often bring a surprise or two in the form of acquiring shooting permission. Also – bizarre as it might seem – don't ignore built-up areas. Find out who owns the run-down industrial mill or commercial units you've seen feral pigeons hanging around. The chances are that they roost in the buildings at night and are causing a hell of a mess. It's always worth asking if there are any problems like that which you can help with, and even though this sort of shooting may not be your first choice, this can have a knock-on effect in that your name is passed on to other people who may have land more suited to the kind of shooting you prefer.

A feature such as a dead tree will stand out on the landscape – as a potential sitty-tree it's an area worth noting

85

First Contact

After a few trips out, you will soon narrow your list down quite drastically. But when you've located suitable farms that fit your criteria, then it's time to make contact. In the first instance, contact the farmer or landowner by letter, not forgetting to enclose a stamped, self-addressed envelope, and also your home telephone number (and your mobile number, if you have one). Take the trouble to have your letter neatly typewritten. Explain your request in a manner that shows you have an understanding of what working a farm entails. Stress that you're responsible, will leave no litter, cause no damage, and will respect crops and livestock. If you belong to B.A.S.C (which I advise you should) or a similar organisation, mention it, along with any insurance cover you carry. Tell them that you can and will supply at least two independent references as to your good character, as a couple of good references can make the difference between securing a shoot or missing it. Remember that you are in effect asking the owner if you can walk around his property with a loaded gun. Ask yourself this: would you let someone who appeared dodgy hang around, let alone shoot an air rifle in your back garden? I think not. Don't expect a quick reply. Farmers are very busy people, and if you start phoning too soon or too often you'll probably put them off.

Obviously the number of letters you've sent out will govern how many replies you can expect to get. For instance, if you've sent out two dozen requests, you'll be doing well to get two or more replies, even with a stamped, self-addressed envelope enclosed. You might think that's a small percentage, but that's the way it is. We live in a world where people are always asking for something. Unfortunately the farmer will probably have been asked many times before, and all too often your request will get put on the same pile, or end up in the same bin. But don't be disheartened. At your

Know your quarry – woodies can cause devastation over farms growing cereal crops

A few collared doves and the like are often tolerated around farms – listen to the farmer and only shoot what he specifies

first positive lead, which is almost certainly going to be because you've telephoned to follow up a written request, follow it up immediately. That hopefully means you'll be arranging your first visit.

Attitude

So you've now got to the all-important point of first contact, and it will possibly require subsequent phone discussions before a face-to face meet. During your initial conversations, don't be pushy. They might not have fully made up their mind, so be diplomatic. Mention you have some knowledge of the farm, tell them you've seen and studied the relevant ordnance survey map and that you're aware of the surrounding land and main features. But don't sound as if you've been spying! Try to convince them that you can offer a free, efficient service that will help in the control of vermin. Though many hunters understandably want to get stuck into quarry such as rabbits, ask first if he's having trouble with rats or feral pigeons. Controlling these species for a farmer can often be a quick route to being accepted on the property for other quarry with your air rifle. Whatever you've noticed about his farm, comment on it if it is relevant to vermin control and something that may be causing him problems. Being fore-armed with some knowledge of the pests that are on his land is where your initial recce will pay off.

Be prepared for rejection at any time, but once a positive reaction has been received, which it eventually will, don't waste the opportunity. Ask when it's convenient to personally visit the farmer and be prepared to meet him anywhere of their choosing, usually on the land. Don't presume that you can visit the house immediately. This meeting will be at an arranged time, not just a 'come round to the yard' sort of invitation. Why do I mention this? A farmer is a businessman, and his business is farming, so it follows that you need to be businesslike in your approach and attitude when you turn up for a meeting. That doesn't mean you need to wear a suit and tie – I've never worn one, never have, and never will – but you can easily dress smartly and project a responsible, respectable image. When you finally get around to meeting the farmer this really is a situation where first impressions do count for a lot. Whatever you do, don't turn up fully camo'd up with your rifle slung over your shoulder. Believe me – I know people who've done this and, incredible as it sounds, they are actually surprised when they're turned away. During your visit be polite, have a friendly manner, and let the farmer dictate the pace of the conversation. At this point he'll probably be 'weighing you up', so to speak. Just in case, take along your gun in its bag but leave it in the boot of the car and out of sight. The farmer might want to see what type of gun you intend to use on his property. As I've said – don't be pushy. But, due to the modern hi-tech look of certain PCPs, I've often found that this in itself can be an ice-breaker, as the farmer usually remembers the old springers and might well find your new-fangled piece of kit quite fascinating. If a conversation develops on this – all the better.

If the meeting has gone well and the farmer has time, he might show you the area you are provisionally allowed to shoot over. You won't (or very rarely) be given carte blanche to go wherever you like, whenever you like. More likely he'll steer you to an area where he's having specific problems with a specific vermin quarry species. This is where it pays for you to know your stuff. Nothing impresses more than a good knowledge of the quarry and what it will be doing that's making it such a headache for the farmer. If you get to shoot, early results are even better, because the farmer will soon realise that having you around is mutually beneficial. On the subject of primary areas you may be shown, and specifically told you can shoot over, pay particular attention to what is said. In fact, don't take it for granted that you can shoot anything that's legally deemed suitable by law for air rifles. Ask the farmer specifically if he wants anything left untouched. Some tolerate and even like to see a few collared doves or squirrels about the place, so don't blow it by shooting something his wife or relative has been feeding for years! Listen to him carefully when he outlines the boundaries of his land. It helps to have a notebook handy, because a hedgerow pointed out on a visit can, if not noted correctly, be mistaken for the next one along when you visit the next time, and you could quite easily find yourself straying inadvertently (but still illegally) onto a neighbouring farmer's land. Ideally, these are the neighbours you will want to impress in the fullness of time. Eventually they too will hopefully realise that your services are very useful.

When all is sorted, and before you take your gun from its case, get your shooting permission in writing as soon as possible, with the farmer's signature. You'll need to carry this with you at all times when on his land. It goes without saying that you should treat the farmer's hospitality with respect, always closing gates behind you, leaving no litter, and taking care not to shoot so as to spook his livestock. This is specialised shooting you might have to undertake eventually, but not one you should even be thinking of doing at the outset.

Only shoot at times that have been agreed, and if you want to shoot at night make sure this is allowed, and always let the farmer know when you'll be there 'after hours'. If you bag a few rabbits or woodies, always offer them to the farmer first, if you see him. A bottle of something at Christmas will certainly be a nice gesture, and is looked upon as a country tradition.

A Word to the Wise

Even now when I secure new land to shoot over I feel I've achieved something. That's because it's the hardest hunting of the lot, and as the years go by it seems to be getting harder. Another factor that many are shy of stating publicly is that, by and large, the shooting fraternity can be very 'cliquey'. More often than not, when you finally acquire your shoot, you'll be shooting over land that already has an established group of shooters present, perhaps rough-shooters or game shooters. They will – rightly or wrongly – guard their own shooting permission with varying degrees of acceptance of your presence or, quite frankly, of resentment. Don't get me wrong, because not all people are like this; but it's all too easy to upset an applecart, no matter how unwittingly, especially in a close-knit community where the shooters may have ties to one another through marriage or even direct bloodlines. You will always be the new boy, and last in really does mean first out. I'm not trying to put a dampener on the matter, but do heed those words as you go about your shooting, and never become complacent. If you hear of another possible shoot, try to get your foot in the door there as well. If it means more travelling than you'd expected you should still pursue it, because you never know when permission to shoot on a farm can be withdrawn. If it is, it isn't necessarily due to something you've personally done as a shooter, and usually isn't.

Shooting feral pigeon can often have a knock-on effect into gaining contacts to the kind of shooting you prefer

Opportunities to Shoot and Learn

Another avenue to try for what can often result in shooting permission, and one that will certainly help you develop your fieldcraft, is to help a fox shooter. Accompanying an experienced fox shooter on night-time hunting forays can bring a mass of opportunities and knowledge. Occasionally you'll either hear through the grapevine or even see an advert in a gunshop or broad-based shooting publication that a person is looking for someone 'enthusiastic' to help him with fox control. Invariably this will mean carrying the battery pack and operating the spotlamp. This might seem to have little relevance to airgun hunting, but you can and will learn a hell of a lot. Watch the way they move over the terrain at night. Listen when they give you tips on using the lamp, take note of their gun handling, watch the way they use the wind to their advantage, and marvel at the way they can actually 'call in' their quarry. It's all fascinating stuff, and much will be relevant to the use of a lamp for your night-time hunting exploits on bunnies. Often for your help, your 'payment in kind' will be an invite onto a farm where the fox shooter has permission to shoot. Here you'll possibly get chances to use your air rifle at suitable sized vermin. The fox shooter rarely has time to keep on top of the rabbits, crows, and squirrels that pester most farmers, but it's his duty as a pest controller on the land to help his host to cull all vermin. More often than not the fox shooter will be grateful for your help, as you're doing a part of the pest control he either has little interest in or, more likely, he's not got enough time to do justice to. Also, many shooters in rural areas double up as part-time gamekeepers. They'll be well practiced in setting traps and snares, and this could well be another area where you'll be asked to help out. You may or may not find this of interest, but it pays to offer help to pest controllers undertaking trapping or snaring campaigns – especially in spring, when it can be a very time-consuming operation. Take an interest in all you see as you progress as a shooter, and always offer and be prepared to help on the land.

So what can you expect, once accepted into these 'inner circles'? Usually you'll first go out for a walk around the surrounding land with your newfound shooting companion. He'll show you the area and watch to see if your shooting, gun handling and safety are of a sufficiently high standard to warrant you being trusted to operate on your own. Eventually he'll introduce you to the farmer and maybe, just maybe, you'll become a trusted part of this shooting fraternity and get written permission for a piece of land to shoot whenever you wish. Always be grateful to that first contact, and to those you meet along the way. By now you'll have come far, and you may even progress to be invited to accompany a deerstalker in his quest for the noble antlered beast. You might be the one who has to drag the culled beast off the hill, but watching a deerstalker is not only an experience, but also your chance to watch and follow possibly the finest form of stalking. The relevance of stalking to the airgun hunter is an obvious one – a basic part of fieldcraft and one you'd always do well to learn more about.

But a word of caution is timely. When you've been lucky enough to be invited as a guest onto a shoot, it'll probably be pointed out to you, but don't ever presume that you can go back unaccompanied unless you are specifically allowed. Don't take it for granted that you can 'nip on' once in a while. Hopefully, it will mature into a fully-fledged shooting opportunity and relationship, but be patient. Let your hosts 'weigh you up', and let them dictate your progress into their shooting world. It's all too easy to blow these opportunities due to over-eagerness, and remember that the shooter who first invited you to join him will probably have spent years gaining the trust of the farmer or landowner. He'll certainly have earned his right to shoot, so be prepared to do the same. Always respect those chances to shoot on 'borrowed land', because soon it may be a place where you can go and shoot on your own.

This is even more basic, but before you even take your first shot against quarry on a shoot, remember that it's your responsibility to be able to identify all legal quarry species in a variety of different situations and from even the most obscure angle. In fact, a handy saying that has served me well and is worth remembering when out hunting is this – 'If in doubt, don't shoot!' Finding a shoot can be difficult, but one thing's for sure: when found, you'll have damn' well earned it!

Chapter 7
Observation and Quarry Location

As a hunter, I used to believe that to be out in the field without a rifle was about as much use as going fishing without a fishing rod. That was until I became involved in wildlife photography and from there on I began my ongoing learning curve and understanding of wildlife behaviour. Not only did I learn the 'comings and goings' of quarry deemed suitable for the airgun around the shoot, but about animal and bird behaviour in general. I can now say that time spent just 'watching' animals will pay the dedicated shooter back ten-fold.

This is of such importance that I'm going into detail on how to properly observe the land you intend to shoot over, no matter what hunting technique you employ at a later stage.

Observation can be as simple as leaning on a wall looking over the fields, or sitting or lying in a comfortable concealed position or hide studying a particular hedge-line or group of trees. But getting to know a particular area usually entails many hours spent out on there, as I said earlier, preferably without your rifle, but using your eyes and ears. In other words, simply looking, listening, observing and learning. If you wonder why I'm stressing you leave the rifle at home, it's because it will be all too tempting to shoot quarry that comes close. And, while this may bring 'instant results', it may just as likely be the reason there's little or even no quarry in that area should you go for a full campaign at a later date. Without a doubt, observation is one of the most important but oft-overlooked factors that contribute to successful hunting. This preparation really is the key to hunting success and, to borrow a biblical quote, you'll eventually be able to 'reap as ye have sown'. Even just meandering around with your eyes and ears open is a start, but ideally you should be much more methodical in your approach to observation.

Map it Out

Following on what we considered in Finding A Shoot, take into consideration that once you've secured that elusive shooting ground you should also make yourself fully familiar with its overall layout by walking the area, and noting all the specific features that may be of interest to particular quarry. In Quarry Files you'll be given information to help determine which animals inhabit which types of terrain and what areas of the land. Pick out these key areas, and lie up under camo or in a suitably 'hidden position' to watch and learn. Granted, at times it will seem boring, but at others very interesting and eventful; and try to learn from everything you see, including the animals and birds that aren't on your hit list. These too will be using an area of the shoot for reasons associated with your quarry. Usually it's because the area is rich in foodstuff, is relatively undisturbed by man, or both. For animals, a combination of the two will represent a safe area.

After the first few visits, draw up a map of the area you are allowed to shoot over. Obviously you don't need to be a master cartographer, but don't think you can get away with just making a quick sketch on the back of a beer mat! Use at least a decent-sized notepad whilst out walking around the shoot, and transfer this in the comfort of your own home to an A4 size sheet of plain paper. A Dictaphone is also a good aid for keeping verbal notes, and much easier to use than continually scribbling on a pad of paper – especially if it's raining or your fingers are numb with cold. As for the

Locate a particularly 'favoured' sitty-tree and you could well find yourself with a steady stream of potential targets

map itself, make a few photocopies of it as standard maps. Then, when you've got an idea as to which quarry species are active in certain areas, mark them on one of the copies using symbols or name abbreviations. Then it's easy to keep them regularly noted by using a clean sheet to amend for any change in quarry activity or locations. Up-dating the map will usually be needed every couple of months or so, depending on your particular area, the time of year and of course how often you go shooting.

The main priority of your map is to show the boundary, which should clearly indicate the perimeter enclosing the area where you are legally allowed to shoot. Unfortunately, at least part of the land probably won't be nice and neatly fenced off. The boundary could be a stream, an old broken wall, a small tree line or even a ditch. Even at this early stage, make a note of these permanent landmarks and features that clearly define the limits of your shoot.

Once you've established the boundary on your map, you can then start to mark in the places that will be of interest to various quarry species – which are, of course, the places that you should also make your first target areas. Begin by marking any wooded areas, no matter how small, and even if they are only a couple of trees standing together. These could well prove to be what are known as 'sitty-trees' (trees used by birds for perching to rest or watch the surrounding area before moving on), that – if approached stealthily or better still to be hidden up near within range – could well see you bagging a few pie-filling woodpigeons, or ridding the land of a bonus nuisance corvid or two once your hunting begins in earnest.

Just Watch

Note down areas that may be appropriate for siting a hide, which will be useful when you've mastered hide-building and the techniques that will be outlined later, and any other spots that offer you natural cover for ambushing and laying baits. All these specific hunting styles will be dealt with in the relevant chapters, so rest assured that you'll be well informed and prepared when the time comes to put it all into practice.

Once you've made the map, do keep it regularly updated. By this I mean keeping notes on where you've seen various species. For instance this may include rabbit activity (e.g. droppings, runs, burrows), or maybe you're lucky enough to have an area of woods used by quarry birds for roosting. Even if you haven't, you're likely to have times when birds will fly over your area on the way to feeding areas or back to roost sites. These, when established, are known as flightlines, usually of woodpigeons but crows also use regular flight paths. You'll certainly not be able to shoot them on the wing as the shotgunner can, but you can tempt them down onto the ground using decoys, or for the corvids a carrion bait. Also, many forget or don't realise that birds, as well as having flightlines, also have regular stop-off points along them. These are usually the sitty-trees, areas to feed, drink, rest or even to await others of their kind before moving on – usually and unfortunately out of your allotted shooting area.

Take time and trouble to prepare yourself properly, and don't underestimate the importance of reconnaissance. An absolutely invaluable piece of kit is a pair of binoculars. A good pair of compact binos with a specification of 8×21 are light and extremely handy to carry at all times. If waiting longer, then a pair with larger magnification and larger front objective lenses will be less of a strain on the eye. Incidentally, whilst I prefer a monocular while shooting as it's smaller, compact binos are a good compromise for using if you're doing a bit of reconnaissance and shooting. For more serious use then a larger pair of binos is the optimum choice. You can even get them in camo!

Creatures of Habit

Now we've established that animals – and especially birds – have set behavioural patterns which they generally stay faithful to, according to season, come spring, summer, autumn and winter. They do say that only mad dogs and Englishmen go out in the midday sun, and they should say that only mad airgun hunters go out in potentially bad weather conditions. But sometimes, taking a chance – and as long as the weather isn't forecast to be extreme – to wait up in ambush in the right position can be well worth the effort. This is because crows and magpies seem unbothered by inclement weather, and even during lengthy spells of light drizzle they move around pretty much as normal on their daily routine. But heavy rain is often the cause of birds disappearing into the woods and animals, especially rabbits, sitting well under cover out of sight. The point is that weather can and does affect how an animal's behavioural pattern changes. But, like us humans, at some point they will need to feed and drink. So, in general, certain animals or birds use some areas more than others for food, to rest and, in the case of the weather, to find shelter. Knowing this and using it to your advantage will put you in the right place at the right time.

Some areas are certainly heavily frequented by wildlife because they are secluded or relatively undisturbed by humans, and only prolonged observation of the shoot will reveal key areas such as this. For instance, with a flock of birds such as woodies, crows and jackdaws, their stop-off points could be a clump of trees in the middle of a field, or a quiet corner of the field itself, where they might only be grubbing around looking for an early feed or late snack. Whichever the case, and I again stress the point, be there at the right time and it could well be their last supper! Correct, dedicated observation and preparation quickly show just how important they are to successful hunting.

Look also for nest sites (in winter, when trees are bare) that betray the areas frequented by magpies, crows and rooks. Corvids return to the same ones year in, year out. The magpie's nest is unmistakeable by its football shape, whilst the rookery will be obvious by its sheer number of nests, and is often heard before it's seen. Crows, though usually in 'paired' twosomes during nesting time, may just as likely be found nesting in loosely grouped colonies rarely exceeding half a dozen nests – a sort of 'crowery', as I like to call them. These tend to be found in twos or threes, with a few in the same tree, quite high but certainly not as high as rooks' nests. Whilst these birds build in the very top of the tree, entwining their bulky structures around the small twigs of the treetops, crows favour the clefts of branches for a more stable base. The same applies to squirrels' dreys, which are often mistaken for crows' nests. The drey, however, is shaped like a small magpie's nest and will have more 'leaf litter' in the structure. Squirrels like their own space so the drey will be on its own, and in a position that allows them good views of the surrounding area. Look too for the smaller 'nut store', once thought of as fanciful; but a squirrel in an established territory can use an old drey above or below the 'new', usually larger drey to store food. But enough on dwellings and nests, as this is just an example of what you can find by keeping your eyes peeled and knowing what to look for. In-depth quarry behaviour will be dealt with in suitable sections devoted to the individual quarry species.

The best times for watching for signs of activity are usually early morning and late evening – and not surprisingly these are also the optimum times for hunting. When you walk around your shoot, looking for signs of life, it's very important you go at the times you will be intending to hunt in the future. It's no use you being in the right place at the wrong time, so to speak. In relation to this, if you do spot areas used as stop-over points or sitty-trees, note down the time the birds are more often there. It could well be a relatively small localised group only stay for 10-15 minutes in that area at the same time each or even every other day. Then again, locate a particularly 'favoured' sitty-tree and you could well find yourself faced with a steady stream of potential targets and be able to reap the rewards if waiting in a carefully chosen shooting position.

There's no way I can advise which quarry species you should target first. Obviously most hunters want to get stuck into rabbits, as that's something for the pot and in many areas abundant enough to be bagged in good numbers. But your initial recces of your shoot should already have indicated what is where, and what is where most often. Young guns should start with rats. That's how many of us started, and even now every time I go ratting it seems to bring back a memory of a trip from my youth. But, remember, in those days we could largely go where we wanted. Restrictions on airgun use weren't as Draconian as they are now, and many a session was spent walking up the 'cut' (canal) on a summer's evening potting rats on the opposite bank or towpath. Today, the newcomer will usually find a shoot with a good few rabbits and certainly woodies and corvids.

If there are trees, then squirrels will also be on the list of possibilities, and for some reason they can be quite oblivious at times to your presence and the threat you pose to them – that is until you've started to make serious inroads into their population! This is when another major skill comes into play, which is fieldcraft, and knowing how to get within range or fool the quarry; and also knowing when to leave a particular area undisturbed for a while.

This might sound like a complete contradiction in terms, but almost as soon as you start over a new shoot you should be considering which areas to rest (stay away from) first. No hunting ground has an unlimited supply of suitable quarry. Granted, there are areas that seem plagued with rats, rabbits and crows, but you'll be amazed how, at the slightest disturbance, that very same area can soon appear to be devoid of all life. Of course if you haven't been there on a major pest control cull they'll probably still be there, and in good numbers. They'll just be more wary or even have moved to a safer spot. Sod's law intervenes again, as often that safe place will be somewhere you aren't allowed to shoot. Experience will show you when it's time to rest an area, but it will probably be blatantly obvious, because you'll not see hide nor hair of anything, even at the most opportune times and in ideal weather. It's called conditioning, and the animal responds and reacts to adhere the basic rules of self-preservation in the wild. The importance of 'rotating' your shoot, especially in relation to the time of year, can often be made simple by looking at the options each season brings. This 'Airgun Hunters Calendar Year' – as it can aptly be termed – can be very useful to know for what should come soon or be just around the corner in terms of monthly behaviour in relation to shooting opportunities.

Preparation and General Fieldcraft

No matter what the hunting method, the hunter must have a plan – even if only a very basic one. In fact, all successful hunters will follow a generally similar line, and this applies to airgunners just as much as to deer stalkers. Depending on the weather and time of year, you'll have to plan according to which areas are most likely to be the most productive. For instance, ratting can be a very slow affair in winter, and in some cases useless unless shooting indoors and where such enclosed areas are relatively warm. Alternatively, rabbits can be out of their burrows for much longer in mild and warm weather, while on very cold or hot days they're either holing up underground or relaxing in a hidden sun-trap. If it's raining your best target quarry species will be of the feathered variety, that will be seeking shelter in trees and hedgerows which afford a decent canopy of foliage from the elements. If it's windy, then look to the leeward side of the woods, especially for woodies and crows. But even with the best laid plans, things do at times have a tendency to go pear-shaped, so do have what the army would call a contingency plan – i.e. an alternative back-up plan.

Rabbits betray their presence in many ways – none so obvious than rabbit holes into well-used warrens

For instance, if you've been keeping your eye on the weather and you've noticed plenty of signs of rabbit activity around a certain area, and even if all seems fine for an early morning bunny bash, you should still be prepared to have another area 'pencilled in' to target. In other words, have a few decoys and extra camo net in the rucksack and at the ready should you get rained off. It could well be that moving to another side of the shoot will bring down a few woodies, or bag a few sheltering from the rain should you scour the outskirts of a wood. Remember, if you've been sitting near a warren, even if the weather has been ideal since early morning, and nothing has stirred, it could well be that in the small hours ol' Reynard has been out and about running rabbits into burrows, and more than likely nabbed a few overnight for himself. In fact, foxes can leave an extremely distinctive aroma – trust me, because you'll know it when you smell it. If even we humans can detect this, with our limited sense of smell, just think what it must be like to a rabbit – a veritable aromatic air-raid siren! Knowing when to move and change the original plan is possibly one of the hardest matters for a hunter to master. Experience will certainly help you decide on a move, but even now I've lost count of the times I've thought 'sod it, there's no way any pigeons are coming down to a decoy pattern' and then, sure enough, I emerge from the hide just as a flock has started to come in to the pattern. Sod's Law, I think that's called!

Quarry Location

Walk along any public footpath and you'll see clear indications of where and how recently a walker has been that way. Unfortunately you're just as likely to find litter, which definitely is a sign that humans have used the route; but this amply illustrates how all creatures leave signs, indication and 'calling cards' that they've passed that way. In the case of humans and litter it's inevitable, alas; but hunters should know the country code and never act so irresponsibly. But back to the quarry we seek and the tell-tale signs to read off the land.

Each specific quarry leaves a part of itself or some other indication that it has used an area, and rabbits are the most obvious. Runs, holes to warrens, gaps under square wire-fencing mesh, hair on low barbed wire or the ground, scratchings in the soil or 'scrapes', nibbled grass, bare patches in grass due to heavy urination, bark stripped from the base of trees and shrubs, and of course paw prints. In the heart of a warren, where entrance and exit holes are most abundant, if the warren is heavily populated the surrounding grass and earth will even smell of them! In fact the smell of rabbits will permeate from the burrows – what a temptation for the local fox population!

Squirrels also leave marks of their activity, and usually these are the teeth marks where they, like the rabbit, have gnawed away to keep their ever-growing incisors in check. Similarly rats are just as big if not more of a nuisance in this respect. Woodpigeons and other birds leave their white droppings on leaves under sitty trees, you'll see the stalks of berries where the fruit has been plucked off, and downy feathers caught on brambles and around trees means the woodie has been there. Spent kernels, half-eaten nuts, berries, etc. scattered on the ground below can also be signs of squirrel activity, and these are just a few of the signs to look out for as you walk your shoot for observation purposes. All living creatures leave evidence of their activities, whether it be tracks, droppings, ground disturbance including scrapings or 'runs', and, of course, their dwelling, be it nest, hole or burrow. It's essential you know the general type of terrain where these more specific 'calling cards' can be found.

This is fieldcraft at its most basic. Always keep in mind the main elements that your quarry needs to live and thrive. Think like them, and you'll soon be finding the areas they favour. Locating quarry isn't an exact science, but more a case of common sense and a little applied detective work.

Birds and animals differ in two main respects when choosing to 'hole up'. Birds favour areas that afford shelter from the elements and, just as importantly to them, a good view of the surrounding area.

Rabbit droppings

Fresh soil outside the burrow – obvious sign of recent rabbit activity

Discarded husks and empty shells

Nibbled fir cones – obviously the doing of squirrels

Classic rabbit damage - bark nibbled and stripped at the base of this sapling

A chewed hole in a feed hopper – typical squirrel damage

The only mammal that also does this is the squirrel because, like birds, it is mainly a tree dweller. The rabbit, the main mammal quarry species for the airgun hunter, isn't worried about 'holing up' in an area it can observe from. Instead, it relies on its deep, safe burrow for protection. All woods will hold birds and sometimes squirrels, and most farm buildings will also appeal to birds such as collared doves or feral pigeons – and often rats.

Here are ten things to look for when locating quarry.

- Animal tracks and well-worn natural paths. Obviously this relates mainly to land animals such as rabbits, rats and to a lesser extent squirrels.
- Half-eaten discarded foodstuffs, empty fruit or nut shells, and droppings.
- Burrows, holes, scrapes, and runs.
- Nest sites, old and new.
- Squirrel dreys and (although harder to spot) the smaller nut stores built from twigs.
- Freshly cropped (nibbled) grass and crops. Crops broken by wings and 'strimmed' by birds eating from the outer edge into the field.
- Scratch marks and partly-stripped bark.
- Tufts of fur or remnants of hair on low barbed wire and brambles.
- Watch for regular flight lines and roosts.
- It may sound obvious, but look out for the animals and birds themselves, as well as listening for their calls and other noises.

Basic Instincts

At the risk of stating the obvious, every wild animal is driven by basic instincts which include the need to find food, water and shelter. The latter varies in accordance with the species and the conditions, but generally during the day an animal may seek shelter from either danger or the weather. Alternatively, it could be to digest food and, especially in the case of birds, a place to rest – i.e. their roosts in the evening. These, plus the drive to procreate (again depending on the seasons) are its basic survival instincts.

Feeding areas are chosen not only because they are rich in the appropriate foodstuffs, but also because they allow the animals good visibility of their immediate surroundings. In other words they feel safe. For these reasons, certain safe, food-rich locations become regular, favoured feeding grounds. So – find this, and you'll find the quarry. There are a few exceptions to the rule as, at times, quarry can be uncharacteristically clumsy and carefree when it finds food. Typical examples are when woodpigeons are competing with others of their kind and crashing around in the trees gorging on ivy berries; but the same rarely applies to the birds when feeding on the ground. Similarly, a group of magpies squabbling over a rabbit carcass can be totally oblivious to a sniper in a well-chosen position. Carefree and careless to the point of foolhardiness, they often don't realise that their numbers are diminishing with well placed shots as they bicker and compete for the tastiest morsels – the rabbit's eyes.

As for feeding areas, locating these is usually the easy part, whereas getting within range of the quarry using them is quite another. This is where the hunter needs to use all his fieldcraft skills to enable him to get within effective range. As mentioned, food is the main driving force at all times of the year for all wild creatures. Whether it is to satisfy their own hunger or for rearing their young, finding and gathering food takes up a large part of their daily (and sometimes nightly) routine. This is when thorough knowledge of your particular shoot pays dividends. Knowing the seasons, which fields have just been sown, which wild fruits and berries are likely to be ripening, where nuts and acorns will be falling etc are all basic requirements for quarry location. Most of this knowledge can be obtained first-hand if you are a country dweller or spend a lot of time on your shoot; but most don't have this

Rabbit runs are well-used pathways that can run for quite a distance between burrows and the animals' feeding areas

luxury, and even those that do will benefit from obtaining good reference works on countryside flora and fauna. These should include naturally-growing trees, shrubs and seed-bearing plants as well as farmed crops – grasses, cereals, vegetables and tree plantations. If you have a good rapport (which you should) with the farmer who owns the land you shoot over, and even though he's a busy man, when you get the opportunity do pick his brains. Ask him at what time of the year he seems most pestered with certain species. He might not know the specifics, but he will be able to tell you to the week what has been sown, where has been or is to be ploughed or cut – and he'll also tell you what he can expect to see in and around that field at that time and immediately afterwards. Another tip is that even if you don't own the necessary paperwork and an appropriate rifle to shoot foxes, still listen to what he has to say about their movements. If they're seen regularly in a certain area near a specific warren you know it may well be that those rabbits are getting seriously thinned out or ultra-twitchy, and certainly worth considering as an area not to concentrate your precious time and effort – at least until the foxing lads nail that particular Basil.

Reference books are important, and I still enjoy reading this sort of material. To some it'll seem like an unnecessary task, but do make the effort. Then you'll be able to easily identify nuts that have been nibbled, pine cones that have been stripped and the shattered shards of beech mast – and, more importantly, by which species. A book I can highly recommend for this is *Nature Detective* by the renowned naturalist and countryman Hugh Falkus. This particular book is excellent for identifying tracks and other 'clues' as to what has been going on when you are away from the shoot. There are many other very good books on this subject, so the words 'library' and 'go immediately' apply!

Just as there are seasonal feeding areas, so there are also those that are sources of food for living creatures all year around. These are the grain stores, domestic animal feed troughs and other food sources around farm buildings. Rats soon learn that pigpens and hen coops contain a ready supply of free handouts. Likewise, grain storage and distribution points are a magnet to collared doves, woodies and feral pigeons. Early and late in the day you can be sure that one or more of these quarry species will be paying a visit to such places. Corvids of course are never far behind, just usually a bit more cautious; but in some parts of the country the jackdaw can be as brazen as the starling in its search for food amongst the sheep and cattle feed troughs, both indoors and out. These are the man-made feeding areas, whereas the natural larders are the other main areas to look to, because this is where your quarry is going to feel safest, in its own habitat.

Another requirement for all creatures is water, and both animals and birds have their own favoured sources. This could be a pond, stream, cattle trough or even just an area of ground that regularly becomes waterlogged. Personally I don't favour specifically targeting these unless otherwise advised, as I haven't found them very productive in the short term. However, if you're the very patient type, lying up in ambush near one of these could well produce the goods, especially during times of low rainfall.

'Gimme' Shelter

Like humans, most wild creatures – especially birds – don't like being out in the wind or rain if they can avoid it. Therefore shelter is another major factor on your quarry's list of priorities. A cold, wet animal can soon find itself in difficulty, so whenever possible they avoid getting themselves into that

No matter what hunting technique you later employ – observation is always the key to success

state in the first place. There are two types – temporary weather shelter during the day, and roost areas at night. On a windy day it's virtually certain that quarry such as pigeons or corvids will be on the leeward side of the woods, and even more so if the wind is driving a significant amount of rain. Although the hunter may not be particularly fond of being out in such weather, the one who does is more than likely in for a productive foray – assuming he's done his homework – and with the quality outdoor wear now available there's no reason it should be a hardship. It's also worth noting that after a good 'blow' in autumn and winter the woodies and squirrels are often found rooting around in the leaf litter for fallen goodies. There is more of this in the chapter on seasons, but in damp, drizzly weather both these species – especially woodies – can also be found perching much lower down in the trees. I'm sure this is to keep the rain off that would soon soak them should they stay high in the uppermost exposed branches. Crows seem to be able to weather the rain well, as the water runs off the glossy black plumage.

Rabbits are notorious for their dislike of rain, but if it's not too heavy look for them along hedgerows and stone walls rather than out in the exposed open fields. The same applies when targeting them at night. The leeward side of the wood is also the warmest area, and appeals to them. The denser the tree growth the more sheltered and cosy it is, and, on the subject of wind, I've found that cold north and north-easterlies early in the day are the kiss of death for a good airgun hunting session. So pay attention to the weather forecast the night before your proposed outing. I know they're not always spot on, but wind direction and the movements and localities of cold fronts are usually dependable. This relates more to winter shooting, of course, but it can help you choose your optimum shooting time. If the forecast is for a drop in temperature and a cold front sweeping the country, or your particular area, you can be sure that the creatures of the fields and woods are out feeding, knowing that leaner times are just around the corner. In other words, try to be there when they are, and not when they've gorged themselves, at which stage they go and find the nearest shelter and sit out the bad weather to come. Squirrels in particular seem to know just when to be out eating, so as to be tucked up snug in their dreys once those biting winds pierce through the trees and soaking rain sweeps with it. Wind direction might not seem so important, but in relation to your particular hunting area it can make a lot of difference. In some areas such as mine – the grim North-West – a west wind coming off the coast will bite hard, whereas a warm inland breeze could well heat up the surrounding area, even in winter, if the temperatures haven't already dropped too low.

It follows that when the weather is adverse look to areas that afford shelter, as the quarry won't be keen to feed in these circumstances, unless driven to it by necessity. However, should the rain subside and the sun come out, their thoughts will turn to food and your attention should again therefore be turned towards the feeding areas you've found from your time spent observing previously. As we've seen, finding your quarry is mainly common sense, and not a science.

Chapter 8
General Fieldcraft, Camouflage and Clothing

Despite all the hype, you don't need to wear the latest hi-tech camo pattern clothing to start hunting with an air rifle. Having said that, effective camo will have a dramatic effect on your performance in the field. Whereas you can certainly hunt with some degree of success in drab clothing, or preferably the military DPM (Disruptive Pattern Material), I'm a firm believer that the modern 'new-era' camo wear definitely does give you the edge when it comes to fooling your quarry. But as camo clothing isn't the be all and end all, this is one reason why this chapter deals with general fieldcraft in association with camouflage and the various apparel that is now readily available to conceal us. I'm approaching this subject in this way because camouflage is of little use if the wearer doesn't know how to move and act in the field. You'll also notice that the term camouflage links with the word concealment. You may think they're one and the same but, by definition, camouflage loosely means 'to 'make something hard to see or interpret', whereas conceal means 'to hide or make something secret'. Consider those definitions and the next descriptive usage of words will be more useful in helping you to understand camouflage in relation to what it is used for and the intention behind its use. In other words, we may 'hide' using camouflage to help conceal us, but camouflage by itself cannot totally conceal us, although it can make us less noticeable if used correctly.

This is because camouflage works by creating visual confusion. It disguises the recognisable human form by blending the mass or shape of the human body into the surroundings and to some extent by breaking up your outline. The need for effective camouflage clothing for the airgun hunter is obvious, because the rifle used has a limited effective range and the hunter needs to get within close striking distance so that the shot cleanly and humanely dispatches the victim. But camo wear is an aid to your concealment, and not a cloak of invisibility. Getting within range also requires fieldcraft, which in part involves camouflaging the body so that you can move across land without being detected. This is a major skill that will be continuously mentioned and explained throughout this book, as we come to various situations where it is needed. To be thorough, at the end of this chapter there's a piece that charts the development of the new generation of 'hi-tech' camo patterns that are now so popular and readily available.

Nature's Own
Animals, and to a certain extent most birds, have a distinct advantage in the fact they have a natural outer protective skin (fur or feathers) of a coloration that helps them blend into their habitats. Naturalists have concluded that brown is the most common colour for any form of wildlife in the natural world. Similarly and more obviously, green is the predominant colour of foliage plants, but also including brown and other similar earth-toned colours of a darker hue relating to the surrounding cover plants, and depending on the season.

In relation to our main quarry species, we can immediately look to the rabbit as a direct indication of how effective brown actually is in helping an animal to blend into the great outdoors. Just try to pick out a rabbit against a dark background such as an earth bank, under a hedge-line or general ground cover. Even amongst a relatively strong colour of green foliage such as grass, if the rabbit

This is taking it to the extreme but camo is an invaluable aid to the airgun hunter

remains motionless it can be very difficult to spot. Often, only the pale creamy colour of the animal's inner ear gives it away, and even then only if it twitches them. So, whereas the green used in camo designs is obvious, you can now see why brown (an earth tone) is used widely as a base colour for virtually all designs. Backtracking slightly, note the use of the term 'motionless', which brings us to another and possibly the most important factor relating to good concealment, and that's movement. For both quarry and hunter, movement is the biggest giveaway. Next on the list after sight for the 'human predator' is sound, and then smell – the latter two changing in importance depending on the quarry species targeted and how far you are from the target. You may think I've used a strange description, but that's what we are when we're hunting – we are predators – and it is like a predator that we need to think and behave so as to bag our chosen prize. Humans aren't naturally coloured to blend into their surroundings. Strip us naked, and unless we have a few bob to spend on frequent exotic holidays we're mostly a pasty white. OK, maybe I speak for myself, but I think you get the gist. In society we wear clothes for decency, modesty and warmth, whereas in the field we wear appropriate clothing that not only protects our rather fragile outer skin but also keeps us warm and dry. As hunters in particular, we use clothing with a suitable colouration to help conceal ourselves.

For sport shooting, camouflage clothing was originally adopted from the Army, firstly because used 'fatigues' such as combat pants and jackets were readily available from army surplus stores and established mail order companies. The bonus was not only the hard-wearing nature of the material the clothing was made from, but that the material was in the army's long used and effective DPM camouflage pattern – in other words it was appropriate, rugged, weather-resistant clothing in a suitable blend of colours and pattern. The army have long known the importance of effective camouflage in relation to their person, their kit – including weapons – and even vehicles. We can in the history of warfare see how the armies of the world first saw a distinct need to have specific patterns on battledress. During and shortly after WWI, the armed forces of most countries developed their own camo designs, mostly based on standard issue khaki. There are many variations of these camo patterns, as different countries have different foliage and terrain specific to their regions.

Also, due to the fact that battles can and would possibly be fought even in arctic climates, the British Army saw the need to develop patterns to suit all eventualities they might some day face. This was the reason we saw the widespread issue of the familiar DPM for use in temperate European surroundings. Other types include designs of jungle, desert, and urban camo. Interestingly, the original Laksen camo (the Swiss Army camouflage) was once quite popular with UK hunters. This is neither a copy of foliage nor fauna, but rather an amalgamation of dappled, coloured blotches. This is a good example of a camo that's effective not due to directly imitating the foliage the hunter is operating among, but because it uses the 'disruption' and blurring of the overall image of the human shape to achieve the desired effect. A pattern that uses this same effect is the German Flecktarn camo. Of the military patterns, it's long been established that British DPM, French Central European and US Woodland are the best suited to the countryside environs of the UK.

In relation to camo for hunting, certain forward-thinking individuals had noticed that army issue camo wasn't suited to some terrain. Indeed, whereas DPM 'confuses' the eye, the new age designs actually imitate your surroundings, and it was this basic idea of imitating the surrounding foliage that spawned the glut of hi-tech 'photo-realistic' camo wear that the modern hunter has to choose from. Many will be aware that it was in America that these designs originated, the most famous being

Being hidden isn't just about the camo you wear but also how you use the terrain as you hunt

the first Advantage® camo pattern, which was readily adopted by hunters and outdoorsmen. This pattern was designed by a hunter himself, Bill Jordan, and this has grown into a worldwide phenomenon in hunting and even angling, becoming a billion dollar industry. Another popular type, and one of the first 'alternatives' to DPM to enter the UK, was a camo pattern called Mossy Oak, and there was also Trebark. As all the major companies and a brief history of their emergence and development will be further detailed at the end of this chapter, it's sufficient here to say that the choice of camo is now very extensive and varied, and continually being developed – and it seemingly gets better by the year, through new camo patterns, the material the clothing is manufactured from, and the design and function of the garments themselves. It's hard to predict how this genre of camo clothing will progress. New patterns will emerge, but I'm sure we're reaching a peak in terms of optimum colour blend and effective pattern type, if we haven't peaked already.

Mix 'n Match

I'd taken a personal interest in camo long before the new age designs arrived, having been experimenting with military patterns as diverse as urban camo and desert camo, and they proved very usable. In hindsight, it seems my findings have proved interesting because the base colours of these patterns are browns (desert camo) and combinations of greys and black (urban). It came as no surprise that brown would become a predominant colour for many new commercial patterns, not only because it's a natural colour in nature, but because my experiences with different army camo showed this. When the early Advantage® pattern arrived, with its base brown colouration, I wasn't surprised at its effectiveness. I also remember thinking as soon as I saw Realtree Hardwoods® 20-200, a pattern largely made up of dark colours including greys, browns and even black, that it would prove very useful. It did, and the rest is history. So my experiments and findings had shown that I was at least heading in the right direction in my thoughts on the colours most beneficial for camouflaging myself in the field. Even now I'll mix-and-match different camo designs in my overall kit. For instance camo that's predominantly heavy with browns and darker tones suits the woods, and certainly if sitting amongst leaf litter it's wise to wear suitable camo trousers of, say, a 'bark' heavy pattern such as Advantage Timber® or Realtree Hardwoods 20-200. Because the foliage growing from the ground is usually ferns and the like, it can often be useful to cover the upper body in a green colour based camo such as Realtree Hardwoods Green® or Mossy Oak Breakup. Interestingly, the American manufacturers themselves recommend this mix 'n' match approach.

Another factor that should also be considered when matching camo to terrain is the angle from which your quarry is likely to spot you. If shooting up into trees, ambushing birds coming to sitty trees, or roost shooting then, as you're concealing yourself from eyes above your position, a more uniform darker hue 'branch and bark heavy' autumnal coloured camo pattern suited to the leaf litter and woodland floor is the best option. The reason is that you'll probably have your back to a tree trunk, green foliage will most likely be sparse, and you'll also probably (and preferably) be amongst the shadows. And remember to keep your pale hands and face covered.

This illustrates the importance of carefully considering your shooting position and studying the terrain you normally shoot over, and then tailoring your camo to suit. As the seasons change so does the foliage, so a hunter should change and adapt his camo accordingly. There are many permutations for this mixing and matching concealment technique. I'll often wear DPM Gore-Tex™ over-trousers because I'm sitting on wet grass or foliage, while my jacket can be anything from Realtree Hardwoods Green, an Advantage Timber, or a Mossy Oak pattern. Whatever suits the conditions and helps me blend better into the surroundings is what I'll wear. It is also worth mentioning the US duck hunters' one-time favourite camo, Advantage Wetlands Camo®. It probably got the least interest from the UK shooting fraternity, especially airgun hunters, but I've found it superb for autumn conditions when foliage has died back around sparse hedges next to and over stubble fields.

There's also the Advantage® Max-4 HD™ pattern to choose. Although it sounds like a computer game, this camo with its brown/ochre base overlaid with reed- and rush-type stems will suit the autumn and, of course, wetland areas heavy in rushes and reeds. How it will fare with the UK's camo-buying public time will tell, as it's the hunter customers who decide what they wear. To some extent I feel the camo industry has reached a point where all terrain and seasons are catered for by these highly effective patterns. And yet I think some hunters are increasingly trend-orientated in their choice of camo. But as time moves on so will the designs that become available, and it's a safe bet to say this is one area of the market that will continue to impress the consumer rather than leading to the ultimate downfall of more vermin! Clever marketing campaigns will try and possibly succeed in convincing many people otherwise, but the selection of camo we already have basically caters for all terrain – at least until we hunt on Mars!

Backtracking, how does basic camo such as DPM now rate in its use for airgun hunting? I still wear DPM trousers, because this pattern is useful for the foliage and fauna of the UK. And, if they're waterproof, they are very practical for the sitting, kneeling, and crawling involved in many situations the airgun hunter encounters. So I find it strange that so many hunters overlook them, as they're relatively cheap and easy to come by. Understandably – in the present climate of realistic foliate patterns, 'imitative camouflage' or 'photo-realistic' patterns as they're known – some seem actively to try and discredit DPM as a pattern. Granted, the new designs look more realistic to the foliage we sit amongst, but what of moving across bare grass fields and open land – both largely uniform 'blank' areas of one colour? This shows that the matter is not as simple as just putting on the latest 'must have' camo gear. We should realise and remember that DPM is universal and useful, as it was and still is used as a base onto which the military would add foliage cut from the land they were operating over. This all helped the soldier to blend into the terrain.

I use the military again as an example, because the infantryman also realised that white faces and hands stood out because they reflect light, but this was soon remedied by the use of 'camo cream' – either green, black, or the American-style multi-colour face cream. Granted, that is for the army, and often the use of camo becomes a life and death situation; but the hunter who realised that his hands and face gave him away would also use this cream even though he'd more than likely receive sniggers from other hunters if he mentioned using it. The truth is that he was better prepared to conceal himself from his quarry. Now, as clothing and designs have advanced, manufacturers have seen the benefits of full concealment and made apparel available to the public that negates the need for big splodges of cream, and these take the form of face-masks or veils. I swear by the use of these camo aids, including gloves. I also reckon the dedicated hunter should wear these at night, as even on nights of little moonlight, a white face and hands at close quarters can stand out like beacons.

The use of full camo is something I feel strongly about, and the only times I think of not using a camo mask or gloves are when shooting from a vehicle, feral pigeon bashing indoors, or some ratting situations – all techniques that are dealt with elsewhere in this book. Let's specifically look at a part of the body that gives everything away – the eyes. Your eyes are a big feature of your face and I have little doubt that the eyes, or maybe the movement and whites of the eyes, can allow another animal or bird to realise that you too are an animal and not the harmless inanimate object you are trying to resemble with the aid of camo. A peaked baseball style cap or, if you prefer, a 'boonie hat' can be used to part-shield or obscure the eyes from your quarry. You shouldn't look directly at the quarry, but rather look up under the brim of the hat or peak of the cap, especially when observing quarry in the trees. The trick is to look up – without making direct eye contact – while you determine the bird's demeanour or

The rabbit is a prime example of the effectiveness of nature's natural camouflage

state of awareness. Once it settles, you can then slowly move to adjust your position, or whatever it takes to slowly sight in on the target. But it must be said that if the quarry is totally tuned in to its surroundings and on high alert, the slightest movement will have it off and away. Even though this can be terribly frustrating, a tip in such situations is simply to wait for it to settle or for a better opportunity to present itself. It is definitely better not to shoot, so as not to risk scaring other potential quarry that may arrive on the scene.

Alternatively, if you're in position and you know the general area where birds are to pitch into the trees, you can have the rifle raised or part-raised towards the target area beforehand. Then you only need make the minimal movement necessary to put the cross-hairs onto the quarry's kill-zone. You're only able to do this if you've got into a comfortable sitting position to begin with. If the ground is uneven or rocky, use a shooting mat or a specialist seat such as a turkey seat to avoid 'numb bum syndrome', and if the shooting mat or seat is black, drape a piece of camo net over it. You may think this a case of 'camo-overkill', but it's not so, because a bare patch of black on the ground with you looking like a bush in the middle could attract the alarmed attention of quarry from above. The optimum position for this style of shooting is to be sitting comfortably, slightly leant back and using the trunk of a tree as a backrest, while your leading arm rests on your raised left knee and holds the rifle pointing upwards in the general direction of the area where quarry is likely to present itself. Obviously, if you're a left hander then use the raised right knee as support. This means you're not straining muscles by holding a rifle up, as it's already rested and little movement will be needed on your part once you decide to take a shot. This again illustrates how movement is the biggest giveaway, and one you should

Notice how the correct choice of camo clothing blends the author back into his surroundings

always be aware of to keep one step ahead of your quarry. Still on the subject of the 'whites of your eyes', you can wear American-design shooting glasses that are transparent from the inside but have a camo pattern on the outside. These allow the shooter to see out but the quarry can't see in. I've used these many times and they do work – an accessory to consider if your quarry has become ultra-twitchy, or you're relatively close. All this might seem like going overboard, but the hunter who pays attention to this sort of detail is more often than not the most successful.

It's interesting to note that many very experienced hunters agree that the ability to blend into the surroundings is most important when at closer ranges, whereas the longer the range (i.e. the distance from your quarry to your position), the more care has to be taken in the prevention of showing your outline. Having established the benefits of good camo, I'll now sidetrack slightly to mention another factor relating to fieldcraft.

If you're a smoker you run a higher risk than a non-smoker of being 'scented' when you try to get close to your quarry. The same applies if you use too much aftershave. A rabbit's sense of smell is legendary, and its nose is seemingly constantly twitching. When really alert, the animal sits up or stretches higher on its hind legs, not only to get a better look around and to listen, but also to smell the air. I'm not coming down on smokers, but if I can smell a smoker – and my sense of smell isn't a patch on an animal's – what do you think? Some advocate the use of the American sprays, or as they're known 'scent inhibitors.' Those who use them swear they work, and on that matter I'd say if you feel they help cover up 'unnatural' smells then use them, because they'll boost your confidence if nothing else.

Also, don't use heavily scented soaps before you go hunting. Just 'cos the good lady is kind enough to leave hers handy in the shower is no excuse. Use it when you come home by all means, but before you hit the field – it's not recommended.

We've now dealt with reducing sight and smell, so what about sound? To mention the obvious rattling zips and buckles is all too easy, and most will realise that needs dealing with. Boots that squeak and clothing that rustles are also out, and nothing in your pockets should make any noise when you move. A major gripe I also have is the use of Velcro. At night and/or when close to quarry, you might as well shout as use large strips of this material. Small tabs are acceptable for added security on pockets, but if you need to open anything and it is fastened or attached with large strips of Velcro, either do it before getting near to your chosen hunting area or don't use it at all. Now we've got everything covered, concealed and silenced – what to wear, and when and how to use it?

Summer and Winter Wear

Experienced outdoorsmen will say there's no such thing as bad weather – just bad clothing! When it comes to purchasing clothing for cold and/or wet weather, this is when you'll discover if the manufacturer's claims are true or not. Always buy from reputable companies with established, tried and tested products. As many companies now produce quality garments, some will be named as we mention their individual garments, while others will be listed at the end of this book.

Camo clothing, like general outdoors country wear, is available in two distinct categories – lightweight summer wear, and heavier jackets and trousers suited to the temperatures and weather conditions of winter and colder weather. The former often involves lightweight mesh suits that can be slipped over existing clothing and, when not in use, pack away easily for carrying and storage. These now come in most of the new patterns, and should at least be shower resistant. When the weather's warm, they certainly offer the optimum solution for comfort, and they're also handy should you need or wish to change camo patterns quickly. A case in point is when stalking hedgerows and then moving across a sparsely foliated woodland floor. It is handy to have a suitable alternative pattern in a large enough size to throw over whatever your main camo wear is at such a time.

Incidentally, using a mesh suit in this manner solves the problem of them not affording you much protection from sharp objects or foliage due to the lack of padding in this lightweight, almost 'skimpy' wear. They offer little comfort when sitting or kneeling on rough ground, or when crawling into a shooting position, so wear something more substantial underneath, and perhaps gaiters to protect the lower legs. There are other forms of overwear which I rate highly, and these are traditional-style 'ghillie suits' and their modern equivalents, but more on those later. For now, we must look at outdoors camo wear suited to cold, damp, inclement weather.

Most quality garments are made up of several different materials, typically an outer protective 'shell' to withstand wear and tear, an inner membrane or laminate for total waterproofing, and in many cases fixed or removable inner thermal or fleece linings for added warmth and comfort. Different manufacturers have their own trade names for these membranes and insulation linings, with Gore-Tex™ being just one of many, and probably the best known. But all are very effective. In relation to the style of jacket, different people have different preferences in the type or even the cut of the jacket. Personally, I don't like parka-style garments, preferring three-quarter length field jackets, and in summer wherever possible I'd opt for a bomber- or blouson-style one. I'm not usually a great fan of using a hood on a jacket, because they can obscure hearing and vision, but if it's removable, either by zip or stud fasteners, then it's useful to keep it in a side pocket should you need to sit out a downpour. Even I am not so stupid as to get wet, but when possible I prefer to use a baseball-type cap to protect me from showers. Some hoods are effective if they come far enough forward over the head to partly shield the eyes by putting them in shadow, and if this is more appealing than wearing a separate item for full-face cover, at least you are using something useful. However, I've usually found hoods a hindrance, not only to hearing but also if you are looking around, as the hood often obscures vision to the sides and thus needs adjustment. Adjustment means more movement, and that's something we're trying to keep to a minimum. The jacket's collar should be of the stand-up 'storm' design, to protect the back and sides of the neck from wind and drafts that can sneak into exposed areas.

Front fastening is usually by a zip or double zip and, as added protection, a stud fasten over-flap or 'storm flap'. The jacket will or should cater for a snug fit around the wrist, with knitted ribbed cuffs or an adjustable wrist strap. All do the job they're designed to do, and that is to keep out the elements; but do remember to put your gloves on first before fastening up the wrist adjustments. The jacket's outer material is also important because it needs to be silent. Materials such as Saddlecloth and Shikari Cloth were amongst some of the first to combat the dreaded 'rustle' but others are now taking their place, and many more will be developed as this side of the sport continues to expand.

The season, and especially the prevailing weather or time of day or night when you're actually going hunting will dictate what you wear underneath a jacket. This may only need to be a T-shirt or sweatshirt, but at other times something more substantial will be needed. Several layers of thin clothing are preferable to one big thick woolly jumper. They allow the air to circulate so that you're not as prone to sweating, but the layers will trap warmth when it's needed. If you're too hot, removing a layer of clothing is the easy solution; but if you only had the one garment then you'd not be able to regulate your temperature as flexibly or efficiently. Companies such as Musto do a fine range of clothing, including some that can be used together as 'cold weather systems'. These separate items build up as layers of clothing of varying degrees of thickness and thermal properties. Many hunters make do with a pair of thermals, one or two T-shirts, a sweatshirt, and a light or medium-weight fleece. The layers of clothing I favour mostly have a zip-up neck opening. This allows the wearer to regulate heat retention by zipping the neck area up or down as required. If you do this, remember to have a full-neck shirt underneath to hide the bare white flesh of the neck.

In colder weather the quantity of clothing needed is one of the reasons I take a rucksack when I go hunting. I can leave it at a known position and, when needed, use it to store clothing I've removed. Similarly, if I need another layer it'll contain a sweatshirt or cold weather shirt at the ready. Extra dry socks are always stored in the pack, as are a spare facemask and pair of gloves. These are very important camo items, and if you hunt regularly in them you'll know how a facemask can become sweat-soaked quite quickly, even in relatively cool conditions, and depending on your exertions. Gloves have a habit of picking up dampness as you put a steadying hand on the ground. It will always seem to find any wet patch of ground!

As for thermal underwear, and thanks to the new materials used, we don't have to make do with those old-style cotton thermals that left you feeling sweaty and clammy after the slightest exertion. Once wet they stayed wet, leaving you feeling chilly and uncomfortable. Clothing has developed to the point where there are thermals that are constructed to allow moisture to pass through from your body – or, as it's known, to 'wick' away - to an outer layer where it is held. The really hot new designs (no pun intended!) use a polypropylene/cotton mix that allows any moisture to wick out, keeping you dry, warm and comfortably mobile.

The trousers I recommend are pretty much standard combat-style or heavier-duty slip/pull over waterproofs. The latter may or may not have pockets, but side access to an inside pocket is very useful. As for the ankle area, you'll often find that combat trousers have drawstring bottoms. If not they should, as there's nothing worse than those with a nondescript straight-leg cut. For the over-pants, these usually are elasticated or zipped so they can be pulled on over boots. We'll come to footwear later, but in my experience anything with a zip is an area that needs to be considered in relation to it being a stress point, and the amount of use it receives. Usually good-quality garments have heavy-duty zips, so there shouldn't be a problem. You'll need to clean these ankle zips regularly so that they don't become clogged with dry mud and earth that will be picked up in the field. A tip is once the zip is clean and dry, rub the teeth with candle wax as this helps to keep them lubricated and working as they should, and to some extent it also helps to limit the picking up of dirt. The same applies to the zips of jackets and pockets.

It cannot be stressed too much that camo wear shouldn't be washed in normal washing liquid or powder. This infuses the clothing with ultraviolet, and will actually make the camo pattern stand out, rendering it much less effective. When clothing needs washing, it should be given a lukewarm or cold water wash with no detergents. I personally leave mine for as long as I can, but I do wash it when needed so that the camo is still effective, and doesn't turn into a bland-looking splodge of mud. Similarly, if over-washed, and although the camo designs are printed using inks and dyes designed to be as colour-fast as possible, eventually all fabrics will fade. A faded camo pattern loses both colour and contrast, and this undermines its ability to present the all-important 'visual confusion' necessary for effective camouflage. A tip to delay fading through washing is to wash the garments turned inside out, using cold water and allowing them to hang-dry naturally, and not on a hot spin-cycle. Although it's not easy when sharing your living accommodation with others, don't worry unduly if your clothing smells of the outdoors. That's the smell of 'mother nature' and God's own earth, and it's the best human scent inhibitor you'll ever find to cover natural human body aroma, which is especially important for an airgun hunter needing to get closer to his quarry. If you can leave them without washing, keep the

'Ghillie style' suits such as this loose leaf design are extremely effective

clothes in a sealed bag or somewhere hung off the ground. The place should be dry, and it's ideal if you happen to have a roomy garage – but do bring them indoors before going hunting. It's surprising how cold and damp can permeate a jacket to the point where it seems you can never get warm in it, especially if a jacket hasn't been properly dried and aired before use.

At the leg area, gaiters used to be popular but are now very much left to deerstalkers and rough shooters. If you don't like wearing high-leg boots then they're worth considering, as they do offer calf and upper leg protection when walking through tall wet grass, prevent nettle stings, and when operating in an area where ticks can nip up a trouser leg. And yes – camo gaiters are available!

With facemasks and gloves we largely have Deben Group Industries Ltd to thank for the best selection of these items. In my opinion this is the company which has really solved the challenge of face and hand concealment. Face veils, masks, neck warmers, cold weather camo balaclavas, 3-D leaf effect balaclavas, sure-grip palm-dot gloves, mitts, neoprene 'cut finger' gloves, full-finger gloves and of course caps, plus jackets and trousers – Deben have the lot, and always in the most popular, up-to-date camo patterns. And let's not forget the UK's largest supplier of Advantage® Realtree licensed clothing – Garlands – for the quality outdoor wear they supply. I recommend light gloves for summer, and heavier waterproof gloves for winter. In warmer weather, I prefer to use light gloves with dot grip palms, but in winter I'll opt for the heavier camo neoprene gloves, again with palm dot grips. Whatever the season, it's beneficial to have gloves with extra long cuffs for full wrist concealment.

A useful tip for any full-finger gloves is to cut off the tip off the forefinger and thumb of the glove for the shooting hand. This allows the shooter to 'feel' the trigger and to load pellets into barrels, loading channels or magazines easily. For the latter I'll also sometimes use gloves where both hands have the specified finger and thumb tip severed. This is often preferable for holding magazines while re-filling and re-fitting them to the rifle. With heavier gloves, even if they are what are termed 'cut finger' types (meaning that you can fold back the first two fingers and thumb, which are split and have a Velcro fold back) I still cut the finger and thumb tips off the shooting hand glove. This is because the folded-back tip of the glove may foul on the rifle's trigger guard, and they have the annoying habit of flipping back over to their original positions – usually at crucial moments. But I must admit that on the left hand I find them useful, and often leave them unmodified. Incidentally, for hunting at night I often now wear a pair of strong yet tactile fingerless mitt style 'tactical shooting' gloves – more on 'night attire' in the relevant section on Shooting At Night.

Now to facemasks: though I don't feel camo pattern to be crucial in your selection of these, I do prefer masks that don't hinder vision. An obvious statement but one that needs further explanation. Some masks have the annoying habit of shifting position on the face as you look from side to side. I prefer a mask with a strong cord tie that fastens around the back of the head, rather than those which use fixed elasticated straps to hold the mask in position. Those just aren't as efficient at helping the mask stay put. Similarly face masks with nose-pieces that clip over the bridge of the nose I find irritating, as I'm always readjusting them – but what doesn't suit one might well be right for another, so see what you prefer. Talking of face concealment, there's also the head-over sock or stocking type headgear, similar to a stretched leg of nylon stocking as used by bank robbers. These come in a basic camo pattern called Spandoflauge®. I've used them, they work, but I'd not recommend them if you tend to feel claustrophobic easily.

As for caps or hooded garments with drop-down faceveils, these are notorious for shifting position and exposing part of the face. This can be remedied by stitching in a couple of tabs of double-sided Velcro, so long as you don't overdo it; but by and large I prefer to cut these out and use a mask. But – and there's always a 'but' – drop-down face veils do actually conceal the eyes rather effectively as well as the face, so if they can be 'modified' to suit your shooting style then so much the better.

The head and shoulders of the human form are unmistakeable, no matter how they are covered. Strive never to show your head or upper torso in silhouette against a contrasting background, because the best camo in the world won't hide your outline. Even though the body is covered by an imitative camouflage pattern against suitable foliage, if you're not positioned correctly you will still stand out.

A Case of the Ghillies

The best concealment to break up the outline of the human body shape is 3D 'leaf effect' over-suits, or as they're commonly known 'ghillie suits'. The loose 'leaves' protrude irregularly from the straight edges of your body, thereby blurring the outline. The origins of these suits are commonly attributed to the US military in Vietnam, as it was around the 1960s that they began to be issued and used by military snipers. Even earlier, they were certainly used by some British soldiers in WWI. However, there has been some fanciful speculation as to their invention and first use by the sport shooter. The name would have you suppose there is a link with Scottish deerstalkers and countrymen of the same name – ghillie. The link seems to be a tenuous one, but it could be that the name was adopted because Scottish ghillies mainly wore – as they still do – traditional tweeds of a colour that makes them less obtrusive on moorland heather. There's also a 'tree fairy' of Celtic folklore known as the Ghillie Dhu, which disguised itself with leaves to play pranks on those who ventured into the woods. That's a nice twist to the tale and a play on words, but not wanting to get embroiled in a controversy over the garment name's true origins, I feel that's one for military historians.

The 'suit' itself is of great benefit, firstly for the soldier. The military version is used by snipers who need a large, baggy, comfortable suit or 'universal' effective camo covering that they can move in and rest under. They also needed one they could swiftly remove when they needed to leave an area in hurry, and these soon became standard sniper issue. Early ones were little more than strips of dark hessian and strips of khaki coloured cloth stitched onto khaki fatigues. As the availability and types of clothing advanced, the military designs were usually manufactured from more modern materials in dark olive, charcoal and even black. Interestingly, the more recent military versions seem to have reverted to the 'hanging cloth' design, using strips of burlap and jute on a mesh suit to obtain the desired effect. There are also rifle covers that use the same design and do an excellent job of concealing a rifle/scope combo.

For hunting, a more formal style of the ghillie suit is now available in a small selection of new-age imitative camouflage patterns. Any ghillie suit will probably provide better concealment than 'flat' cloth camouflage, because the first function of a ghillie suit is to add a sense of depth to the otherwise two-dimensional human outline. No printed cloth in the world can duplicate this, even though some HD (High Definition) patterns are now almost reaching a level where they have 3D characteristics. As well as creating depth, the second essential purpose of a ghillie suit is to make the resulting three-dimensional form blend as undetectably as possible into its immediate surroundings, whether that happens to be ground characteristics or vegetation or both.

Much of the effectiveness of a modern hunting ghillie suit is due to the 'loose leaf' design, as the texture of the outer material won't look flat or block-cut. In the natural environment few things have clean-cut edges. In certain cases I would choose a ghillie suit, but only if not moving through heavy undergrowth or sitting up in tangled vegetation, as brambles in particular have an annoying habit of catching in the loose-leaf build of these suits. Some manufacturers have tried to remedy this by using a half-and-half design – i.e. loose-leaf for the edges of the suit, while the back is of flat cloth camo so that you can push yourself backwards into undergrowth. Fine in theory, but there's always a stray branch or twig that'll catch on the side of the suit, so if you're going to move about regularly use a more conventional design of camo wear. If lying up or sitting still in ambush, they can be deadly effective. Interestingly, you can purchase ghillie-type garments that just conceal the head and shoulders, and these do go some way to eliminating the problem of getting snagged on foliage as you stand and move position.

One downside of military-type burlap and jute ghillie suits is they can be heavy and warm, and unfortunately if they get wet they can absorb a lot of water, rendering them uncomfortable and even heavier to wear.

No matter what camouflage you've chosen to help conceal yourself, let's take an example of a scenario that facilitates its use with the terrain you're operating over to stress the importance of body positioning, and the part your use of other cover plays in concealment.

Always try to position yourself, when seated or even when moving, with branches or other such objects half-obscuring your body from the area you're targeting. Branches and low foliage that runs across the front of your outline, as long as they don't obscure your view and shot to the target, are helpful in breaking up the unmistakable human form. Remember, there are no straight lines in nature, especially ones that move like we do, so anything that helps you blend into the surroundings should be used. Branches, small shrubs, a patch of high nettles, ferns – anything that's there, use it as cover.

Good camouflage will help conceal you, but using it with the terrain also allows you to make small, slow and subtle movements, especially when in a position to make final adjustments for your aim – the crucial moment for any successful shot taken in the field.

Suited? Now Booted!

We can't discuss clothing without mentioning the importance of good quality footwear. For most, a strong pair of hiking boots will suffice, and a pair of softer-soled shoes or dark coloured trainers for stalking in summer. You'll be surprised how quickly you can amass a selection of boots, including high-ankle field boots and maybe even camo boots, to cope with the terrain and situations you hunt over. I've got as many different pairs of boots as there are months in the year, and I swear I've a use for them all.

The two specific types of field boot are low- or high-ankle design. Lower-cut boots give more flexibility for slow, stealthy stalking while high-ankle, as the name implies, affords better ankle support to avoid sprains and similar injuries should you go over into a pothole, rut or rough ground. Another important feature of any boot is the sole or, as the treads are known, the cleats.

Whilst a stalking boot requires a soft, flexible sole, boots with a harder, tougher and more rigid, thick rubber cleat are more suited for wet muddy fields. A word of caution is that some cleats and the material the sole is manufactured from are notorious for being slippery on wet stone. Although many realise the importance of correct design, few realise that the colour of the soles is equally important. You should only select hunting boots with a dark-coloured sole, as the bottoms of boots are more often than not very visible when you're sitting on the ground, and may therefore possibly spook your quarry. Another factor to take into consideration is that wet boots can often be shiny, and their glint will give away your position. This may seem overly cautious, but I'm sure quarry notice these things. Consider this: no matter how wet, when was the last time you saw a shiny fox? Case proven, I think.

I always prefer to wear field boots that offer ankle support, and as camo boots are now available, these are often a good choice. Just pay attention to the undersides of those soles.

Some prefer to wear traditional Wellington boots, but I personally wouldn't recommend these for airgun hunting due to their lack of flexibility, but there are alternatives I do wear, especially the field boots that are manufactured as a half Wellington/half field boot. These have rubber soles that come midway around the ankle, providing superb protection in waterlogged fields, tracks and ditches. The special sole is stitched onto a more typical leather or Cordura field boot for better flexibility of movement. Whichever you choose don't skimp on the quality of the socks you wear underneath.

Mesh suits are ideal for summer and facemasks a must if you're getting up close and personal

Frankly, some socks sold as thermals are about as thermal as my chest hair! A couple of pairs of thinner, good-quality socks are better than one pair of poor-quality thick ones. As with underwear, you can obtain socks to be used on the layer principle, and these give an impressive performance in terms of comfort and heat retention.

So as you can see, the choice is huge, but the dedicated hunter needs to be prepared for all situations.

Hardware

Most hunters will have seen full camo-covered hunting combos. They look workmanlike, and in the field they really are effectively camouflaged. Long before these were available many like myself had taken a leaf from the military handbook and were concealing our rifles with strips of tied-on scrim scarf. Useful as it still is, you can now make use of camo tape such as the No-Mar (No-Mark) Camo-Tape made by the American company H.S. Camo (Hunter's Specialities) to break up the outline of the stock, action, scope, barrel or silencer. Even if you only wrap it around the barrel and put intermittent 'stripes' on the stock you're going along the right path to concealing your kit. Another bonus is that tape can easily be changed for another pattern, thereby adapting to suit a particular terrain. In fact, the best camo I once used was while shooting where there was minimal cover at the side of a barren field. To remedy this I used camo tape around the silencer and the appropriate dark brown pattern camo netting draped around the rifle and over myself! The army realised the importance of camo on weapons, and it's all part of the concealment of what is in effect a foreign object in the terrain you're operating over. The camo you employ will imitate the surrounding foliage, and does break up those give-away straight, black outlines of what is in effect a mainly black-coloured object with well defined lines and edges to the action, barrel, silencer, scope mounts and scope. Some think this is going too far, and many feel it's unnecessary. In some ways I can agree, as a rifle with a matt finish and dull colour stock is very much like a branch – as long as you're not waving it around. But on the subject of movement, move your combo, say to raise it to your shoulder, and it does give off some glints no matter how much it seems to be matted down. Also, nothing in the natural environment is made of plastic or metal, and everything is more noticeable when it's moved. You'll also not often stumble across a luxurious piece of London-quality, hand-finished, oiled walnut stock wood whilst on your shoot.

Camo net draped over you and the rifle can be a very quick and useful aid to concealment

We've noted the importance of movement as a give-away of position, but consider this. Slowly moving a rifle combo that's been camo covered is less likely to be noticed than an 'untreated' one, so, in situations such as relatively close-quarters hunting – and especially if shooting from cover below aiming up into trees – I'd say having the rifle combo covered in camo definitely gives you an edge. If you're really serious about this aspect of cover, you can go the whole hog and have the combo specially dipped in the camo pattern of your choice by the specialists in this field – Hydrographics. This company can cover virtually anything by the ingenious dipping process of immersion coating. The item to be covered, be it rifle action, stock, scope, mounts etc., is immersed in a liquid which has a 'film' of the desired camo design floating on the surface, that adheres to the item when immersed in it. After coating, a finish is applied to give the camo a protective skin. This is so fine-tuned that it can be made matt or, even more useful, a finish called 'soft touch' can be applied. As the name implies, this gives a sure grip and another bonus is that once treated the outside of your rifle and scope are waterproofed. Even accessories such as spare buddy bottles, scope mounts and bipods can be treated – in fact your whole kit and caboodle.

The History and Development of 'New-Era' Imitative 'Photo-Realistic' Camouflage

Although most patterns originate and are made into clothing under license from Bill Jordan's hugely successful Jordan Outdoor Enterprises, the UK does have its own independent manufacturers, although most use these Jordan patterns in the clothing they manufacture. It's therefore worth mentioning Bill Jordan's multi-million dollar camo empire.

Contrary to popular belief, Jordan Outdoor Enterprises doesn't actually manufacture any clothing, or even the material the clothing is made from. Their specific area of expertise is the development and design of the hi-tech camo patterns we've seen flooding into the UK. After they've created a design they feel is suited to a particular terrain, they license that pattern to specialised outdoor clothing manufacturers who then supply the cloth and garments to the trade, and in turn to the end consumer – you! Before leaving the subject of design, you'll notice that new patterns seem to be appearing on the market every season. As is the way in an ongoing business, designs are constantly being improved, and further designs such as Realtree Hardwoods Green HD® (High Definition) and Advantage Timber® make the original Advantage pattern look quite bland, nondescript and even dated – even though it's still an effective pattern. By the time this book has been published, new patterns may already have appeared. But how and where did it all begin?

Bill Jordan, an American outdoorsman, originally founded a company called Spartan Archery Sportswear Products Inc in 1982. He started by selling camo gloves and headnets from his father's boatyard, in addition to a few bowhunting accessories. Like many hunters he was dissatisfied with the fact he had to make do with military camo. Always looking to improve his success in the field, he concluded that for hunters to be more effective they needed to wear a camo that would closely resemble the environment (mainly dense woodland) in which it was to be used. This led him to embark on an intensive study of North American foliage, particularly tree bark patterns. This meant comparing hundreds of photographs to identify common characteristics of North American flora and fauna, and the configurations and patterning of the many types of tree bark. Still convinced that the secret lay in the bark of trees, he isolated the most prominent traits shared by bark patterns. From this he developed the very first original Realtree® pattern, and changed the company's name to Spartan-Realtree Products Inc. This early pattern was developed and changed a few times, and began to slowly infiltrate the UK market in the late 80s. You could say that we were quite late in realising its benefits, as in America the secret was well and truly out and hunters embraced these new designs eagerly. In the mid 1980s a company called Mossy Oak sprang up, with a camo pattern simply called Mossy Oak Bottomland. Headed by a man named Toxey Haas, who did the initial research into the most common natural colours found in the outdoors, Mossy Oak have also developed new patterns and are still producing successful new designs today, under the Mossy Oak brand name.

But back to the enterprising Mr Jordan, as due to the success of Realtree, he started another camouflage business called Advantage® Camouflage Inc in 1994. He now had an extraordinarily extensive knowledge of camouflage, and this showed in the fact that these designs soon came to rival the original designs released by Realtree®. So why were the Americans the first to realise the need for a specific specialist 'civilian' camo for sport shooting? It can partly be credited to the fact that it was primarily designed for wild turkey and whitetail deer hunting. There's an American hunting saying that maintains that if a wild turkey could smell, you'd never see one; so I think that amply explains why camouflage was of such importance to American hunters. Also, if an American bow-hunter can get so close to his big game quarry as to kill it humanely, then these new camo designs really are effective. If it can help a bow-hunter get within those close ranges, then it's more than capable at helping an airgun hunter to achieve his goal too.

Interestingly, Paintball games enthusiasts first used the early US imitative camo patterns here in the UK as far back as the early 1980s, and paint-balling is a pursuit that had long been enthralled by all things camo, even without any official importers of the garments at the start. It wasn't until the mid 1990s that the UK shooter was targeted (pun intended!) and first properly introduced and educated to the benefits of what was then simply known as Advantage®, and later known as Advantage Classic and Realtree All Purpose® Brown. The former really did take the UK by storm as it kicked off the trend and demonstrated the technology and practical effectiveness of these patterns.

It's worth noting that Trebark was another US camo pattern that came into the UK courtesy of the now defunct Simmons UK company (now AirgunSport). It is known as Superflauge and manufactured by the US company Lynch. Simmons-branded Superflauge camo clothing was at the time a huge success for the company, and was based on the well-known US 'Trebark' print design, consisting of a blend of bark, branches, twigs and leaves to give an almost 3-D effect camouflage pattern that blends well with British and European foliage.

In this competitive, expanding world of camo, deals are struck and specialist camouflage companies change and merge. Mossy Oak now own Trebark, and while the 'MO' brand and designs had experienced a lull in the U.K., it has once again become increasingly available.

New patterns seem to take over from those that were previously the recommended favourites, and it seems to be the Jordan way of business to have four patterns in circulation. We have three of these in the UK, but the fourth, being 'snow' camo, is obviously not as popular or as readily available here. But the good news is that there's always a camo to suit the season and terrain, and I would say – choose wisely, and wear with confidence.

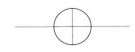

Chapter 9
Hunting Accessories – Kit Bag
Essentials and Useful Extras

As you progress as a hunter you'll soon come to realise the need of certain accessories and to carry a few essentials besides the obvious such as extra ammo. There's various bits and bobs, gadgets and gizmos and all manner of little extras that will help you perform more efficiently in the field.

Accessories fall into two distinct categories – those that are small and compact enough to fit into a jacket pocket and those of a size that'll warrant you buying a rucksack for their safe storage and transportation. Fortunately, the accessories you'll find of most use to have immediately to hand will fit into a pocket of your clothing. Incidentally, kit specifically associated for lamping and night shooting is dealt with in the relevant sections – here we look at accessories all airgun hunters should consider having from the outset. But be warned, it's all too easy to start adding and adding to your hunting kit until you start to overburden yourself. Especially as with each passing year new products come onto the market that do seem too handy not to have. Indeed with the popularity of 4 × 4s I have to admit like others I often take far too much gear than I need or in fact actually use. Often spoiling myself using the vehicle as a base camp to return to for a brew, extra clothing, collect decoys, hide poles, camo net, pop-up portable hide and even to change hunting rigs! But that's the extreme, or the highest level some will want to attain.

A reasonable size rucksack will hold all the accessories – as shown – that you'll need on a hunting foray

The general airgun hunter should be more concerned with items that can be classed as 'kit bag essentials' and will easily fit into a small to medium sized rucksack for carrying with him onto the shooting ground.

Before going any further - there is of course the all-important factor of the gun itself being carried. Even while in a vehicle it needs to be in a bag. If that's the only journey it makes – from the house to the vehicle – and then you're fortunate enough to be able to step straight onto your shoot – then you can use a gun slip. These cover a rifle but offer little in the way of real protection. But whichever you choose – it's required by law that you carry your gun in a gun bag at all times if travelling in or through a public place. Every gun shop will have gun bags of one sort or another. Virtually all gun manufacturers produce or have bags built for them and 'badge' them up as their own. These range from simple gunslips to padded cases with extra pockets for kit and special carrying attachments. Take my advice and buy the best you can afford. Often it's better to opt for a specialist type of padded case: granted they'll be more expensive, but for the protection it affords your combo, it's well worth the price.

So what to look for in a gun bag? Obviously it needs to be manufactured from tough weather resisting synthetic or canvas material with high strength fittings and preferably have reinforced stitching. Where applicable clips should be metal or at least toughened ABS and zips need to be heavy-duty. On better quality bags you'll find a fleece lining or better still high-density foam padding to ensure that maximum protection is given to the rifle in transit. Many bags have cargo pockets or zipped outer sleeve type pockets – some more than others depending on type. These are handy for carrying extra 'bits' but more so once on a shoot I leave my bag in the 4 x 4 or in an area I know it's safe and where I can return to it easily. In that respect I don't carry anything major in my gun bag other than items

The hunter who chooses and uses the right accessories is better equipped to be more efficient in the field

that relate to the specific rifle it contains. This can be extra pre-filled magazines, spare ammo the combo is used with but both these items are transferred to a jacket pocket or bum bag as soon as I set off on my foray. Incidentally, if you have a few combos it's advisable to always keep the same rifles in their own 'set bags'. Reason being if you chop and change it's all too easy to set out with a gun in a bag containing the wrong magazines and ammo. And yes, even after all my experience I've done it so maybe I do own too many rifles? Look to the specialist shooting publications and grab a look at various wholesale supplier catalogues to see what's on offer – and certainly check in at your local gun shop. Incidentally, if total protection is needed for the journey in transit, there are ranges of semi-hard soft boxes with egg box type foam linings, and even aluminium strengthened 'lock-able' flight cases. So as you can see, the choice of keeping that valuable combo safe is many-fold.

Semi-Detached

One piece of kit that I feel is essential and hunters should consider fitting to the rifle from the outset is a set of quality sling swivel studs. Not only to use with a sling and Quick Detachable (QD) sling swivels to ease the burden when walking around your shoot but more so to use for attaching a bipod. This is a very useful addition to your equipment for ambush if using a PCP air rifle. And there'll be much more on these 'rests' later. The best swivels by far are the QD sling swivels and swivel studs manufactured by Uncle Mike's, a company who also make a variety of rifle slings. Even so you have other makers of specialist slings that offer other benefits. Deciding to fit a sing is personal choice – more often than not, for general work, I prefer not to use one due to the fact the sling can be more trouble than it's worth. They can snag on clothing when you shoulder the rifle, catch undergrowth as you move, swivels 'click' making noise at a crucial moment or the strap itself rubbing against the body can be a potential 'noisemaker'. However, for longer standing shots some prefer a sling as it can be used to steady aim and QD sling swivels do allow the sling to be removed in an instant should you need to be 'clutter free'. Where I find a sling of most use is when you need to 'carry' the rifle on your person and be hands-free for negotiating very rough terrain, or even driving a quad bike possibly climbing up to a high seat or tree position. These situations will be dealt with further in this book, suffice to say a sling can be handy to have at times and the quick detachable facility means they can be removed in seconds and put in a pocket.

Rucksacks

Since I first began seriously hunting I've taken my 'bits and bobs' in a rucksack and carried off my game in a plastic bin bag. In the early days I used ex-army ruckys in DPM. Then I began using various sizes of Bergen's, and even a selection of rambler's waterproof packs. However, now we have dedicated 'backpacks' designed for the hunter, some made in America but distributed over here, hence the availability of fanny packs (no sniggering at the back) or as we know them 'bum bags'. A good selection of top quality 'ruckys' are available, manufactured by British company Napier of London. We've now got access to the American manufactured Flambeau Rucksacks – a very well respected name in the manufacture of outdoor sports carryalls and utility boxes. There are others and most are now available in the modern new age camo designs so even your rucky will blend in with the terrain.

While you'll soon recognise a good rucky from bad, like gun bags the best will cost that little extra but you'll find them worth it. One feature you'll find useful and is incorporated in many well-designed bags is a moulded rubber or heavy-duty rubberised base. This ensures the contents inside at the bottom keep dry when placed on the ground. A simple but clever way of keeping out the water from damp grass or should you inadvertently plonk the pack down in a puddle. The size of pack you choose depends on how much gear you intend to take with you but as with a gun bag it can be left in a safe area to return to – to get larger items when needed such as extra clothing or even food. A medium bag with a 30litre or preferably 40litre capacity will suit most shooters. Look for padded shoulder straps if you intend walking far with it on your back and outside cargo pockets are handy so you can access certain items quickly without having to rummage through the bag. One factor pertaining to rucksacks is I recommend you don't leave them on to shoot. Not only will you find this tiring but it will interrupt and hinder the shooting stances and holds you've taken the trouble to master. Even a small bag can catch a slight crosswind knocking you off balance – usually at a moment you are going to take a 'snap shot'; shoulder straps catch and hinder rifle hold at the shoulder – numerous problems can be encountered. But as with most accessories they can be useful. As they now come in very effective camo designs I often use a pack as a rest and as part concealment – forward of my shooting position. Even so – and as I've recommended earlier – best to take out the kit you need and leave the bag in a 'set' safe place. Just don't leave important items such as wallets, car and house keys, shoot permission or FAC licence in it.

I've already mentioned bum bags and they are handy for taking a few extras with you. Especially useful if wearing a ghillie suit or mesh oversuit that has few or no pockets. They're handy for ammo, spare magazines, spare faceveil, gloves, quarry calls, your shoot permission and other personal items including your mobile phone. More on these accessories later but suffice to say bum bags – like back-packs – are very useful.

Before looking at what you should be carrying in your pack – a quick word here of carrying game off your shoot. You've probably read many times how you can carry rabbits in a rucky after you've shot them. I've done this but even three and certainly four full-grown rabbits get very heavy and a rucky soon starts to whiff. As I've already said, I don't continually 'yomp' around my shoot with the pack on my back, the rucky now being a convenient way to carry kit further towards the shooting area – for me an extension of the off road vehicle. In relation to shot quarry – rabbits are usually hocked and hung on a branch or fencepost, woodpigeon are placed above ground, wrapped in a small swing bin liner bag to keep off the flies – all are collected as I return to my starting point. Other non-edible species such as crows and magpies are thrown in ditches for scavengers or if there are a fair few I'll bag them up and take them to an incinerator. Fortunately the main shoots I frequent have incinerators on site meaning I have easy access for the proper disposal of the carcasses and my hosts see how much I'm helping alleviate their vermin problem. Unfortunately on a bad day they see I've not done that well – but as they say '*c'est la vie!*'

Kit Bits

Some of the following are essentials while others can be added when finances allow or indeed if you feel you need them. Also not everything will be needed every session – so you can 'tailor' your pack to suit the circumstances but always be mindful of the unexpected eventualities that may and can occur. Another factor in choosing what to take is the duration you intend to stay in the field. From past experience I'd say, if not tied down to a specific time, if for instance you need to get to work or pick the wife or kids up, if it's going well or you're just happy to be out and about in 'God's Country', you'll possibly stay longer than you first expected. Also, the weather forecast and of course season of year will dictate what extra in terms of clothing you'll need or should consider taking. In no specific order here's a run down of accessories that I'd consider for virtually all hunting sessions.

Firstly an observation aid such as a pair of compact binoculars or monocular is in my opinion a must have piece of kit. Scanning around using the scope isn't the most advisable way of observing your shoot. Better to have a dedicated observation aid for scouting the land up ahead or looking up to scour the treetops.

Compact binos are most popular, the usual specification being 8 × 21 and rubber armoured outer casing helps protect them from knocks and scrapes. A good quality pair won't cost the earth and most scope manufacturers have good quality items including small rubber armoured monoculars. Usually, they come with leather carry case, and have a lanyard for hanging around your neck. If you've read through the previous section on observation then you'll certainly realise binos are essentials. But when observation is done, when out shooting I'll as likely and more often than not choose a monocular. I personally prefer a monocular as it's very small and can be stored to the side in a pocket, taken out for a quick scan around when needed. Just as useful is a fixed magnification laser rangefinder monocular. There are some very good value for money models should you require them. And, if anything takes the guesswork out of range estimation then in my book I reckon it has to be a useful aid. Granted you should be sufficiently skilled in range estimation before even attempting hunting but there's no law in saying you can't add a rangefinder to the kit list. Both Bushnell and Leica have a range of similar devices that are very reasonably priced – both of the monocular or compact binocular style.

Next up is a small first aid kit. This doesn't need to be overly comprehensive but the contents should be kept safe in a watertight container and at the least this should include wet wipes, antiseptic wipes, small bottle of antiseptic cream or spray, painkillers, selection of plasters, sterile gauze, small roll of bandage, an army field dressing kit is a very useful addition as are tweezers and small scissors etc. – the usual basics.

Spare ammo is an obvious requirement. You can tip a few in a jacket pocket or better still use a pellet pouch. Whatever you're carrying them in make sure it won't rattle around to potentially make any noise and store pellets so they won't get damaged. If you're a longer session hunter, take a cold drink for warm weather, but avoid sugary drinks and certainly no alcohol, they'll make you thirstier, the latter also of course impairing judgement. A water bottle is simple basic kit. Not only to hold

Use good camo, fieldcraft techniques, knowledge of quarry and the right accessories and you'll be successful

water to quench a thirst but to rinse hands and face. Include a small container of liquid soap and a small hand towel, along with the obvious uses you might have for tissue and some toilet roll. Some take rubber or disposable surgical gloves for messy tasks such as gutting. If you use these, keep a few zip-lock plastic bags handy to put them in when used and take them home to dispose of in the proper fashion.

If out and about in cold weather it's certainly advisable to carry a hot drink. A stainless steel flask is the one to use – many makes around and you'll find even cheaper ones last a reasonable amount of time. For the flask, seriously consider investing in a flask cover. The camo covers available might seem gimmicky but their thermal properties really do keep drinks warmer longer and help protect the flask from knocks. The camo being helpful for concealing the shiny stainless steel so this means you don't continually need to store the flask back in the pack. It can be left out to hand. If hunting in cold weather it's advisable to pack a spare jumper or fleece. Neck warmers are also useful to keep out drafts.

As clothing has been dealt with fully in the previous section, I'll just mention that it's handy to have a few extra items or layers of clothing not forgetting spare socks and gloves in your rucky. And always carry a set of waterproofs, even if wearing cold weather gear. A sudden and certainly prolonged down-pour isn't easy on any quality all-weather clothing. You'll probably have to or decide to stop 'actively' hunting, so waterproofs don't necessarily 'need' to be rustle free as if away from any reasonable amount of cover, you'll by and large have to put them on and just sit it out. An ex-Army Poncho is often ideal and rolls up a compact size for storage. If you take a two-piece set of waterproofs, look to obtaining a larger size than you normally take. This is because you'll be putting them over clothing already worn. A generous fit, especially the trousers make them much easier to get into quickly. If opting for the two-piece, choose a jacket with hood, preferably with a peak and drawstring as it offers much more protection from the elements.

Incidentally, another bonus of a Poncho, is after the shower, if you intend to lie on the ground in ambush, use as a groundsheet so as not to get damp due to 'pressure transfer' through contact with the ground. It'll usually open out further and offer a solution to lying on the gunbag.

Now while many cover themselves, they forget to treat the rifle with similar respect. You can slip it back in the gunbag, but as I normally use carbine size rifles, I've found slipping it into a waterproof landing net cover as used by fishermen is ideal for keeping these moderate size rifles totally dry and it folds away to nothing when not in use.

Next up is a knife. A traditional and now familiar Swiss Army 'style' knife or Opinel penknife is always useful in the field, especially for paunching or preparing 'baits'. Ideally have a folding lock knife and a small (3–4-inch) fixed blade 'skinner'. Also, don't forget the sharpener as knifes have an infuriating habit of losing their edge at the least opportune moment.

Now to the many useful pocket-size multi-tools: There's an abundance of these from various manufacturers available, but do buy a quality tool, as properly looked after it will last many years. They're handy for field repairs and all other manner of tasks that can face you as you go about your shoot. It's surprising how often you'll find the pliers, wire cutters and the various knife-edges and screwdriver heads they contain of use. However, I'm sure others have seen it written they're useful for 'nipping up screws on the rifle'. That makes me cringe. There's no way you should need to be doing quite intrusive work on your rifle body or action while in the field hunting. If so, you've not been keeping the rifle maintained properly. Screws don't just suddenly decide to become loose so that you notice while out hunting. See the chapter on General and Routine Maintenance for advice on combating potential troublesome hunting session faults before they start.

Secateurs are handy as is a compact folding wood saw – ideal for trimming hides or cutting foliage to use as cover. Just don't hack away willy-nilly and leave young shoots and saplings well alone.

Possibly the most useful accessories of all – compact folders and fixed blade knives not forgetting the very useful multi-tools

There'll be plenty of abundant foliage and dead or excess wood around to use.

Just as handy to have in the kit bag is a reasonable size camo net, even if you don't initially intend to build a full size hide. You need something that packs down small and will still fold out to offer a reasonable amount of screen should you find yourself requiring the use of extra cover. Many companies offer a handy size piece of net and the correct pattern of camo netting has for me often saved the day. Just draped over to disguise my static position. You often need to cut a few slits here and there for shooting through, but throw it over your person or some branches and foliage and you've got yourself an instant covered shooting position. More on the use of netting will be found in Hunting Techniques.

Also let's not forget how handy a roll of camo tape is – indeed H.S No-Mar (No Mark) tape is a must if you want to cover or break up the outline of your rifle action, stock or barrel. But, camo and its uses have been fully dealt with so I'm sure you can see taking those extra 'bits of kit' can often add the final touch to your concealment.

Even though you don't intend to hunt at night, dusk soon turns to dark and if you haven't packed away your kit a small torch such as a Mini-Maglite or better still a small headlamp is also very handy to have. It not only makes the walk back to the car less hazardous but light sources are very useful if you spill pellets in a hide. You'll hardly find the lion share in the gloom but the lead will glint in torchlight meaning more can be found.

There are of course many other accessories to aid the hunter such as Para Cord, flip up scope covers, eye piece shades, quarry calls, bulkier items such as decoys, hide poles etc. but these can be added as and when finances allow and you feel you need them. In other words – when you feel ready and feel they will help you hunt more effectively.

Get the basics of your kit sorted first and add those extra more expensive and not as necessary accoutrements later.

Silence is Golden

A major accessory to have is a silencer or as they're more appropriately termed – sound moderator. Some rifles come with integrally fitted silencers whilst most others, especially PCPs have the muzzle threaded or have an adaptor to accept their own 'optional' silencers or another company's as long as it has a standard ½ inch UNF thread.

Now the reason we as hunters use a silencer on any rifle but more so an air rifle has I feel become mystified and the facts somewhat distorted. In truth, you'd hit your quarry with an un-silenced air rifle because almost instantaneously after firing, if your accuracy is of the required level, then your quarry should be dead! But, the reason silencers are beneficial is because they allow the airgun hunter to go about his business without overly disturbing the area. Trouble is this doesn't hold much weight when you consider the sound a pellet makes on impacting with a rabbit's skull can often be as loud as an un-silenced air rifle and what has to be considered is the sound is usually right next to quarry feeding or sitting alongside the one targeted. Moreover the major plus point of the silencer is that it doesn't betray your shooting position. So once quarry has scurried for cover or flown off after a comrade has fallen, the specific area they've vacated is the place the quarry is watching – not your shooting position. Should both remain undisturbed, by you not giving away your position, say by movement – and in some cases it only needs be a matter of minutes – quarry will return, especially if it's a favoured sunning spot or has rich pickings. This often allows you more shots at quarry in approximately the same area and at the same range as the first. Because of this behaviour, it's also one of the reasons you shouldn't be in too much of a hurry to retrieve shot quarry. Only if it has fallen badly in an untidy manner or you need to administer a coup de grace. Also, a rabbit lying on the ground doesn't seem to deter others from returning back out to feed. Indeed I've had rabbits come out to actually go over to sniff and nose around the deceased scut tail. Many times I've had crows and magpies fly in to take advantage of the freebie meal giving me even more quarry to target. So where does this leave us in respect of the silencer as a hunting aid? Well, it's due to the afore outlined that should have us obtain and use the one most suited to the rifle we're using

The subject of which silencer is best is very much now down to personal choice as the quality of brand name silencers is of a very high level. Most experienced airgun hunters have a favourite brand.

I suppose I'm no exception though I have noticed certain brands of silencer tend to fare better on some rifles than others.

Whichever you choose, by and large the majority of sound moderators are made up of equi-spaced sound absorbing baffles. Some companies try to surround the construction in mystery but on the whole – that's what 'absorbs' the muzzle blast, and in turn quietens muzzle report.

Sandwell Field Sports manufacture a range of remarkably quiet moderators and will custom make anything you care to order – so too will the Venom Custom Shop. Off the shelf you'll find the Logun Silencer is pretty much

Silencers are an essential and come in all shapes and sizes

doing the business across the board on PCPs, but there are others worth considering. Needless to say you'll soon come to appreciate the need for a silencer on a PCP, and the benefits of using a silenced air rifle in general – especially when hunting at night.

Before moving on, always carry a copy of your written permission to shoot and though I've already made mention of it, and many feel them intrusive, a mobile phone is a valuable friend to have. You can always turn it off when not needed. But don't rely on the phone exclusively for the fact it can help you should 'god forbid' you have a hunting accident while out on your own. What if the battery runs flat or you can't get a signal? 'Pay as you go' has a nasty habit of running out just when you most need the talk time. So take a back up, a few coins for use if you can reach a public phone – but for safety sake, an emergency whistle is the least you should have and the torch can be used for signalling when night falls.

But enough 'doom and gloom', now to finish on something I feel is one of the most useful aids second to the silencer. Though some associate more with fullbore shooting, used wisely all 'rests' such as shooting sticks or monopods can be invaluable shooting aids, but, none so useful and handy as the bipod.

Basically this is a detachable unit comprising of a mounting plate and two stabiliser legs that attach to the rifle to form a rest to steady your aim, usually while shooting in the prone position. But, extendable models allow more height and can be used for shooting from a sitting or kneeling position.

The basic bipod available is little more than two toughened plastic legs attached by a hinge with a half open cup that clips onto the barrel. More beneficial are bipods with spring loaded legs that fold up out of the way when not in use and adjustable legs. These usually fit to the rifle by attaching to the front sling swivel stud. In fact 'sniper' shooting from a hidden ambush position with a PCP on a bipod and using a silenced rifle the hunter can soon put a good bag of bunnies together. Used this way these are two accessories that perfectly complement each other – especially with the added aid of good camouflage and fieldcraft.

Before we leave this section a quick word or two on other accessories often mentioned for use in a hunter's pack. You'll probably have read it wise to have a 'space blanket', a compass, mirrors for signalling and other such 'boy scout' motto fuelled paraphernalia. Take these if you must if they help make you feel secure but why this 'advice' continues to be foisted around is anybody's guess. Granted, if hill walking, they can save your life. But, the average airgun hunter will probably never venture that far that he'll need these survival aids. In fact more in your mind should be to hunt sensibly and safely and certainly don't venture into or onto areas that are ridiculously remote or so obviously unsafe. I've hunted over some very 'rough' terrain but I've never once felt under equipped or ill prepared. But then again I've not stalked the banks of the lower Zambezi or in a Peruvian rainforest – yet!

But seriously, do take the basics, the essentials and in the least have a spare full change of clothes in the car, spare shoes or trainers, a car travel blanket should you get snowed in and a folding shovel is handy if you need to dig out the back wheels.

Keep safety as a watchword for your shooting – equally be watchful to your own well being as you go about your sport.

You need to wear the right gear if you want to hunt during the winter months

Chapter 10
The Changing Seasons – An Airgun Hunter's Year

Now it's time to examine the changing landscape and weather that the different months bring, with the effect this has on the quarry you seek. Also outlined are the year's countrywide farming and agricultural 'landmark times' that indicate where, when and why airgun hunters should be actively using certain hunting methods and targeting specific quarry species. But, as seasons seemingly aren't as cut and dried as they once were, we can even have summer-like conditions in late September, and winter weeks that are so mild you'd be forgiven for thinking it was spring. Take prevailing conditions into consideration when planning specific hunting trips, but use the following as a guide to what is most likely to be happening through the months of the year.

January – February

The calendar year starts in January, of course, and as the airgun hunter isn't currently governed by any game laws or close seasons unless he is shooting seasonally protected quarry, I'll start here. Most if not all parts of the country will almost certainly have experienced not only their first hard frosts of the year, but the more northerly areas will also have had snow. Hunting in these conditions isn't impossible, but it is impractical enough for me to advise only the extremely dedicated to try their hand in such extreme conditions. I've been out late at night fox shooting 'on the lamp' and been amazed at the lone rabbits that venture far out into frost-ravaged fields. Why they're out and what they find to eat is a mystery to me. The rabbits I've shot at this time of year aren't on my most frequented shooting areas, but when I've been kindly invited to join others shooting over moorlands with all-round rabbit activity, and areas with large rabbit populations. It seems the rabbits that inhabit the upper parts of the Pennines and both the Highlands and Lowlands of Scotland are a hardy breed! It goes without saying, at this time of year if I'm hunting in these situations I'll be very well wrapped up, but to be up and out in time to witness a bright wintry sun breaking through a clear blue sky over snowbound hills or frost tinged fields is a wonderful sight to behold. When shooting in such extreme conditions, I'll hole up in ambush near any natural cover. Usually dry-stone walls or hedgerows are favoured locations, but then only if I've been told by my host that it's near a spot which rabbits regularly frequent for their brief spell in the early morning sunshine. It's not uncommon to encounter crows or magpies, and this is a time of year when baiting them with a slit-open rabbit carcass will do the trick. Corvids are used to finding carcasses, especially if the weather has been particularly harsh.

January must be amongst the worst, if not the very worst, of times for planning any hunting trip. Woodies can be found huddled in sitty-trees, but you'll have to hope you can get near them, or preferably have done some serious planning so as to be hiding in ambush and waiting for them to fly in and seek shelter.

By February, if your land has pheasants on it you might have to put woodpigeon roost shooting on hold until the pheasants have left the trees. Not only do you not want to disturb the 'stubby-winged ones', but also it doesn't help your relations with the keeper if you shoot one by accident. The air rifle is often the best option for dealing with certain types of vermin in the woods, and although the shotgun is still widely used, at this time of year many keepers are coming to realise the benefit of the air rifle, because it's almost silent. Nothing is so sure to have pheasants high-tailing it to live in another wood than shotgun blasts! Rooks will be returning to re-establish themselves at favoured nests at the rookery, and the young that escaped the previous year's short springtime 'brancher' cull will swell their ranks, building nests anew.

At this time of year, my 'outdoor' shooting is usually limited to roost-shooting woodpigeons, wandering around the woods for opportunist shots at squirrels, and shooting corvids over baits or, where possible, on feeding areas. Crows will still be flocking together as they move around fields in search of food, usually in the company of other corvids such as jackdaws, and they'll be finding food in the creep feeders that are put out in the fields to fatten up the sheep. If you get within range of one of these areas in a suitable hide, a good few sessions can be had before the birds move to steal feed from a safer feeder.

Even magpies seem unusually sociable in February, hanging around together in small and sometimes very tight-knit groups. But by the end of the month it's typical to see that some will have paired up and be back repairing old nests in preparation for the coming breeding season. Note where their nests are, and keep watch for activity around them. However, if you're not overrun, don't disturb magpies too early as there can be opportunities later in the year to bait-up nearby, as soon as the young leave the nest. Alternatively, you can annoy the whole family with a strategically placed little owl or kestrel decoy, which they will mob. As February progresses, you'll see them less frequently over open areas of land, as the pairs will be staying close to the nest areas, often with another noisy suitor in tow.

But don't ignore the open fields for chances of shots at other vermin. Stubble fields and set-aside areas left from autumn can see a glut of flying felons, and for the shooter in a well chosen hide position they can yield surprising results. Typically, in the woods the woodpigeons will be stocking up, probably feeding on the last of the ivy berries and the like before eventually moving onto rape fields later in the year. (There'll be more to consider on berry feeding woodies towards the end of the year.) If it's windy, you'll find them sitting out the bad weather on the lee side of the woods, and depending on how severe the weather is they'll sit lower in the trees, because they don't like getting bashed around by the stormy elements. Rainy conditions will also see them perching lower than usual. Squirrels can often be found scratching around in leaf litter on the woodland floor, and at times even seen foraging alongside the woodpigeon which will be frantically pecking around the bases of the trees. The squirrel can be taken by surprise by the soft-footed shooter, as it may have its head so deep in the leaves that it won't hear your approach. The woodie, on the other hand, is never so obliging or foolhardy when on the deck.

February is definitely a month of change. Many airgun hunters of my acquaintance – and I must generally agree with them – feel this to be one of the best times of the year for hunting, mainly in wooded areas before the branches become covered with leaves. Walking these areas comes high on the list, as you can encounter a variety of species ranging from most of the corvid family to the wood-pigeon and grey squirrel. If you're fortunate enough to be able to shoot around old buildings in rural areas, you can often encounter jackdaws, and in some areas certain broadminded representatives of the clergy will allow airgun hunters to take discreet walks around their churches and grounds, as they know that vermin do not respect such places. They can be havens for feral pigeons, crows, jackdaws, rooks and squirrels to name only a few. Obviously, in places such as this you need to use your discretion as to when to go shooting. It is not good practice to be seen sauntering around in full camo just before or after worship. But go when people have gone home, and your quarry will still be there. Many a productive afternoon can be spent walking around taking opportunist shots.

By the end of the month, spring will definitely be in the air and the daffodils and snowdrops will already be well on their way to flowering, a sure sign that a change of season is underway.

March – April

With more light to shoot by in the mornings, and a little more in the evenings too, the countryside is waking up for the airgun hunter. It's a good time to be out and about as the fresh smell of spring hangs in the air. The typical weather is more accurately described as pleasant rather than really nice, but on the whole a vast improvement in conditions will be seen as we progress through the month. But as the weather may still change suddenly, it can catch out those who are too optimistic and not prepared for variable weather. During these months rain can be the hunter's downfall.

The 'mad march hare' of lore and fact will be seen in certain parts of the country, and although it is a legitimate species to be tackled with a powerful FAC-licensed air rifle, many now recommend the animal best left for the .22 rimfire rifle or the shotgun. If you want to try your hand with an FAC hi-powered air rifle and there are plenty of 'long ears' around, I say keep the range sensible – and don't forget your game licence!

Corvids will have paired off and be getting ready to lay the first clutch of eggs, while the first young rabbit kits will be out and very innocent and foolhardy as they learn the ways of the natural world. Many fall easy prey, being mopped up by foxes, stoats, weasels and buzzards. The sporting shooter will leave them until they're of a size worth preparing for the pot, but take note of the area as it's a place to target later in the year.

Generally this is the busiest time of year for serious pest control, because the adult rabbits are easier to target before the foliage starts to green and thicken up. Rabbits will also now be much more active at night, and at dawn and dusk. You'll notice that the burrows are starting to be re-dug and run through. Fresh scrapings and earth near entrance holes shows that the rabbits are back in business. They're likely to be much more active during the night, and the optimum times are the first couple of hours before and after dawn, which comes earlier as the weeks pass. But if you're targeting them at night, it can be very cold and temperatures can quickly drop below freezing, just as happens in autumn, even though the days may have been pleasant and at times very sunny.

Come early spring and corvids such as magpies are soon back repairing nests

Tackling the corvid population is important before they breed. Unfortunately you'll have to rise early, as the dawn still seems to be trapped in the night and it can be hard to get up in time to be in position to catch these earliest of risers. Try baiting or ambush tactics for both crows and magpies, although you will find that these will decrease in effectiveness as the birds find mates or re-establish acquaintance with old flames, and go off to do what comes naturally. But baiting can be done again with a vengeance once they've raised a family. The woodie roost shooting will have all but dried up by now, not only as the trees get their leaves but as the birds pair off and leave established communal winter accommodation to find individual nest sites.

By this time in the season, if not earlier, you should have either repaired natural hides, or be building new ones for reaping rewards from summer into autumn. If you see rabbits establishing a new warren, now's the time to build a hide within comfortable striking distance, and by late summer you'll have a hidden shooting position just waiting to be used.

May – June

They say 'don't cast a clout until May is out'. Many will have heard this old saying, and it's one that usually holds true. Rain can come at any time, but those fresh spring mornings can also still bring a chill, as will the evenings. But on your shoot this is definitely a key time of year to hit vermin hard. Corvids are preparing to raise further broods of potential problems. Gamekeepers cull magpies with Larsen traps, and even large crow traps nab their share throughout the breeding season, but where possible airgun hunters should use their rifles to help eradicate those birds that dodge the traps. The first rabbit kits you saw not many weeks ago will soon be ready to breed themselves. Everywhere you look the countryside is growing greener. Bluebells erupt into full bloom, forming carpets of colour wherever they're found along hedges and the woodland floor, while the fields are getting full of long grass and tall stalks of barley, wheat and oil seed rape. Land animals have plenty of cover now to hide

When the weather starts to warm up, time can be better spent during the day shooting around the farm buildings

in, and tree dwellers have much more foliage from which to call and watch.

May 12th is still known by many as 'brancher day', and the annual beginning of shooting young rooks preparing to leave the nest is part of the tradition in many country areas. Although the young branchers in many areas can now be seen to emerge as early as April, May 12th is still the particular date that many choose to go out and stand underneath a rookery waiting for a youngster to venture forth. Rook shooting is a controversial subject, however, and some are now of the opinion that there should be some control over this practice, especially if the species isn't in plague proportions locally. It seems that more and more 'officers of the countryside' are deeming rooks the farmer's friend, not that I've met many farmers – especially sheep farmers – who'd miss their presence on their land.

Young rabbits are naive to the ways of the world and betray the presence of warrens

As for activity in the fields, this is my favourite time of year for hunting rabbits with dedicated night-vision equipment. Early summer nights are very appealing, and this is a very exciting branch of our sport that is certainly worth trying once you're proficient enough. Rabbits are very much more active by this time of year. If the weather is fine, they'll be spending much more time above ground, both day and night, and that means many more shooting opportunities. Ambush shooting near warrens, feeding areas, and the sides of crop fields they're invading is very productive, and at times it can seem as though you're almost tripping over them. At others, they're very wary; but look for signs that they've been around and it could indicate nocturnal activity.

During the day, woodpigeons in particular might seem to be quite thin on the ground, although there will actually be many about. Rather than settling into flocks to feed on the fields, they'll now be raising their young. The birds feed sporadically to produce the regurgitated 'pigeon milk' that is food for the young. Magpies that have escaped your attentions or the gamekeepers' Larsen traps and gone on to breed will now be seen in family groups. Often the adult birds will fly along hedgerows with the brood following in an undulating line. These are opportune times to lay baits, and often you can make a good bag, especially before the young birds get too educated and wary. This also applies to young crows, which can be quite comical as they make their first solo flights.

Many grassy fields around the countryside will now have had their first cut of grass for silage, or will soon do so, and this makes rabbits easier to get at once they stray onto the freshly-mown, lawn-like expanses. With a keen eye, the shooter should be able to see them right up until last light; but many rabbits will stay near the rye grass that always escapes cutting. They frequent these areas to feed as well as to utilise the little bit of cover it affords on otherwise flat fields. If the grass has been swirled around and left by the cutter, you'll find good sport spotting them between the rows of cut grass left in the fields to dry. Alongside hedges that border crops, especially alongside rape fields, the rabbits can cause havoc. This damage often goes undetected until the end of May, when the crops are cut only to reveal large semi-circular patches of barren ground, because ever since the seed was sown the rabbits will have nibbled their way out into the field. The airgun hunter should take opportunities to watch for the beginnings of this damage before the rabbits get too established. Carefully walk the edge of a field, looking for signs of rabbit activity, and you can then ambush them over these well-frequented feeding spots, saving the farmer costly losses.

As we come into June the morning light really does break much earlier and the sun goes down far later in the evening. The longest day is approaching, and high summer is just around the corner. All those lovely daylight hours to hunt in! But in reality, especially during a sudden warm spell, quarry can be quite scarce over the fields, while only the dedicated will rise to be out before dawn. That means 3 am (or even earlier in far northern Britain) starts to get into position if we're ambushing, and not many will or can endure that for long. Time is better spent in the longer evening bunny-bashing sessions, while a mooch around the farmyard and outbuildings can often be the most productive way to find quarry during the day, especially as we get into the progressively warmer months that follow. Birds regularly visit farms and outbuildings to feed or drink at this time of year. Collared doves, feral pigeons, woodies, jackdaws, crows – they'll all gravitate to the outbuildings and areas holding livestock, and corvids especially will hang around cattle and sheep pens. Sit in the open-plan 'hangar-type' barns, maybe using some form of hide, and await intruders. Many a time when it's sweltering in the fields, time spent sitting indoors in the cool shade produces a steady stream of winged quarry throughout the day.

In some places I've had superb sport shooting jackdaws coming to steal the protein-rich pellet feed put out for livestock. Uncannily, they know the exact time it'll be spread into the troughs, and in some places they'll perch outside on fences, telegraph posts and overhead power cables waiting to descend, after the farm workers have left the building after putting out feed. Be in there, hidden and waiting, and you can have some very hectic, fast-firing early morning action.

Take care on your way to and from the shoot as you travel the country lanes, as farm machinery will be coming and going at all hours to get the many seasonal jobs done. If bales are left bagged-up on grass fields, you can often find magpies and crows pecking around the base and even attacking the plastic, and a cluster of bales is possibly a place to consider hiding up to ambush them in the early morning. If well hidden in ambush at the side of a newly cut field, don't be surprised to see corvids dropping down to sift through scattered hay if it hasn't been baled.

At the end of June, and certainly as we reach July, they have their young with them, often two and occasionally only one juvenile bird that follows the adults, cawing to be fed. The adults busy themselves picking through the freshly cut grass for anything edible to stuff into the cackling young bird's eager beak. If you're there hiding up in ambush, make the most of this and put something else in the way of its bill!

If you have an appropriate vehicle and the weather is fine – and, of course, if the farmer or landowner gives you permission – now's the time to drive around picking off rabbits at the side of the hedges backing onto the cut fields. You can usually shoot without the aid of a lamp until it's quite late in the evening. Alternatively, if you're fortunate enough to own or have access to one, you can be out roving those inaccessible areas on an ATV such as a quad bike. Yes, summer's here and it really is getting close to the time for reaping the rich harvest of shooting opportunities that are not only just around the corner, but have already begun. With the longest day past, you're now hunting in high summer.

July – August

Warmer weather should be predominant but as this is the UK, our unpredictable climate can throw up many surprises. The only sure feature of these months is that there's more day than night, and the sun lingers low in the sky during the evenings. Woodpigeons have bred, and you'll start to see the young birds (squabs) flying with others of their kind, which are recognisable by the lack of a white neck flash.

The squabs aren't too cautious, and if you encounter them away from the more worldly-wise adults they can easily be picked out of trees, and off the ground if they land amongst decoys. As the crops will now be standing tall, it's time to try decoying birds onto setaside fields.

At this time of year, it can seem as if the fields are alive with rabbits. Depending on the weather, geographical location, and when the seeds were sown, grassy fields could still be being mown.

This is a busy time on the land, and you don't want to be getting in the way, or putting anybody working on the land at risk. Let them know you're there, because with modern camo you can literally disappear in the undergrowth. Remember that many accidents occur on farms, and you don't want to be one of them. If fields are being tended, keep well out of the way, as you don't want to be a hindrance. You're there to help the farmer and the other people whose livelihoods depend on the land.

August can be a strange month, with autumn just around the corner. Quarry creatures can be found anywhere and everywhere as they search for food, with their numbers boosted after the breeding period. The mornings can be surprisingly chilly, as can the late evenings, especially if aided by a chilling breeze combined with little cloud cover to help the earth retain the warmth of the day's sun. As the month ends, spring-sown cereal crops such as barley, oats and wheat will be harvested. The long-stemmed, drooping ears of the crop first take on a rusty appearance and soon thereafter ripen. And then, as if the fields were never green, they'll soon be turned back to stubbles.

September – October

Fieldfares will by now have begun to arrive, and it can often seem that these members of the thrush family are bobbing around everywhere. But whilst September must rank amongst one of the busiest months of the year for the farmer, for the airgun hunter autumn yields many opportunities. However, due to the unpredictability of the weather it can also be very frustrating. The weather can drastically change and ruin any hunting plans you might have. Squalls, rain, freak gales and thunder storms are always a possibility - certainly at this time of year they're never far away. So expect the unexpected!

Know the times crops are sown and you'll find the quarry that visits to feed

Farmers will be cutting late crops, and ploughing ready to sow others. Most will have harvested all their rape, wheat, barley and other cereal crops, and by the end of the month the new seeds of winter oats, barley and wheat will be back in the fertile ground. Grass fields will have had yet another cut, and probably been tilled for another. These are the ever-continuing cycles of the agricultural calendar, and the airgun hunter needs to learn them so as to be in the right place to ambush and target quarry.

With all this harvest and sowing activity, it's hardly surprising that September is woodpigeon time as they descend like locusts to feed on freshly-cut and freshly-sown fields alike. This is always a time the shotgunner looks forward to, and the same should go for the airgun hunter as well. The woodpigeon is a worthy adversary and, better still, is very tasty. By this time of year I'm nearly fed up with eating rabbits, and a bit more woodie is a very welcome change. Decoys used under flightlines and over the fields the birds are visiting are the way to target these crop-guzzlers. I've learned many of my pigeon shooting tricks from watching experienced shotgunners, and I recommend airgun hunters to do the same. It pays to keep an open mind and remove the blinkers, because the keen pigeon shot will possibly have years of experience, so watch and listen – and when the opportunity arises, join in. Shooting over stubbles can bring all manner of sport, with rabbits, crows and woodpigeons being the most common.

Planting and harvesting are a never-ending cycle for the farmer, and as I'm sure you're now realising often open up many opportunities for the airgun hunter. These windows of opportunity are at times relatively small ones, as in many places no sooner is the corn cut to stubbles than it's ploughed in again and promptly planted with rape or winter barley. Similarly, grass fields once harvested are superb areas to go lamping over, but within weeks the farmer could have tilled them again to get another crop of grass, or the lush new growth won't benefit from much 'pounding' so there's no more rattling across the bowling green-like surface in your 4 × 4 vehicle. Whilst we need to take advantage of the opportunities, also be mindful of what the farmer has done. He'll not take too kindly to you tramping over freshly seeded fields, and your muddy boot prints or wheel tracks will always give you away. If you are continuing your shooting around these fields, then 'around' is the key word. Shoot quarry on the edges of the field, and when moving your position walk around the edges, keeping well off the seed.

If myxomatosis hasn't reared its ugly head, rabbits will be plentiful. However, if they've been shot regularly during the year, by now they'll be very twitchy. Once the crops and grass are cut at least you have a quick chance at getting at them before they dive back into cover. Ambushing them in the early mornings and the short evenings, once you've established the areas they still use, can be productive. However, the evenings start to close in very quickly now, with shooting time being reduced steadily with every passing week. You can at times shoot by moonlight, and if positioned correctly you can shoot woodies silhouetted in the treetops. It's not always possible or practicable, but it can be done. Also, at the end of September into October, woodies will be feeding heavily during the day around and actually in the trees that hold acorns, beech mast and rowan berries. Again this is one of those small windows of opportunity the forward thinking airgun hunter can take advantage of. Find the right area and wait up in ambush and a good bag can be put together. Shooting will be demanding as the trees will still be in almost full leaf. Alternatively put a few deeks out around the base of these trees and try to entice them down onto the deck.

Many hunters now see autumn as the start of the lamping season, the time to 'turn the lights on' and focus your attention on shooting rabbits at night with the aid of an artificial light source. This can be done either by going out in pairs, with one holding the lamp, while the other shoots or, as I prefer to do, go it alone with a gun-mounted lamp.

Once again, remember that as the farmers are busy, cutting and bailing there will be more activity on the country lanes, so be careful on the way to and from your shoot. Remember my earlier warning on weather – note too that September days can go from one extreme to the other as regards temperature. The afternoons can be gorgeous and even hot, and you may be sweltering under camo when decoying pigeon, yet shivering when dusk comes and you ambush rabbits. It often feels very chilly during night-time lamping sessions.

If grass fields have been left after the first cut they could be cut again as late as the first week of October, before rain becomes more frequent. Winter corn, barley and oats will all be sprouting in the fields – a good time to watch for flying vermin visiting. The rabbits will be hefty, having now put on body fat in anticipation of the lean winter months ahead. As for weather, rain will sometimes put paid to shooting, and may curtail a lot of

As autumn comes down in the woods – it's not only squirrels that forage around in the leaf litter

hunting plans when we have lengthy periods of wet weather. Trudging across sodden fields isn't ideal or fruitful, but for those who have indoor shooting opportunities for quarry such as rats and feral pigeon – go to it! Alternatively, look around the woods and even small pockets of trees or copses. Now's the time you'll see squirrels as they go about their daily routine of eating and travelling the routes they use along branches which will by now be starting to lose their foliage. They'll be preoccupied with gathering food, especially beech mast. This is as much a favourite with squirrels as it is with wood-pigeons, as it has a high protein and fat content – just what wild animals need to help sustain them in harsh winter conditions. As we saw at the start of the year, you can once again find squirrels amongst the leaf litter frantically gathering up the nuts that fall from split husks to stash away for use at a later date. The same applies to jays and woodpigeons too. The best tactics are to find where your quarry is making regular visits to feed, and then wear full camo, sitting quietly with your back to a tree to hide your silhouette as you silently wait in ambush.

Woodpigeons will still be around, but those that are will be very wary. If they've escaped the shotgun or your airgun they'll be more difficult to decoy than ever before. Try deeks on setaside fields that look barren, as a well-placed deek pattern might just fool them down to investigate if their brethren have found food.

As the foliage starts to slowly disappear, tall ground cover also dies away. Now you can target rabbits under hedges that are usually impenetrable during the summer months. Night frosts will more likely than not increase by the end of the month, and the trees will definitely be looking increasingly bare.

If September has been particularly mild you can be pretty sure October will see winter arrive with a vengeance. Rainy conditions will be the norm, with much colder temperatures in the mornings and evenings as well as during the day. Cold, strong winds are usually most prevalent as well, but if you head for sheltered areas such as copses and woods you might be pleasantly surprised at what can be found sheltering there. Dawn breaks later, so an early morning session can be profitable if you can stand the cold. By the end of the month it's dark soon after teatime, and as the clocks go back, another hour of light is lost in the evening but gained in the morning.

As food becomes harder to find, you'll discover corvids are easier to entice to baits. Woodpigeons will readily come down to deeks placed almost anywhere, especially as they'll be visiting setaside areas in search of wild flowers, shoots, seeds and clover.

By the end of October we'll have done well not to have a smattering of frost over nearly every field in the country, and that means swapping from lightweight camo wear during the day to insulated jackets, trousers and gloves at night.

November – December

Nowadays, the climate is such that in late autumn and early winter we almost have what can be considered a rainy season. A prolonged period of rainy days will not only affect you while it's raining, but will also quickly turn many fields into muddy bogs. It can take up to a week for the land to dry off afterwards. Indeed, in some years it's only dry when the weather has turned cold enough to harden the soil by freezing the water it holds. When these rains come, which can be earlier or later than November, you can be sure of one thing – that they'll put a huge dampener on your sport, unless you've got access to indoor shooting. These will be lean times for your trigger finger until the rains lessen and the cold, sharp frosty mornings herald a return to outdoor shooting for the hardy hunter who can go back out into the fields and woods in search of sport.

But even then, quarry will be hard to find on the ground, and the targets will be mostly corvids, pigeons or squirrels.

Again, baiting is a favourite method for corvids, but now is a good time to establish a baited area for squirrels, although wood-walking among the bare trees can also yield a nice bag of 'tree rats'. Decoys still work

When the colder weather arrives it's time to head back indoors to catch up on the rat and feral shooting

for woodpigeons, especially lofted deeks near sitty trees; but as much thought as goes into hunting should also go into your own welfare – in other words, keeping warm and dry in the cold weather. If you're cold or wet not only are you uncomfortable but you won't hunt efficiently either. There's no shame in admitting that it's too cold and admitting defeat. Far better to go home and come back to hunt another day, than to end up with short- or even long-term illness.

Come December, the woodies will be even easier to target in trees with very sparse foliage, and easy to spot against ivy-covered tree trunks. They can become uncharacteristically quite careless of their own safety as they take the opportunity to gorge once again on ivy berries, so if you find trees they're regularly visiting, being in the right place at the right time can produce results.

You only get the opportunity of a few sessions at them in these situations, as they'll soon wise up to the danger and visit other more inaccessible areas to feed.

As the weather closes in, especially when cloud is very low and it's damp and drizzly, squirrels will come down from the trees and be much more active on the woodland floor again searching for food. The same applies to woodies which can often come down onto glades, clearings and tracks alongside the trees, and not only in the search for food. I side with those who believe they also come down from the upper branches to escape the damp air. If an animal or bird gets wet through, it can have disastrous consequences so it follows that a small animal such as a squirrel or a downy-feathered wood pigeon would be susceptible to saturation and chilling. The weather can be downright miserable and will steadily worsen, and unfortunately it will tend to remain much the same until late January. And that's where we came in – at the start of the year.

Now that we've reviewed the seasons, I'm sure you've realised that both the beginning and end of the year can be very dour times, and unproductive to be out on your shoot. But these are opportune times to take advantage of the lull in activity by making a thorough check of all your kit. If your camo clothing's looking worn and battered treat yourself to some new garments. Even though regular routine maintenance of your rifle should be done periodically throughout the year, most shooters opt for a thorough annual check up. See the chapter on Gun Maintenance for useful advice on keeping your rifle in tip-top condition. If you've spent all year hunting regularly with a PCP air rifle, now's the time to seriously consider having it sent into the manufacturer or a good specialist airgun-smith to have it properly serviced. That way, when it comes back, it'll be working as well as ever to take on the fresh crop of vermin that each new year brings.

There's no way I can be described as a fair-weather hunter, but when winter has gripped the land, with hard frosts the norm, possibilities of snow and the Met Office issuing the familiar stormy wet weather warnings, there's not much to tempt even the hardiest or most optimistic out into the fields. When this happens I do as nature indicates and head indoors with my rifle, and that means catching up on feral pigeon clearance jobs and late-night ratting sessions. Remember, in colder weather these are the times when the rat will seek shelter from the elements and will be getting well established in places where the farmer doesn't want it. It's time to prove your worth as an airgun hunter and earn your right to shoot on the land when more conducive weather returns. When I do occasionally venture forth at the back end of the year for sport, it's really for the challenge and I recommend that anyone who does the same should keep sessions short.

Chapter 11
Quarry Files

As mentioned at the very start of this book the airgun hunter has a 'specified' selection of quarry species classed as vermin that are deemed legal to shoot with a 12ft lb air rifle on land where permission has been granted to shoot over.

It's the responsibility of every hunter to be able to quickly and easily identify all quarry species in all conditions from a variety of angles. In fact if you take time to study the quarry species as a naturalist studies the behaviour of animals and birds you'll soon notice your hunting tally grow as you realise why certain creatures react and behave the way they do pertaining to variation of seasons, weather conditions, even their tolerance to sensing danger.

For instance, the first crow you examine close up (which will be the first one you shoot) will remind you of every Hammer horror film you've ever seen. The bird's gargoyle-like features, its 'reptileanesque' legs and almost demon-like claws all betray the bird's lifestyle and true character. There really is nothing to like about the

The back of the head, neck and between the shoulder blades – a crow shows the 'Achilles' heel' kill-zone of all flying felons...

crow. The only thing to respect is its wariness and intelligence. While a magpie's curiosity can often get the better of him most times a crow will never be so stupid, neither will the adult rook or a large gathering of jackdaws. It really is amazing to watch a flock of jackdaws descend into the treetops as they fly hither and thither on their daily search for food. Hardly have they alighted on the trees than one of their number spots something untoward below and the flock take noisily to the skies. In fact further in the chapter on Hunting Techniques you'll soon come to appreciate you'd rather be in a position worrying if one pair of eyes has spotted you than three or even four. So imagine how you'd cope worrying on upwards of a hundred!

Even the humble rabbit can be a source of endless fascination. There's always something to be learned from just watching your quarry even without a rifle in your hands. Granted, you'll be amazed at the animal's voracious appetite as it nibbles and gnaws its way over the ground. These fluffy 'hoovers' seemingly do nothing but eat, but often as not they'll sit motionless seemingly doing nothing but listening and watching. Then, in the blink of an eye it can either start to groom itself, resume feeding, start to doze in the sun, huddle down against the rain or just simply leg it to the nearest hedge cover.

Observing animals equally shows their destructive sides, which is the reason they've become classed as vermin. Rabbits chew, eat, nibble and scratch at everything, squirrels similarly so and they climb. Rats are possibly the most abhorrent – the urine and droppings being a particular cause for concern due to the health aspect. This is where birds come into the equation. Droppings from feral pigeon and collared dove spoil grain; woodies eat masses of it and are responsible for other cereal crop damage as do corvids particularly crows. Those who suppose crows only scavenge for carrion should forget the first 'C' in the birds' Sunday name as along with the woodies this is the biggest cause for concern on barley and wheat fields at certain times of the year. Its wings easily beat down crop stems and left unchecked they can 'strim' the fields from outside in, or inside out with a matter of weeks. Even in a few days a mass of destruction can be caused by a large enough concentration of these pests. And so when you see this destruction know the financial burden this puts onto the farming community and realise you are doing a service and although pursuing a very absorbing sport you do put a lot back to your hosts who allow you to shoot on their land. Before going any further a word on the importance of kill-zones and the knowledge needed of what is in essence each and every animal and birds' Achilles heel.

Some of what you have probably read in certain publications is tempered with caution or inflated with flowery prose to make up for a lack of practical know-how.

It must be remembered that quarry rarely presents itself perfectly side on or fully facing you. This is sometimes referred to as a quartering target, meaning it will often be at a slight angle. However in some cases this can work to your advantage as it can help you place the shot past protective feather, fur or bone into a specific kill-zone area. As we come to each individual quarry species you'll clearly have it detailed where and when each kill-zone is a viable and suitable area to aim for.

This will ensure you hunt as effectively and dispatch your quarry as humanely as possible. This is of utmost importance as you need to have respect for your quarry until the very end. And, though I have a favoured calibre I'll detail which are suitable to use for each.

But not wanting to get too bogged down with the ultimate result, time now to look at each quarry species in turn. In other words a closer in-depth view into the lives and behavioural patterns of the 'eleven' most wanted.

RABBIT (*Oryctolagus cuniculus*)

Where better and with what better animal to start an in-depth look at our main quarry species than with the rabbit, because unquestionably the rabbit is the mainstay of the airgun hunter. And why not, it's usually found in abundance, it can often be a very challenging adversary and to top it all – its very tasty.

The rabbit belongs to the family of mammals known as the order of Lagomorphs, which actually means 'hare like'. In actual fact they belong to the same family as the hare, which is leporidae. Despite what some presume, they're not 'true' rodents as rodents such as mice and rats have four incisor teeth whilst lagomorphs have six. However, it does share a major similarity with any rodent – when in large numbers it can be a great pest. Everybody knows what a rabbit looks like but commonly, rabbits are covered in a grey brown colour 'fur' with an orangey patch on the nape of the neck and an off-white underbelly. Not forgetting the little brown topped, white tail known as the scut – often seen disappearing before the hunter's had chance to take a shot. In some areas black rabbits aren't uncommon but albinos and piebald are very rare. Rabbit can be distinguished from its close relative the hare by the fact it has smaller ears, shorter hind legs and is much smaller in build.

When to target the animal is very much up to population on your shooting ground and the farmer's or landowner's instruction. Usually you need to make inroads into a large population in early spring, but if not totally overrun use your discretion and don't over-shoot the land. Their numbers will soon dwindle under heavy shooting pressure even though they are prolific breeders giving rise to the familiar phrase – 'breeds like rabbits'.

Due in part to the fact that a sexually mature female can produce up to 30 offspring in a year, it's no surprise why the rabbit is an animal that farmers and estate managers keep a weather eye upon. Breeding can begin as early as January and continue into early autumn. At the start of the season the female rabbit is continuously fertile. In less than half a day after giving birth the female is once again fertile. Hence the ability to breed in such large numbers as it's not uncommon for

The rabbit is the airgun hunter's major quarry species

a healthy doe to produce over 6 litters a year, each containing on average half a dozen kittens.

Even in certain urban areas it can and will cause havoc on cricket pitches or bowling greens – sports centres being a particular favourite as for some strange reason best known to 'ol bugs' it just loves to gnaw on the very expensive all-weather Astro Turf. In the countryside, in badly hit areas, cereal farmers have been known to experience a 20% reduction in crop yield. Despite its numbers, the rabbit can at times be perhaps the most infuriating quarry to bag, quickly wising up to the methods you employ.

Habitat

Rabbits can be found almost anywhere. A very adaptable mammal, it's found amongst hedgerows, fields, and scrubland. Certainly over most arable land and amongst foliage that provides the requisites for survival, those being cover and a plentiful food supply. Basically, its diet consists of anything that's green and edible ranging from grass to seeds, berries and in deepest winter when other foodstuff is hard to come by, even the bark of bushes and trees. By and large they prefer soft sandy soil to build warrens that are usually found on slopes to provide drainage. Contrary to popular belief the rabbit isn't the world's best burrower, and that's the reason loose sandy soil is ideal for them to excavate and build the 'warren', its communal home. It is an accomplished climber, scrabbling up saplings to get at shoots, quickly clambering over dry stone walls and has even been known to swim short distances when the need arises.

It's an extremely sociable animal, which in many areas generally spends most of the daylight hours underground. Depending on population, it can be seen at any time of day but the early morning and late evening, especially in spring and summer are times to turn your attention to a spot of rabbiting. Where population is at a reasonable level the rabbit serves as an important part of the 'open' country-side's eco-system, but left to its own devices it can become a disastrous nuisance, particularly to the farming community. This is where it needs to be kept in check and the reason it offers such widespread sport to the shooter of all disciplines.

Location and Behavioural Patterns

Finding rabbits is relatively easy as like most animals they leave clues as to their presence. These are holes to burrows, dense round pellet droppings and runs. Runs are basically flattened pathways rabbits regularly use to move around to and from a feeding area. If left undisturbed rabbits tend to be quite unadventurous travellers preferring to use the same route day in, day out as they venture from their burrows to feed. Feeding areas are easily identified as closely cropped grass or bare patches in newly sown crops at the edges of fields. Also bits of fur on low barbed wire fencing or at the edges of brambles will indicate areas of rabbit activity.

Rabbits don't like the wind on them, so on blustery days you will normally find them in a sheltered position. Look for them on the leeward side of anything that offers a windbreak – stonewalls, hedgerows and high embankments – all fit the bill very nicely indeed.

The rabbit has many natural enemies so has developed a high level of detection systems. These are, in the following order – ears, nose and eyes. The three Ss of sound, smell and sight. Reputedly a rabbit can smell a predator, especially a human from up to a hundred yards away and its hearing is even more acute. Little wonder it can make such challenging quarry, especially when you consider, due to the eyes being positioned at the side and towards the top of the head a rabbit can virtually see all the way around and above its position. The animal is usually in a constant state of alertness, the only time you can stalk up on them successfully is by approaching downwind, keeping low and hoping the animal is either dosing in the sun or preoccupied with feeding. Interestingly it's now known a rabbit's status of alertness changes depending on its location. If close to cover you'd think it'd be more relaxed. Not so as it realises here a predator could spring from the same cover it can take refuge in. Also when far away from its burrow it'll also be very alert as it knows it's got a longer distance to travel to safety. The animal will only relax in areas it has found to be relatively undisturbed and when in such a position it feels comfortable. If you regularly observe rabbits you'll soon recognise that their body language is a give-away if they are anxious or untroubled. This is where being out and watching animal activity can reap dividends for you as a hunter. Just watching lets you see the animal in its natural state going about its business and if you remain unobtrusive as possible you'll be surprised at how much you can learn and how close they'll come. The body language of a rabbit is also the biggest giveaway to the way it reacts to its surroundings. Once the ears droop onto the back of the head it has relaxed one sense, the next are the eyes which won't actually close but like a dozing human it will half close them and then it will drop its head onto its chest or even lie flat out on the ground. You often see this behaviour during hot weather and through the longer summer evenings. But it only takes the slightest hint of danger for the situation to change. Whether that is because it has detected a suspicious movement, foreign smell or sound – it'll prick up its ears, get up onto its hind legs in readiness to bolt for cover. Learning the body language of a rabbit is very important as it can often save you a lot of wasted effort in maybe stalking a rabbit that just isn't a suitable candidate for your attentions.

Methods to Use

The rabbit is a candidate for virtually every hunting technique. You can come across one while opportunist shooting or wood-walking. You'll most certainly need to stalk closer to take the shot and ambushing them in appropriate areas can be a very productive method. They can be targeted at night with the lamp or dedicated Nightvision riflescope. If you are allowed and can drive around a particular area of the shoot you can shoot them from the cab or passenger seat of a 4 × 4 or going solo on an ATV such as a Quad Bike.

In most cases stalking can be productive and is a skill that needs to be properly learned. There are times it's 'unstalkable' and this is when you should try lying up in ambush.

But one thing that we have in our favour is its habit of 'freezing' when it first senses danger. This can either be its saviour from predators or if we spot it – its downfall. To have any measure of success with hunting rabbits it is essential to know where they are likely to be at certain times of the day and/or night.

Ambushing is a much more relaxed way of shooting rabbits and can be very productive as long as you've chosen your shooting position with care. Always reconnoitre the area you intend to shoot over and establish where the rabbits are found and at what time of day. Get into position before the rabbits usually appear and a good bag can be on the cards.

As a hunter I feel there's nothing like the first adrenalin rush after watching a hedgeline for a lengthy period, you see a flicker of movement. It could be a twitch of an ear or the tentative first sight of the animal's twitching nose, slightly poking out from the undergrowth to sniff for danger. Alternatively it can just suddenly lollop out into plain view to sit and survey the scene or even start to spruce itself up. Sometimes however, that flicker of movement that sets your pulse racing can just as likely be a robin or wren searching out insects. On more than one occasion these busy birds have charged me up to have my head on the cheekpiece getting ready to sight in on what I have thought to be the first potential bunny of the day.

Lamping can also produce when the rabbits are active at night. Alternatively if the rabbits are wary of the lamp (lamp shy) more and more hunters are realising the benefits of using dedicated Nightvision equipment such as NV scopes to target quarry in total darkness. Suffice to say, in the relevant chapters to come, all these hunting techniques are outlined fully to help you deal with this most rewarding of quarry species. And at some time or another the airgun hunter will thank it for the sport it offers.

Calibres and Kill-Zones

As I used the rabbit as an example of where pinpoint accuracy is of paramount importance in placing a pellet into a kill-zone way back in the chapter on pellets and calibres it's now the place to explain the reason for that and to explain kill-zones in general.

While choice of calibre is a hotly debated subject amongst airgun hunters, nobody can disagree, that to hit any animal correctly in the kill-zone with any calibre 'slug' and it'll be dutifully dispatched. Therefore all calibres will be more than a match for the rabbit as long as your accuracy puts the lead into the areas detailed here. Incidentally, it's very fitting we begin with the rabbit in Quarry Files pertaining to kill-zones as this animal's vulnerable areas are surely the most misunderstood.

With a legal limit 12ft lb air rifle, more often than not, when targeting the rabbit, this is where it's advisable to adopt an all or nothing attitude in your hunting and take only headshots. A wounded rabbit can quite easily get to cover to perish in its warren or similar area of safety. This is an unacceptable situation that you must strive to prevent from happening at all costs.

But to glibly say headshot isn't explanation enough as a more detailed look at rabbit anatomy is needed to describe exactly where the pellet needs to go. Although the head of an adult rabbit looks quite large, the kill-zone of the brain is approximately only the size of a walnut. To hit this area with deadly effect, imagine a line from eye to the base of the rabbit's ear. The area to aim for is just off centre behind the eye, on that line towards the ear. This is why I mentioned the need for precision with the smaller .177 calibre pellet. Hit dead centre with .22 or even slightly further forward or back and it's also fatal. Move further to the front with .177 and you could actually go into the nasal passage of the animal. Now I'm not purposely trying to be controversial, and I know this has never been written about before but I feel a book intended to be highly comprehensive should address these matters. I've shot rabbits that have obviously recovered from these wounds but is it fair that they've been injured in this way – no and I'm sure the majority of responsible hunters agree. So that's the 'side-on' headshot fully explained. Now if the rabbit presents itself 'head on' facing you from the front we can take a line from just above the eyes to just below the neckline and again achieve a clean kill with any calibre from a 12ft lbs legal limit air rifle. Sometimes, especially at night while lamping the rabbit can infuriatingly turn its back on you, adopting a position where it can move directly away from you – usually this is when they're near cover so they face back into it. If they do, put one straight into the back of the 'napper' or base of the neck before it does a runner.

Now to the thorny subject of the body shot, and it is one that some shooters take with a 12ft lb rifle and feel is a valid kill-zone. That's fine if it works for them, but personally a shot I'd only take using a high power .22 calibre air rifle of say 22+ft lbs.

If the rabbit is facing you, and if it is standing on its hind legs you can shoot directly into the centre of the upper chest to place the pellet between the front forelegs. From the side, it isn't as easy. Here you 'follow' the line of the foreleg to where it meets the animal's body. Then place the cross hairs so the shot will impact the rabbit approximately a third of the way back on the body. This will place a shot straight into the boiler room – the heart and lung shot. These shots are acceptable due to the fact the rabbit's rib cage not being overly strong at this point coupled with the lower amount of body tissue surrounding these organs. But in autumn when the rabbit has usually piled on the pounds with extra body fat you do have more to contend with. This is where I'd not take this shot with anything but a hi-power air rifle and then only when necessary. There is a section devoted to hi-power (FAC) rifles much later in the book, also you'll notice as you work through Quarry Files that a hi-power air rifle gives you more options on pellet placement for a variety of species.

But I digress. When a rabbit presents itself full on, sat up looking in your direction, a hi-power FAC rifle really does give you the edge allowing a very specific shot. Imagine a line drawn across the head just above its eyes and one drawn down the centre of the animal's body – making a cross, the centre of which being just above the rabbit's eyes on its forehead. From here (the brain) to approximately 3 inches on the vertical line down its chest to the heart and lungs is all exposed kill-zone. If you're rangefinding isn't the best, that's a fair 'drop' of allowance and certainly a reason some choose to use FAC air rifles for rabbits. But as this is for the majority who hunt with 'off ticket' rifles, the headshot is still the optimum kill-zone.

Incidentally, for those who really want to understand the reason these 'body-shot' areas are effective, when you shoot a rabbit, dissect it by slitting straight up the front and middle with a sharp knife or game shears. Cut up the sternum to expose the chest under the rib cage and look to see exactly where the heart and lungs are. And this applies to other species, dissect them and you'll have better understanding of the quarry's anatomy giving you better insight into these vulnerable areas known as kill-zones.

Myxomatosis

You can't talk about the humble rabbit without having to mention the horrendous plague that all but annihilated them in this country in the 1950s – that being the insect carried virus Myxomatosis.

Myxomatosis or 'Myxi' was used to clear Australia of the plague of rabbits. It was introduced here in the early 50s – some pin it down to 1953. It was brought to Europe by a French physician called Dr Delille to control the rabbits on his country estate near Paris. Many presume or have been told it was intentionally brought and introduced here. Granted it has been 'put down' in some areas. Sometimes legally others not so; what did happen was when farmers realised how effective it was in eradicating pesky scut tails they moved infected rabbits to other areas where the rabbit flea just went aboutits business spreading the disease. But it's not just the rabbit flea that carries the virus as most other blood-sucking

insects can also to some extent spread the 'plague'. It can take up to two weeks after being bitten for the rabbit to contract the disease, which manifests itself on your shoot when you see misty and swollen eyed rabbits. The eyes stream with mucus that they continuously rub and scratch at often until they bleed. The rabbits quickly weaken and eventually die of starvation or lung infection. Rabbits carrying the disease can look healthy up to a few days before death when they show
characteristic signs of lethargy, blindness, stumbling weak movement. Unfortunately the disease still rears its ugly head today but tends to crop up in localised pockets and then will not totally wipe out the area as more rabbits survive as generations have developed a tolerance. The fleas still carrying the disease can over-winter with the rabbits in burrows ready to infect the next generation. Pet rabbits can now be vaccinated against it and as it's highly contagious they should. But for the wild coney – shooting rabbit in this state is an act of mercy as if not picked off by natural predators; they otherwise meet a lingering and unpleasant end.

BROWN RAT (*Rattus norvegicus*)

The wood pigeon, magpie and carrion crow surely top the list of farmers' 'most unwanted' feathered pests, but undeniably the brown (or common) rat is surely the most detested of all terra-firma based vermin. Not only will/and does it eat anything, but it also carries all sorts of infectious diseases, including the potentially fatal Weil's disease. It's caused by the Leptospira virus hence its other name, Leptospirosis. It is carried in the rat's urine, so humans only have to come into contact with something it has soiled and they can become infected. For this reason, never touch any you've dispatched. Handle them only with protective gloves or tongs. Dispose of them properly, preferably by burning, or bury them with a shovel full of quick lime.

Man's mortal enemy – the brown rat

Despite or because of its deplorable ways, you could say that along with the feral pigeon, we have it to thank for the public accepting the valid use of airguns as a tool for controlling vermin numbers. Virtually all airgun hunters have a tale to tell and I'm sure you've heard the 'rats as big as cats' stories. Well that's a bit of an exaggeration, but adults can weigh up to 2 pounds and be up to two feet in length, from tip of its whiskery nose to end of its scaly tail. Its ability to survive and thrive is staggering.

Habitat

Wherever there is human habitation you will find the rat, living in unhealthy (for us) harmony with its unwitting hosts. During the summer months they, like all mammals are spread far and wide across the countryside. When the colder weather comes they head for barns, grain silos and outhouses, in search of warmth, shelter and of course food. Although they are found in sewers or beside drainage ditches and canals, they aren't the greatest lovers of water – preferring warm dry accommodation. Farms make ideal rodent environment. Spilt grain, chicken and pig feed – all make a ready food supply for the rat, whilst outbuildings, barns and chicken coops make ideal homes. In fact, your average farm could be considered a Five Star hotel for a rat. There's little more to say on the subject other than they can live above or below ground, the holes and runs they use can at times seem too small for them to pass through or use and they are everywhere they are not evicted from.

And consider this – as they have no breeding season or seeming limitations to breed here are some frightening facts. The brown rat becomes sexually mature in little under 3 months and most females produce at least five or six litters each year, with each containing up to ten young. This means that in an ideal habitat a pair of sexually mature rats can easily produce over 60 offspring, as a pregnancy can last as little as 24 days. Taking into account the relatively short time it takes them to reach sexual maturity this knock on effect can mean a

Rat droppings are unmistakeable and betray areas of heavy infestation

pair of rats, including their offspring in one year can theoretically be responsible for creating well over a thousand rats. A staggering thought! There's also the widely held belief that rats can sense disease in a potential mate so healthy rats don't mate with poisoned rats. A reason they say modern poisons are becoming less and less effective.

Incidentally its close relative the Black Rat (*Rattus rattus*) responsible for the 'Black Death' is now a protected species (cough!) and thankfully only found on the Island of Lundy.

Location and Behavioural Patterns

On the farm, the first sign of rats is usually amongst the pigpens, cattle feed troughs and hen runs. Later or simultaneously they'll appear in and around grain silos and hay bales. You'll probably catch sight of one out of the corner of your eye as it scurries along the base of a wall, across a beam or girder making its way to food or back to an entrance to a communal home. Hundreds of these rodents can occupy an absolute labyrinth of tunnels and 'scrapes'.

Rats just love dark, gloomy places – all the better if they contain straw such as the aforementioned hay bales stacked in storage over winter. Any of the animal pens or outbuildings are worth a try for locating them but as extreme caution is needed if shooting near livestock, first check if you can target them elsewhere.

Within the confines of the farm buildings and outhouses, rat holes can often appear as if overnight where the rat is usually finding its way in from the fields. In fact I'll take this opportunity to dispel the popular misconception that the rat lives indoors all year around. You'll more often than not find a few in and around the farm all year long, but come late spring and the onset of warmer weather it returns to the fields. Often then only returning to farm buildings because of the food it can find. Once the food source is taken away – in the case of grain used and sold – then so too will the rat – like Elvis – 'leave the building' until the colder weather once again returns.

The rat is an unwelcome guest around the farm due to two major problems it will cause. One is damage and the other the foodstuffs it will spoil. Granted it will eat a lot of grain but the major problem is the droppings left on top and the faeces that permeate down into the valuable stored cereal. The other damage is the rodent's penchant for gnawing into anything that it comes across – electrical cable, sacks, wood and particularly its burrowing into bales of hay – not only to rip out material to take away for nest building but simply to find a cosy spot to raise yet another brood.

Incidentally, be warned: indoor close range shooting isn't as easy as it first seems. No sooner will you see one, than it will disappear into the little hidey-holes they use for safety. Despite its abhorrent nature, the brown rat is a clever, intelligent and at times infuriatingly cautious critter. It's also a socially structured animal that can pass on information quickly to others concerning areas that hold food or once you've shot a few times – the area that carries danger.

Methods to Use

By and large the brown rat is a nocturnal creature, spreading its nastiness under the cover of darkness. There are two ways to bag them, both involving shooting at night using some form of artificial light source. However, now with the availability of hi-tech Nightvision equipment the true 'specialist' has even more options. But first the tried and trusted traditional methods – the most widely known, being 'baiting out'.

Before going any further it must be said that although this method works and works well to some extent it isn't nearly half as effective as targeting them on their established runs and self-appointed feeding areas which will be dealt with in the chapter on Shooting At Night.

As the name implies 'baiting out' is a method whereby the shooter puts out a suitable bait into an area with the objective of establishing a feeding area the rats feel safe visiting. Similar in reasoning why a dead rabbit is left out to bring in carrion feeders.

The baiting process is quite straightforward. Food should be left out regularly for up to a week, before any shooting is done. Anything will suffice from bread to rotten fruit. Most who've done this type of shooting prefer certain foodstuffs. But the experienced agree that putting out bait that can't be dragged away and eaten out of sight is far better. Some favour bread or a chicken carcass in a net bag suspended a few inches off the floor. This has the rat work to get at the food above its head and to get into the bag. Similarly a big tin of pet food with holes punched in the side so the rat has to struggle to get its nose in is another good bait. But if there's one treat they can't resist it's grated chocolate and peanut butter. Peanut butter is ideal as it sticks to the area you place it and the rats have to stick around to nibble and lick it up. As an added incentive the grated chocolate is like icing on the cake sprinkled onto it and the combined aroma wafts around to easily be picked up by the whiskery rodent's nostrils. There are others including grated cheese or groundbait used by anglers. This small 'crumb' bait keeps the rat nibbling away on the spot. The kit and employment of the method is simple. You need to choose a hidden shooting position within range with a shooting angle that gives you a sturdy backstop behind the target. If needed put a big piece of heavy wood covered with carpet behind the bait to absorb the impact of pellets. For many situations such as this you don't need a gun lamp as you can shoot by the illumination of the low power light near the bait. In these cases I'll opt to use a springer with open sights or preferably a multi-shot PCP with red dot for the fact they allow you to get a 'quick fix' on the target. However, I'll more often than not use a scope with a gunlamp onboard so as to target those detected in the areas out and away from the baited area.

As well as preparing with bait, the area to be baited should initially be illuminated with a low light on a regular basis so the rats become accustomed to it. Most barns have a power source for illumination so all you need to do is put a low wattage bulb of no more than 40W in a suitable holder such as an old bedside lamp or car inspection lamp.

I set the light to the left of my intended shooting position and no more than 12 yards from the baited area. The light source is then blocked out from my direct view so I'm never able to look directly at it, thus saving my 'night-vision'.

Baiting out tactics can bring quick results when first employed but soon lose effectiveness after a few shooting sessions.

This is when you need to search the rats out in their natural runs they're using to and from the natural food they've discovered. In fact it's often the case that where rats have established food and a way to and from shelter they'll not respond well to baiting out tactics anyway.

In this situation you'll need some extra and specialised accessories other than rifle and pellets. These other methods will be detailed in full in the relevant sections.

Calibres and Kill-Zones

Though I'm a great fan of .177 calibre I must admit it wiser to opt for the .22 calibre slug when targeting rats, especially if taking them 'on the 'hoof' so to speak. Usually a pellet into the front third of the rodent's body will dispatch it but if it's 'moving' that's a very small target. The .22 allows you more leeway from the exact point of kill whereas a .177 pellet needs to go straight into the brain or heart. If the rats are hanging around, then I would use .177 calibre but take full on head shots and preferably the best shot by far is directly into its whiskery snout from the front as it peers down or up at you. However, if the range is within 25yds I choose to use .22. Some even advocate .25 but though you're getting a pellet giving extra weight and mass, I don't feel the pros outweigh the cons. So that brings us back to the two most popular calibres and equally as important where to place the lead. Obviously headshots are preferable and with the .177 calibre essential. However, with larger calibres and at closer range hit the rat in the front third of the body and it isn't going to go far!

'Ratting' can be very challenging and satisfying as every time a scaly tail snuffs it – you've done a public service – no arguing with that.

Know your Voles

When hunting near rivers, streams, lakes, canals or any body of fresh water make sure that you don't confuse the brown rat with the little bank vole or larger water vole. Both are becoming quite scarce in some areas, they do no harm to the environment and are largely protected.

It's easy to distinguish between rats and these friendlies. A full-grown bank vole is only about 8-10cm in length, including its furry tail – more the size of a mouse than a rat. The water vole is a lot bigger, with head and body about 20cm in length and a hairy ringed tail of about 10cm. Its head is round and blunt in appearance (vaguely similar in fact to a guinea pigs), with tiny ears. In contrast, an average sized rat has a head and body length of 23-28cm, a pointed whiskery nose, prominent ears and long scaly tail.

GREY SQUIRREL (*Sciurus carolinensis*)

A prolific inhabitant of our forests and woodlands, the grey squirrel has been nothing but trouble to our forestry industry since its introduction to this country from its native North America in 1876. It's a busy little rodent that will gnaw and nibble at anything, it has a penchant for biting the growing shoots from young saplings, resulting in a stunted, unsightly tree. It also has another particular annoying habit of stripping the bark even though it doesn't eat it. Most of these random acts of destruction are due to the fact that like other rodents it needs to wear down the incisors due to the continual growth of these effective gnashers. It eventually was recognised as such a huge problem that in the 1960s a bounty was put on its head as the Government actually paid people to shoot them. Incidentally, it's approximated there are now over two million greys in the UK at any one time, despite the pest being well and truly classed as vermin.

Easily distinguished from our native and protected red squirrel it has a uniform grey fur coat, with a dirty white underbelly extending up to the throat and face. It has a characteristically long bushy silvery grey tail. Its small almost indifferent ears are a big contrast to the red's ear tufts which are in relation to the ears of the animal, large and very distinctive. The grey is also much larger, stockier and even in silhouette has an unmistakable outline.

Come spring before new foliage fully takes over the trees, the squirrels can feed on buds or gnaw to get at sap just under the bark. This is where, when and why they cause such a problem to plantation owners. But it's not only due to the damage they inflict on trees because come the breeding season for birds, they're notorious egg thieves and fledgling killers. Often we punish and blame corvids such as magpies and crows but just as likely the culprit is the squirrel.

The grey squirrel is little more than a tree-rat

They're also a nuisance on 'keepered' estates where they will steal the grain spilled out for game birds and in harsh winters will even chew holes at the top of the feed hoppers to get inside.

As you can see, definitely not a fussy eater and couple this with the fact that it serves no constructive natural purpose at all to the woodlands eco-system, and you have on your hands a right royal pest!

Habitat

Where there are trees, there will usually be grey squirrels – especially in deciduous woodlands. An extremely resourceful creature, it is equally at home in a town park or urban garden where it delights and thrives in raiding bird tables for nuts, fruit and seeds. A popular misconception since its arrival on these shores is that this larger 'alien' species of squirrel has ousted the more timid native red squirrel. This is only partly true. The 'red' was actually in decline before the introduction of the 'grey'. Also it's now coming under threat from the Parapox virus and to top it all, our native species prefers coniferous woodland – a habitat in somewhat of a decline in most 'lowland' counties. Another misconception is that squirrels hibernate during the winter months. Again, this is definitely not the case and one of the reasons it provides excellent sport for the airgun hunter during the colder months. It can be seen out foraging even in the snows of deepest winter. However, it does prefer the warmth of the drey during harsh wet weather but if hunger dictates it must feed, it will be out rummaging around in the leaf litter.

The drey is usually quite a modest sized ball-shaped construction of twigs and leaves, usually built in the cleft of a tree. In the safety of its lair, two litters of one to seven young are reared between January and June.

Location and Behavioural Patterns

Signs of squirrel activity in the woods on your shoot will be easy to spot. They usually have a particular branch or stump from which they keep an eye on the trees around them. This can often also be a favourite feeding spot.

Around the bottom of these areas you will find pieces of stripped bark, broken husks, chestnut shells, split and gnawed fir cones etc. The drey is also easy to identify and locate once the trees have lost some of their foliage. This can look like a small nest but will often only be a scruffy collection of twigs, dead leaves and even pieces of bark jammed into the fork of a tree. Usually they're not very high up, maybe midway up the tree as the squirrel isn't keen on repairing wind damaged dreys perched in the upper branches. Occasionally you'll find established dreys with 'nut stores' close by usually higher up and smaller in size than the main drey. Like the animal's separate outhouse cum larder. Sometimes the squirrel just takes up residence in an unoccupied crow or magpie nest adding fresh building material when needed. In fact, find a drey in spring that has had some recently added fresh vegetation with green leaves showing in the construction, and you know it's being used.

Squirrels, like rats have no difficulty in finding food. They have an acute sense of smell – one of the reasons they easily find hoppers full of grain and any 'spillings' or leftovers that are freely on offer. Then again, the squirrel is so adaptable and intelligent it can soon work out a way into most containers of food storage – usually by chewing their way in. As with any form of hunting, location and patience are the key to success. A quick walk around a small copse or wood will soon have you find the tell-tale signs of squirrel habitation. If near coniferous trees, you'll find the fir cones neatly stripped, gnawed down and discarded like an eaten apple core. Small scratchings at the foot of trees in any wood betrays their presence especially if accompanied by signs of bark being stripped. These signs aren't always aloft; as squirrels often have a favoured fallen log or branch they'll gnaw away at like hungry little beavers.

But it's the feed hoppers themselves that come regularly under attack and regular replacing even the toughened plastic types is a troublesome chore for keepers not forgetting an extra expense. Find these areas and you'll undoubtedly have some squirrels. Look up aloft as you walk through the trees and you'll soon find its bulky home.

But it's not only outdoors squirrels can be found as they can and do cause a right problem when they've taken up residence in roof space of country houses or even more in urban areas. They can ruin loft insulation by scratching, gnawing through wiring – all potential fire hazards.

Methods to Use

The airgun hunter can target them in the trees, and where possible bait them down to a natural or artificially 'created' feeding station. There is a technique known as drey knocking. This is more often used by shooters working in pairs whereby they 'knock' the drey with lofting poles to send the squirrel out to meet an end with the shotgun. Though some airgun hunters try this method, by and large I'd leave this for the shotgunner as we want them to be still, rather than running for cover. However, the method is detailed in Hunting Techniques for reasons of thoroughness.

Wood-walking is just as the name implies and can be allied with opportunist shooting as the technique involves you walking slowly through woodland scanning the trees for signs of activity. These methods are outlined in the suitable chapters. Needless to say, the best time to hunt squirrels is from autumn through to winter.

When beech mast is ripening early on in the autumn squirrels can and will stay in the trees but once the split open husks fall they'll follow the food source to where it's fallen on the woodland floor.

It's plentiful food and the trees are bare so take the opportunity to reap results until the buds start to green the trees up come the spring when squirrel shooting becomes nigh on impossible due to the foliage.

However, it's at this time of year you can sit up near an area you've found they're feeding and wait in ambush. Sitting quietly within range in full camo is the way to succeed. If it is a feed hopper they're visiting, then they'll come down to feed near it, but it often pays to give them an extra incentive to bring them to the shooting position.

Spend time in a place frequented by squirrels and you'll soon notice they have favourite walkways to and from areas. They'll come down or go up the same trees and use the same branches to keep moving around while still keeping off the deck.

Whether it follows its own scent or just knows its way around a familiar area is debatable but they certainly do show a preference for travelling along the same routes. They also definitely have favourite positions to sit and eat foodstuffs. These can be in the fork or cleft of a tree, anywhere that gives them an easy place to sit on their haunches as their front paws are busy holding and manipulating the food for getting their greedy chops around. Alternatively, in spring they'll go to the very tops of trees to get at the most succulent buds.

I don't think there's any animal or bird classed as vermin – with the exception of the rabbit – that can't be tempted by a free meal.

The animal's inquisitive nature can often be its downfall which is one of the reasons they're sometimes easily trapped but squirrels are very clever and soon learn to avoid the cage traps that are regularly set in any one particular area for them.

Usual baits for traps include corn, any cereal grain, ground or whole peanuts and would you believe some swear by chocolate.

Use ground up nuts, assorted nuts and raisins or cheap brand breakfast muesli and put it out at the base of a feed hopper or favoured tree they use for descending from the canopy. Then carefully select a spot, under another tree within range and just sit and wait for events to unfold.

Make yourself comfortable and prepare for a long wait. I'll use the same tactics I employ when sitting up near a 'sitty-tree' waiting for woodies, that's full camo, including facemask and gloves but ready to take shots along the horizontal as soon as the squirrels come to the feeding area. When shooting in this way, I prefer to use a low light scope, with the magnification wound down to its lowest setting so as to take full advantage of a big objective lens's light-gathering capabilities. Even on the brightest days it can get quite gloomy under a tangled canopy of even quite bare branches. When the squirrel does, and don't worry, it will eventually make an appearance, aim carefully depending on how it presents to your shooting position and you'll have ambushed the first of hopefully many bushy tails.

Incidentally, in my experience it doesn't pay to leave shot squirrels near a baited area so though you need to break cover, look to check there aren't other potential targets moving around before removing it.

But like any animal, squirrels soon sense danger and wise up to the fact hanging around on the deck isn't a good idea once a few have been shot. But, thankfully for the shooter, they're predictable little varmints and if they don't sit and hold on the ground, they might nick a piece of the tasty treats left out and high tail it to sit high up on a branch nibbling the prize. And once up aloft, in familiar territory, a squirrel's confidence rises dramatically, even to the point of arrogance.

Calibres and Kill-Zones

For squirrel shooting any calibre, be it .177, .22 or the less popular .20 will suffice as long as your accuracy is up to the mark. Targeting these rodents isn't easy because the kill-zones aren't that large, and if up aloft the shot could be a tricky one.

If the squirrel is sitting side-on, the prime spot to aim for is the head down to the shoulder but if it presents full on the little white chubby underbelly is a very exposed tempter. But the squirrel is a deceptively tough critter and even here the pellet can't be allowed to drop below the animal's front paws or else you'll miss a vital organ. If facing away, flat to a tree trunk, drill one right into the back of the head or neck area and it won't be clinging on for long.

THE COLLARED DOVE (*Streptopelia decaocto*)

The collared dove is a relatively recent visitor to our shores, but has now become firmly established as a most common and abundant breeding bird. It's hard to believe that it was once strictly a bird of the Balkans (the hilly region encompassing Bulgaria, Greece etc.) and lowlands of mainland Europe. The first reported nesting pair in the UK was in Norfolk in 1955. Its colonisation of this country since that time is staggering and there can't be a farm, park, garden or urban estate roof that hasn't been graced with its deceptively pretty presence at some time or another. The main reason for its amazing population expansion is largely due to its ability to breed all year round if the food supply is plentiful. Not to be confused with

The collared dove is a deceptively pretty pest

the protected and slightly smaller turtle dove, the collared dove is distinguished by the black and white edged half collar around the back of its neck – hence the name. This collar, which sets off the creamy grey brown to buff neck and body plumage make it a very attractive member of the dove family. Unfortunately, appearances can be deceptive, as left to its own devices this bird will eat a store of winter grain.

Habitat

Whatever the species, bird population usually declines due to the fact they either can't adapt or they are too shy to live in close proximity to humans. The collared dove, however, is perfectly designed to live near urbanised areas and feeds on anything from grain, corn or poultry feed to household scraps and bird table offerings. In fact it's now officially classed as a bird of town parks and gardens. In areas where dairy farming is the norm, the collared dove easily adapts to live further out into the fields on anything from weed-seeds and young shoots to elderberries.

Why are collared doves so unpopular then? Well, they can and do actually steal the feed from free-range hens, where they are often seen feeding right amongst the domestic fowl. Even though it's a pro-lific breeder, its nest building skills leave a lot to be desired. The usual nest structure being little more than a flimsy platform of woven twigs high in a tree, on a ledge, on a fluorescent tube light fitting or in the rafters of the barns and outbuildings. An insight into its self-procreating potential is that some recognised ornithologists have stated that, in the case of collared doves living in a high yield food enriched habitat, female birds can be in a state of near permanent fertilisation. Somebody really should tell them about birth control.

Location and Behavioural Patterns

The collared dove is a very easy bird to find, due to the fact that it never strays far from its food

Hardly sport – but the collared dove is now so common partly because it can breed all the year around

supply. So it follows, its need to be close to a regular source of suitable foodstuffs is the key to this 'pretty pest's' location. This is why they have taken (like feral pigeon and some instances woodpigeon) to frequenting town parks and gardens. For obvious reasons the law prevents you from shooting them in these public places. Therefore, the main place for the airgun hunter to target them is around the farmyard and surrounding buildings. Short observation recces will soon show where it prefers to feed. The bird absolutely detests bad weather, and will always be found sheltering from the wind and rain. The unmistakable relatively high-pitched double 'coo', so common to doves of all varieties, or the repeated 'cu-coo-cu' call will usually betray their presence. The collared's call is also a quite lengthy repetition of this set pattern. It has another quite raucous 'crying' call which is used when flying off or landing – it's used as both an alarm signal and telling all and sundry it's 'arrived' on the scene. Like many other feathered felons, it will also have favourite 'sitty' trees, ledges or beams where it will sit and digest large meals. In a sitting this relatively small dove can get through an enormous amount of seed, corn or grain. In fact, when they are in this 'digestive mode' after a good feed they can be quite easy to sneak up on.

Methods to Use

Firstly it must be said that although the collared dove is a pest in certain areas similarly when targeting other quarry species use your discretion as to what exactly constitutes a 'threat' to the farmer's livelihood or health. I only consider shooting collared doves when they are present in seriously large numbers and known to be 'spoiling' or taking an unacceptable amount of grain. I say this because shooting collared doves is relatively simple and in my opinion an act of sheer pest control, not sport. Their 'trust' of humans is their downfall and they will hang around much longer than any other quarry species apart from established feral pigeon colonies.

If you are asked into an area to shoot them, then the three main methods of dealing with or dare I say 'hunting' this prolific dove are roost shooting, stalking (around the farm buildings) and baiting down with grain. As soon as the dawn starts to break they'll probably already be out and about feeding. Although the bird tolerates human presence, it still has keen eyesight and if it does sense danger from you it will flutter up to move onto another part of the farm to feed. This can be infuriating but it still won't be as shy or wary as any of the other legitimate quarry species. Roost shooting isn't anywhere near as productive as the other two methods, as collared doves tend to roost in very small numbers, usually twos or threes. However, this is also the most unsporting and again a method to use if shooting for sheer pest control. In fact, when the birds have paired off, especially when they have eggs or young they often roost together on the nest. In the day the female sits on the eggs, the male hanging around outside the barn in a tree or on the building roof. At night he comes in to snuggle up against the female but the birds often sit facing in opposite directions. The sitting arrangement is presumed so the birds can defend the nest from rats that will also be up there in the rafters and roof space. The collared dove is very brave for its size and they'll fly at magpies and even rats keeping them away from eggs and chicks. Unfortunately in the kafuffle they often knock their own eggs or even fledglings out of the nest so they achieve little. However, such is the prolific breeding pattern they soon have another clutch of eggs, usually two laid shortly after they lose any. They're also, once paired off very affectionate to each other, preening one another and generally sitting and staying close together. But I digress and back to shooting methods.

Baiting down is the most efficient method of making inroads into the bird's population where it has become troublesome. Once you have established an area that the birds frequent regularly, it's just a matter of putting out feed for them and leaving them undisturbed for a few days. This form of ambushing obviously necessitates the use of shooting from cover. This can range from a perimeter wall, from inside an outbuilding or from behind any type of static farm machinery. I stress the term 'static' as it's no use if the tractor gets driven away on the morning you plan to shoot. Large bags can be built up shooting this way as the collared dove, even when scared off, will usually return quite quickly. Whether this is pure greed, or they are just plain dumb is anybody's guess. I reckon it's a combination of both with a liberal sprinkling of plain old gluttony! However, a trait they do display which is their downfall is they tend to stay together in pairs and even when you shoot one, often the other won't fly far sometimes only fluttering up to immediately settle back down strutting around near the fallen comrade. These are the times a double shot or multi-shot rifle are a godsend as a quick back up shot will usually end in you bagging a brace a time. As I said, shooting collareds is hardly sport.

Once you've shot a few birds, these can be used as decoys using chin sticks set up as you would using shot wood pigeon as natural deeks. Try to sit the birds in a head down feeding position. Unlike decoying woodies, the pattern you lay collareds out in isn't critically important. One tip though is to arrange the birds as if feeding in a loose circle, heads facing inwards towards each other. This seems to be the dove's natural feeding pattern when congregated in a small group.

Stalking is the most demanding method for dealing with the birds. Even though the doves might at times seem to be untroubled by the human presence, a person intentionally sneaking up on them is something else altogether. If the weather has been inclement for a few days then this could well work in your favour, as the doves will shelter amongst the buildings and surrounding trees. When moving around the farm buildings themselves, stay close to the wall and move slowly. Plan your route in an anti-clockwise direction so as to approach corners with the ability to peek around them rifle half-mounted at the ready. This allows you to keep most of your body concealed. Of course for 'lefties' the opposite direction will apply. For once, full camo gear isn't needed, but do wear drab clothing to suit the farm buildings, rusting metalwork of silos and outdoor machinery as well as the darker areas in shade. Whichever attire you choose, when 'sneaking' quietly around the outbuildings in this fashion, be mindful to the possibility of coming across any other people who might be working in the area. Remember, safety at all times!

Calibres and Kill-Zones

I'll always choose the small .177 calibre pellet time in and time out for the dove but any of the popular calibres will suffice. Headshots and full on breast shots will see this bird cleanly dispatched. Remember though the headshot is very small. This takes accuracy especially shooting at awkward angles so more often than not I'll always take this bird with a shot that punches straight into the upper part of the chest cavity.

When you've shot your doves, don't waste them as the breast meat is quite tasty. Tougher than woodpigeon but cooked slowly and for a longer period it's worth the trouble of breasting enough to make into a stew or casserole. Mixed in with a bit of woodie, rabbit meat and root vegetables you've got a tasty meal and the farmer gets to 'lose' yet another cause of potential loss of earnings.

WOOD PIGEON (*Columba palumbus*)

On a dull overcast day the wood pigeon, or as hunters affectionately know it, the 'woodie' can appear to be little more than a plump large grey bird with a patch or two of black and white. When the sun hits the plumage, marvel at the attractiveness of its beautiful pink/mauve breast feathers, the brilliance of the white neck patches and glistening iridescence of the green/blue feathers that surround those attention grabbing neck flashes. Even the bold black bars of the wings are boldly etched with broad white bands giving the woodie an almost regal appearance. Yes, the collared dove might beat it hands down for cuteness but you can't deny the woodie its place in the countryside as a very distinctive and attractive bird.

The wood pigeon is a major agricultural pest

Unfortunately, it's the scourge of every cereal farmer, crop grower and market gardener in the land. The woodpigeon may be a dreaded agricultural pest, but it's a firm favourite with the shooting disciplines of shotgunners and airgun hunters – and as an added bonus it's very tasty. In fact alongside the rabbit it surely now rates as the airgun hunter's staple quarry species for year-round sport. With thought and know how, decent bags can be achieved as you pick them out of the trees as they rest, or off the fields as they feed. Wherever and whenever you encounter the 'woodie', you can be sure it will prove a very worthy and wary adversary.

Habitat

As its name implies, this is primarily a bird of the woods although depending on season it will feed and readily move over and onto fields. Due to its massive population figures it can also be found even in relatively treeless areas, including towns and even some cities. Like the collared dove it's becoming a much more common sight in urban areas. I suppose it's safe to assume it realises it's not in threat from the gun there! For nesting, it usually builds a small platform of twigs high up in the trees and will raise two to three broods. Unlike most other birds the adults feed the young on pigeon milk they produce during and throughout the breeding season. This can start as early as March right through to October but depending on availability of food they have been known to breed even in winter. The young birds are known as 'squabs' and can be seen over the fields come summer. They're easily distinguished from adults due to the lack of white neck patch and of course are a lot smaller. Some shotgunners consider it unsporting to shoot these naive inexperienced birds but I don't think a farmer in the land would thank you for giving them a reprieve. The reason being woodies can eat an amazing amount of food, stuffing their crops to bursting at every opportunity – especially when feeding on oilseed rape, corn, wheat, young pea or bean shoots and ivy berries in the winter. Woodies feed three or four times a day, so ambushing them can be a very effective tactic when you've learned the areas they use as flightlines to the fields they feed over. Unlike a lot of other birds, its habitat is not in decline or under threat. Although some woodies are lost to foxes and cats, it has few natural enemies – most commonly those being the sparrow hawk, peregrine falcon, kestrel and buzzards. The latter especially can cause havoc when decoying, as the buzzard will spook the birds but as it's nature's way we have to put up with the goings on around us as we hunt and adapt accordingly. Needless to say if a buzzard is soaring and gliding around the area, the woodies aren't likely to be feeding confidently.

However, none of these raptors pose a major problem to the bird's population figures.

Location and Behavioural Patterns

The movements of wood pigeon are very much dictated by the seasons and their need to find food and shelter. They can usually be found over fields during the daytime, and around woods and copses in the evenings where it will return to roost. And depending on season not forgetting weather conditions, it will often spend a lot of time in the woods. This is when the bird's distinctive and repeatedly used throaty 'cooo, coo, coo – coo, coo' call will more often than not give its presence away long before you see it. But the woodpigeon's voracious appetite and specific dietary preferences, coupled with the annual availability of those foodstuffs, are the definitive key to its location. Basically if there's grain on the soil or crops growing in the fields then you'll find pigeons on them. It pays to know when the farmer is sowing, as the birds will descend like a plague as soon as the grain is on the ground. This is because, unlike some other birds, the woodpigeon isn't keen on scratching about deep in the soil, it rarely if ever will dig into the soil for food. It prefers to take easy pickings of seed kernels and grain off the top where and when it can find them. It also doesn't like getting its feet wet or muddy so when conditions dictate, look to the sitty-trees for sport, the edge of woods or dry areas of fields with good drainage – a factor to take into consideration when choosing an area to set-out decoys.

It stands to reason that to ambush them effectively you need prior knowledge of potential feeding areas, and the flightlines that the birds regularly use. A few days watching the land will soon indicate which 'lines' the birds fly up and along. They often follow hedgelines, a line of trees – even along roads. In winter the birds really do have to search for food and can from day to day be found either foraging on the woodland floor, around the base of trees and hedges before they get the chance to descend on the winter rape fields.

Methods to Use

The successful pigeon shooter must be organised, well informed and disciplined in both their approach and methods. Though major methods are decoying and roost shooting, the airgun hunter can have superb sport if favoured sitty-trees are located. You can also encounter the birds while out wood-walking or opportunist shooting but more often than not as you 'sneak' stealthily around, the first indication any are near is the sound or sight of them clattering out of a nearby tree.

Talking of trees – when the birds are preoccupied, feeding on ivy berries in the colder months you can often, with prior knowledge be waiting for them to arrive, well concealed to pick the birds off when they're gorging themselves. Or if they're staying deep in the wood because of wet, harsh or cold weather conditions. Know the areas they frequent when this weather arrives and carefully slip from tree to tree until within range. This is particularly challenging but very rewarding if successful.

Ambushing near 'watering holes' isn't a method I'd rely on but if the birds have been feeding on cereal especially corn they seem to get quite thirsty. Discover a place they use to take on water, which unlike most other birds they actually do by sucking it up and you could well have a few good sessions. It could be a pond, stream or water trough but I'd rather recommend you find the 'feeding' fields they're coming from or going to and ambushing them there with the aid of decoys. If you want to get serious about woodies – then check the crop of the first few birds you shoot in a session, as this will give you good indication of where the birds might be feeding.

Decoying, roost shooting and my preferred method of picking them out of sitty-trees – they're all very productive methods for bagging a few birds.

Calibres and Kill-Zones

Either .177, .20 or .22 calibre is suitable to cleanly dispatch woodies at sensible airgun hunting ranges but the pellet needs to be placed with precision in one of three major 'kill-zone areas' depending on how the bird presets in relation to your shooting position. Crop shots shouldn't be taken as the food-stuff in the bird's onboard storage tank can be packed so dense it can deflect or stop a shot being fatal. First and foremost is the side-on shot at the head and neck. Next is the upper chest cavity but only if you can slip the pellet up between a wing fold from below and the angle into this area also has to be right so the pellet enters the heart and lungs. If the bird has landed on the ground, aim for just forward of the shoulder/upper wing fold to put a pellet into the chest cavity. Alternatively, if shooting from behind, put one right between the shoulder blades, into the neck or crack it in the back of the head.

If you don't mind spoiling or bruising some of the breast meat then there are times a hi-power FAC rated air rifle in .22 calibre would be my rifle of choice. This doesn't mean you can let power override sloppy shooting technique but it does allow two very different target zones and when you've not that much time to select the kill-zone it's handy. To save continually repeating myself I'll mention here that when using a hi-power air rifle, these kill-zones also apply for all the larger members of the corvid family.

These are a side-on shot in the frontal chest area where a pellet can actually crash through the front of the wing doing deadly damage to the bird's heart and lungs. Similarly, the full-on chest shot, aiming from the lower neck to just below the crop. For corvids, aim slightly off centre to the right or left of the upper chest.

A heavyweight .22 calibre pellet fired at 28-30ft lb out to 40 – 50yds retains a lot of energy meaning the lead projectile really can smash through the bird's protection to enter the chest cavity causing massive internal damage. Some might think this not the most sporting way to tackle the birds, but then again, what's the difference in that or a shotgun blast?

FERAL PIGEON (*Columba livia*)

As unlikely as it seems the feral pigeon's original ancestor is the protected rock dove but nowadays the 'ferals' are just as likely to be related to domestic pigeons escaped from medieval dovecotes, or wayward homing pigeons. The word 'feral' simply means gone wild. Due to this, the coloration of the plumage can be extremely variable. It could be brown, slate-grey, black or even dove white. Any combination of these colours can be found, but the pigeon will usually still have double black wing-bars and traces of an iridescent purple green front/side neck patch and/or white rump, proving its rock dove ancestry. Don't be too worried about mistaking a feral for a 'rocky' as the latter is now very

Indoors or out, the feral pigeon is a terrible nuisance

rare confined to a few colonies on the sea cliffs of Scotland and the West of Ireland. More likely it could be mistaken for the stock dove, or a bedraggled racing pigeon. The stock dove is usually more uniform grey with no white rump patch. The 'stock' also has a double 'grunting' call rather than the traditional cooing of a dove or pigeon. In the case of mistaking it for a racing or homing pigeon, check the bird has no rings on its legs. If you're unsure and you don't have a clear view of the bird's legs, then don't shoot.

Habitat

Feral pigeon are found everywhere and anywhere. A veritable avian avalanche of these flying rats flood our every town and city. So you'd be forgiven in thinking these felons stay around the streets all year round – not so! Like their close relatives (woodies, collared doves etc), they move where the food supply is most plentiful. In winter they do stay in the cities and towns where they feed on scraps of food, usually fast food leftovers disposed of onto the floor by the thoughtless. Come the spring and summer, many birds periodically head out for the country to feed on freshly sowed grain as well as general farmland stubble. It's also not unusual to find them in the company of woodies and I've shot countless ferals over the years that have landed amongst decoys. Though they usually nest on beams and amongst the roof space of disused buildings they're not fussy where they site their sparsely built nest of twigs. Any hollow or sheltered ledge will suffice but they do prefer it to be indoors.

Location and Behavioural Patterns

Due to the bird's ability to adapt and its inherent nomadic nature, ferals can crop up almost anywhere on your shoot. More likely than not around farm buildings where they can often be found in the company of collared doves. When you find them in the open country, the best time to try to thin them out is in the spring before they drove back to the towns to breed.

And for pest control purposes – this is the main place you'll be able to shoot them in any great numbers when they colonise abandoned buildings, factories and industrial units. Gaining access to shoot here isn't as difficult as you may think as any small business owner with a feral problem is worth approaching – as long as you do so in the right manner. If you gain permission, wherever practical and possible shoot them off the roof as inside work is specialised stuff but not beyond the capabilities of the practiced and disciplined shooter – more of which later. But before going inside to 'find them' you'll first see them sitting around the same areas for most of the day. The same applies to the barns and outbuildings on your shoot. Look to the ledges, ridging tiles and the sheltered 'sunnyside' of the roof. They certainly seem to have favourite 'sitty' areas, especially in the colder weather where they can take advantage of the expelled warm air from chimneys and factory extractor fans.

Step inside a disused building and you'll have no trouble locating the birds as under the areas they roost and rest the floor will be a quagmire of droppings. This is one of the main reasons you'll be asked and allowed to shoot inside an old building they've taken over and you'll have to take them out. And depending on the building you're in, you could find yourself in some pretty nasty conditions.

Methods to Use

It's hard to believe that you need official sanction to dispense with feral pigeons. According to DEFRA – Department of the Environment, Foods and Rural Affairs – it has to be confirmed they are causing a major problem as specified by the department. Usually they are but you are only authorised to shoot them by the building owner's permission and the fact other methods such as scaring and netting are failing to contain or evict them from the premises.

Obviously the main qualifier for culling is they present a major health hazard which they undoubtedly do due to their droppings containing a multitude of dangerous pathogens and diseases. And it goes without saying, like rats when you shoot any don't pick them up without gloves and dispose of them in the correct fashion by burning.

We're now getting very much into the realms of serious pest control and a situation the majority of sporting airgun hunters won't ever want to be in or find themselves asking to do. However, it's worth remembering that 'doing such a favour' can have the knock on effect that your name is passed onto somebody who might have some land. Word of mouth usually means another feral clearance job or some rat shooting is in the offing. If the latter is around a farm barn or outbuildings this could well score you some field shooting depending on how you conduct yourself.

As we're back at the farm, around the farmyard the method for dealing with ferals is exactly the same as for collared doves – these are stalking around the outbuildings and even baiting them down with grain or even bread. But we still come back to the fact most serious feral bashing and rat shooting for that matter will be done indoors. Due to this I'm purposely going to deal here – as a prelude to the chapter on Hunting Techniques – how best to go about your shooting inside old buildings, barns and around the farmyard itself. Take note of the latter as ferals are partial to sitting around on the farmhouse roof so we'll check out the etiquette of shooting around the farmyard. But first, forget ferals for a moment and consider the opportunities of being allowed to shoot inside the big main barn on the shoot you've maybe recently gained permission to shoot over. This is a big chance for you as an airgun hunter to prove yourself. No live round sporting gun is needed here, just the precision modern day air rifle running within the 12ft lb legal limit in your hands. And that's why you're here looking at a 'feral job', so before you go lumbering in, double check your zero, your accuracy, your kit – everything. Most of all be sensible and show how responsible you are as you go about your sport. Firstly though – the C & Ks of the feral pigeon.

Calibres and Kill-Zones

As I've stuck to a formula for these Quarry Files, and though the feral is a nasty disease ridden pest it still deserves to be dispatched correctly. Incidentally, it's worth mentioning some shooters use detuned (lower power) rifles due to the fact the birds are shot at such very close range, especially indoors. This is to lessen the possibility of over penetration at the target. That's a specialised route, and one to consider, but for the majority of airgunners who get the chance to go feral felling, a standard hunting combo will be more than adequate.

Though I favour .177 calibre for most hunting situations, for this work I prefer a good old .22 slug. This is also one of the only times I'll mention the .25 calibre as an option. Here it can be useful as if a building hasn't been cleared for a while, targets will more often than not be encountered well within 20yds and that big piece of lead drops them like a stone.

Kill-zones apply exactly the same as they do for the wood pigeon but with one big exception. If you think the woodie a tough bird then this is the 'Arnie' version. OK, somewhat of an exaggeration but it is true to say whilst the woodie has soft downy feathers the feral has a relatively thick layer of full and very strong feathers all over its body – a sort of avian armour plating. These feathers can absorb quite a lot of the pellet shock value – so place those pellets carefully, especially if using the chest kill-zone.

Shooting Specifics – Indoors and Outdoors

First Up – Indoors: This form of 'hunting' opens up a whole new range of opportunities for the shooter. Invariably you'll be shooting for pest control only as your targets as we've outlined will mainly be feral pigeon and of course rats. However at times when the weather isn't very conducive to outdoor work, having the opportunity to shoot legally indoors can be a welcome and challenging alternative.

In some cases you could get the chance to cull collared doves but in most cases you'll be evicting feral perils and scaly tails.

First major factor to take into consideration when shooting 'indoors' is your own personal safety. Ricochets can have dangerous consequences and if shooting inside abandoned industrial units and even places you are unsure of always note if you see bare wires. You can't be a hundred percent sure a wire isn't 'live' until it's too late so don't go near them. Also watch for rotten floorboards, rubble underfoot, rickety stairs and dodgy ceilings. As this isn't a manual on feral pigeon clearance I'll stay on the sporting side of advice but even so. In the years I've been shooting indoors I've been into buildings that quite frankly should have been condemned. So be warned. Also, you always need to pay particular attention to what lies behind the target. Airgun pellets punch nice neat holes in corrugated or plastic roofs and no farmer wants his outbuildings to have roofs like colanders.

If you walk in during the day and there's still a few about, then that's fine – shoot them off the beams they perch on. Until they wise up they'll sit there thinking you're a farmhand or factory worker depending on location of shoot. At night it's a different matter altogether and of course you'll need a lamp. Incidentally, a word on the use of lights for indoor feral pigeon shooting: under the 1981 Wildlife & Countryside Act, it's an offence to use a device for illuminating a bird to shoot it.

The aftermath! The scene after a feral pigeon cull – not a glamorous job, just sheer pest control

However, provision is also made in the act for the grant of an annual licence that allows – amongst others – feral pigeon to be culled with the aid of an artificial light source and sighting device for purposes of pest control.

So, once all legalities are satisfied, before getting in there to shoot you need suitable clothing. A disposable 'boiler suit' and a dust mask are sometimes needed such are the conditions but many times an old pair of combats and jacket will suffice. If it's a factory unit, presumably it won't be 'too' disgusting and the occasional walk around with the permission of the owner to curtail the numbers is good to tone up your shooting practice. Incidentally, in many old outbuildings and disused industrial units there'll be no light – hence the provision for the use of a lamp. Some opt to work with another person, one shooting while one 'spots' and operates a hand held lamp. Others prefer to go in solo with a gun-mounted lamp. If unsure of the area, the building and even if you feel more at ease I advice you go with another shooter. But if in pairs or alone, the correct way to deal with pigeons at roost in buildings are the same. That is to enter the building sweeping through the areas or rooms methodically, then after shooting all those you pass, move out to rest the area for a while. After a reasonable amount of time, repeat the procedure until the ferals are sorted. The entry points they've used which are often broken windows, holes in the roof etc need to be covered or else they'll be back in before you've finished showering at home. After shooting collect all the dead birds, using gloves and 'sack' them up to be disposed of properly by incineration. Those that drop stone dead up on the beams should be retrieved or else you've provided free rat food.

I know, it's not sport, it's not exciting, but it's a job that at times needs doing and with the air rifle you have the perfect tool to do it with. Talking of which, this is an ideal situation to use a quality springer with open sights or gas ram powered rifle with a quality red dot sight. No messing around finding the target in your sights and you won't need to magnify the target anyway. Even if using a multi-shot PCP I've often been thankful of the super-fast target acquisition the red dot sight affords and believe me, get amongst a colony of established ferals and the action can be fast and furious! Similarly, if using a scope a laser is useful for giving a quick ranging reference.

Incidentally, this brings me to a much-overlooked nuance of indoor shooting and another reason to use these alternative-sighting systems. As with shooting outdoors at night, enclosed areas can play havoc with rangefinding. Shots can seem closer or further than they actually are. In fact, optical illusion will make upward shots seem closer and shots along to quarry on the floor will appear further than they actually are or vice-versa. And that's with the building lights on. So as you can see, 'ranging' difficulties aren't something you'll only experience when using a lamp.

Outdoors – Close To Home: Usually, unless stipulated the farmhouse will and should be out of bounds unless you're invited in for a brew and a chat. Remember this is your host's home. By all means when allowed stalk around the barn, storage units, pigpens and cattle sheds but respect the farmer's privacy. If you are going to be shooting around the farmyard always ask and let the farmer know. You may be lucky enough to eventually be given carte blanche on the land, but near the farm and inhabitants take no liberties with your host's generosity. Also, farmers and their workers start early. That means there'll often be people around from first thing in the morning to possibly late evening. Sundays are better as even the farm hands at most times of the year can be scarce on this day. Even so, never take a risky shot – don't presume someone won't walk around a corner. Let the lads in the yard know you're there even though you may have told the farmer and always let them know which part of the farm you'll be going to next. Again ricochets can be a problem if a misplaced pellet deflects off a concrete wall. Watch while taking upward shots, plastic guttering, lead flashing, asbestos roofing, security lights – all are 'no-no's' if near or behind the quarry targeted.

As outlined in 'Seasons…' many quarry species will be found around the farmyard, especially in summer. Corvids can crop up anywhere looking to scavenge food, especially around dung heaps. Woodies stop over at anytime and of course the collared dove is virtually guaranteed to be around. It's not only opportunist shooting though as for the flying felons you'll often need to plan your trip with more care and more often than not build a hide. Yes, a hide isn't only of use in the open countryside. You might even need to build one in a barn itself if targeting feed stealing jackdaws, collareds or ferals. Luckily there'll be plenty of materials in the outbuilding to use such as wooden pallets, sheets of corrugated iron, heavy-duty cardboard sheets, old empty grain and feed sacks – anything that blends in with the surrounding area. My preferred material, if present, and more often than not they are in abundance are hay bales. With a bit of ingenuity, a few hide poles or garden canes and suitable amount of camo netting you can construct a hide that allows you to be fully hidden yet affording a good view of the marauders' comings and goings. But, I must again stress the importance of letting others know where you are and what you're doing. If there's the possibility the area will be used by people, the utmost caution is needed and every precaution taken to ensure safety of those concerned.

Every so often the farmhouse garden may even need a periodic ridding of pests. Squirrels and magpies that come to a bird table are easy targets and need 'evicting' if becoming troublesome. With you the airgun hunter around – they won't be there for long and you'll earn yourself some brownie points with 'the boss'.

There are a few tricks to shooting around farm buildings that have been detailed in the section devoted to the collared dove so all that was written there obviously applies here.

Another tip though is when shooting around machinery – if resting your rifle on anything to steady your aim, take care not to 'knock' the rifle on anything so as to cause any noise. In the early morning, metal-to-metal contact of an air reservoir, cylinder, barrel or silencer on the side of a tractor can be all that's needed to give your presence away. And as for the birds that don't tumble off the roof but lodge in guttering, ask to borrow a ladder and get them down. Nothing worse than leaving quarry in this situation as it'll cause blockages where it lodges. And the owners won't thank you for a blocked drainpipe should it wash into one after a downpour.

Shooting Near Livestock

Whether shooting indoors or outdoors when faced with this form of shooting there are obvious safety aspects that need addressing. It certainly needs a degree of shooting discipline as there are many times – infuriating ones at that – you'll need to 'hold off' taking a shot because the quarry targeted is too close to livestock or the backstop behind the target isn't safe. Whenever possible, always shoot away from livestock and try to avoid even shooting over the top of the animals. Obviously there are times you'll need to shoot over them but use your commonsense and discretion. Don't ever drop your rifle 'too' low and don't think you can 'skim' over the animals. Upward angles are fine but as always consider the likelihood of ricochets. Animals in pens will be unpredictable, sometimes they'll stay put at others walk to the far side of the pen. If they start getting too twitchy, stop shooting.

Some animals – such as pigs – can be quite tolerant to you shooting near them – others not so. The farmer won't thank you for scaring his prize heifers or having his sheep constantly jumping around. Be sensible, and always think before you shoot.

CARRION CROW (*Corvus corone corone*)

Reputedly capable of living for up to 20 years, it's little wonder the crow is so wily and cautious as it has plenty of opportunity to learn that humans pose a major threat to its survival. It's undoubtedly got very keen eyesight, which it uses to continually scan for feeding opportunities or danger, but don't discount the bird's uncanny ability to 'detect' dead carrion, of which I'm not the only one of the belief it does due to an acute sense of smell. Seemingly the bird can 'home in' on carrion, not clearly visible, from hundreds upon hundreds of yards away. Little wonder that baiting down with a slit open rabbit is so effective at drawing them to a shooting position.

The carrion crow is the wiliest of the wily

The carrion crow is the largest of the corvids (crow family) that airgun hunters are legally allowed to shoot. With a large thick-set stocky body, uniform blue/black plumage and a lighter shiny black bill. Older birds look bedraggled and often have white feathers in their plumage. I've even seen all-white crows that couldn't be classed as albinos.

I'm sure most hunters have heard the saying 'lonesome crow.' Well, study the behavioural pattern of this corvid and you'll soon come to realise this is only partly true. Crows will gather, move, feed and roost in large numbers at various times of the year – especially after breeding in summer and in autumn into winter. Although generally it doesn't flock to nest, like its close relative the rook, it can sometimes be found nesting close to others of the same species – and on the outer limits of large rookeries. But by and large, when breeding, crows prefer their own space and both noisily and aggressively guard the territory around the nest.

Habitat

The carrion crow is at home over fields with a few trees as it is in dense woodland, moorland or even close to and at the seashore. At the shore it takes on characteristics more attributed to the gull familiar beachcombing the estuary and sand flats for foodstuffs such as small crustaceans, lug and ragworm. This is one of the reasons it has been so successful in colonising areas and becoming so plentiful. It is just at home scavenging on an inland rubbish tip as it is in the woods, over farmland and on the coast. All but absent in Ireland, and not too common in parts of Scotland where it's replaced by the hooded crow (corvus cornix), it is nevertheless, widespread in the rest of the UK. Incidentally whilst it was once supposed the 'Hooded' was a sub-species of the 'Carrion' it's now widely acknowledged that they're both species in their own right.

During late spring, 'unattached' crows pair off (apparently staying together for life) and will then move regularly in pairs. During the colder months they cover quite a distance between feeding areas and the communal roost. Although it roosts in numbers, on the whole it can often appear to be quite solitary and at times single birds (hence the 'lonesome' saying) seem to wander lazily and aimlessly over the land – especially in the daylight hours of winter. In that respect, despite the obvious similarities, it is not like the rook. In fact its behavioural patterns ally more closely to the magpie than any other corvid. Indeed it's quite common to see a few magpies, moving around or feeding with a crow noisily bringing up the rear.

Having said that, when it comes to being with its own kind, the carrion crow does display a very complex social infra-structure, especially when large numbers descend to feed over fresh cut grass fields, cropland or amongst pasture land used for the grazing of livestock in the summer months. And the behaviour of the crow is very much dictated by the seasons. For instance, large numbers can be seen in the company of jackdaws and rooks feeding over fields in summer. Similarly loose packs join up on their way back to roost, a place where once again the bird's complex social behaviour is very evident. Interestingly, it's believed that certain individuals take it upon themselves to act as sentries sitting on the outskirts of the roost or feeding area to watch out for any potential danger. I've noticed this and it does have some credence. It's also worth noting that when crows are found in small groups these gatherings are known as a 'Murder of Crows'. And taking the birds loathesome nature, a very fitting term it is too.

Location and Behavioural Patterns

Look over the five-bar gate to the far fields where the sheep or cattle are grazing and the black 'dots' strutting and pecking incessantly around are more often than not crows.

Indeed, if there is one certainty – where there are sheep, you will always find crows, jackdaws and to some extent rooks. The stories told of crows sitting on the backs of a young sheep pecking at their eyes are based on some truth. Not only do they sit on sheep to peck at ticks and insects in the sheep's wool, but they'll also attack the new borns, sick and weakly.

The birds will attack the lamb, first pecking out the eyes then attacking the soft flesh of the throat. Once the hapless lamb is debilitated to a degree it cannot stand the crow singular or in groups will descend to finish off the animal pecking at any soft areas of flesh. They certainly seem to have a liking for the tongue. Needless to say, lambs or adult sheep that die by natural causes are absolute magnets to these birds.

It will however more readily kill and eat other small animals such as frogs, voles and even young rabbits using its heavy, big black beak as a formidable instrument of doom. And whilst the crow's 'varied' diet does consists of grain, seeds, worms and beetles. It will always prefer to take eggs, nestlings and gorge on carrion of any description. Hence its name!

Crows usually nest alone and upon high

But it's not all carnage when they're next to livestock! They follow flocks of sheep around primarily to pick up anything edible the grazing sheep might disturb. This also applies to the reason they follow cattle.

Finding a roost isn't difficult either, as when evening starts to draw in they will come lazily flapping over the fields making a beeline straight to their communal roosting site. Hence the origin of the phrase, 'as the crow flies'.

During autumn, you can almost set your watch by them as they fly home to roost. If you're lucky enough to have a roost site on your shoot then you'll be in for some cracking crow action come the colder months when hundreds upon hundreds can often be found heading back to stay at the same roost. Be warned though, as the crow learns very quickly and seeing a few of its own tumble from the trees will soon cause it to rethink its sleeping arrangements, probably never to return to that area of the wood again.

Its feeding areas tend to be much less localised. In summer when the younger birds have paired off for the first time they establish and stick to their own definite territories.

When the crow is nesting, even if it hasn't as yet got chicks to raise both adult birds still only tend to search for food within a few hundred yards or so of their nest site. This is quite a small territory but it serves it well at this time of the year.

Crows display very strong paternal instincts towards their young during early summer. They feed them on the ground and show them how to feed – the young cawing incessantly for attention and food. The adults peck around the ground near the young bird encouraging it to do the same. The birds will frequently stop to preen the youngster eating the ticks that infest the bird's coarse thick feathers. But this cosseting doesn't last long as the adults soon start to ignore the sibling realising it needs to become independent in order to survive.

When the young are reared, then they all wander far and wide – a time when most hunters can encounter them and attract them within range of a shooting position. A very productive time is late summer after the young crows have started to fly and follow the parents. Large flocks of adult and young birds can descend onto fields of barley, corn or flailed maize. They will also, like the wood pigeon, take advantage of flat spots caused by wind or rain. They can even flatten low growth areas and cause even more damage as they progressively tread down the crops as they 'eat out' into the field. Find an area such as this and set up a suitable hide and you could well score yourself a couple of memorable sessions before the flock decide to move to safer feeding areas.

In built up areas, like the magpie and in some areas the jackdaw, it's found in and around human habitation. All scavengers know that they get easy pickings in these areas but obviously these are not the places for the hunter.

Methods to Use

For hunting this particular corvid you have quite a few options. Baiting down, ambushing them from a hide next to a feeding area or established sitty tree, or an opportunist shot when hiding up in or next to woodland awaiting squirrels or woodies. Forget trying to stalk up on the bird, it's the wariest of the wary, even if in the trees, so stick to the methods outlined in full later in the book if you don't want to be ripping your camo gear off in frustration.

And, like the magpie it's the early riser of the bird world. That means whether ambushing or baiting down you need to be up well before dawn and in position to reap the rewards.

The daily nomadic scavenging nature of crows means they can crop up unexpectedly anywhere on your shoot – just one of the reasons an opportunist shot can always be a possibility.

The crow's scavenging and curious behavioural patterns can sometimes be its undoing. Often when using decoys to bring woodpigeon within range shooting in autumn over stubble fields, and especially if using a 'confidence crow deek' I've had crows drop down for a quick look. They don't stick around long but if you've 'downed' a few woodies you should be tuned in enough to sight in on the kill-zone and successfully take the shot.

To bag a crow or two is always a true test of your fieldcraft, hunting and shooting skills.

They don't call 'em 'crafty' for nothing you know!

Shooting Techniques Specific to Crows

During the summer into autumn, shooting crows over feeding areas can be very time consuming – specifically in relation to how long you need to wait in the hide between shooting spells. This can vary depending on how frequently the area has been shot. Now whilst they come to fields holding sheep where they raid the creep feed troughs, they also like bovine company. Take advantage of this by setting a hide near an area of a cattle field they're known to frequent. They will systematically work over a field pecking through cow dung; this distasteful habit shows the carrion crow for what it is. The birds will appear from the roost to congregate in the tops of trees and on power lines and pylons adjacent to the field they intend to feed over. As if a switch has been turned, the birds will then land in the field in twos and threes, with a continuous flow of birds arriving and most if not all will land next to the birds already feeding. They'll be seen to land almost on top of one another seemingly looking to take the other bird's food and squabbling over the foodstuff found in that area. Slowly but surely they'll work their way over within range but you need patience as sometimes this can take quite some time. Once the birds are within range, shoot the one that seems the most dominant. Easily distinguished if there are younger more inexperienced birds near it. Once you've downed a crow the rest will take up to the sky but more often than not, some birds can often hop over to peck at the downed bird whilst others wheel around in the sky cawing loudly from above. This affords another shot and if successful even more will come to harass the dead birds. While this can happen, alternatively, after maybe a minute, but it always seems a lot longer the birds will eventually leave the area to sit high up in nearby trees or on power lines to survey the scene from a safe distance.

From here they'll eventually return – hopefully for you to pick more from the flock. In fact, if you shoot with a partner it can be very productive for one shooter to be positioned hidden at the side of the wood, within striking distance of the sitty-trees and one in a hide adjacent to the field they're feeding over. This can often keep them moving but they don't fall for this trick too many times before feeding on safer areas or infuriatingly coming down to feed again but always keeping out of range.

At times action can be hectic as you knock one crow over, then another. A magpie might zoom in as if from nowhere to stand stock still next to a dead crow. This peculiar behaviour is only displayed by members of the corvid family but is certainly one that the airgun hunter should be aware of so as to take advantage when it presents itself.

But as fast as the birds are seemingly oblivious to danger and preoccupied behaving in this uncharacteristically reckless manner 'one shot more' can see the birds vanish to safety. In this and other situations it seems corvids – and in this I specifically include the crow, rook and jackdaw – all display a very complex pattern of social interaction. One minute they will squabble over the feeding area but fast establishing a pecking order. The next, it can appear to be a mass free for all during which the shooter should take advantage of this confusion. After many, many years watching and shooting all the 'black' corvids I reckon there's still a lot to learn of their complex behavioural patterns.

Calibres and Kill-Zones

The main kill-zones on this wily old bird have to be the head or heart lung shot. When possible take a side-on headshot or full-on neck to upper chest shot. If the angle presents itself a 'slug' in the base of the back of the skull is equally effective. One of the traits the bird shares with other corvids, is when sensing danger it will turn around showing its back, while looking over its shoulder – usually just before it flies up and away. It's at this point you have a chance of the deadly kill shot into the back of the neck and between the shoulder blades. If shooting from below, slipping a pellet up into either side of the bird's upper chest under the wing fold will find another weak spot. It has little protection here at the chest under those heavy wings.

Some say .22 only but place a .177 or .20 in these kill-zones and it's goodnight Vienna for this crafty corvid.

When using hi-power air rifles, the same alternative kill-zones apply as outlined earlier in full for the woodie.

JACKDAW (*Corvus monedula*)

The jackdaw is a very intriguing bird

Of all the quarry species airgun hunters are legally allowed to shoot the jackdaw must surely rate amongst one of the most intriguing. That grey neck-cape giving them a look of a balaclava-clad burglar ready to get up to no good. Despite its noisy, troublesome behaviour the jackdaw is quite a pretty bird with its glossy black plumage, grey neck and head feathers and when seen close up you can't fail to be charmed by the pale blue iris of the bird's very keen eye. Their 'coughing' call is quite unique to this bird, seemingly being an alarm call as well as a call for general location and contact between individuals. This metallic 'tchak' or intermittent 'tcha-ak' sounding call usually heralds the bird's arrival on the scene but equally if being cautious it can almost appear as if from nowhere. And being one of the smallest of the corvid family, when keeping quiet, they're equally expert at unobtrusively going about their daily routines. But during the breeding season, especially during the mornings or evenings the birds can put on fascinating acrobatic aerial displays as they fly, flit, glide and soar, twisting this way and that around a church spire or high above a group of tall trees on the wood's edge.

Habitat

Jackdaws are nomadic in nature but will flock readily with their own. Primarily a bird of woodland it ventures out to feed and in many areas to breed. This is when the jackdaw often presents itself as a problem when nesting in buildings in rural areas – doubly so if they've taken to regularly visiting farms with livestock and large outbuildings. And when near human habitation, the jackdaw's fondness for nesting in dark crevices often has them nesting in chimneys or ventilation outlets of houses. This means they are a potential fire hazard not forgetting the raucous racket they make eventually having the most tolerant of homeowners in despair. In fact in many rural areas, the chimney outlet is covered with mesh to prevent birds nesting. Church spires often have 'ledge spikes' installed by professional pest control companies – primarily to prevent the intrusion into the holy building from feral pigeon. Unfortunately the smaller jackdaw can easily slip through these and sometimes they actually use them to secure their untidy bulky nest to the building.

Although all viable hunting methods are discussed later, I must make mention here of correct procedure for dealing with a situation where a pair or group of birds are nesting in an urban or rural dwelling. It must be stipulated even on a 'one-off' localised 'house' shoot you need the property owner's written permission. Targeting them in these situations isn't difficult as long as you adhere to a few basic rules of safety. Firstly, ensure no stray pellets leave the area you're shooting in which by and large can be a medium to even a large estate garden. Also, be thoughtful to the neighbours. Without fail, go around the houses that overlook the property or those nearby to let them know the situation. This has not only assured the people that all is above board and safe but can also even gain the responsible airgunner a few extra 'jobs'. These can range from dealing with pesky squirrels or even 'eviction orders' placed on other unwanted neighbouring jackdaws and magpies.

In respect of problems for the crop farmer, they cause damage to newly planted cereals but they have to be present in large numbers. More so – like crows – they're drawn to the presence of sheep. Not only in the fields, but where the sheep are fed on sheep pellets the jackdaws can acquire a taste for this high protein foodstuff. It's not uncommon for the birds – by learned behaviour – to know when the feed is being put out and be there ready and waiting to suddenly descend to steal the amount they need. They'll also invade the farm outbuildings if the sheep are inside at lambing and if left to their own devices will swarm over the sheep pens picking at anything that looks even remotely edible.

Pairs and even small flocks of 'jakes' can put on fascinating acrobatic aerial displays

Location and Behavioural Patterns

An unfussy feeder you'll find 'jakes' anywhere they can find food. Scavenging for scraps around picnic tables, walking amongst pedestrians in the rural areas picking over fast food leftovers, or out in the country – hanging around the creep feed troughs in sheep fields – yes, they know where life is easy. That's why when they find a free meal – they'll regularly come back to it.

Locating the roost sites around buildings is simple as you only need find the white splashings familiar to all roosting birds. It applies to some extent for woodland roosts but these are more readily found by observation in the evening. The birds 'coughing' call rings out over the fields as they fly into the woods to flock tightly together in chosen trees. Roosts can be well established, deeper in the woods than a wood pigeon's and often shared with crows. But as with other roosting birds, once disturbed by shooting they'll very quickly move to a safer area. Come the spring and jackdaws are easily located due to their untidy nest building. Underneath a church spire, house roof space or tree with dense foliage you'll find thick twigs and sheep wool littering the ground – the two main materials the bird uses to build its very bulky home. In areas near human habitation the nest is also padded out with any manner of 'litter' it can find in the area such as bits of plastic, crisp packets, bits of cloth – the jackdaw isn't house-proud.

Though the birds pair off for breeding, and to some extent nest alone, they will often be found in localised groups. Unlike the crow, seemingly no dominant birds have a specific territory, rather they share the feeding areas around them and seem to communicate and move as a flock especially after breeding and when out feeding when the juvenile birds boost the 'group' these can number considerably.

They feed liberally amongst other corvids, particularly rooks and crows. It's also not uncommon to see them feeding over pasture with woodies and even starlings.

Methods to Use

The time to target jackdaws, like other members of the crow family is in the spring as they prepare or are actually raising young. However, the sport with the birds in jackdaw 'plague' areas can last all year around and once you've found areas the birds regularly visit to feed you can be sure of some satisfying yet challenging shooting. If the jackdaws are visiting these feeding stations, whether outside or inside buildings, you need to be in position and shooting from a hidden position or if outside using a hide – wearing full camo clothing and using all and any natural cover that's available. The birds will noisily arrive very early in the morning in large flocks to initially gather on sitty-areas close to the source of food before dropping down to dine. Then they'll leave to sporadically return throughout the day in twos, threes or fours.

Not all the birds will disappear over the fields or back into the woods after the early morning feeding raids. In fact even during the hottest of summer days a steady but dwindling procession will visit the area throughout the day. By mid afternoon the birds will usually show up very infrequently, and when they do, it'll be in very small groups.

Outside you need to wear full camo wear, and if there is any hedge cover to shoot from, use this or alternatively erect a hide near the sitty-area. Small portable 'pop-up' hides are great for quick concealment at times and in situations such as this. When shooting in this manner, better to have the birds come in small numbers, especially pairs as often you can shoot one from the 'sitty-area' or feed trough whilst the other will at first 'fly up' but circle around the area calling down to the fallen bird. Sometimes it will land on the sitty-area (which will be high structures such as telegraph poles, overhead wires, rooftop etc), still calling to its mate. The second bird will only land briefly to survey the scene below before flying off, rarely if ever landing near the shot bird as can be the case with crows or magpies. If the second bird is going to land, it will almost certainly land up aloft so keep your eye on the circling 'jake' while keeping your rifle raised towards the area you expect it to land. Reason being, in this agitated state, it won't tolerate the sight of any movement on the ground. So as soon as it folds its wings to land you want to have the muzzle pointed in the general direction, positioned so as to be able to just carefully take aim and shoot.

Roost shooting isn't as profitable due to the shorter time slot you have to shoot them and their intolerance of intrusion when disturbed. But again this is an area they can be targeted.

Calibres and Kill-Zones

Like the jay and magpie this is a relatively small bird, therefore the kill-zones are equally small. Any popular calibre placed with precision into the head or upper chest cavity will see it cleanly dispatched. The chest shot will be most practical as the bird hardly keeps its head still constantly searching this way and that for something of interest to see or find. If shooting when they've entered a building then all safety aspects (dealt with in the relevant section pertaining to indoor shooting) apply. Same for shooting near livestock.

JAY (*Garrulus glandarius*)

It's debatable whether the jay should even be on the airgun hunters 'hit list' as it's not nearly as common as it once was in many parts of the country. But as it's deemed legal vermin for control with the air rifle – and considered one of the main 'target' species – it warrants inclusion here in Quarry Files. Personally I rarely shoot these birds but I presume it's been tagged as vermin on the list for pest control because of its somewhat 'tenuous' links to the rest of its relatives in the corvid family. But rather than preach my own belief, I'll say the decision to shoot this species is best left up to the individual.

The jay – a technicoloured corvid

Originally there's little doubt the bird was and is targeted for its plumage which was used for decorating hats and still is used for the making of fishing flies for sea trout. A pity its coat of many colours then has put it in our sights but it does cause 'some' upset in a habitat it is in over abundance.

However, the bird's beautiful coloured plumage betrays the fact it's a member of the corvid family at all. So unique it's hard to describe the bird with almost peach/pink brown coloured body, white bib, with thick black stripes leading from each side of its beak. The wings are the most prized for fly tying, with the striking blue side flashes with white patches and black wing trims and broad black tail feathers.

Habitat

Found in both broad-leaved and coniferous woodland there's no doubt the jay is at home in the heart of the wood. Now resident throughout the UK except in Northern Scotland it rarely leaves the protection of the trees. It favours established oak woods but is equally at home around beech and hornbeam woods. In the areas these habitats are being 'reduced' it will then move into suburban parks and gardens. Interestingly, the resident population figures fluctuate quite wildly because at times, large numbers of Central European jays migrate here during early autumn.

Location and Behavioural Patterns

A shy and cautious bird, the jay must surely be one of the most difficult quarry species to intentionally find. In summer you'll most likely only hear its harsh screeching call as it sweeps through a glade or alternatively in autumn through winter you can often see them flying in their characteristic bouncy fashion across your path with an acorn in their beak. Like the squirrel, in autumn the jay will bury acorns for retrieval later when food is getting scarce. But obviously they don't remember where every one is so the upside for the natural environment is the jay is actually one if not the most important 'natural planters' of acorns therefore actually helping to conserve and distribute natural oak woodland. This in itself leads to why in some areas the jay is best left to its own devices.

Even though it's so colourful, a jay can miraculously disappear in a tree, even one with sparse foliage. Whilst it will and does steal eggs of small finches and songbirds, it's nowhere near as bad as the magpie. It can easily thrive without thieving and pillaging due to its love of acorns, hazelnuts, beechmast, seeds and insects.

Methods to Use

Of all species the jay is probably only ever going to be encountered whilst opportunist shooting and wood-walking. Whilst at times quite nomadic, make note of an area you see jays frequenting as the bird is very territorial and staid in its ways, staying within its own territory to feed and breed. During the breeding season it can be annoyed with a little owl decoy placed within its territory. Be in position and it could well show itself for a clear shot. Alternatively, at other times of the year due to their habit of carrying off food to bury, wait around these areas and pick them off as they go about their business. In fact, when feeding, they often carry food in their beak up to a favourite tree branch to pick out the kernels. Again, locate one of these through very dedicated and careful observation and this can be an area to wait in ambush for that lone solitary bird.

As this is a very shy but 'busy' bird the first indication a hunter has a jay is close by is often only when the technicoloured corvid flies past to disappear into the trees and foliage. In winter, this gives the bird away and those quick and keen of eye can watch the bird land amongst branches then flit upwards until flying on hardly before pausing for breath. Jays hardly keep still. This is the main reason this bird is so hard to target. Also, it has the uncanny habit of keeping twigs and branches in between you and it. In spring and summer, the only time you get to take a shot is when it peeks its head up above the leaves to take a look around before flying off.

In fact, truth be known, hunters targeting squirrels deep in the woods will often be the ones who encounter most jays.

Calibres and Kill-Zones

As this is a relatively fragile and small bird, same kill-zones apply as with the jackdaw and magpie as do calibres. And if you do shoot the birds at least know someone who will use the feathers for fly tying or a retailer who will take them off your hands for this purpose.

THE MAGPIE (*Pica pica*)

The most notorious of the corvids, the magpie can't be mistaken for any other bird native to the British Isles. With its iridescent blue/black and white plumage, long narrow wedge shape tail and raucous call, it is bold, brash but very wary. Like other members of the crow family, landowners and gamekeepers persecute it due to its fondness for the eggs of gamebirds. Equally, it will and can totally decimate the songbird population of an area it is becoming a nuisance in. However, a born survivor it'll just as happily feed on grain, seeds and insects which in actuality at certain times of the year make up the greater part of its diet.

But there's no disputing the fact that the magpie is undoubtedly a nest raider, taking eggs as well as chicks of all species. This behaviour is thought to be the reason it builds its own nest as a doomed roof structure so birds flying over cannot see into it. But that doesn't mean it's totally safe as I've personally witnessed other magpies invade and plunder another magpie's nest.

The 'maggie' is widely credited with hoarding food and to taking a liking to shiny objects. Again, this is largely based on truth. In old England the bird was known as the 'maggot pie'. Supposedly maggot alludes to the name Margaret and pie is derived from pied, an allusion to its black and white plumage.

For the airgun hunter this bird will, at times, test your fieldcraft skills to the full, not to mention your patience to the limit.

The magpie is a notorious egg thief

Habitat

In recent years the magpie, like the fox, has adapted well to urban existence, and is a common sight around housing estates as well as city-centre parks and gardens. In its natural habitat of deciduous woodland and hedgerows, it's perfectly designed to prey on the weaker, smaller inhabitants. It is active throughout the year, but will retreat into woodland in harsh winters and come the breeding season in spring into early summer, will haunt the bushes and hedgerows that surround the woods. The magpie is most commonly found moving around areas in a seemingly non-stop search for food in small and even quite large groups. The latter gatherings are more commonly seen in winter, when like its relative the carrion crow it can flock with its own kind or mingle in with crows to feed over grain fields. The birds will eventually pair off to breed, which can be as soon as late January when they start to build, return to repair old nests or take over nests of others. The usual breeding and laying takes place in April or May.

As mentioned before, the magpie will eat virtually everything and anything be it animal or vegetable, and although predominantly a scavenger, it will, like the crow, kill its own prey when the need arises. Chicks of song and game birds present no difficulty, but on rare occasions – 'a pack' of them has been known to kill a young rabbit.

As for an agricultural pest it can be a nightmare. Although it isn't a problem over serial crops the time it really causes damage is at bailing time. When the bails are wrapped in black plastic, in many areas the farmers need to get these off the fields as quickly as possible because the magpie and to a lesser extent the crow will peck holes in the covering thus allowing the elements in to spoil the hay. It's presumed the bird sees its reflection in the black shiny plastic and attacks it. As it makes a hole in one area as soon as it catches site of its reflection in another it pecks at this. As both birds are very territorial this explanation seems a very valid one. Either way the magpie like the crow is a major pest species that needs to be kept under control.

Location and Behavioural Patterns

Finding magpies is an easy task. Not only are they highly visible birds when moving but also they can initially betray their presence by their distinctive 'chack, chack, chack' alarm call. When caught out in the open or suddenly alarmed the response from the bird is usually a noisy one. However, in wooded areas, they are more likely to slip silently from tree to tree. The magpie is very sharp eyed and will not stick around long, especially if it suspects even the slightest hint of danger. This coupled with its preference for sitting high up in trees to survey the surrounding area, make it almost impossible to sneak up on. In fact the birds have favoured sitty-trees or areas in trees where they can regularly be found watching. If you're patient and know these areas you can hide up in ambush but it's still not the easiest of ways to target this corvid.

Nests are easy to find and are usually returned to year after year. These bulky domed structures are sometimes taken over in winter by squirrels and a fair kerfuffle can be heard and seen whenever the twain shall meet.

Methods to Use

The two main methods of dealing with magpies are wood-walking and the more effective and dedicated method of baiting down. Both these techniques will be outlined in full in the relevant chapters. However, it's worth noting that as with all hunting methods, prior knowledge of the area to be shot over can pay handsome dividends. The birds will more often than not be active at set times of the day – being in position at the right time can save hours of fruitless searching or waiting. Birds of a certain area will tend to have localised feeding spots and routes to and from them. Indeed, as the wood pigeon establishes a flightline more often than not you'll find magpies seem to use the same route as each other. Sometimes birds will follow other birds in five to ten minute intervals. Some naturalists presume they're birds from the same brood but whatever it is they're definitely moving and searching around in the same areas as a form of 'connected' team.

However, as the corvid is a scavenger it can stop off anywhere it sees may provide a likely source of food. One of the reasons baiting down is so effective. Like the crow, the magpie is definitely one of the earliest risers of all flying quarry species. They are often active on the shoot a good half hour or more before dawn breaks starting their scavenging activities looking for leftovers from other predators from the night before. Also some believe they're active so early because it gives them the opportunity to search out nests to raid as sitting female birds call out to males for food or similarly fledglings are easier to hear at this time. Whichever it is, if targeting these wary adversaries you need to be out on the shoot or even in position if baiting down at least an hour before sunrise.

The black 'n white terror has a varied selection of calls from the familiar chack, chack, chack call to the chattering cackling call not dissimilar to the sound a box of matches makes when being quickly shaken.

Indeed some use the 'rattling box of matches trick' to entice or annoy the bird within range.

But as for the bird itself, like any other clever scavenger they can when they prefer, be silent and quite discreet in their movements.

Calibres and Kill-Zones

The calibres .177 and .22 including .20 are suitable for dealing with this crafty corvid. And in most situations, to cleanly dispatch the bird you have two choices of kill-zone – depending on its attitude to your shooting position. If it presents itself side on then a headshot or just forward of the wing fold will give an instant kill. But like all corvids it rarely stays still and the headshot is a very small kill-zone. Alternatively, a full-on chest shot in the upper chest cavity is my preferred area of pellet placement and deadly effective

Though they don't have an overly strong breastbone, care should still be taken in placing this shot accurately. It's easy to see where the shot should go as you can't fail to see the bird's large black bib extending from head and neck down to end approximately mid point on the chest area. Directly below you'll clearly see the bird's strong muscular legs as there's a clear defined line that centres down from the bib. I mention this to illustrate that anything below the bib is a wounding shot, ideally half an inch up into the 'black' of the bib in the chest is straight into the heart and lungs. Another fragile area on the bird is from the back and like other corvids this is a position it often adopts when alighting in an area it isn't too sure of. It puts its back to potential danger, but with its keen eyes watching around and behind. This is so it can fly off in the blink of an eye or if on the ground hop quickly away in the opposite direction. Little does it know – again like other corvids – it's 'offering' its weakest spot. A well placed pellet into the base of the neck, between the shoulder blades to even approximately an inch down its upper back will quite literally 'break its back' and result in a clean kill. This is quite a large kill-zone for such a deceptively small but fragile framed corvid and a superb kill-zone for any other flying felon.

On the subject of size – the magpie isn't much bigger than a blackbird. Like other feathered predators, it belies its size by fluffing out its plumage and sitting bolt upright.

ROOK (*Corvus frugilegus*)

The rook is a noisy but noble looking bird

Few sights or sounds so epitomise the traditional view of the British countryside than the raucous activity that surrounds an established rookery set in a lush woodland setting. High in the treetops, large bulky nests of twigs can at times seem to almost merge into one because of their close proximity, whilst great black birds circle high above the treetops cawing incessantly to each other. This rural scenario even extends to the old traditional country recipe for the dubious culinary delights of rook pie! There can't be many more birds that have steeped themselves so firmly into our countryside's heritage and lore. Whilst crows and magpies are treated with the disdain they so rightly deserve, the rook seems to have slipped through the cracks to earn the airgun hunter's respect. It's a clever, almost noble looking bird with purple-black glossy feathers and that characteristic grey white bill. Contrary to popular believe the bird is actually a tad smaller than the carrion crow, and arguably much less gregarious in nature. Its cawing is also of a higher pitch than the crow and it seems to have a much wider range of calls.

Habitat

The rook is a bird of the wood – only leaving the sanctity of the rookery to search the fields for food. Deciduous woodland with farmed cereal fields lying on the outskirts makes for a prime rook environment. An extremely social bird, it nests in the colonies known as rookeries. Some can number over a hundred nests, but in each season a lot will be uninhabited, although on record there are some absolutely astronomical examples. One rookery in Scotland was once reputed to be home to nine thousand pairs of birds! Now that's what I call communal accommodation.

The rookery in winter can be an eerie place

Although the rook is extremely sociable, with its own kind – living in such large numbers, and in such close proximity – it still defends the small territory around its own bulky dwelling. In fact, this communal life is so well developed that it has given rise to fanciful stories of 'rook parliaments'. It was once actually believed that if one bird in the rookery had been, for want of a better phrase, 'out of order' in some way then the others would sit in judgement and dish out appropriate justice.

Although responsible for attacking freshly sown fields when it digs up shoots and seeds, not all the rook's activities are harmful to the farmer's livelihood. Due to its taste for leatherjackets (crane fly larvae) and wireworms, it can serve a very useful purpose. But like all other members of the corvid family it'll pretty much eat anything. And this is the major problem. Unfortunately, like crows, they batter down the stems of growing corn and barley with their wings or simply land and walk forward primarily to get at the grain and seeds, but the 'flattening' damage to the crop left uneaten means it can't be picked up by the combine harvester. Over fields they dig around for worms and larvae and scavenge for the eggs of nesting ground birds.

They're also attracted down to freshly cut grass fields; ploughed crop fields, and areas with an abundance of molehills showing can attract birds on a regular basis.

Why you ask, have I not mentioned carrion as part of their diet? Well although it does eat carrion, it isn't as keen on meat as its other close true carnivorous flesh-eating relatives.

Location and Behavioural Patterns

Most deciduous woodland will have a rookery or two; so established woodland especially with tall oak, birch or yew trees is the place to look. Finding a rookery is easy – if the birds don't give themselves away with their non-stop cawing, then sooner or later, walking through a wood scanning the tree tops, you'll spot those big, bulky, untidily built nests that the birds return to year after year. In winter the rookery can be an eerie place with all the blobs of nests dotted above you, an uncharacteristic silence as the birds are feeding elsewhere. In fact, by mid-summer, once the young rooks have left the nests, the birds form into huge flocks and leave. They usually roost in another location but in some parts of the country, as early as January, the birds start to return to the rookeries. At first they tend to use the trees nearby as sitty-trees as if getting used to the area again. Then in preparation for breeding they start to repair or rebuild a nest for the season's brood. This can be a clutch of up to five eggs, and laid so the fledglings don't all hatch together. This way, more are likely to be able to go on to survive – unless you're there to knock them from the trees.

Methods to Use

Methods for hunting rooks aren't as simple as those for other corvids such as baiting down. You can find very few birds opportunist shooting as you 'woodwalk' but more likely and more traditional amongst the shooting fraternities of all disciplines, the main method for controlling population numbers is what is known as 'brancher' shooting.

Brancher shooting takes place around the first couple of weeks in May. For some reason, certain country folk like to pin this down to a specific day – that being May 12th. Well, we all have out little foibles but whatever you term it or date it brancher shooting is a very short season. To be there at the right time you need to keep a close eye on the rookery so as to take advantage of the young rooks clumsily emerging to hop about near the nest. But, it's widely recognised as the only worthwhile method of curtailing their numbers. Before we deal with that tried and trusted method, I'll explain my previous declaration as to why the rook doesn't fall to the usual corvid curtailing techniques.

Of all the corvids (jay excluded), the rook has the keenest of eyesight. And that's saying something, as all the corvids seem to have bionic 20/20 vision on the worst of days. However, whereas a magpie's curiosity will sometimes get him nailed, the rook will never be so foolish. Also, although you'll regularly see them feeding over fields in summer, autumn and winter you'll often not get within a bazooka's distance of them.

However, if you're fortunate to get onto land where they haven't been 'shot at', you could well bag a few before they give the area a wide birth. This can also apply to when the rooks are 'sitting' tight near the rookery early in the year. Again, you'll only have a few chances before they immediately fly up on your approach and not settling at all unless sitting atop a nest out of sight.

Suffice to say the rook is a crafty and very challenging adversary for the airgun hunter. However, don't let me mislead you into thinking it has got supernatural powers. It has not – like any living creature it does have to sleep – so yes what would we do without the chance of roost shooting. Even then you'll only get the chance of a few shots and only a few sessions before they move on to roost elsewhere in the wood or maybe even a wood in the distance.

In fact it's worth me relating a couple of behavioural patterns of rooks when at the rookery that makes them so difficult to target even when repairing nests and indeed when roosting there.

Firstly all the birds are seemingly constantly wheeling over the area, never still except for some which will be sat on the uppermost branches, as high as possible, and amongst a labyrinth of potential pellet-deflecting twigs. You'll rarely see adult rooks sat low in the trees or in plain sight. They're far too clever and wary as to make that mistake.

When the birds are actually back roosting at the rookery, depending on the season they'll only come back late so the light is all but gone by the time the main body of birds arrive. Also, such is their cleverness and wariness of character that as the birds drove into the rookery virtually all will land in the top of the single tallest tree giving them the best view of the rookery. Even here they're on their guard, the treetops black with hundreds upon hundreds of rooks. This would be the shooters' only chance of a shot when they're behaving in this manner. As after the birds are satisfied the area is safe, and as if given an order they then split up and spread out throughout the rookery to sit out the night in the security of either the nest they're re-building or a handy abandoned one. Within minutes hundreds of birds can disappear into the bulky structures leaving the rookery as quiet as the grave. Once in the nest, no amount of normal activity on the woodland floor will spook them out until they're ready to rise before dawn to repeat the season's particular routine. This can be to leave the rookery to wander around and feed or to establish with mates in the mating ritual and rebuilding and re-establishing their position in the colony high in the trees.

I'm sure you're now beginning to see why shooting the young birds (branchers) in spring is the most practical hunting method. Basically if you've done your homework you'll know the time and place to employ this tactic. So how do you tackle it?

Brancher Shooting

When the young rooks first leave the nest, taking their first clumsy steps onto the branches as the name implies they 'hang around' the nest on the surrounding branches. That's why they get the nickname of branchers. While in this fairly vulnerable position they're sitting ducks for the shooter below. Though we have a yardstick, this 'brancher season' can actually start sometimes as early as the end of April into mid May, depending on which part of the country you live in and how the year's weather conditions have affected the colony during the early part of spring.

The only reliable method to catch the branchers napping, as it were, is to keep a regular watch on the rookery at this crucial time. Only then will you be ready for the young inexperienced birds' emergence. Don't get the impression that's it's overly easy though as the shots are often very challenging. After shooting you'll have a crick in your back and a pain in the neck with continually looking upwards. But done correctly brancher shooting is by far the only effective method of keeping the rooks' numbers in check.

Though some might scoff – I recommend you wear full camo with gloves and facemask. Anything that helps you blend in below is a useful aid and don't go crashing about in the undergrowth beneath the rookery as you shift shooting position. It will keep the birds twitchy and have adults less likely to settle back. They'll constantly be calling an 'intruder alert' which the young rooks take heed of.

Shooting upwards at awkward angles is difficult at the best of times, but couple this with the fact that the type of trees the rook inhabits means the twigs are plentiful, even starting to bud and sprout leaves makes it even harder. There's plenty of opportunity for a pellet to get deflected off a branch or twig on its way to the target. Always be aware of this and carefully place your shot. A recoilless multi-shot PCP air rifle will be a godsend as you can rest the rifle on the side of a tree trunk to steady your aim and no need to keep loading after each and every shot. Choose a rifle you can shoulder easily and one that won't be too straining to lift up. Also, as you begin shooting the adults will noisily take up; with the branchers scrabbling to higher branches or clumsily hopping back into the nest. There often can be relatively long periods you can't find a target. Rest by sitting down for a while until things settle – which they eventually will. Even take shots from this seated position, much easier on the back muscles and a steadier hold and aim can often be achieved

A tried and time-tested method, but it's certainly not as easy as you might think.

Calibres and Kill-Zones

As with the crow, it's often said that the prime kill-zone is the head. This is usually credited to the fact the bird has a strong breastbone (keel) easily capable of deflecting a pellet so head shots should be the name of the brancher and rook shooting game. After much hunting experience this is yet another myth that I feel can be dispelled. Whilst the crow and rook have fearsome solid heavy-duty beaks for smashing young fledglings and digging around in the ground their skeletal make up is nowhere near as robust as the head and beak. The skull of a corvid is reinforced and is certainly thick to accommodate the proportionately large heavy bill. But the chest bone is only as strong as a bird of a similar size such as the woodpigeon. Its ribs being just as prone to damage so heart and lung shots can be taken if the bird presents itself at the correct angle. Obviously a pellet will deflect off a heavy bone such as the central chest bone or keel. Look under those heavy wings of the corvid and there's a lot of flimsy unprotected flesh. Place a pellet of any calibre up into the chest area of these birds will result in a clean kill so don't be fooled into thinking you only need try for a headshot.

So whilst the rook is a quarry species to have on your list for spring and the chance to shoot it as a brancher short, you will encounter adults atop trees.

While we're now at the end of Quarry Files I'll just reiterate that although an FAC rifle shouldn't ever be thought of as a tool for getting longer range what it can do is give you less to worry over with awkward angle shots and trajectory allowances. When the birds are high, and you're taking these shots then this is certainly a case where the hunter shooting an FAC rated air rifle could get the chance at shots hunters using a 12ft lb air rifle couldn't dream of attempting. Look to the same kill-zone areas mentioned for the wood pigeon in relation to using a hi-power air rifle.

OTHER SPECIES

Before the Quarry File is fully closed, I feel I should briefly take a look at what other species are legally classed as vermin and still deemed suitable for air rifle. Reason I feel they should be dealt with in this way is due to the fact you may encounter them as you go about your shoot and might be asked to deal with them when and where appropriate.

And though there's a specific section at the end of the book detailing the law pertaining to airgun use as it currently stands – still worth a few cautionary words to the wise on the subject in relation to your shooting and the land you hunt over.

Responsible Attitudes

Firstly, remember that we are only allowed to hunt any species because permission is granted to us by the powers that be – in other words it can just as easily be taken away from us. As a responsible airgun hunter this should always be at the forefront of your mind and whilst out in the field we should all act accordingly. Just one stupid reported incident or action could have serious repercussions, not only for the perpetrator, but also for the whole of the sport.

Mink are best left to be managed by a dedicated trapping campaign

It's easy to inadvertently fall foul of the law whilst out hunting. For instance, you can get so engrossed in stalking that you inadvertently stray 'out of bounds' as it were.

And always – repeat always – keep aware to the possibility of others in your vicinity. While you may know the boundaries of your shoot, ramblers and the dreaded inconsiderate dog walker can have the nasty habit of appearing as if from nowhere. I'm sure others have experienced this. A pellet will travel with sufficient energy in flight to inflict possible serious injury for up to 200 yards or more – and that's from a 12ft lb air rifle. Before you shoot at anything, carefully consider where a missed shot might go. If shooting around buildings, that's a usual worry, but in the open fields are you sure the hedge line is thick enough to 'stop' the shot or is it so sparse that a pellet can fly straight through?

Know where the footpaths and rights of way across the land you shoot on are. Though some may hardly if ever be used there's always the possibility they will at some time attract the walker. With the 'public right of way law' even I'm surprised at areas being opened up I presumed closed indefinitely to unauthorised persons. In that respect, even if shooting in your allotted area you can still technically commit an offence if you are shooting within 50 feet of a public footpath, roadway, bridlepath etc. And as there is the current mentality of the non-shooting public to think that a 'man with a gun is up to no good'. Especially if clad head to foot in camo!

One of the major reasons that DPM camo first fell out of favour was due to 'incidents' giving this attire and 'look' a 'bad public image'. In turn this tarnished those who were seen wearing it. But in part, we can be thankful that this helped inspire the wider acceptance of the new-era 'non-aggressive' camo patterns most airgun hunters now use.

On the subject of the general public – and the fact they might 'just appear' on your shoot. My own personal code is a simple one, if I can see another person (in any direction from my shooting position) I don't shoot. This applies to anybody who might not know who I am, what I'm up to and why. In fact I'll lower the gun and wait for them to pass, then phone the farmer to enquire who is on that part of the land. It could be a disoriented walker but also maybe even a poacher.

Fur and Feather

Of the eleven quarry species fully detailed in the previous pages, you can of course add a few other birds and animals to this list depending on time of year (season) and status of both yourself and the situation you find yourself operating under. For instance you could find yourself in an area infested with starlings. As vermin, the starling comes a very close second to the feral pigeon and can totally 'pollute' the areas it roosts in. Nothing specialised about shooting starlings you might think. However, the starling is a very difficult bird to keep in check. Even some of the major pest controllers opt to scare them away rather than eradicate them. Interestingly in rural areas they tend to drive them off with smoke – a method unsuitable for built up areas. Around buildings, ledges can be smeared with a sticky jelly that is apparently unsettling for birds coming in to land.

However, like most of nature's survivors they soon wise up to these tricks. If you do have to deal with them at moderate range, a hit anywhere on the head or body will see them dutifully dispatched. As with feral pigeon shooting, dealing with starlings is more a public service than a sporting opportunity.

Other vermin such as the mustelids including weasels, stoats and the mink are also animals that can be dealt with by air rifle hunters. But, despite the times, wherein non-thinking Animal Rights activists 'free' mink from farms, they're still generally not a common sight. However, when they do emerge over an area it can be very localised and their presence felt very suddenly. Usually, a well thought out and deployed trapping campaign sorts these vicious destructors but if caught in live catch traps – the air rifle is the tool for dispatching them humanely. To hunt them is very, very challenging and more often than not will prove a pointless exercise. I have shot mink, but in over 20 years probably not enough to make a decent hat!

The airgun hunter is also allowed to shoot the hare which I've made brief mention of in the chapter on Changing Seasons. A game licence is needed and even then it's a point of contention if the 12ft lb air rifle is up to the job in hand. As I've said previously, certainly one to consider with an FAC rifle, but largely best left to the rimfire shooters and shotgunner. In fact the hare isn't as common as it once was in many areas – so the hunter will have to use his discretion. But consider this – anatomically the skull of a hare is much stronger and thicker in bone than a rabbit's. Not only that but the chest area is generally covered in a thickish layer of fat and of course muscle, body shots therefore being out of the question to responsible airgun hunters.

Gulls and Waterfowl

For the record, of the other feathered pests you are legally allowed to shoot as listed under the current 'directives' these include house sparrow, herring gull, greater black back gull and lesser black back gull. In fact in some seaside areas, council refuse tips have days in the year set aside to cull the gulls. Permission is needed to shoot and sometimes in the past a small fee was required. Now as to the house sparrow – surely we all realise this little bird isn't half as common and prolific as it once was. Its habitat not seemingly in decline, its numbers though are dwindling. I like the sparrow and I still think it strange for me not to hear the constant cheeping of them around the houses. I'm sure many remember when they were in plague proportions – they surely were when I was growing up. So I like to see these around and I hope others feel the same. Even though as kids a sparrow or starling was probably the first feathered pest we chalked up on our first rifles.

In some parts of the country waterfowl such as the coot is considered a tasty dish. And when in season lawful quarry for the airgun hunter

Now most hunters don't realise you're also allowed to shoot both moorhen and coot. Many might not consider these waterfowl 'suitable' airgun quarry but they are a legitimate species – when in season. These closely related water birds come under the Game Laws which means the close season is from February 1st to August 31st. This allows them, like game birds, to nest and breed unhindered. This 'royal' pardon is strange as they were originally shot in truckloads by river keepers as vermin, due to the damage they do to nesting ducks.

The coot will rob ducks' nests and even kill the young. Some say it's aggressiveness other say it's because they are competing in the same territory with the more timid duck. And in comparison, though slightly smaller than an average mallard duck, coots are very aggressive and territorial. Just watch the birds in the breeding season – mad as a coot – no surprise why that saying came about! Interestingly, of these two birds, the moorhen does in winter venture into the fields and meadows to feed, especially over waterlogged areas. You'll often see them in moderately sized groups of four or five scavenging over muddy ground. This is when one might just well present you with an 'opportunist' shot. Head or full-on breast shots being suitable for both species.

I'm reliably informed that coots and moorhen can be quite tasty, and the dish is still a favourite in parts of the Norfolk Fens. So maybe this is why they originally became classed as game? If this has sparked your interest in these birds, bear in mind that they are mainly only ever found on or near water. If you do have a 'duck' pond or some such waterway running through your shoot – then do take precautions when shooting around water. Specifically be aware of the risk of ricochet from the water's surface.

Real Game

While the law doesn't stipulate that game birds such as partridge, pheasant and grouse or some species of duck can only be shot with the shotgun, many feel the airgun hunter partaking in the shoot is little more than a poacher. The reason for the 'unsporting' label is certainly due to the fact, these game birds especially, aren't very clever while on the ground so offer little sporting challenge as a static shot. But to take them on the wing with shotgun, flushed up by beaters and dogs is the way to take on these birds as it does give them a sporting chance.

If your shooting ground has 'wild pheasant' then as long as you ask the farmer, landowner or gamekeeper if you can take the odd one for the pot should you encounter it. This sensible attitude to the situation, shooting etiquette and commonsense will be duly noted and you'll probably be allowed to do so. But, a pheasant is a big stocky bird and rather than get myself embroiled in controversy I'd say headshot only at medium range. But do ensure you're not upsetting any shooting 'syndicate' linked apple carts.

As I've said way back in an earlier chapter – 'Finding a shoot is the hardest hunting of all – and the easiest one to lose!' If ever in the slightest doubt – don't risk it.

Chapter 12
Hunting Techniques

The tactics and techniques you can employ when hunting with an air rifle are pretty much the same as they have been for years. However, as air rifles have become more accurate, and precharged pneumatics much more affordable certain hunting methods can be used that weren't viable in the past. Also let's thank the 'gods' for the sound moderator (silencer) and of course multi-shot air rifles.

Even if you're a traditionalist, once you've been hunting a while you'll soon realise the benefits a 'multi' affords. Not only those extra quick back up shots but the fact you don't need to 'fiddle around' to load a pellet for each shot. In that sense and definitely from a personal perspective I'm achieving results in my hunting I'd have never thought possible. But back to the matter in hand and techniques you can use to bag quarry.

Whilst there are many variants, no matter which method you employ it will fall into the major classifications of either active or sedentary. Active – which obviously means actively pursuing quarry such as Opportunist Shooting, Wood-Walking or Stalking to the sit and wait 'sedentary' methods of techniques such as ambushing or hide shooting. Some techniques cross into others such as baiting down corvids whilst using a decoy placed near the bait to lull the birds into a false sense of security. Also decoying woodpigeon to a shooting position then shooting them from a hide shooting position. As you can see the possibilities are wide ranging. So let's take a look at the basic tactics and the main quarry species they can be used for. Firstly, those that require a bit of legwork.

OPPORTUNIST SHOOTING

By far the most suitable way to acquire more knowledge of your shooting ground and probably give you the most chances of 'targets' is a method known as Opportunist Shooting. This can range from something as basic as a walk around the farmyard and outbuildings right up to the outermost fields and hedgelines of the land you're legally allowed to shoot over. But, contrary to certain misguided belief it's not just a case of wandering aimlessly around your shoot in the hope you'll get the chance to take a 'pot shot' at whatever presents itself. Rather it's about reading the land, watching, listening and taking advantage of any opportunities that may present themselves. I realise many readers will probably want to get straight into sneaking (stalking) up on feeding rabbits they see out in the fields. But to get within effective range takes fieldcraft and much of what is outlined in this section will be relevant to those scenarios.

As outlined in the chapter on Observation, when out 'oppo shooting' always look around to be aware of what's going on around you. If you see the woodies landing in the next or a few fields away, plan your route accordingly and using whatever available cover there is, make your way over there. Don't worry, the specific methods of using cover to mask an approach are outlined further in this section.

If bunnies are appearing out of the hedgeline adjacent to the one you're shooting along – carefully stalk over to that area. Incidentally I think it worth stressing the word 'stalk' refers to walking with slow careful deliberation and upright as it does in the half stooped position. You'll come to realise which posture suits the situation. So back to the theme – getting to quarry. This will mean plotting a

Tread carefully, quietly and slowly when opportunist shooting and stalking

route, often not a direct one and using any and all natural cover as an aid, along with your camo clothing for concealment. You can see how hunting methods can cross over – one moment slowly and attentively adopting the role of an opportunist hunter – the next – purposely moving towards a target. Needless to say this is stalking at its most basic, keep low and always try to prevent yourself showing as a silhouette. Approach from down wind and move slowly and quietly. All are basic requisites of good fieldcraft.

There are times you need to go out with a specific plan, but there are times when even the best laid plans can go badly wrong. This is when the hunter who notices and takes advantage of the opportunities that arise can score over even the most careful tactician. For example, if you've planned to lie up in ambush near a feeding area or woodie or corvid sitty-tree, the prevailing weather conditions could well dictate whether you have a productive or non-productive foray. Therefore always be adaptable. If you think you'll be wasting your time waiting around for something that isn't going to show then it's definitely time to become an opportunist hunter.

Doing this has resulted in some of my most challenging and memorable hunting forays. One moment you might come across a twitchy rabbit that takes all your fieldcraft skills to stalk up on, or alternatively you can be carefully walking through woods and spot a cocky squirrel sitting well within range on a branch thinking it's untouchable until you drop it with a well aimed shot.

Alternatively on a walk around the farmyard, just what might be sunning itself on the far side of a barn roof or outbuildings, and what might be mingling in or hanging around near domestic fowl looking for a quick feed – get the picture?

You may think it strange that hunting techniques has seemingly dived in at the very deep end as this method of hunting tests your shooting skills and reflexes to the full. But as I said earlier, this method employs fieldcraft techniques that apply across the board. One such is to never let your concentration wander. It's uncanny that just when you stop for a breather and turn your attention to wiping a blade of grass or dirt off the rifle barrel, a rabbit bolts out from well within range or a woodie leaves the trees nearby. If you'd taken more care, been more attentive, maybe you'd have seen them – who knows – maybe an opportunist shot was on the cards. But, you'll always get caught out like this – just pay more attention to the 'job in hand' and you'll start to find you're not caught out as often. Also, and this is something that is dealt with in more detail later is the need to avoid direct eye-to-eye contact with your quarry until ready to shoot. And then you should be looking through the scope, cross hairs locked on the position to send a pellet into the kill-zone. The reason for this is the animals' uncanny ability to sense danger. The times a magpie will let you walk past – usually when you're out walking without a rifle –- but still keep an eye on you and it can let you stray unusually close. Now try that and slowly raise your hands as if pointing a gun and the same bird will be away. This is the animal sensing and reacting to what it has come to learn by inheritance of genes from previous generations as a threatening gesture. Threatening postures will be outlined further but the one that can give you away, especially with wary rabbits and corvids is direct eye contact. They know that you looking directly at them is prelude to potential danger. Add threatening posture of the body – stopping with arms rising – and that's one legally deemed vermin species that will live to cause problems another day. The next bit of advice may sound odd but in certain cases it does work. If you catch sight of a potential target out of the corner of your eye – don't whip your body and head around to look but try to act as if you haven't noticed it. But, still be ready, when you get within range to take a shot. Try to walk up within range, without overly changing direction. Have the rifle pointed down, but in your shoulder, so you can position yourself to take the shot. Squirrels are particularly susceptible to this technique. Even though most hunters like myself will try to adopt a more stable kneeling, sitting or prone position – when opportunist shooting a high proportion of shots invariably need to be taken standing. Reason to be well practised in all shooting stances and holds before targeting live quarry. Another factor to take into consideration with this form of hunting is not only quick target acquisition, but also recognition. From certain angles the sparrow hawk can look uncannily like a wood pigeon, the green woodpecker can in silhouette be mistaken for a jackdaw, jay or even juvenile crow. Books on British birds are commonplace so invest in one – it'll pay you back in terms of the knowledge you will learn from it even though only a few it contains are legally classed as vermin. Incorporate knowledge such as this with what you observe in the countryside yourself and it will help to make you a better countryman, let alone hunter!

Remember also the importance I've placed on movement in a previous chapter being the hunter's biggest giveaway. So move slowly stopping at regular intervals, only stopping if you're sure there are no potential targets near the position you decide for this studied position. Look up ahead, look around and even back along the track or hedge line you've moved along. The key watchwords are concentration and observation – even if walking over ground that in your experience hasn't produced much during other hunting forays, don't discount it by rushing through. With opportunist hunting you just never know, this time there could well be quarry everywhere – that's part of the thrill and challenge – as you don't know what you could happen across next!

For this form of shooting, like many other experienced airgun hunters I personally favour a carbine sized air rifle. The reason is obvious – that being its compact dimensions and lightweight make it ideal for carrying around and its fast handling. I also now choose to use a PCP multi-shot as it'll give me the 'opportunity' to access quick back up shots and if quarry has stuck around longer than is wise – sometimes it can be 'two down' in double quick time.

It goes without saying that full camo wear is the order of the day. Also, holding the rifle at all times is preferable so unless I'm 'yomping' any great distance to a specific area, I prefer not to have a sling fitted or remove it – thank heavens for QD sling swivels.

For scope choice you need an optic that allows you to quickly acquire the target when spotted. This is definitely when you'll appreciate a wide-angle scope. There are a few very good compact optics on the market, but a general specification scope is often just as handy wound down on a lower magnification setting for optimum width of view. Then if you require you can wind up the magnification for a more studied longer range shot if the situation allows. Also, let's not forget the fact you'll often walk into a dull area or be operating under canopy where the light is low. As most optics have good coated lenses I'm not saying opt for a specialised low light scope but one with good light gathering capabilities is always, and should be at the forefront of your selection list. Though you'll often take 'quick select and fire' shots, never take 'chance shots'. If there's the slightest possibility the quarry may be wounded and get away, be disciplined and leave it until another day.

As I'm sure you now realise Opportunist Shooting requires a high level of fieldcraft, shooting skill and of course experience brought on only by actively practising the method. Importantly, address your body language. The half stooped slow walk is exactly the right way to move once you've sighted a target such as a feeding rabbit which of course you intend to get closer to. However moving across any ground in such a way will be sensed and seen by other quarry species as threatening. Anything that spots you moving along a hedge-line or through undergrowth instinctively knows you are a predator switched on to hunting mode. This might sound bizarre but consider this. Animals such as rabbits and to a lesser extent birds will quite happily carry on feeding or hold position as a deer or even a cow ambles past them. Reason being the deer or cow will not only be familiar to the animal but has always/usually behaved in an unthreatening manner. This reaction and acceptance is learned behaviour. Not that I'm suggesting you dress up as a cow or deer but as you will/should be fully camo'd up, walk with an unthreatening posture as you try to almost 'drift over' the ground. Stooped with rifle half at the ready isn't always the way. I know I've used a few military references in this book already, but the army adopt a walk in 'sensitive areas' that allows them to appear unthreatening but ready to respond should the situation dictate. That is rifle across the chest, muzzle pointed slightly downwards held in half folded arms, walking slowly, whilst their eyes study everything around and above them. Adopt this alert but seemingly relaxed posture and you're halfway to blending in with your surroundings. Also, pay particular attention to the ground you walk over. This obviously also applies to stalking when you've spotted a target you want to get within range of. Stepping on a twig can make a sharp quarry alerting 'crack'. Noise can be created if stepping on gravel, loose stones, piece of tree bark, dry leaves – the list is endless. Virtually every writer on hunting has written how the shooter should place his feet when walking. The basics are – move slowly, and step forward, first placing the ball of the foot down on the ground. Then carefully roll the weight forward onto the sole of the foot, then step forward again and repeat the procedure. You need to 'feel' the ground beneath your feet as you look at the ground you're walking over. All fine in theory but only experience and practice will enable you to 'walk' quietly as possible over a variety of terrain. The footwear you choose also makes 'some' difference. Although as a rule of thumb a soft-soled trainer style shoe can be useful for stalking in summer, in the winter every hunter should wear a pair of suitably heavier duty style field boots. Most offer a good compromise of support, grip and flexibility. Again, you'll discover which suit you as you progress as a hunter. By and large following the basics will help you adopt the style of walking that best suits your build and agility. Firstly you walk an area with your eyes. Look at the 5 yards forward of your position, making mental note of what lies on the ground and the consistency of the terrain. Then slowly use the ball, sole, forward rolling movement. If you feel anything on the ground underfoot about to slip or snap – stop and look at what it is. Carefully retract that foot and place it suitably in another place and progress on your way looking ahead, around and in many cases above for any sign of quarry. Again, remember you still need to stop at regular intervals to again visually inspect the area you're about to walk over or around. While doing so take this opportunity to check around your position for any signs of life. It may seem nigh on impossible but this slow 'drifting' walk will eventually become second nature.

Walking over soft long damp grass is much easier than any woodland floor. That is until the frosts have the ground scrunch with a sound as if you're walking on cornflakes. You'll soon come to realise stalking in the frost is a definite no-no. From my experience of walking over frost ravaged fields at night lamping foxes with a fullbore has made me realise that trying to get within range with an air rifle for any suitable quarry is nigh on impossible. Know when it's impractical to walk up on quarry. This is the time to use other methods such as hide shooting using decoys and/or ambush techniques with bait for corvids. Again, even though we've come away from the main thread the fact that hunting techniques often complement each other or blend well together is an all too obvious one.

But back to 'hoofing it' around the shoot actively searching out quarry – now as the way you move around your shoot on foot is of such high importance so is the use of cover – and as they apply as much to opportunist shooting as they do stalking. I detail movement as this is a very important part of fieldcraft and in actuality, stalking is in definition different for the deer stalker as it is the airgun hunter trying to 'stalk' closer to a rabbit to take an effective shot. It's only the last but very stressful distance whether it be as many as sixty or only ten yards to get to the final shooting position, usually crawling on your belly on the final approach until you are within range.

I'll further detail how to think about planning your route and how to use hedgerows, small copses or tree lines, using the cover these natural features provide. I've nicknamed this technique 'hedge-hopping' – which is simply slowly stalking or walking along hedges, walls or any other perimeter that will offer cover, keeping an eye out for quarry in front of you, that you may walk up on, or even come across on the other side of the cover you are using. Whenever possible, always walk away from the sun, into the wind and keeping in the shaded areas. And that applies wherever you're moving around looking for quarry. And when stalking around hedgerows do so in an anti-clockwise direction (clockwise if left handed) as this allows you to have the rifle ready mounted in the shoulder to be ready for a shot should you spy an opportunity as you round a corner. This is opportunist shooting in its most applied and dedicated form.

Applied Opportunism

At certain times of year, an area that could have been relied upon to 'hold' a few likely targets may suddenly seem to become devoid of all legitimate quarry species. This is dependent on how much disturbance it's been subjected to, either by too much shooting pressure or by other factors such as an increase in natural predators – foxes, stoats, weasels, feral cats, birds of prey etc. Waiting around for quarry to turn up in this sort of situation can be fruitless and one occasion ambushing techniques are nigh on useless in these areas. But this will be dealt with in the relevant section. So as I'm sure you can realise, this is when a 'hedge-hopping' stalking technique can come into its own, as you are actively seeking out a shot.

Creatures of the outdoors survive on their wits, so they will soon start to avoid areas you've had a field day in only a few days before. This is very noticeable amongst rabbit that have been over-lamped at traditional times of year. And yes lamping is another technique that will be covered in detail later, so back to the matter of opportunist shooting. Due to disturbance, they can become much more wary becoming reluctant to stray too far from their burrows or cover. This is especially the case if you share your shoot with other airgun hunters, rimfire shooters and/or shotgunners. In the main you'll find that at first light 'twitchy' rabbits will remain close to home. More often than not these will be sited under hedgerows or shrubbery or right inside bramble thickets – favourite haunts for rabbits in many parts of the country. If rabbits are your main chosen quarry species, look for sand banks or soft disturbed soil leading up to these hedgerows or shrubbery. Similarly the well used 'runs' through the grass. These flattened grass pathways lead out to feeding areas and the regularity the quarry use these routes can often be their downfall, not only because you can ambush them as they come and go but they're clear indication that there may well be a hidden burrow system in the heart of the bramble bushes or whatever dense cover the runs lead in and out of. The following information could have been put in the chapter on Observation, but opportunist shooting is as much about observing and learning from what you see as it is about getting more quarry in the bag. In that respect, be advised that around an 'active' warren, rabbits can be found feeding on the grass near the cover of hedges and bushes at most times of the year. This is because it will probably be lusher and more nutritious, not being as exposed to the elements and feet of grazing livestock as much as the grass further out in the fields. Plus, and perhaps most importantly – they also feel safer near their homes.

Note that the grass can be quite long near the hedgerows, so when taking a snap shot in this opportunist way although I've advised where possible to adopt the kneeling position for extra stability, the downward angle of a standing shot may sometimes be the only and optimum option. The rabbit's head may be all that's visible when it stands up to peek out around. In that case the only sure route for an un-obscured flight path for the pellet to the target is when the shot is taken from the standing position. In the section on stalking we'll further deal with 'eyes from above', feathered quarry that may spot you from the trees. Suffice to say woodies and magpies can be an awful nuisance – even though legitimate and challenging targets if your attention is always on the ground, they will give you away when they spot you approach. Woodies are canny creatures – almost invisible amongst the branches –

and with the annoying habit of suddenly taking off, wings clapping alerting everything in the vicinity as to your presence. So by and large, if opportunist 'stalking' around hedges for rabbits and I know the woodies have taken a liking to a particular area of hedgerow or copse, I'll usually steer well clear. I know this may sound contradictory, as you are supposed to be opportunist shooting and looking for any quarry. But, unless working through a wooded area, I'll keep away unless I've decided to lay up in a pre-dawn ambush for them. Reason being, it's very difficult to sneak up on birds unless you've decided to attempt the seemingly impossible. But, further in this section there are a few tips to help you assess the worth of targeting a bird spotted while opportunist shooting in the woods.

So, suffice here to say if the intruder alarm goes off, bang go your chances of coming across land bound and ground feeding quarry.

However, by slowly and stealthily making

Rabbit on the alert, sitting bolt upright, ears pricked up

your way along or around the perimeter of hedgerows and bushes, it's a fair bet you'll find a bunny or two. And when I say near, I really do mean as close as possible. Once again a word on the shooting position. If a rabbit is spotted close up under the hedge it's likely shooting alongside will be deflected by a straggling branch as much as a tall heavy piece of undergrowth. Here, depending on terrain you have the option of lowering yourself to the floor to take a shot under the canopy of the hedge cover that can often be very bare. Here the rabbit could just be sat outside its warren watching or even dozing. Worst-case scenario is the cover is such that you need to physically move out from the cover you've walked along to take a shot inward to the rabbit's position. This is fraught with variables. Firstly in no way can you step out. You need to make yourself as low as possible and move slowly, usually crawling flat to the ground on your belly, moving 'side-ways' out into the field. It may only be a few yards, maybe even a few feet but the rabbit will notice any movement as it will more likely be side onto your original position. Once far enough out you then still have to contend with ensuring the pellet has a clear path to the target. The words 'challenging' and 'why do we put ourselves through it' come to mind but when you get it right and the end result is a bunny down with hardly a twitch of a back leg – then it's worth every drop of sweat on your beaded brow.

A word here on using areas of low light to your advantage – or you could say lurking in the shadows. Every natural predator knows the importance of staying in the shaded areas. Be it a lion in the African grasslands or a fox scouring the English hedgerows. There's also the use of shadow in the woods, which we'll come to later. So in respect of using the shadows of the hedges and low foliage, notice which side of the hedge the sun casts the shadow, and stalk up this area. It may well be the rabbit is sunning or feeding on the other side but as you'll soon appreciate you'll stand a better chance coming up in these darker areas.

Typical hedgerows that suit this technique have to afford you enough cover (be sufficiently thick and dense in foliage or branches) to prevent your silhouette being spotted by quarry feeding further out in the field. Again we are already coming to a juncture where as I mentioned in the introduction to this section how hunting techniques can often merge or be used together for a successful outcome. Incidentally, this 'cover-hugging' technique works well when stalking/walking slowly along old dry stone walls overgrown with ivy or other creeping cover plants. Even plain dry stone walling itself can be used to conceal your silhouette, providing at these areas you stay low. While opportunist shooting in this way there are many times you need to move low and slow. Breaks and gaps in badly maintained walling offer the chance to scour the field on the other side. If there's no quarry on your side of the cover, periodically take a peek over the other side to see if there's anything around in the field adjacent. This must be done very slowly, your eyes leading the way, with only the slightest amount of your head showing above to allow you to look over. This way if you spot quarry, you can watch its demeanour as you bring the rifle over to sight in on the kill zone. If the quarry begins to look twitchy, freeze – as soon as it relaxes, leave it at least a minute before resuming bringing the rifle into position. Rarely, you might just surprise a group of feeding woodpigeon – magpies and crows will more likely be off and away at the first glimpse of your eye – even the top of your head. But pigeon especially and of course rabbits and squirrels can often get totally lost in the urge to feed and the wall allows a nice steady rest to shoot over. In fact, when and wherever possible, take the opportunity to look around and scour both sides of the cover you're using. Stopping at frequent intervals to take stock of the situation is of great importance if you are to reap dividends from such an applied approach to this method. Ideally you are striving to spot quarry before it has chance to spot you.

Unfortunately, when you do encounter quarry it often has 'noticed' something amiss, in many cases it most likely is aware of your presence. I can't stress this highly enough but movement is the hunter's Achilles' heel. If you sight quarry and it has also seen you then all you can do is completely freeze. I know I'm repeating myself but patience is of the essence in this situation. It can be infuriating, almost like a battle of wits who will break first but never be tempted to carry on sighting in or moving when the target is so 'tuned in' to your position. At this stage it probably and most likely isn't recognising you as danger – but certainly realising you're something to keep an eye on. All you can do is remain totally motionless, avoiding direct eye contact hoping the quarry will soon relax and resume whatever activity it was engaged in before being attracted by your 'seen' or 'sensed' presence.

If you have a shoot that includes un-managed hedgerows which have had the opportunity to grow to a decent height, these can be a nightmare to stalk along. Woodpigeon can be uncannily invisible in even sparse foliage. If you do spot a bird dozing, sleeping off a good feed – a rare opportunist shot this is indeed. In this situation, slowly raise the rifle, assess range by eye then take the shot.

I'm sure you're now thinking for this form of hunting you not only need eyes in the back of your head but the top as well. In a situation a bird does suddenly strike out, if you are close to hedge cover then keep still. Quarry around that hasn't seen you and is near cover itself will possibly hold position or only nip into the very edge of cover. It won't necessarily disappear for the day. This watch and wait tactic has paid off for me many times and it may well seem fruitless to spend any amount of time in this position but surprisingly, if the area isn't usually shot over quarry can be surprisingly tolerant. You'll discover in the stalking section that quarry is rarely as tolerant when out feeding away from cover.

Natural breaks in the hedgerow and man-made passes such as gates should be approached with particular care, as these give the hunter the opportunity to take a studied look into the adjacent field. More often than not, rabbits also use these areas to cross between fields – so they are also areas to consider as an ambush point. In these breaks in cover, again look for rabbit runs and beats (narrow pathways with flattened or bald patches in the grass) going out into the field. These will usually cross the hedge line close to the hedge itself or at the base of gateposts and either side of broken dry stone walling. And for those strange rabbit runs that disappear at the base of a wall – no, the rabbit hasn't walked or maybe I should say 'hopped' back on itself – more so it's probably gone over the wall. Until you see it you probably won't believe it but rabbits are good climbers and will when necessary go over such an obstacle. They'll even swim – something that has surprised many countrymen who've seen the phenomenon. Then again, it's usually when being chased they'll do this and not a regular route they'd prefer to take. So in respect of opportunist shooting for the land borne quarry it's very much a case of expect the unexpected. The prize you seek could be just at the other end of the hedge you're walking up along. Tread carefully – walk quietly and keep your wits about you at all times.

All scenarios mentioned have leant more to shooting around cover and along the hedgerows that form borders to fields. Now to opportunist shooting in the woods.

WOOD-WALKING

It's hard to categorise some methods as they're a mixture of elements taken from the others. One such is wood-walking which can be construed as a form of stalking. This is used when opportunist shooting squirrels, magpies, woodpigeon etc as they go about their routine in the woods. Also don't neglect the perimeter (sides) of the wood. Here you can find a variety of quarry from rabbits to woodies at the edge of fields to corvids in the tops of the bordering trees.

Again this is a very challenging form of shooting that needs stealth, keen eyesight and good marksmanship. Best carried out in the months between and including October and March because the trees have less foliage for quarry to hide in making spotting much easier. If you're looking for squirrels at this time of year a walk through an area will usually send a few squirrels scampering up back into the trees. A 'wood-walk' can be described as an alert but leisurely stroll – slowly walking through the woods stopping at regular intervals keeping eyes and ears open to the sights and sounds around you. Often all you'll see is the flick of a silvery grey tail, enough to give the squirrels' presence away. At others, dead branches can mysteriously fall from the trees on windless days or you'll hear scuffling sounds coming from the forest floor which could be a squirrel foraging amongst leaf litter. Soft-soled shoes are the norm if not too muddy and full camo wear including faceveil and gloves a must.

Once a squirrel has been sighted you can be 99.9% certain it has spotted you no matter how well camo'd you are. As you 'freeze' in position, the camo creates the effect of blending you back into the wood giving the squirrel a false sense of security as it will be unsure what to make of what it 'thinks' it has seen. Either way it will have seen you and will react in one of two ways. It will either stop perfectly still or scamper up a tree to a position it thinks is safe to observe your intrusion. If you have stopped still at this point, you're in with a chance of a shot. Continuing towards the squirrel as it watches you will see it disappear higher up or into heavier foliage if available or even into a hole, crevice, small hollow – anywhere it can to give it cover from you. In squirrel shooting patience is a virtue as eventually, with you keeping quiet and motionless it will carry on feeding. The squirrel's habit of freezing is usually its downfall, as if he's within range you should slowly raise your rifle, aim and have

dispatched the tree rat. Often they scamper around the tree to put it between you and itself. Sometimes it will scurry up the tree only a few feet, then poke its head around again to check if you're still there. This curiosity can be its downfall and possibly the reason they can respond to special calls. Here a quick word on quarry calls. If you can't spot any squirrels, or one has gone from view, try one as it might fire the animal's inquisitiveness to the point it shows itself. These calls, when used correctly emit barks and chatters similar to the animals. I don't particularly think you're talking 'squirrel speak' but it does seem to interest the rodents enough for them to take a closer look.

An old trick often recommended is to drape your coat over a small bush and walk around the other side to confuse it. In practice, this is utter 'BS' as the squirrel isn't completely stupid. Anyway, who wants to continually take their jacket on and off every time a squirrel is spotted? This is when shooting in pairs is beneficial and this is one of the few times I personally enjoy the company of another shooter.

When stalking the woods, even in autumn keep the sun behind your shooting position so you're not squinting

The correct way to hold the rifle as you belly crawl into final position to get within range of the target

when aiming at targets. No need to worry over it casting your silhouette forward as your quarry is likely to be above you. Stop at regular intervals to scan the trees (and ground) ahead. In fact, when walking the woods it's worth keeping an eye on the woodland floor for spoor – tracks – in the woodland loam. Also, gnawed fir cones or 'scratchings' that may indicate the area is well inhabited by the 'grey ones'. Looking up aloft as you walk through the woods, you'll possibly find the squirrels' bulky home – the drey. Not dissimilar to a magpie's nest but smaller. In fact it's not uncommon for squirrels to take over old magpie dwellings. If shooting in pairs one can poke the drey using lofting poles, there's even an attachment unimaginatively called a drey attachment to put onto the end of the poles instead of the wire arm used for deeks. The technique is a simple one. One assembles the sections of the lofting poles together until you've got enough height to reach the drey. Then 'knock' the drey or poke the pole right into it. Incidentally, if there is any breeze or even if there isn't the guy using the poles should stand away from the tree so the dead leaves and debris that knocking the drey will create isn't continually falling into his eyes. The shooter then stands ready in preparation of a shot when the tree rat emerges. They'll sometimes leave the drey very lazily or come rocketing out. Sometimes they'll stop within a few yards, in plain view trying to suss out what has caused the disturbance. This is the time to take the shot as they'll soon head straight for the treetops clinging to the thinnest of branches or disappearing far out of view. Just a few important pointers on drey knocking – ensure there are no overhead power lines. It only takes a brush with one of these and your hunting days are over. Also keep a check on the ferules where the poles join together. Make sure the spring loaded ball catch (if fitted) is strong as losing a lofting pole amongst the branches might sound unfeasible but it's easily done.

Though I've detailed this technique for reasons of thoroughness, by and large I leave this for the shotgunner.

Now, a major problem facing the 'wood-walker' is sound on moving through the wood. Dry leaves are impossible to walk over without causing sound but that doesn't mean you can't cut down on audible disturbance. Like other forms of stalking, don't drag your feet – don't scuffle the leaves unnecessarily but lift and place your feet carefully being ever cautious to avoid those 'ear splitting' dead twigs that can send a 'crack' echoing through the trees. Wet leaves can also be treacherous so watch your step. Consider each footstep as you stealthily move through the wood. There's no hurry and I recommend the hunter stops at more frequent intervals to take a studied look around his position than when out on open ground.

You need to look all around your position at all times, at what could be on the woodland floor, flat against the tree trunks, sitting on limbs and branches. From the ground up – everywhere around you has the potential to produce targets. Shooting in woodland holds many different attractions than the open fields and can be quite exhilarating. If you're lucky enough to be able to walk through a large old mature wood in this way – give thanks to the owner as every time you visit you're entering a magical place – full of things to see and hear. A jay flits across between the trees to disappear in even the sparsest of cover. How the technicolour corvid manages this is a mystery until you realise it uses shadow, cover and remains motionless. A magpie chack, chack, chacks from a position high above, squirrels scamper busily around doing squirrelly things – it's an airgun hunting heaven. For the challenge and variety of targets you'd be hard pushed to find better hunting for the air rifle than the English wood. Not only do you need almost extra-sensory senses but also remember there are particular tricks to employ when a potential target is spotted. For instance, if a bird pitches into the trees it'll head straight for the area the twigs or whatever foliage is available is most dense to give itself as much cover as possible. Depending on species of bird but sometimes any can do this but more likely corvids, such as the jay and magpie mentioned, will head for the upper branches before flying out. Woodies usually just head straight out. A tip for targeting an opportunist shot such as this when the scenario arises is don't try to scan the foliage where the bird entered the tree but train your scope to scan the top of the tree where the branches are more bare. Here you might just get a crack at the bird as it makes its way up, before heading out. If not alarmed it could sit up there looking around. However should another follow it in don't start dithering over which to sight on – choose the area you feel one particular bird will appear from and stick to it. Sweeping your rifle from left to right will only have you unready and miss the small opportunity you have. If it's a pair or lone woodpigeon that's flown into a heavy foliated tree chances are it'll just flop right out again anywhere so don't waste time waiting for this to climb the tree as it won't. Jays and magpies are birds that use the 'climbing' tactic but woodies will land in a tree to rest or feed. If they're resting after feeding these trees can be known as sitty-trees and for a woodie it can return to the same tree time and again. These are easily found by the amount of bird droppings or 'splashings' as they're known found around the base of the tree along with the birds' downy feathers. To sit or stand quietly and patiently within range can produce good sport.

Other areas to 'hang around' are feed hoppers. These can be found in woods for game birds and those that have duck pits. Everything will come to know these 'bins' are packed with food, indeed squirrels and even rats will gnaw their way in to get at the food inside especially during a harsh winter.

Another form of shooting I find very enjoyable around the woods is shooting woodpigeon when they've taken to the thick ivy covered trees to feed on the ivy berries. The birds can become so preoccupied as they jostle each other for the berries that they sometimes don't notice the first few shots or birds dropping from the tree as birds are continually crashing into trees near them to feed. Once you've found a place this is happening stand with your back to a tree in full camo and wait for the best shot to present itself.

For once, the birds are easy to spot in the bare branches and also stand out against the lush green of the ivy leaves. The best time to shoot these birds is before they've been disturbed. Birds new to the area are cautious but not as cautious as ones that have seen comrades fall or you walking beneath the tree canopy picking up your hard earned prizes. When birds are new to an area they're flitting around looking and generally taking over the trees. They'll barge anything out of their way to get at ivy berries because in a harsh winter the fruit can really be their saviour. Unfortunately for them, but fortunately for the well-organised and observant airgun hunter, finding woodies feeding in this manner can result in challenging and exciting sport.

Again don't overshoot an area taking what you need for the pot as depending on region, weather conditions, and density of pigeon population in relation to the food supply you'll have a good few months at them in this manner. When it's over, an area can be completely stripped of berries with just bare stalks and the downy feathers below bearing testament that they've been. In fact these are signs to look for amongst the berries that remain to indicate the birds are frequenting and feeding confidently in the area. Some use lofters (see lofting) to encourage birds to the shooting position or install a feeling of safety so they land near the shooting position. However, when the birds are feeding in this manner I've never found that deeks were needed – the birds are coming and feeding anyway.

STALKING

The word stalking has already been used quite frequently in this chapter as generally it's the term used to refer to the way we stealthily 'walk' up on quarry undetected in a myriad of circumstances. Many will know the word in association with sportsman hunting deer. A deerstalker of course being a hunter who purposely walks up undetected within suitable range to shoot a deer with a suitable calibre of firearm. In relation to airgun hunting – stalking in that respect specifically is used as the term to describe a technique that is widely and mainly accepted and employed for targeting rabbits. Basically,

The crucial moment at the end of any stalking situation – taking the shot

walking up undetected within range to shoot the rabbit with a suitable power of rifle – in this case the 12ft lb air rifle. This requires the shooter to get much closer to the quarry due to the relatively limited effective range. One of the major reasons why stalking up on feeding or 'sunning' rabbits is by far one of the most demanding of hunting techniques the air rifle hunter needs to master.

Most usually this method is employed during the spring right through to late autumn. Incidentally, although stalking is in essence 'sneaking up' to your quarry without it seeing or sensing you – I think we shouldn't kid ourselves as the truth of the matter is, most times it probably has. However the secret of effective stalking is to get within range without your movements overly alarming your quarry with the result it bolts for cover.

The basics of stalking are – always and whenever possible approach from downwind, keep as low a profile as possible, move slowly and quietly taking advantage of every bit of available cover including 'shaded' areas on your way to the target. The use of 'natural cover' will be dealt with in greater detail later.

Whilst camouflage clothing is by far one of the most useful aids in the airgun hunter's kit bag – in summer lightweight overwear such as a mesh suit is ideal, but as you'll be walking and then crawling through and over rough ground, it's always advisable to wear something more substantial underneath. Incidentally, the pattern of camo isn't overly important as long as you're using an appropriate colour blend suited to the summer hues of the open fields and hedgerows you'll be stalking along. As we've touched on previously in the chapter on camo and fieldcraft, obviously soft soled dark green colour trainers or lightweight fieldboots are a must for 'feeling' your way across the ground. And importantly the whites of the body – hands and face – should be covered if you're to get up close and personal with ol' bugs! That means facemask and gloves.

Any quality spring powered, gas-ram or PCP air rifle with general specification 3 – 9 x 40 scope will suffice for this method. Although I always prefer to use a PCP carbine with a good low light scope as you'll often find stalking most productive in the early morning or late in a summer evening when the light values fade.

One of the first mistakes the novice bunny stalker makes is to attempt to creep up on rabbits that are so obviously to the experienced eye – 'unstalkable'. Let me explain that further: Firstly the ground may be unsuitable for a stealthy approach, the rabbit may already be on high alert or there are other factors to contend with such as ground feeding or nesting birds interspersed amongst the feeding rabbits. If so, leave them be and move on until you find rabbits that are 'stalkable'.

As for the ground you're going to have to move over. Stalking can and often needs to be done on ground that is completely or relatively flat with no cover. Rabbits that are feeding out in a fresh cut grass field during daylight hours might appear confident but don't mistake their apparent nonchalance as foolhardiness. It's anything but, as the animal's every sense is ready to detect anything approaching that resembles danger. This is why you need to adopt the stalking walk and learn how and when to use the various stages – those being to half stoop, then to progressively lower yourself as you approach. On sensing your approach the rabbit will freeze, could immediately bolt for cover or lie flat to the ground. If its ears are pricked up, it's heard you and is listening for danger. If it has stopped feeding you can be sure it's also looking at or in your direction. Here's the right way, to get within range to make the 'telling' shot.

Going the Distance

If there are bushes or trees behind you, use these to prevent showing yourself as a silhouette – basically don't allow the rabbit to see you in outline. If there is no 'backdrop' to use, then you only have one option and that is to reduce your size to distort what the animal can see. Whilst camouflage works and works well at breaking up or disguising the unmistakable human outline – unfortunately, against a blank or uniform background of either sky or the field behind you, even if wearing the best camo available, you will show a certain amount – if not all – of your body shape in hard outline. This is a situation why and where you need to break up the human form and still move forward. It sounds impossible, but it isn't. Also you can never put a definite range to target that you should change to these different 'levels' of approach. But there are basic guidelines to follow – these are:
The closer you get to the target the smaller you must try to make yourself appear. This means, almost as soon as you've spotted quarry, you should adopt the half stooping posture as you begin to carefully make your approach.

Once you get closer, continuously watch the animal's demeanour – is it, or are they, showing signs of being 'worried' at your approach? If so stop. If not then the closer you get to the target, reduce yourself lower, walking as low and close to the ground as you can. This is straining on the thigh muscles and you'll soon need to get down to your hands and knees to crawl closer to the target. Certainly towards the end of the stalk you will have to belly crawl into a final position, using your elbows and knees to move forward.

Whilst making the final approach, you should adopt a move, stop and look procedure. Keep an eye on all rabbits, especially the closest to see if it has sensed or is disturbed by your presence. If all is well, choose the rabbit in the feeding group that presents the best shot, and then when within range, take careful aim and take the shot.

And the golden rules of engagement are to check – a rabbit on the alert will sit bolt upright, ears pricked, nose twitching as it uses its exceptional hearing and sense of smell to detect danger. They really are wary little critters!

Now, in a perfect 'hunting world' all would go according to plan, you would reach a distance to take an effective 'killing shot' and the rabbits would remain perfectly still to let you achieve this end. But it's hardly ever that 'text book' simple!

For a start, the most infuriating factor of stalking is not only have you to be mindful of the quarry you are stalking up to (old bugs!) but quarry that might spot you on the way there. Rabbits in the field that you haven't seen may bolt for cover, bobbing up as if from nowhere.

Similarly, as mentioned before, woodpigeon can suddenly crash out of the trees with clapping wings sending your intended quarry scuttling for cover. Likewise the magpie can be an infuriating nuisance shouting its alarm call to all and sundry that an intruder is in the area. If you're hunting over or around a field in spring into summer that has nesting lapwings, forget it. The 'pee-wits' aren't deliberately spoiling your sport, only thinking of the family. Either trying to divert you away from the nest or the flightless chicks that you will encounter scurrying across the ground. It can be frustrating but all these factors need to be addressed and taken into consideration in a stalking situation. Even unseen song and game birds could flush out of cover to signal your presence to everything in the area and beyond.

If that wasn't enough to contend with there's also the possibility of birds flying over at the last minute – this can be a nightmare. In summer – especially – crows can drift over at the most inopportune of moments their raucous 'kaarr, kaarr, kaarr' cawing alerting anything within 'crow shot' that everything isn't as it should be down below. Even woodies flying over the same field – if they veer off their flightline close to the feeding rabbits – the rabbits will notice and carefully look around for danger. If you notice birds flying into the area don't for any reason look directly at them as they will invariably react to your attention. In these situations you can only freeze, keep your eyes and head lowered. As rabbits are creatures of habit, if they do bolt at this type of disturbance they'll often only nip into the nearest cover or lower themselves flat to the ground. Whatever the reaction – 'freeze' – keep totally still, as if you don't make any undue movement, the rabbits more often than not – if they aren't worried by the 'blob' lying on the ground (you) – will soon resume their previous activity.

Stalking isn't only a long distance option and more often than not isn't. Just as many times it can also be adopted in situations when you might encounter rabbits quite unexpectedly – often while opportunist shooting. Usually they'll bolt on your approach as your sudden appearance in the area will have surprised a small group or a solitary feeder – a case of being 'too close for comfort' so to speak. But if you aren't 'too close', and the rabbits aren't 'too twitchy' they'll probably hold on the alert or hop further down the hedge line or field. As they have not bolted for cover, it means they know you're there but haven't particularly identified you as representing danger. In this situation you could try the 'disappearing act' of slowly lowering yourself down to your knees, then onto your stomach, eyes facing the floor. Again, it's nigh on impossible to put a time frame on moving closer in these situations because the behaviour of the rabbits will dictate your next move. Always bear in mind that you should never rush. The speed of your approach isn't only dictated by the proximity of the rabbits, but also the terrain you're moving over. It could be 'smooth' fresh cut grassland or uncomfortably rough pasture – both obviously have their own particular nuances for using the stalking technique.

Over rough hilly ground you can at times travel quite quickly between areas, using hillocks and clumps of foliage to mask your approach, then slowing once again to a belly crawl to carefully peer over to see what may be feeding over the brow of the hill. Unfortunately in this type of terrain, a rabbit can seemingly hide behind the smallest clump of grass, suddenly darting off in a zigzag to disappear into the distance. The times this will happen will far outweigh the textbook stalks. Also a rabbit when flat to the ground, even on a relatively flat grass field can be virtually invisible – only being seen when it bolts. You might think it incredulous how they manage to make themselves so invisible but remember this is how and why they survive detection and capture from natural predators such as foxes and stoats. And whereas some would look over a set of fields on land relatively flat and see nothing but a few trees and hedges, the experienced stalker's eye will notice every bump, bush, nettle patch or fencepost. These are all objects to be used to mask an approach.

Using a row of fence posts you can get surprisingly close to a rabbit feeding on even the flattest field. Move when the rabbit is relaxed stopping at each post. Stand side on to disguise your shape and if downwind from the rabbit it will find it difficult to detect you as long as you remain completely motionless. And whilst the rabbit will notice movement, it will also, as you get closer detect your approach felt as vibration on the ground. Remember, rabbits signal to each other by thumping their hind legs on the ground as a danger signal. They're tuned into the vibration of anything unnatural or running. Sheep that run across a field on your approach will send rabbits to cover. A flock of sheep moving in such a manner is thunderous to a rabbit. This illustrates the importance your footsteps and how quietly you walk has on a successful stalk. And as your movements need to be slow, steady and fluid, so to your footsteps need to be light, carefully chosen but purposeful.

Walking on long damp grass can be done quite quietly but as always there's the possibility of a broken branch or twig if near hedges so still pay attention to the terrain as you move. If walking over marshy, sodden ground place your feet on the highest clumps of grass as these are the driest and will make less sound. Don't if you can help it step into deep mud. The sound of your boot coming out will make more noise than when it was carefully placed down into it.

Stalking is also very strenuous and will test the level of every hunter's fitness. In fact realising your own limitations, and certainly knowing when and when not to stalk can save valuable time in the field and from the time you have in which to participate in the hunt.

Another factor is how much movement will the rabbits tolerate – rarely will they be unaware of your presence. As we've established movement is the hunter's biggest give away and when in a position to take a shot – bringing the rifle on aim correctly is crucial if you don't want to blow it at the last minute.

Presuming you are now in a prone position, and have read the chapter on shooting positions, then you'll be manoeuvring the rifle forward of your position to sight onto the target. The rifle must be kept low, flat and side on to the ground with the right hand side of the rifle upper most. This is so you don't catch the cocking lever. Few PCP air rifles have dedicated left hand bolt actions so I'm sure most will have to use this method of bringing the rifle to bear. Alternatively if you've stalked along a wall or hedge and are now in a kneeling position there's another factor to address in bringing the rifle on aim. That is to bring it slowly up to your shoulder directly in front of your body – this way your body acts as a backdrop behind you so the movement of the rifle is screened. That means not allowing even the tip of the muzzle to present itself forward of your position outside your outline as you bring the rifle to bear.

You may feel foolish but the best way to practise this procedure is while watching yourself in a big mirror – full length if possible. Stand in front of the mirror and practise bringing the rifle up to your shoulder to shoot from different angles. kneeling, sitting, lying prone and even standing.

Also, remember that when lying prone you're at the same level as quarry on the ground. Many wonder why at the end of a stalk and in this position the quarry spooks. It can be the simple fact that it's alarmed at the movement of the rifle along the floor. Alternatively, the rifle catches on something and makes a sound – it can be that simple. This is one of the reasons I rarely use a rifle sling when hunting in this way.

Another factor that can make or break a successful stalk is how you observe the target as you approach. As mentioned previously, when looking at any animal, if it detects you try to avoid making direct eye contact. Keep the rabbit in your peripheral vision but don't stare intently at the animal as it will more often than not realise you're another animal and combined with any movement, smell or sound it may have detected will act accordingly. In other words – 'leg it'. Only when its body language shows it's relaxing and for instance has resumed feeding should you continue the stalk towards the target.

How a rabbit visually 'sees' the stalker can only be imagined. Obviously it hasn't got the benefit of seeing you as a standing average sized adult would. This is why a ground dwelling animal such as the rabbit relies so heavily on its other senses of hearing and smell. I'm sure the fox is detected by smell more than visually detected. If you get the opportunity, watch a fox stalk a rabbit and you'll not be far wrong copying the way it carefully chooses a path, hugging the ground using all cover before launching forward to grab the bunny.

The effort needed to stalk is not only a strain on the muscles but on the nervous system – the adrenalin will have you shaking. As you reach a position you feel you can make an effective shot – lie perfectly still and rest. Calm yourself before even attempting to put the scope cross hairs on the target. Once within a reasonable range, which for most airgun hunters should be within 30 yards, you should always go for a headshot.

Another of the last 'checks' you need to do before taking the shot is to ensure the path from muzzle to target is clear. At ground level a mound of earth could deflect the pellet as could coarse heavy grass or foliage.

Slightly tilt your head to one side of the scope to visually check the terrain. The scope can often give you a false sense of security at this stage so double check all is as it should be. Don't lift your head above the scope as that'll show more of your body. A quick but studied look should be all you need to do, then settle those cross hairs on the kill zone and it's yours.

There are times though when stalking within range of rabbits is impractical, nigh on impossible or both. This could be due to many factors – the terrain is unsuitable, wind isn't in your favour or just the fact the rabbits have become very, very wary. But no need to despair as the airgun hunter should be a king of adapting to the situation he faces. And for times such as this there is at least one other technique at his disposal – one being the next we'll look at – that being the art of ambushing.

Incidentally, another challenging method for targeting rabbits is not only shooting at night with a lamp but also stalking with a nightvision riflescope.

These 'nerve wracking' techniques will be dealt with in the coming chapters, so suffice to say practise hard and long during daylight hours and you'll soon find yourself wanting to take on the challenge at night.

AMBUSH SHOOTING

Sometimes known as static hunting this requires the airgun hunter to wear full camo clothing, use some form of hide or make use of natural cover – usually a combination of all three. The ambush shooting position obviously needs to be chosen or 'built' within effective range of where the quarry is known or expected to move, frequent or feed. Ambushing from a hidden shooting position is used in conjunction with many other methods to bag wary quarry. These can range from decoying, baiting down and in some instances – even indoors rat shooting. So it follows, the most important requisites of successful ambushing are a well chosen shooting position, good camo techniques and sometimes a well-constructed hide.

Ambushing gives the hunter the advantage of surprise and in most cases if you choose your shooting position correctly you'll also know the approximate range of the species targeted. This is most prevalent when baiting crows or magpies down to 'bait' at a known fixed position – further details for shooting corvids are in the section devoted to that technique.

Similar ambush tactics can be used to set up in wait near a rabbit warren. If you've located the main entrance holes and runs to a large, well-populated warren this form of shooting can be very productive. Again cover and concealment is your major concern. In many cases you should be able to position yourself under a hedge or heavy cover within range of the target. If you've got a sling swivel stud

Ambushing can be a very productive hunting method

attached to the forend of your rifle, and it's a PCP you can take advantage of this and shoot using a bipod. Otherwise use a camo rucksack as a rest – this can also help partly conceal you from the forward position. Whilst – by and large – ambushing is a set 'hidden and sniping' technique – depending on what quarry species you intend to 'take by surprise' there are certain factors pertaining to various situations that need to be addressed if you want to operate to the optimum level. Ambushing our main land borne quarry the rabbit is a much more straightforward affair than sitting in wait for flying felons. Typically, what you can 'get away' with in the form of what can be termed 'usable cover' for sniping rabbits will often be totally unsuitable for crows or woodpigeon. Often you only need a camo screen forward of your shooting position to pot rabbits as they emerge from a warren or a hedge line, but if you don't have complete cover around you and are completely hidden from prying eyes from up above, then you'll not stand any chance of ambushing quarry landing in trees. A crow's eyesight is legendary and the woodpigeon's equally keen – as much on the lookout for danger as they are food. Firstly, we'll deal with the animal that hops and jumps – the rabbit.

Although knowing quarry movement around an area is essential to successful hunting, to reap the best rewards from this method, you really must know the movements and specifically the time of day most rabbit activity can be expected in a given area on your shoot. You don't want to be lying or sitting up for hours on end with no activity. Often, you need to be up before sunrise to get into position and many times within the first half hour or so of daybreak you can have a couple for the pot. It goes without saying then that in summer when dawn breaks 'very early' only the dedicated regularly get up at such ungodly hours. By and large though when the sun is hot and up high in the summer sky, the fields aren't the best places for the airgun hunter but that's been dealt with in the chapter on Seasons – I mention it here as a reminder.

But, they say patience is a virtue and nothing worthwhile comes easy – none so true than when you've made the effort to ambush on a summer's morning. But whatever the season, it takes careful planning, fieldcraft and a disciplined shooting technique if you are to achieve optimum results. Note the use of the word 'discipline' as this is only second to patience in order of importance when ambushing. When you've stuck it out and waited three or even more hours and not had a sniff it can be tempting to take on a 'dodgy' long shot or one that tempts you to try the impossible at an awkward angle. In the right circumstances in ideal conditions you might well be lucky enough to hit the mark. But luck should never be relied upon when you're at the moment of slipping the trigger. After sitting or lying for hours on end, then to thankfully at long last 'spy' an opportunity it can be all too easy to grasp at straws. For instance, shooting rabbits as they emerge from hedge lines can be very rewarding but challenging. You've got to drop the rabbit where it 'stands' as one kick off those powerful hind legs will see it lost in the undergrowth or straight down the hole it emerged from. Wait a while and it'll more likely than not move out that little further to present a more clear shot. That's the one to take and the one you should wait for.

Even when you've chosen a suitable shooting position, the nature of ambush shooting means it can be very frustrating just sitting or lying in wait. In my experience it's best to allocate time spent ambushing – especially in winter – to shorter applied sessions. And I know from bitter experience – as I've sat or that should be 'lied prone' for well over five hours on a bitter cold February day waiting for a solitary bunny. The reason I remember that particular month and session is because although the rabbit did eventually appear – which I duly missed – in hindsight I now realise I also experienced the first stages of hypothermia and believe me it's no joking matter. I'll recount the tale because it's certainly a cautionary one. After forcing myself to stay awake and I'm sure I must have at some stage started to doze – I eventually got the chance of a shot. Although well within range, again with the advantage now of hindsight I realise my clumsy clear miss was due to tiredness and the fact my co-ordination was affected by the cold weather's effect on my body. Stubbornly I carried on waiting in the vain hope I would get another chance before nightfall. Eventually it became too dark to see with the scope so I finally relented and admitted defeat. As I tried to move – not only was I numb and shivering – but also for a second or two nothing moved. No I wasn't paralysed but rather my clothing had frozen to the floor. When I peeled myself up off the deck a layer of soil was stuck to the front of every part of my body that'd been in contact with the ground and in the gloom you could clearly see the outline of my prone shooting position in black soil on the surrounding hoar frosted floor. It looked eerily similar to the chalk outlines you see of a dead body in the movies. If I'd stayed there any longer who knows? Some unlucky farm hand could have found me the next morning, and that as they say would have been that.

Needless to say take warning from that story.

So with the doom and gloom out of the way – high time we now get into the nitty gritty of successful ambushing. Also – I reckon it's worth you have a quick re-read of the section on Observation – a very important requisite to all methods of airgun hunting.

Previously I've mentioned how 'an overly uncomfortable shooting position isn't conducive to accuracy'. This certainly applies to the shooter waiting in ambush. Experience has taught me a few major factors pertaining to this form of shooting. Firstly prepare for the unexpected and be ready to adapt accordingly and while waiting – wait in the most comfortable and relaxed shooting position you can. It may sound obvious but if leaning on anything for any length of time, put padding between you and the hard surface. This is where shooting mats or cushions are a godsend. Also keep strain off the arm muscles until you need to use them to alter your aim. As I've mentioned previously, holding a rifle up for any length of time has been dealt with in Shooting Techniques – where possible use a branch as a rest until you need to take control of the rifle to place the cross hairs on a selected target. A typical scenario for this being those potentially long waits for birds coming to sitty-trees. More specifically, here I'll address the use and positioning for using and correct deployment of a bipod.

Give it a Rest

Some are of the opinion that you plonk the rifle down on the ground on the 'pod', lie behind it and wait for a shot. All fine in theory, but body positioning and even height of bipod need to be considered for both shooter comfort and effective use of this super accuracy-aiding accessory. For instance, if shooting out of a ditch or over the brow of a hill, there is one very important reason to use a bipod. You are already able to lie in a way that puts your upper body in a natural angle so you can comfortably look around the area you're observing.

Also, the rifle is already elevated high enough off the ground so you're not tempted to lower the rifle (as could happen if holding it) too low to the ground when you take the shot. At longer range there's no reason to keep yourself 'too' flat to the ground. If you do, the pellet could well be deflected by something – a sod of earth or other such ground obstruction or foliage – on the way to the target. In fact where possible I always recommend the use of a bipod over 'propping up' the forend with your leading hand. Talking of propping up this nicely brings me to the importance of your body posture and position behind the rifle. You'll not always have a handy ditch to drop the lower half of your body back into. So, don't be tempted to overly arch or bend your back to lift your body to look through the scope. If you have to do this you've adopted the incorrect shooting position. The strain might not be felt within the first hour but you'll pay for it when you try to move later the same or next day.

You can easily damage back muscles lying or sitting in awkward positions. Optimum body position for bipod use is to lie with the forearm of your leading arm flat to the ground at 90 degrees facing across the body or bent slightly inwards but comfortably forward or at shoulder level to the ground. This supports the weight of your raised upper torso. The other hand can rest naturally by the side, underneath the rifle while waiting for quarry to appear, letting the rifle's butt pad sit in your shoulder under its own weight. Then when a shot presents itself, slowly raise your trigger hand to take the grip, line up the scope cross hairs and gently squeeze off a shot. But pay attention at this stage as even though the rifle is steady on a rest, your body behind this 'fixed point' needs to be equally stable. No flinching on taking the shot, dropping the shoulder, or moving the head. Even though you're steady at the forward position you need to keep just as steady at the rearward position to achieve the ever-important follow through. The shooting position may be different but the theory and physics for firing a rifle always remain the same. Lock onto the target, squeeze the trigger and freeze while you watch the pellet slam into the quarry's kill-zone. A tip for those having trouble in keeping the shooting hand steady is to bring the leading arm hand up to support the wrist of the shooting hand or underside of the rifle butt therefore forming a secure cradle for the rear of the rifle. You'll soon discover which works best for you.

Incidentally, some bipods come with leg extensions for extra elevation and there are even extra long legged 'specialist' bipods that allow you to adopt a sitting position and still shoot the rifle off a steady rest. And whilst there are various heights of bipod you can even obtain steadying aids that allow you a rest while standing. These are shooting sticks such as monopods, extra long bipods or tripods. Though you might find these useful for rare occasions or if your standing shooting stance is particularly 'shaky' I'd recommend you not start to rely on one as it means carrying extra kit around and more to 'sort-out' before you take a shot. At least the bipod when not in use, folds flat up to sit neatly under the forend of the rifle. Choose a lightweight model and it won't unduly affect handling when shooting off hand and you can still fit a rifle sling to the bipod's 'extra' sling attachment point. So in that respect, you tell me – can any airgun hunter ignore the benefits a bipod affords?

Where and When

As different quarry species have different routines it follows there are better ambush areas for specific species. Here are some examples and ways to tackle the areas from a perspective of ambush.

A good ambush point for rabbits is obviously and as outlined earlier near their warrens but I also favour surprising them as they emerge from hedgerows or as they cross both farm and dirt tracks. The obvious signs to look for are well-worn 'runs' out from cover. As well as flattened grass stems look for soil worn flat and shiny under a hedge, wire fence or side of a vertical wooden fence or gatepost.

In these positions they cross where they have the best view to the front and to either side. But hold up within range near a well used crossing point and you could reap rewards. When they've decided to leave cover, they'll either bolt straight across the track or – and this can often be the case – most often they'll either just sit on the edge of the track or sit almost in the middle. The reason for this behaviour I presume is because they're 'weighing up' the area – deciding if it's safe to enter the field they're facing or move to the area they're intending on feeding over. This is the opportune moment to snipe them from cover. The optimum shooting position is to conceal yourself on the nearside of the hedge line next to the track so the rabbit has left cover before having any chance of spotting your position. If the undergrowth is thick and tall, position yourself within this cover but with a clear path for your pellet from muzzle to target. This ensures no mistakes shooting alongside dense undergrowth and it also gives you a better angle of fire.

Utilising Natural Cover

Cover you've walked beside while opportunist shooting the fields is also typical cover you can use for 'hiding in' while waiting in ambush. I'm sure after a few 'walkabouts' you've established the warrens so you'll know where best to settle down to await your unsuspecting quarry. Not to put that 'big a deal' on it but this form of hunting isn't for the shooter who might be wary of scratching their treasured rifle or getting the odd knock, scratch and scrape themselves, but if you want the results... no pain, no gain, as they say. Seriously though getting amongst thickets, brambles and even thick ground cover with stinging nettles isn't the easiest of tasks. But quarry – specifically rabbits – are often found in these 'inhospitable' areas because they realise that these places afford them the safety they require so you can be pretty sure they won't be far away. A note of caution though when moving through nettles – don't presume to use even gloved hands to move them aside. Light summer wear will often be too flimsy to afford your skin protection against the aggravating nettle stings. Instead use your rifle, or if wearing a suitably padded jacket, the back of the forearm. If settling into position amongst foliage with nettles, avoid applying body pressure onto the plants unless suitably padded. In this situation a padded gunbag can be used as a seat as can a shooting mat, rucksack or one of the specialist padded ground seats.

As always, stealth and slow movements are of vital importance. Even though you plan to use 'sit and wait' or 'lie and wait' tactics don't go stomping straight into the undergrowth or trampling the cover down as this defeats the object of entering the cover. Take the least disruptive route you can take into it. This way you're less likely to get too many scratches or scrapes not only to yourself but it also helps avoid damaging the rifle and snagging your clothing. This is where a pair of secateurs can be very handy for making a pathway that can be regularly pruned for future and continued use if the site proves a good point of ambush. Unfortunately there's no chance you won't disturb the area to some extent as you invariably will but once in position in the thicket or bushes you've chosen you're in one of nature's very own hides. If you think it strange to chose these areas for ambush once again consider the fox that will lie up in this cover, awaiting a rabbit to emerge from the very same area.

Try to position yourself for optimum manoeuvrability, so that you won't have to make too much noise when you want to change position. This is more important should you be choosing a smallish thicket of foliage or bush in a wooded area when you may be using it as a completely self-contained natural hide from eyes above. For this, ideally the thickets you choose should be smallish so you have what is in effect natural cover surrounding you and a canopy of foliage concealing you from above – but not so much cover that you can't virtually do a 180 degree turn with your rifle if the need arises. Also, and I know I stress this but ensure shots out from this cover aren't in danger of being deflected by long grass, twigs and the like. Similarly if shooting upwards at anything that may pitch into trees always ensure the path to the target is clear. Other forms of utilising cover can be as simple as shooting from behind fallen or up-rooted trees, dry stone walls or even out of drainage ditches found on the side of fields. The idea is to hide or conceal yourself. You can even do this in plain view using suitable camo in conjunction with a large enough 'backdrop' such as a hedge, bush or even large tree trunk. The objective is to shield your figure being silhouetted so light doesn't show your upper torso or body as a 'hard outline' as it would if you were 'backlit' so to speak.

Another tip is while holding up in ambush always use your ears as well as your eyes. You'll notice I often mention this – 'hunt with your ears as well as your eyes'. Rabbits will be heard moving through or underneath thickets, scratching or plucking grass from the surrounding area and you'll likely hear woodpigeon land in trees. Granted, they can slip in undetected but often the clapping sound of the wings as they seemingly clumsily alight into the trees gives them away. Don't look up immediately as you'll be seen. Wait a while, until the birds have done their initial neck craning, eye scanning recce of the area – then slowly look up to try and spot the tell tale white patch on the neck. But they'll be hard to spot, no matter what the season as even in trees with sparse foliage the bird isn't one that's easily detected. Choice of rifle for ambush shooting is again a matter of personal choice but as it's a static method standard length rifles give extra shots. They also balance out nicely for bipod use. Carbines can also be used off a bipod and for shooting freehand – can be more manageable in confined spaces – especially useful in the confines of a hide.

The construction of hide is detailed soon, but first, to one of the most basic of hides – the use of a suitably sized piece of camo netting.

Camo net has progressed a hell of a lot since the days of heavy 'tank mesh' used by the army to conceal vehicles and positions from the enemy flying planes above. But the theory of the use of camo net is exactly the same – that being to disguise and hide that which lies behind or beneath. Modern camo net is lightweight, offers some water-resistance and very, very effective. A length of net approximately 10ft × 5ft (however 12ft × 56 inches is a commonly found and available size), is sufficient for covering the human form whether thrown over branches or just thrown over the shooter lying prone. The more net you use then granted if 'constructing' a hide the larger the interior can be but the more you'll need to carry. In many situations I prefer to use a stalk and sit technique. A cross between stalking and then 'sitting up' in ambush as you wait in a likely position. This is when full camo wear and/or a suitable piece of camo net is very useful. If it can be rolled up to fit in the rucky all the better – here's just a few instances where camo net really produced for me when there was little natural cover to use.

One of my most useful ambush tricks is to use a suitable dark pattern of camo net thrown over myself with my rifle on a bipod. Alongside a freshly ploughed field it completely breaks up the outline even though you'll appear as a 'blob' on the landscape – you're still accepted as an unthreatening object.

Another method I learned to use was due to a problem I encountered one autumn and which I eventually solved. There was a huge warren teaming with rabbits. It had been built in the most inaccessible areas. A tangle of roots surrounded the warren and bramble and ferns littered the entrance holes and runs to other areas. There was no cover to snipe the rabbits from with the only shooting position that would afford a direct shot being from the open field – unfortunately in plain view. For a time a pop up hide did an excellent job. Left for a few days it was accepted and a good few fell to the lead before they began to question the Tardis-like object. Then I discovered the desert sand coloured camo nets. Pigeon shooters swear by these for putting across or around a few bales to form a hide in autumn. The way I used one was to lie within range, in the prone shooting position actually in the stubble field facing the warren. The net was draped completely over me like a blanket. This was amazingly effective as birds flying over ignored me because they couldn't make out a human shape. Rabbits had no idea where I was and the trick to consistent, continued sport was to regularly change my shooting position. Another tip I found for comfort was to use a shooting mat. Reason being, after my first session with the thick-cropped stalks of stubble digging into me it felt like I'd been lying on a bed of nails.

Talking of Positions…

If looking to do some general pest control then setting up ambush within striking distance of a feed trough can be very fruitful. Virtually all the flying quarry species will come to visit a feed or indeed water trough at some point during the day. Corvids, wood pigeon – even rats and squirrel can put in an appearance. And considering the fact rabbits use the paddock for grazing and gate access as a crossing area – you could possibly find everything here at one time or another dependent on season. Always a good area to try especially if you've had limited time to recce the whole area.

There is also ambushing in a way that gives you two options or better put two arcs of fire into two different areas around your shooting position. A 'double whammy' approach you might say. Obviously this can only be done for those with the luxury of two rifles but referring back to my chapter on combos if you have two set ups and you've taken my advice and fitted at least a front sling swivel stud then another combo can be employed to use in the double shooting ambush technique.

There are a myriad of options in setting up two rifles but the basics are the same no matter how you're shooting. Firstly and obviously once again the ambush position needs to be chosen with great care. Both rifles need to be set on bipods and preferably and I'd now say by necessity should be precharged pneumatics – unless you have the option to hold one when shooting. You can lie up in full camo in the undergrowth with rifles pointed to either side along opposite lines of the hedge you're lying up in or both out to the front at different angles or in a few cases if you can find the appropriate spot you can lie up in ambush with a rifle set in front and at the back of your position. The method is quite simple but does take concentration as you're watching both areas and depending on what presents itself you need to get behind the rifle to take the shot. Difficult shooting but very productive for covering a wide arc of ground once you master the method.

ROOST SHOOTING

Basically this is just another form of ambushing as you're waiting for the birds to come back to an established resting place in the woods for the night. By and large winter into very early spring are the optimum times for roost shooting, reason being there's less foliage on the trees. But, when it's particularly cold woodies have a crafty habit of preferring to roost in conifer trees meaning targeting them here is impossible. Incidentally, note the chapter on 'Seasons' and advice given therein on roost shooting – particularly the months that the method is least productive.

And so, once again observation is the key to success as you watch where the birds fly out from the wood at dawn and return to in the evening. You need to be out in good time to see the birds on their early to late evening flights back to their chosen areas. This will probably be on the lee side of the wood

The author blends back into the wood and takes careful aim on a woodie at roost

amongst large mature trees. Other favoured spots are where conifers, ivy strangled larches and oak trees – any of which break up the usual sparse foliage of the season are sited. But even when that's established I recommend you enter the wood shortly after midday without the rifle to find the trees they will be actually using. Watching from outside the wood, the trees you presume they're landing in might not be the ones they settle into. The usual white splashings at the base of the trees give this away. When these are established, locate the best spot to sit or stand which gives you the optimum shooting position when they do return. There's nothing more infuriating than to be there waiting and find a few gangly bushes or trees in your line of fire or be 50yds to the left of the best position. No point going and walking around spooking the birds before you begin so cover all the options. Once you've established this, enter the wood this time armed, at the same time as your initial visits and take up position in the area you now know gives you the best chances of bagging a few. In many areas the birds can be quite obliging and the perfect roost site can be right on the edge of a wood. I say 'perfect' as this allows the shooter to take up position within the wood, the gloomy inner woodland floor often helping with concealment.

Preferably sit or stand with your back to a tree to disguise your body and needless to say as a 'back-stop' for concealing your outline. Your head and hands should be covered as uncovered they will stand out like white warning beacons from the woodland floor. And to prevent a fruitless wait, whilst the shotgunner prefers blustery days to carry away the blast, we do not want to contend with shooting in those conditions, so check the weather forecast before your trip.

And don't think the birds will only come back in the evening as a steady trickle of birds can start to return depending on how they've fed during the day as early as mid afternoon. And as often as they do, don't expect them to always announce their arrival on whistling wings or by them clattering into the branches. They can just as likely alight above and around you with hardly a noise. Many times, after taking a shot on what I thought was the first bird to 'come home to roost' – an eruption of clapping wings set up from the branches of trees all around me.

On textbook days a few will arrive and one will present itself perfectly. Let the bird settle, take careful aim, checking the path is clear of twigs to the target. Even a thick leaf can deflect a pellet enough for you to miss the vital kill-zone. Then once certain of the shot, squeeze the trigger and the bird crashes to the deck.

Don't be in a rush to pick up as others could be coming in within minutes or less. For the airgunner that's how it works best. On other days a whole flock could come whistling in, fly around the back of you and then settle into the roosting trees.

An exciting moment as you anticipate the challenging shots ahead, and although you'll be eager to take the first shot, you really have to let these birds settle as you now have many eyes that could detect your movement as you sight in on a bird. However, when the woodie has come into roost in such a way, even if a few birds notice your first movement as you take aim if you see them getting twitchy, as long as you hold the position and no single bird flies up to take the others off with it they'll tolerate this as something natural on the woodland floor and carry on to settle down to roost. This really is one of those 'heart in your mouth' moments as you freeze, wondering and waiting for them to fully settle so you can settle the cross hairs on the bird you'd already picked out and hopefully bag it. Then they will be up and away! But that's the name of the game in roost shooting.

In most woods you don't need a hide, if anything a hide restricts your movement and angle of fire on the birds in the trees. Like many other hunters I often prefer to stand while roost shooting as this allows you to edge around into a better position to take shots on birds alighting into the upper branches. However, if you are certain and sure birds will land within an area you can comfortably see and target while seated, this is less strenuous and more comfortable on the neck muscles as you wait.

Once you've become adept at roost shooting which is a very skilful form of airgun hunting, you could shoot on into the night if there's light cloud and backlit with bright moonlight. These conditions give you an ideal backdrop to sight the 'roosters' against. Only target those showing as full body outline silhouettes as these will more likely have few twigs to deflect the pellet. This is exciting and demanding shooting, the birds often more unwilling to fly off as is usually the case when they've only just settled in. But note – never shoot with a gun lamp as this is illegal.

Once you've shot a particular roost site, leave it a good few days. If you can, best to wait a full week before returning because the birds wise up quickly and will find another suitable area to roost. And sod's law says usually an area 'off limits' for the shooter as they'll be further into or away to another wood.

A very important part of the kit for the roost shooter is the choice of scope. A good quality 3 – 9 × 40 will suffice but a special low light scope is handy for when the light begins to fade – and during autumn and winter the light is gone all too quickly. Sometimes you have a very limited amount of light for shooting. Granted shooting at silhouettes can be done but as I've outlined, only in perfect conditions when you are very experienced at this form of hunting.

Another factor to contend with is judging the range of the bird. Judging distance is hard enough at the best of times when you have objects near your target to relate to. However, when all you have is a blank sky behind and around your quarry, range estimation becomes very tricky indeed.

That aside, presuming you've 'nailed' those upward angle shots and are confident in your aim points roost shooting involves little else except common sense, fieldcraft, a steady nerve and an even steadier aim!

As for roost shooting corvids – this is similar but has its own perils and pitfalls. If you thought woodies are hard to target then crows are more so. However, at times, because of the racket all the birds make as they come into roost you can take the birds from trees and the sound of others joining easily overpowers the resultant crack of lead hitting crow kill-zones. And whereas the crow is a noisy 'rooster', jackdaws can have loose roosts but in total contrast are almost silent as they flit into what they feel to be a 'safe' area for the night. Targeting jackdaws at a roost site can be almost impossible – there are much better places to tackle these corvids as you'll have read in Quarry Files.

Sitty-Trees

Whilst there's no denying the effectiveness of shooting woodpigeon at roost during the evening, many airgun hunters won't even have a 'roost on their shoot'. However, woodies also have routes (flight lines) to get to and from the various feeding areas. But, and most importantly to the airgun hunter looking to 'nab a few' for the pot – in-between times, the woodpigeon use what shooters affectionately term sitty-trees.

Not only found in woods or amongst small copses these trees can be a small standing group amongst fields or even a lone tree on a landscape all offering the airgunner this accessible alternative to roost shooting. In fact it's surprising how the birds can often prefer a lone single tall tree in the middle of fields or a dead tree with hardly any leaf cover. It's safe to presume this is because both afford such a commanding view of the surrounding area.

Optimum times for shooting in this manner are in autumn through to spring before the trees 'leaf up' as the woodies can be picked off the bare branches with a precision shot. But if it's a dead tree with no cover – perfect place to shoot all year around as long as you don't overshoot.

You can only establish the areas and specific trees the birds use with dedicated observation by scanning the fields and trees of the shoot with a good pair of binoculars – preferably from a reasonable distance. It won't take long to spot the trees the birds favour and note the times they're used. A quick recce on foot around the trees should show bird droppings and downy feathers, dead giveaways that woodies are alighting here with some regularity.

Incidentally, whilst sitty-trees are used by woodies to sit in to either rest and digest food, they are also as much used as an observation post, or stop over point before flying onto another area or simply await others to catch up and join them. A 'good 'un' is likely to attract other species such as crows but never be tempted to 'raise your sights' on these until they've fully settled into the tree. While woodies can sometimes zoom straight into the tree the crow is never so foolish and on seeing anything untoward near the area will veer away, cawing loudly – crows can indeed be a good indicator as to the effectiveness of your camo or the hide you've built.

And that brings me to the next important issue after establishing the sitty-trees – to determine a shooting position for the relatively limited effective range of the air rifle.

Whenever possible I prefer not to shoot from the confines of a hide even though there are times that's the only way to keep you concealed from the woodpigeon's incredible eyesight. Thankfully though there are times full camo wear or a modern ghillie suit and face veil will do the trick. But the white of the face and hands must also be covered with facemask and gloves. Next giveaway is movement. If you're constantly raising your rifle or craning your head up and looking around you'll be spotted immediately. Similarly to roost shooting, ambushing woodies coming to sitty trees can be done standing or sitting, the former is only viable in dense woodland where you can stand with your back against a large tree trunk to disguise your silhouette and remain under any foliage canopy to hide in the gloomy area on the woodland floor beneath. Usually in copses and amongst or near a small group of trees, a seated shooting position offers the better option for being able to blend into the surroundings.

Find yourself a sitty-tree and you'll be in for some good sport

If seated on the ground rest the rifle on your knee so minimum amount of movement is needed to place the cross hairs on the bird's kill-zone.

Another tip is before the birds arrive, and this can apply to roost shooting; take a few shots at chosen small branches. Hit these and this will give you a confidence boost that you've 'sussed' the correct adjustment of holdunder needed for the different angles of fire.

Patience is the name of the game and you'll often hear the birds come into the trees as they whistle in or the clapping of wings as they clatter into the branches to waddle along into a comfortable resting position. Unlike roost shooting the bird isn't going to be as relaxed once it has landed. Even before looking up, give the bird time to settle, you'll probably hear it call or be joined by others. It can seem like an eternity but wait until the birds are in position until you slowly look up to seek the giveaway white neck patch in the branches. When spotted, slowly raise the rifle and sight the bird through the scope – again and I know I'm sounding like a stuck record, ensure the path to the target is clear of twigs or leaves that could deflect the pellet. Incidentally, an amber colour front lens cover for the scope is useful to prevent the possibility of any light reflecting off the objective lens and possibly spooking the bird. If a few have arrived choose the one offering the optimum shot or closest to your set zero – done correctly the slipping of the trigger should be followed by a satisfying 'thud' as the bird tumbles from its lofty perch. If the tree is surrounded by undergrowth no need to retrieve the birds as more could be coming in.

Now there's an important trick you can employ to bag more birds in these situations and that's as follows. When you shoot a bird, don't drop your rifle when the others clatter away out of the tree. Woodies are notorious (as are crows) for looking behind and down at any movement as they fly away.

Watching and waiting – patience can be a virtue in airgun hunting

If they spot you, and they will if you move your rifle, then they can mark your shooting position. This might sound far fetched but believe me when I say I've had woodies fly out to come around and land in a tree behind or to my side but well out of range – plainly sitting craning their necks watching me. This still might not sound important but any birds alighting afterwards are likely to quickly spot their comrades staying away from the tree and quickly fly over to join them. I speak from experience as a 'lapse' in concentration like this once bagged me one woodie while I had to watch bird after bird land in the tree on the opposite side of the field clearly watching my position.

But this is just one example of the various tricks you'll pick up yourself through experience out in the field. You will make mistakes but as your fieldcraft and knowledge of your quarry increases you'll know instinctively by your 'target's' behaviour if it's going to sit tight, settle or fly! Incidentally, as we've been discussing the tactics for taking birds from trees worth remembering those variables for upward angle and longer-range high shots we covered in the chapter on Shooting Techniques. Not that easy is it? So, that's the shooting method, but there is still more to say on this subject as anything that helps fool the birds into the optimum position for your shot is useful. This is where a technique known as 'lofting' could well boost your bag.

Lofty Aspirations

I'll mention this technique here, but it could equally be at home in decoy techniques or even previously in roost shooting. Reason being a few lofted birds near an established roosting tree can often keep the birds coming in even though others have flown up after a shot indicating danger. The technique is not as widely used by airgun hunters as some would have you believe – it's a trick borrowed from the shotgun shooters – probably due to the kit required and whilst the shotgun shooter often has a 'few poles' and a 'T' bar, the airgun hunter may only have plastic deeks. We'll come to decoying later but the intention and basic reason to use any decoy is to give the bird a false sense of security. It sees what it thinks are its brethren and has confidence to come in to join them.

Although I prefer to sit and wait within range of an established 'natural' sitty tree and wait for the birds to arrive, there are times it can be beneficial to use a few carefully placed decoys in this manner to pit the odds in your favour. The intention in using these birds is the same in theory as why decoys are used on the ground – it triggers the bird's 'flock instinct' – where it sees others it presumes that place must either be safe and/or there's something there to interest them. The difference in this example of using decoys being the birds are 'lofted' up into the trees and birds flying over within range to visually see these plastic pretenders drop in to join them in what appears to be a nice cosy area to rest. The method is a simple one as long as a few basic rules are adhered to. First, the decoys are placed on a 'T' shape cross bar, but they must be secure as you don't want to have to keep bringing the birds down to re-adjust them because they've drooped or shifted into an unnatural position in the breeze. Lofting poles are usually 5 – 6ft in length and made from aluminium painted green to disguise the shiny alloy. They have a spigot at one end that fits into the next, where a spring-loaded pin locks the poles together. The next procedure is a bit tricky, especially if breezy as you loft the arrangement higher. A tip is to find a fork in a branch to use as a rest then lift the first pole with the T-bar and decoys attached. Once high enough the next pole can be slotted into the underside of the first and this pushed further up until another pole can be inserted into the underside of this. Once the required height is achieved the 'deeks' should be positioned facing into any breeze and the pole leant onto the tree and pushed into the ground for added security. Don't be tempted to loft them too high as decoy birds obscured with a few branches look very realistic and a pigeon's keen eyesight won't miss them in the bare branches. Anyway, in a breeze or when resting up, woodpigeon tend to sit lower in the trees.

There are decoys that have eyelets on the back that are used for 'hanging' the birds onto branches with wire. Alternatively, fishing line can be tied to a brick and the brick thrown (or catapulted) over a branch. The 'brick end' of the fishing line is then tied to the eye on the back of the deek and the bird pulled up into a position in the tree with the line being secured to keep the bird in place. Although this method means you don't have the encumbrance of carting lofting poles it's a poor alternative as you need a calm day else the birds will likely swing unnaturally on the line or wires. I mention the method here only for reasons of thoroughness.

HIDE BUILDING – HIDE SHOOTING

Of all hunting methods, hide shooting can probably be classed as one of the most productive but only by having a very good knowledge of your shoot will you be able to select the best area to build a hide to gain the best from it. These 'buildings' can take the form of the simplest structures of a framework of thick branches leant against a backstop such as a large tree trunk or thick hedge using extra foliage for front cover, or a few hide poles draped and surrounded with camo netting or even permanent sited structures resembling little purpose built bungalows.

Alternatively natural cover can be embellished and made more impenetrable to quarry with a suitably patterned, well-placed piece of quality camo netting. There are even commercially available 'portable' hides – all types will be detailed later and all have their uses. Suffice to say a hide is often more substantial than just throwing a piece of camo netting over the surrounding foliage or your body – even though as you've read previously the latter can at times be very effective. Reason being, modern camo nets – both in pattern and design – are far superior to what was once available. Choose wisely and you really can be hidden from view even in places quite scarce of natural vegetation. And that's the main purpose of any form of hide – to allow the hunter to get within range of wary quarry in situations where there is little or even no natural cover.

Where, When and What Type

One of the major considerations of choosing the hide position is where the sun will be in relation to the time of day you'll be shooting. I know of more than one person who's built an extremely good hide, got into position only to discover the sun coming up to rise in their face and stay shining at them all morning. Ideal shooting position for dusk but at dawn – big mistake. So firstly plot where the sun rises and sets on your shoot, including where it could and will be most intense midway through a bright sunny summer's or even winter's day. Remember, the sun in winter can be even more 'harsh' than summer. And don't build where the sun in summer can keep baking down on you – you'll swelter inside. But you should be avoiding this already, as you should look for an area that affords natural shade to build the hide. You'd be surprised when you look around an area how many places fit this description due to surrounding bushes and/or the position of nearby trees.

Once you've established the basics, observation, which has been dealt with previously will have given you all the information you need on the quarry activity on your shoot. Preferably the hide should give you control of the shooting situation, so you are well within range of the quarry targeted. Once you've taken everything into consideration, it's time to build the hide.

Unless building a permanent hide – first important factor to address is to judge how much the building of it will disturb the area. Some quarry will tolerate quite a reasonable amount of activity whilst others won't want to see you around at all. Similarly, depending on species targeted you need to take into consideration at what time of day you undertake construction and how long you take in building the hide. For instance if building a semi-permanent hide within striking range of an established wood pigeon sitty tree then build in short sessions and use sparingly. Don't use it every time you go out on your shoot – no matter how tempting. However, build a hide near an established crow roost or feeding area and you'll be lucky to have more than one or at most two sessions before the crows will move on. If it's a field they use for feeding, they soon wise up and just move further out into the field – and infuriatingly always just out of range. A tip here is to build the hide near the trees they use to sit before dropping into the field to feed. But I'm sure you're now realising, winged vermin are always more confident 'off' the ground.

Alternatively, rabbits can often be quite quick to accept even a crudely built hide in their area. Woodies are more aware but the corvid family really will notice any structure so the hide needs to be the best you can build.

Obviously if it will only be of use for a short period, or if you have a short period of time to build it, you need build the most basic of structures but always remember that any hide is only as good as the amount of concealment it affords the shooter inside. Always better to overbuild a hide even if it does take that little extra time and effort.

If building near a warren, build when the rabbits are least active. If possible have another hide built so you can alternate shooting positions. If you're tactful you'll be able to cover most of the major entrance and exit points from both shooting positions but when the rabbits decide to move on because of over-shooting, they'll be gone as if by overnight. But a semi-permanent hide – say built for decoying woodies you've noticed that are feeding over a particular area – should be quick and easy to build. Some 'hides' especially for rabbits need only screen you from the forward position. There are even portable camo screens with poles attached that stretch out to form a wall of cover. If this will suffice for a few sessions, then they are very handy, quick and simple to set up.

Incidentally, a hide can be built anywhere including around the farmyard or even within a farm outbuilding or barn. If building around or in the barn, then obviously certain factors need addressing such as other people's safety and the fact they need to know you're there and when you are there shooting. There's more on building hides around the farm in the relevant section but I mention it here to stress that it's not only over open land where a purpose made hidden shooting position is of use.

Hide shooting can often be the only way of getting within range of targets

Size Matters

Spend any length of time in a small and cramped hide and you'll not want to use it again. The hide needs to be large enough to comfortably accommodate you and some essential equipment, be roomy enough for you to move (within reason) around and take different aiming positions. But it also should be small enough so that it doesn't overly stand out from the area it's built in.

When looking to build any hide, ideally look for a natural recess or gap in a hedge line – one that you can blend a structure back into. It's always better to build around a natural feature. When you've chosen such a position sit on a hide seat in the area that would be the centre of the hide and using the rifle swing through an arc of fire. If building with hide poles place the front poles that will form the framework to the sides and forward in relation to your sitting position so you have a comfortable and acceptable field of view. It needn't and more often than not won't be 180 degrees, but do allow yourself room to manoeuvre to shoot. Also, more often than not you'll probably have your gunbag, some other utility carryall such as a rucky and small hide chair in there with you so allow for this when building the hide. Once you've decided on the internal size of the hide, don't forget to allow yourself enough headroom when sitting. Use an extendable hide pole and stand it next to you at head height, then extend above that – whichever height you feel comfortable with – then you can use this as a 'yardstick' when building.

Also look to see if there are points that could be useful to shoot up into. If there aren't any and you only have the forward area as a firing zone then begin building.

Clear what will be the floor area of any runners and straggling branches from the hedge or cover you're building near. The reason being you don't want to trip on anything while in the hide, certainly not stand on anything that may snap to cause noise and kneeling on brambles or nettles is never recommended. If you're going to sit on the floor rather than a hide seat, clear the area of stones as afterwards you can sit on a small camping mattress – preferable green but definitely a dark coloured one. This will keep out the cold, wet and help prevent you getting a numb bum – but do make sure it doesn't cause any noise when you move.

At this stage consider which position you will use as the entrance. This should preferably be from the side and to the rear but discreet enough so you can drape a piece of camo netting across as a door blind when you're in residence. Equally though it needs to be large enough for you to take equipment in, and for you to enter and exit with ease.

As we are now at the building stage, you'll hopefully recall in 'Hunting Accessories' I mentioned the 'kit' that would become useful once you progressed as a hunter. This is one such situation as for hide building you need a few basic tools and equipment. Firstly a pair of garden secateurs, a wood saw, twine, camo tape, and the obvious such as hide poles and camo netting. If building a permanent hide – add to that your toolbox including hammer and a plentiful supply of nails. But this is the extreme – for most structures it's the basics you need and always the basics of correct hide building you need to remember. Another factor to consider is that before you even think of building a hide although you have permission to shoot on the land, don't take it for granted you can go building on it. If it's a permanent hide you'll obviously need permission of the landowner but in some counties they can even be classed as a 'dwelling'. It's common courtesy to ask the farmer if you can construct anything on his land. More times than not he'll gladly agree if it helps you eliminate more vermin. Also, he might just have a few pieces of material that could help in its construction such as old fence posts and even railway sleepers – the latter being ideal for the building of more substantial hides.

Here I'll stress the importance of the hide needing to have a solid impenetrable back section. If not quarry can see you clearly as you move inside as you cross the chinks of light passing in from the back. This is where many new to hide building make their first mistake. It's all well and good wanting to be able to see all around your shooting position (if shooting from natural cover you can often achieve this) but it will be to the detriment of total concealment. So, when hide shooting, there are sacrifices that have to be made for the cover it affords. So it follows the hide needs to be built with the base knowledge from the outset which way you will be facing to shoot. It's here that you'll need small openings in the foliage to shoot from or gaps in the netting you poke the barrel through. Note here not to have too many 'shooting' positions. It may seem like a good idea but if you can see out, wary quarry is just as likely going to see in and the shooting 'slits' or holes you make shouldn't be overly large – no more than fist size in a hide built from natural cover. Far better to have them 'closely' covered with camo net with the intention of just poking out the barrel to shoot. This means less foliage is needed so as not to obscure sighting the target through the scope but enough to conceal your movements – a case for compromise.

Now we come to choice of cover materials for the hide and net types. Firstly natural cover: If you find dead branches lying around use these and if possible leave then without trimming. Nothing looks worse than a regimented row of cut 'sticks'. For weaving into this framework use weed trees of alder and hazel but whenever possible, as camo netting has become so much more advanced, I often prefer to use extra natural cover only to embellish the netting.

As for netting itself – best nets in my opinion are what are known as cut leaf open weave. These already have openings wide enough for you to shoot through and the 'leaf design' has a natural 'break-up' effect around the open weave. This means maximum visibility out, allowing you to gain a sight picture while the shooting 'opening' is still quite concealed.

Once built, stand away from the hide and visually check to ensure there are not any unnatural looking straight edges formed by either framework or netting. If there are, disguise them by using natural foliage you can add from the surroundings. Also when gathering natural foliage, take it from a reasonable distance away from the hide, rather than at the sides. If you don't, this will make the area look less natural and will have the hide stand out rather than blend in.

What you build depends not only on the time you can spend in construction but also the time of year you've chosen to construct it. For permanent hides, it's widely accepted that early spring or even earlier are prime times as then when the surrounding foliage springs into life the natural growth actually adds to the hide and over the years if you keep a hide maintained a very natural look will eventually be achieved. So, let's look at the 'hide' options to build or buy.

Natural

A framework is always needed and like a 'house' has walls, these are the supports that hold the structure up and give it strength so use thick branches. Once in place, as you're going to use what nature provides, dead braches that easily snap off or are found on the ground are useful for shoring up at the front, sides or even building a roof but if you need to cut 'flexible' branches for weaving into your framework you need to know which trees to cut. It's not good practice to cut everything you see that looks useful as in effect you're damaging the woods you should be there to protect. If you're going to use live trees know which ones that are known by some forestry workers as 'weed trees'. These include most soft woods such as elder or hazel as they are most common in most areas. These woods are nice and flexi and you'll find enough straggly branches to use in the construction of your hide. But take note to ensure the leaves stay the natural 'dark' way up. Most leaves have pale undersides and even this can be just enough to deter quarry coming in closer.

If the farmer has removed any old dying trees or just cut back an area for any reason, this is the time to ask if you can use the 'dead wood' as he'll only probably burn it for disposal. You can in fact do the farmer a favour in clearing the cut wood. And although this is mainly a 'natural' built hide, if necessary, I'll also use old camo netting as extra concealment. Incidentally, if you've left a natural hide for a while it'll more often than not need some repair and you'll possibly also notice the dead wood will have dried up and look different to the natural 'live' foliage growing around the area. In that respect, a bit of titivation with some fresh greenery will soon have it spruced up and looking like new.

Semi Permanent – Using Poles and Netting

This is the most popular and versatile as you can have a hide erected quickly in any area you choose. The ability to build where you choose is made all the easier thanks to the large selection of quality hide poles and effective camo netting easily and commercially available. One item definitely to add to the kit are cross support bars which means a firm framework for the roof can be formed once the camo net is draped over. This will help prevent the net 'sagging' down into the hide. Hide poles can be lightweight or heavy duty, standard fixed sizes or extendable. Some come with kick plates for pushing into hard ground. So as you can see there's a large variety to choose from. All are useful in various situations. Similarly there are many types and different patterns of camo netting to suit the varied terrain – usually these are either autumnal colours or more 'green heavy' for summer foliage. There are sand coloured nets, and these are ideal for using over stubble fields – more often by pigeon shooters draped over a few hay bales. More often you'll be building against a hedge so use the appropriate coloured foliage netting. I've already mentioned my preference of net design but with the additional use of natural vegetation and a hide such as this can be erected in no time at all. A word of warning though. When you add foliage to make the hide look more natural don't weave the foliage and branches into it unless you want to spend a day removing straggly branches from a net you need somewhere else shortly afterwards. Only do this if it's to be left in situ for a fair amount of time. If not 'lean' the natural foliage against the netting – it's just as effective.

Permanent

The beauty of a permanent hide is it can be built to a much higher standard and in some cases be able to fully withstand the elements. Also, as the seasons progress, if built near growing hedgerow of bramble or hawthorn, nature really will soon encroach onto and around the structure blending it into the natural background. And one built in a well-chosen position can often offer all year round sport. The ideal places to consider for these hides are within range of where quarry crosses from one area to another. For positioning, the usual type of areas such as natural gaps in hedgelines that might accept a hide into the surroundings as a continuation of the hedge are ideal. As it will be there – in some cases for some years – you need to build from much more substantial materials. Thick fence posts make an ideal framework and should be driven well into the ground. The lower base surround of wood ideally needs to be made up of substantially sized logs or old railway sleepers. They can also usually be much larger than semi-permanent hides, even have enough internal space to accommodate two shooters. A seating arrangement such as a small bench can easily be made and I certainly recommend you build a fixed strong roof of either weatherboard, or shiplap construction with a slant to allow rain to run off. You can even build a proper doorway but let's not forget the outside. This should always be repaired to suit the seasons. No matter what the main construction – even it was made from breezeblock – the outside still needs to reassemble the outside vegetation that surrounds it. Think along the lines of a birdwatcher's hide but one that blends in with its surroundings. And the longer an object is in situ on the landscape, no matter what it is, be it a hide, tractor trailer or discarded oil drum the more it will be accepted by the local wildlife. This is a major bonus of permanent hides that work in the hunter's favour as they are there much longer and therefore have more time to be considered 'just part of the scenery'.

Pop-up hides are quick and easy to use – not forgetting very effective

Portable Hides

The main benefits of using portable or as they're often known 'pop up' hides is the fact you can erect a hidden shooting position in literally seconds. Some even fold down into a carry bag the size of a very large pizza. Arrive on the shoot, 'pop-up' the hide and use it.

If you've chosen a bad position or you spy a better area to shoot from it can be moved just as quickly so you can constantly take quarry by surprise, vermin never knowing where you could strike next. These hides have given me some excellent shooting and have proved to be very usable for many hunting situations. Set up and leave it in an area for quarry to become used to it for a few days, arrive before dawn, get settled into position and reap a few hours of quick fire action. They come in a small but useful variety of camo patterns and designs. Whichever you choose, all have 'windows' for shooting out of that can be opened or closed depending on how much or little you want to see out. All come with pegging points, guy ropes and pegs and most are quite secure until it really gets windy. If this sort of weather is forecast best to take the hide down, rather than leave it set up or a 'good blow' could see you traipsing over the other side of the fields to collect your hide next time you arrive to use it.

Another downside is these 'one-man' hides tend to be quite small and cramped inside, good for short sessions but you'll feel the strain on your back the longer you're sat in there, waiting to see what is going to appear.

Always handy for when you spot an area pigeons or crows have suddenly started feeding over – so don't discount this option.

The Hide Shooting Technique

Once you've finally built the hide, depending on type, a few words on maintenance. If it's a natural hide or even a permanent hide, before entering, give it the 'once over'. Check to see it still blends in with the surroundings. Hopefully vegetation will have 'grown up' in front or over your hide helping to make it blend more into the surroundings. If all's well, fine. If it looks a bit shabby, give it a spruce up. If you haven't used a hide for a while certainly check the shooting 'points' aren't obscured. Embellished slightly with a bit more naturally growing cover is no bad thing but to the point of obscuring your vision – no way. If the foliage needs trimming back then do so with secatuers or adjust the netting accordingly. After that check the back is still impenetrable to light. Incidentally, if you're after the dawn feeders, you'll almost always have to be in and settled a good half hour to in some cases an hour before dawn.

But before even starting to use a hide, a routine check that I advice shooters do, and one that can be done on a day prior to shooting is to 'range' certain objects from the shooting position. You can do this from inside with a laser rangefinder or purposely pace out and set out markers at different positions from the front of the hide. Markers can be stones or even wooden pegs. You can be as frugal or comprehensive as you prefer, with range markers set out at your set zero, then at 5yd increments closer and further out from this mark. And I'm sure you will realise the benefits of this and that 'ranging' can be used when just lying prone in ambush near a warren.

However, specifically in relation to hide shooting, depending on the 'field of fire' you can comfortably target, you'll possibly want to set out markers to the left and right of the hide as well as directly in front. These will form a semi-circle around the front of the hide. Don't put out too many as they'll become confusing – too few and you'll not get a reasonable indication of a range should quarry present itself too far to the left or right of a set range marker. The way you set this out is up to you but try to envisage the effective shooting area you have as a block grid map of set ranges. When quarry is within a grid ref on the area, you'll know the approximate range to target. Once you've assessed the ranges – time to use this knowledge and the concealed shooting position you've now created.

The two major requisites that will aid success and your enjoyment of hide shooting are the need to be organised and comfortable. You're likely to be in there for some time, so set out the gear you need so everything is to hand. That way you'll not have to rummage through a bag for extra ammo or to get a drink. Also, there's nothing more infuriating than settling down in position, have been waiting patiently for first light than to suddenly remember something you've left in the car. As you progress, learning and developing your skills as a hunter you'll soon realise the accessories that are useful to you. We've dealt with the general accessories available in the relevant chapter but certainly as you do more hide shooting you'll know which accessories suit the task.

Obviously, unless you've built in some form of seating or are sitting on the ground a small light-weight portable folding hide seat or pigeon shooter's bag combined plastic 'tub' seat will certainly be a must. The latter being very handy as these holdall carry bag/seats will accommodate poles, netting and your deeks. A small rucksack or carryall will still be needed to carry extra ammo and other bits and bobs such as a flask, food, extra clothing – anything you might need during your stay as you work under cover. Incidentally, although the hide should ideally be built in the shade, inside it can still get hot in summer and certainly cold in winter. As you're not moving around much, in winter it can be very cold indeed. So take appropriate drinks depending on time of year and certainly consider a soup flask for some warming nourishment in winter. But don't be tempted to take too much gear into the hide as what at first may have seemed to be a fairly roomy construction can soon become crammed with kit.

Different shooters want different things in the hide but there are basics. Have a checklist so you don't forget something obvious. If you've a bad memory, no shame in checking the list before you start a session. It'll certainly be a better proposition than having to leave the hide for something you've forgotten – usually just as a woodie or two are just about to drop into the area you're decoying over. In fact leaving the shooting area to retrieve a kill can be infuriating. If dropping birds from trees and the grass is quite long around the base you might get away with leaving them. Sometimes it'll be a necessity and need to be done immediately after the kill – especially for birds that fall unnaturally in the open to be seen by others flying in.

However, just as many times it pays to hold off a shot for the fact the bird or for that matter rabbit lends itself to being a natural decoy. A scraggy lone feral pigeon in the trees isn't that worthy a target, but wait a while and it could soon be joined by woodies. Similarly a crow you hear just out of sight behind or directly above isn't worth spooking by undue internal hide movement as it'll probably soon drop down into the field in front – especially if using baiting down tactics. Also it can possibly attract others into more suitable shooting positions. That brings me to mention the fact even though you are supposedly fully hidden, don't think the cover of the hide allows you to move around freely, try to stay as quiet and still as possible at all times. This is often known as 'hide discipline', adhere to it and it will pay dividends.

Now, even though you're hidden I recommend the use of full camo wear including facemask and gloves. No matter how good the hide, no point in taking the risk of blowing it due to your leading hand flashing white across a shooting area. Don't go looking out of the hide showing hands or face – even though concealed your movements will be noticed. Too many get impatient and look over or around a hide even putting their face right up to a shooting point – don't. It's easy to become inpatient but this is a waiting game. Remember – 'hide discipline' at all times.

When it comes to rifle choice, carbines are the optimum rifle type as they are suited to manoeuvring in smaller spaces. Even so, when pushing the rifle through to shoot, do so slowly and only far enough so you can sight in on the target.

Only the very end of the muzzle should need to poke through as sometimes you don't need to push the scope right up close to the inside of the netting or front cover foliage to see out. If so, this is also a situation when once again the front scope lens can be a cause for concern, even on dull days a bird, especially one as wary as a corvid, can see the sky reflected off the front lens and even catch a glint from the finish of a rifle barrel. Use an amber scope cover or piece of loose 'see-thru' camo material wrapped and secured with a rubber band around the objective lens to prevent this.

Also, in the least I recommend camo tape around the silencer and maybe a bit on the barrel immediately behind. Also, if using a rifle with a buddy bottle, cover that as well. Slip on covers of brown or camo can be bought for the major rifle models. I'm sure quarry can spot the black outline of a barrel or even tip of a silencer moving in or against camo. No use blowing it for something so trivial. Another bonus of shooting from a hide is you often have more time to take the shot. Without fear of detection you can take more time in waiting for the quarry to present itself better so you can put the pellet smack bang into the kill-zone.

As with other techniques you hunt with your ears as much as your eyes. The magpie will often noisily herald its presence to the more discreet rustling of a rabbit. Alternatively the sound of it plucking grass from the ground can be quite loud and tell you there's one close by. Another giveaway are the clapping of a woodpigeon's wings as it lands in the trees and crows usually can't help but start harshly cawing to see if one of its own is about.

Depending on the size of your shoot, the permission granted and the length of time you've been shooting over the area I'd advise most hunters to construct at least one permanent hide and maybe one or two semi-permanent hides on their shoot. More hides means you can rest areas and rotate the use of hides so as not to overshoot an area.

Now to the subject of using a rest in a hide – and an old camera tripod is useful for this. A camera beanbag or shooting beanbag on the head of the tripod will allow you to slide the rifle back and forth and swivel it right around. If you had the rifle on a bipod – even with extended legs and swivel facility you'd not get this level of movement. Then again you could use a small compact monopod.

Going for a 'slash?' Sorry to sound crude but it's a natural bodily function. You can bet sod's law says you've waited three hours and as soon as you leave for a call of nature quarry will appear in a position you could have drawn an easy bead on. A funnel into a length of plastic pipe set to the back and running from inside to out is better than using a old container and throwing it out the back door. I know it may sound unpleasant but you need to take these things into consideration. That's hide shooting.

DECOYING

As the name suggests, decoying is a way of 'attracting' (in some cases 'distracting') a bird with an imitation bird (known as the decoy or 'deeks'), of the same species so the intended quarry targeted is brought within range. In the case of the woodpigeon – the bird most associated with this method – attracting them down to an area is nothing new as shotgunners have been doing it almost since they first seriously began targeting the crop guzzlers. Alternatively using a crow deek positioned near a suitable bait such as a slit open rabbit works to give the corvid a sense of safety near the food – the same applies for magpies. For corvids, there is the alternative decoy method where a bird is used – such as a little owl or raptor – placed in their territory or near a nest sight to 'annoy' the corvids to show themselves as they mob the intruder. Those 'peripheral' and 'off-shoot' decoying methods will be dealt with as we come to the relevant section. But, there's no doubting both methods work well, at the optimum times of year in the right locations. First the use of decoys for our most popular pie filler – the woodpigeon.

The theory behind the method is quite a simple one. Arrange a pattern of decoys in a field to look like feeding pigeon so the 'real live' ones flying over will come down to join them. Then hole up nearby

Decoying woodies in autumn is now as traditional for airgun hunters as it is for shotgunners

within striking distance – more often than not well hidden in a purpose built hide. Eventually birds flying over see the 'imitation' birds, assume their brethren have found some grub and come down to join the feast. Sounds easy if you read it quickly doesn't it? Well obviously it isn't – unlike shooting with the shotgun, as you're using an air rifle you need the pigeon to land and stay still long enough for you to take a shot. This is the main problem that faces the airgun hunter using this technique. If they've come in 'en masse' so to speak, always let a good few settle amongst the deeks before choosing a target. But there are times small groups or even lone birds will land with more confidence. And as I often say, less eyes to potentially see you is much better than numerous pairs. So now, let's go through the stages to set up the woodies for what is in effect a most crafty deception.

As with other hunting methods observation is of major importance. You need to watch and learn where the pigeon feed but more importantly learn the regular flightlines the birds use to and from feeding areas. Once you've established a pattern of behaviour in your local woodie population you can make a start. But take advantage of any sudden feeding areas you observe the pigeon use. They might even be off a regular flightline because they've found 'lays' in the corn or barley. These are flattened patches caused by wind or rain – even 'tramlines' caused by the tractor left after spraying are wide enough for the birds to drop into. Watching from a distance you'll see the woodies drop like stones to disappear from view gorging and ruining more of the crop field. If left untroubled by shooting attention woodies and of course crows and rooks can 'strim' crop fields from inside out and vice versa. Like other methods of hunting, make the most of the opportunities you see and get over there as soon as you can, set up a hide and put out the decoys. That is if you can get to the position without trampling over precious crops yourself! If you can't, you need to wait until the fields are harvested.

But it's not only a method for the autumn as decoying can work at any time of year when crops are cut. You can even decoy birds down onto the barest set aside field.

A few decoys and hide building material will get you started. If you get the 'bug' you'll soon be buying all sorts of paraphernalia – 'floater' poles, bird cradles, possibly even one of the electric rotating pigeon attractors or 'whirly-gigs' as they're often referred to.

But let's take a look at basic decoys, the types available, and patterns to set them out in.

And though the art of decoying hasn't changed much since its early use, the types of decoys available to the modern shooter most surely have. In fact, back in the very early days of the sport, keen pigeon shooters made do by making their own from bits of wood and feathers or either used dead birds, or carved wooden ones. Trouble was you had to either shoot a few first to set out in a pattern or lug heavy wooden ones onto the shoot. Fortunately, the decoys you can buy today are much more user friendly – either plastic full body, plastic or rubber 'shell' or EVA foam outstretched winged 'silhouette' types. The latter for use as 'floaters' or to put on a 'whirly-gig' machine if you haven't already bagged a few birds to use as 'naturals'. Methods of usage will be outlined presently. Incidentally, there are plastic decoys that are treated or 'flocked', this is the term given to the fact they're covered in a soft felt-like material or 'flock'. This makes them very realistic looking and in situations of bright light and direct sunlight can often work better as they don't glint or shine unnaturally. In fact 'flocked' decoys are now available for most species.

The Art of Deception

Decoys should be placed out in the field under an established flightline. And set out in little groups or 'patterns' as they're known, always facing into the wind. Don't position them too close to your shooting position – but obviously keep the nearside edge of the pattern well within range.

Unfortunately, birds often come in textbook fashion but veer away because there's something not quite right about the set-up. Maybe they caught a glimpse of you, the hide doesn't blend in well enough with the area or the decoy pattern just isn't quite right for the day. However, you'll not have long before woodies do land, but they often don't hang around long before they realise their mistake. As soon as the bird settles and raises its head, take the shot – slightly poking the muzzle of the rifle out of the hide netting, an adrenalin rush of a moment as you'll be 'willing' the bird not to move or catch sight of you.

At first, this shooting technique can be very frustrating but very challenging. If all goes according to plan, the shot bird has dropped and hopefully not showing breast feathers or wings outstretched. If it has, leave the hide so as to retrieve it, or better still, if it's not during a warmer month set it out as a natural decoy. I mention the season as birds soon get 'fly blown' if left out in the field. For setting out dead birds as decoys, you can either use a special 'cradle' that supports the bird on the ground, or simply tuck its wings into its side and lay its head out at a right angle or better still prop it up using a chin stick. But don't have the head stuck up too high as this is the posture of an alert or unnatural look-ing bird. When used correctly, real or I should say 'shot' birds certainly do make the best deeks.

Incidentally, even though hide building has been dealt with already, the importance of a hidden and well-constructed hide can't be overstressed. It must 'obscure you' from prying eyes, especially from above as birds fly over. But, so good are the new camo nets that I've had birds land in the pattern spook at something or they're twitchy from past experience and fly up into the trees on my left or right clearly visible from my shooting position. But due to their position in relation to the hide they can't see into the gloom beyond the net as you've got a full dark colour backdrop – the ground. Many times I've taken them from the trees shooting through the net roof of the hide.

Now, as this is not an in-depth look at 'advanced decoying techniques' but more a guide to help you try your hand at the method, I recommend anybody who seriously gets into this form of airgun hunting get a quality book on the subject of pigeon shooting. Knowledge is power in this game and even then the reason to employ certain 'tricks' will only become apparent after much experience.

The basic patterns I use are variations on a theme that most shotgunners use and that's what can best be termed as a 'loose horseshoe, a staggered 'L' shape or a pattern in the shape of a 'comma'. All so named due to the appearance of the pattern from above. In all cases the deeks at the front of the pattern form a barrier to the front so incoming birds drop into the open space behind. But watch how birds react to the pattern, have a bad pattern out and they'll let you know – they'll hardly give the area a second glance on their way over. It could be they're determined to get to a specific area but often a good deek set-up will turn them in. So don't be scared to experiment with the pattern, slightly enlarging it, narrowing or even changing its shape.

Also, when setting the deeks out, if there is any wind, face the birds into the breeze. Don't make the pattern too regimented or have birds too close together. Have some at a slight angle to the others, some with heads up and some with heads down as if feeding.

Now, specific to this form of shooting with the air rifle – as not to cause problems further down the line, the decoys shouldn't be overly spread out. I set them out so the closest birds in the pattern are 20yds and the furthest edge of the pattern of birds at approximately 40-45yds out from my shooting position. The pattern itself is no longer than approximately 40yds from front to back. The reason for this is when you're in position, even in a hide; movement is your biggest giveaway. Unless you're totally concealed even carefully moving the rifle to the left or right will spook them and up and away they'll go. Using a more 'tight' pattern usually brings the birds or at least a reasonable amount down as close as possible to where you're ready to train the scope. This should be towards the back of the pattern. This is probably the major difference between setting a pattern for air rifle shooting instead of targeting them when using the shotgun.

Remember, of all quarry, woodies are amongst the wiliest and unlike a rabbit that knows it can bolt to run for cover, the woodpigeon on sensing, hearing or usually seeing anything untoward will just fly up and away – and not always to a tree where you can 'pick it off'. It won't sit there thinking on the ground. This means shooting is very demanding, often as soon as the bird lands and stops moving you've got to take the shot. However, plus points the air rifle hunter has over the shotgunner are shots can be taken at greater distance and using a silenced airgun there's very little sound to disturb the peace. In fact many times I get the bonus rabbit or two that comes out of the nearby cover to my shooting position while pigeoning. I presume they see deeks in the field and it gives them confidence to come out as well.

As an alternative, and whenever possible I relish the opportunity to shoot over decoys from natural cover. It'll be obvious that there aren't many times you will find an area with an ideal shooting position 'ready prepared' such as this. Obviously you need to wear full camo wear and it needs to be somewhere where you can get right back into the hedging at the side of the field, under overhanging trees to use the hunter's friend – shade.

If you've found an ideal spot where you don't need the encumbrance of a camo screen then not only have you been very lucky or been vigilant in your observation but you can adopt a shooting style very similar to the shotgunners. Once you spot a bird or two are coming into the decoys – and you really do only want them to come in small numbers for this technique – put the butt of the rifle into your shoulder and follow it keenly with your eyes as it drops into the pattern. As the bird is landing, slowly raise the rifle, pointing it in the direction of the bird and drop your head onto the rifle cheekpiece to sight 'alongside' the scope. Incidentally, this is the only time the bird will tolerate 'movement' from your position – though you should strive to keep it minimal – as its eyesight at this moment is concentrated on the landing area.

If you've smoothly followed the bird's path on landing you should only have to shift the rifle slightly to sight 'through' the scope and the woodie will be in the sight picture. This is the ideal scenario as there's nothing worse than waving the rifle around trying to spot the bird. If you haven't got the bird in your sights, carefully look to the side of the scope, find the target, line up the muzzle and look again. Hopefully the bird won't have spooked. But as they're so inconsiderate it probably has! It will certainly by now be walking and moving wondering what's going on. This is the most nerve-racking moment because it'll feel like an eternity until it stops still or 'lingers' in a feeding position long enough for you to line up on the kill-zone. If hide shooting or using alternative cover, I recommend you take heart lung shots as believe me head shots are almost impossible unless it does what I've now termed the 'vacant stare'. Watch woodies feeding or even when in sitty-trees – every so often they just stop with the head slightly cocked to one side with the most vacant look in their small yellow-rimmed, black spot eyes. However, don't be fooled, as the bird's anything but vacant, as at this moment it's using all its senses to take in everything going on around it. That's why you can't be moving around or even wavering the muzzle. If it catches sight of you, a glint off the barrel or the scope lens it'll be off. At this point you should be on target and it's definitely only during 'vacant stare' moments I'll consider taking a headshot on a woodie that's landed.

There are also times you can get back in heavy cover, or under a camo net shooting from a prone position. This is one of the only times shooting lying down when I usually prefer not to use a bipod because the pigeon can land anywhere and for once the bipod would be an encumbrance.

In these situations, some natural cover could well be needed cut from foliage placed in front, anything so those keen eyes don't spot you as the woodies pitch in.

Incidentally, if lying prone, or shooting from a ditch at ground level a wood pigeon doesn't stand very tall as a target. To be most flexible you should whenever possible find a position where you will be slightly above the shooting area. In this situation there's no following the bird or birds as they come in – it's 'head down' and let them land. Then slowly sight a target and take a shot.

It's worth mentioning that if the birds are not coming to decoys, also keep your eyes peeled as many times a lone buzzard, kestrel or sparrow hawk will spook them. If so, time to switch plans. I'll usually opt to go for a spot of opportunist shooting because if they're really twitchy they'll not land in the pattern when there's a predator around.

Nothing's ever cut and dried with any hunting technique. It can be a long wait

A dead natural set out as if feeding is the best deek of all

or at others you can just put out the deeks, have turned on the pigeon machine and just entered the hide when they come flying in. And that nicely brings me to the subject of rotating pigeon machines or as they've become affectionately known 'whirly-gigs'.

Magic Roundabout

I first became interested in the use of pigeon machines through their use in shotgun shooting but primarily, as an airgun hunter, I noticed a few things pertaining to how the birds reacted towards them. Admittedly when the machines were first used, birds absolutely zoomed into the area. Presumably they work because of the movement of the 'whirling' birds on the machine, in theory resembling birds 'circling' maybe to land or lifting off jostling for position over an area heavy with feed. The pigeon machine is used with traditional deeks on the ground and where you set it in relation to the pattern is personal choice or judged by experience. Most set it to the rear and to the side. Now the thing I noticed was birds that 'snuck' in under the noses of the shotgunners without detection would actually fly at the machine and land underneath. Strange behaviour or some natural feeding characteristic or both. I prefer to think the birds come zooming in to get under the 'flying' birds circling above to get at what is presumably a food rich area underneath. Birds that do this will often sit longer – possibly because they're puzzled at the birds that are still circling overhead and the fact there's probably nothing much of interest where it's landed.

So if using one of these machines, watch for this, but also watch for birds landing more conventionally into the pattern. It's now generally accepted the machines, in some areas, are losing effectiveness. I think this will come and go with seasons and as new birds come along with each and every year. In other words, like other quarry species, some birds have learned to stay away because they associate them with danger, possibly being shot at in the past but ones that have been lucky enough to be missed. The pigeon soon wise up. If you're keen, get yourself one as they don't cost the earth and they certainly, at times, will work. But as with most things, experience will show when and when not to use them.

Special care and attention always needs to be taken when shooting near or around livestock

Incidentally, the rotary pigeon machine often attracts crows. Unfortunately crows tend to lazily float over the area watching more than the sometimes-foolhardy woodie, and can infuriatingly glide off as lazily as they first arrived. However, let's leave the 'machines', and return to more traditional decoying methods. What can often bring woodies down to a pattern is a crow decoy placed well back at the outside edge of the birds. This is known as a 'confidence deek' and works to give woodies a feeling of security as it does to fool the crow one of its kind has found something edible. It gets the nickname of a 'confidence deek' as every animal knows how wary the crow is, and if woodies see a crow looking comfortable on the ground then the area must be safe.

Another useful device to use with decoys is a floater. This is just an extending pole that has a cradle on the end. Onto this you 'set' a dead pigeon with wings outstretched as if it was 'floating' down to join the others on the ground. You can also use an EVA foam silhouette deek if you've no naturals. You can even mount a crow on the floater. Whichever you use, in any sort of a breeze, they bounce and sway about resembling a bird about to join the flock below. Needless to say it pays to position the floater to the back, even quite well behind the main decoy pattern depending on conditions and area being shot over.

Come October those that have survived will have probably seen a lot of pigeon machines and been shot at by traditional methods so will associate them with danger. This is where a very small tight decoy pattern and a couple of floaters can be very effective. While on the subject of floaters, it's this movement that attracts other birds in when using these decoys as the wind raises and lowers the floater giving it a natural look. That's why you can often see these decoy set-ups referred to as 'bouncers'. You can now get electronically operated floaters that even flap their wings as if landing. Some that can be set with a timer to flap every so often. Also 'peckers' that as the name suggest peck at the ground, operated by battery – all clever stuff, and I'm sure other ingenious deeks will be developed and designed and all will be useful at times. But even simple half body shell deeks placed on their stakes rocking in the breeze can often be enough to trigger response from birds flying overhead.

And though at times infuriatingly difficult, decoying woodies down to the air rifle is now amongst my favourite form of airgun hunting, especially through autumn into winter. I can't describe the buzz you get as you'll need to be out there and experience the feeling for yourself as they fly over, then circle around to take another look at the deeks on the ground. Your heart will be in your mouth as you wait for them to drop into the pattern. Sometimes they touch down but take off as soon as their feet hit the ground but they'll do another circuit of the field before returning to land hopefully this time with more confidence. Don't try to watch them fly around, just follow them with your ears as you'll soon know when they've come back. It might be the clapping and whistling sound of wings or glimpse of shadow and dark shapes sweeping overhead but then they're back and it's your opportunity to put the pellet into the target.

Though using established and traditional decoy patterns are a good starting point and will produce results, experiment with your own if you're not having much luck. One of my favourites is to huddle a small group of no more than half a dozen together near the base of a sitty tree or in a quiet corner of a field. Be in a hide within range and birds often fly in but veer away from the pattern to sit in the nearest tree to watch the area from above that's if they don't land next to the deeks. Remember, it's natural for the birds to be seen feeding at the base of trees, especially come the autumn into winter when berries, beech mast or nuts are falling. If coming in but preferring the safety first approach and landing in the tree – a good bag can be had taking them from the branches in this way. In effect you've created an 'artificial' but inviting sitty-tree. If you prefer, a few lofted birds in the closest tree to the pattern can be used as an added attractor.

Annoying Habits

As mentioned at the very start of this section, another method to use with decoys is one of annoyance. This is used to trigger the attack and mobbing instinct familiar to all corvids – especially magpies, crows and to some extent jays. The method couldn't be more straightforward as you simply locate a nest area or territory you've seen birds regularly frequent after feeding and position a little owl, kestrel or similar raptor. Some even have had success with teddy bears with the target trigger presumably being the big glassy eyes staring out of the trees. You can position the deek on a pole which I prefer to put close to cover in a position the corvids will have chance to sit on a branch to call angrily at this intruder. It's at this stage you can pick them off and of course it hardly needs saying you need to shoot from a well-hidden shooting position. This is also a shooting situation where the use of the suitable quarry call can be employed to further agitate the birds into making a foolhardy mistake! There'll be more on the 'conventional' use of decoys for corvids in the Baiting Down section.

So as you can see, many uses for decoys and I'm sure many will agree that it's definitely a case of 'never leave home without your plastic!'

BAITING DOWN – CORVIDS

This is the most popular method for bringing wary corvids such as crows and magpies within range. But in lean hard times even woodies, collared doves and squirrels can be brought to suitable bait, as of course can rats which has been dealt with in Quarry Files. As a matter of interest, some reckon they have success using 'baiting techniques' for rooks but in my experience the rook is too clever for that and can seemingly always find a meal somewhere safer.

In its simplest form you put out suitable bait – which for corvids is most often a slit open rabbit – wait in a well-hidden shooting position (usually a hide) and pick them off as they come to the bait.

However, a much more methodical and thoughtful approach is required if the hunter is to reap the most for his efforts – which in the case of baiting down corvids – none the least is the fact you need to be up well before dawn as the magpie and crow are surely, like their close relatives, veritable insomniacs of the bird world.

To get up to use this method in the depths of winter takes commitment. And it's during this period that this method really comes into its own because like other species, corvids find food harder to find. But, don't despair; if you enjoy a lie in, when the birds have reared young it becomes very effective again from midsummer onwards at any time of day. Evening sessions can also be very productive in summer before the sun drops too low.

In fact starting a 'baiting' campaign again once the birds have reared young can be deadly. Young magpies and crows are surprisingly naive and can be caught out nearly as soon as they've sampled their first found free meal – especially if you're waiting to greet them with some lead that is!

Reason for the lull in early springtime before the method becomes 'killer' again in the summer is although it seems maggies and crows are everywhere you look on your shoot; come late February and certainly by early March both species will have paired off and not be spending as long over the fields looking for food. Much of their time is spent in breeding pairs rebuilding nests and preparing to rear young. And as more and more of these nest sites are in town gardens and cities – a major reason you now generally see less of them over the open countryside.

Incidentally, in some parts of the country, at certain times, rabbits can be quite hard to target and shoot, especially for use as bait. To save the effort or indeed the waste of good rabbit meat, you can use pet food or chum mixer. Unfortunately these make easy pickings for the birds to grab and quickly fly off with. Better still – when I can find them – I'll use road kill rabbits as bait. However, you can try a makeshift bird's nest using straw or scrunched up dying foliage and put out a few hen's eggs. Corvids

Baiting down is a deadly effective technique for bringing corvids such as crows within range

are used to raiding any nest including ground-nesting birds so it isn't unnatural for them to find food like this. A trick that's worked for me is to use at least one white duck egg with a couple of hen's eggs – the duck egg helping the bait become more visible. Also a trick is to put down cling film and crack open one of the eggs to expose the contents to make it even more appetising. If there's one thing these egg robbing corvids detest it is another of their kind getting to the spoils first. Alternatively, a piece of raw bloody liver, the rubbery the better nailed down onto a log or fencepost so it can't be dragged off also brings in the corvids. The texture of the meat isn't easy for them to break up so they have to work to get pieces off, giving you more time to target them.

But it must be said a dead rabbit is by far the best. Preferably 'bait up' in an area already regularly frequented by the targeted species. And you need to bait an area for a good few days before shooting – better still a week or more so the corvids will get used to finding free meals but just as importantly be confident feeding there. Then when you've got the birds feeling the freebie dining area is a safe place, you simply get yourself into position before feeding time to pick off the carrion eating critters. A major advantage of this method is it allows you to dictate the range the quarry is to be targeted. Obviously, before the baiting out process begins, you'll need to have either built a semi-permanent, natural hide or have left a pop-up portable hide in position in readiness for use. This has to be accepted by the local corvids as a natural part of the scene. And as both the magpie and crow are always moving around looking for food very early means you need to be ready and waiting in the hide with fresh bait in position even earlier. Once you're in position with your cross hairs trained on the bait, you should-n't have long to wait until a chack, chack, chack will herald the magpies' arrival. But at times they can arrive as silently as the crow. Whichever way they come, they will usually land away from the bait then hop up to it when they've had a look around to check the area is safe. As magpies rarely travel solo, they rarely come to the bait alone and it's best to let a few start tucking in before starting to shoot. When using slit open rabbit – don't empty too much of the rabbit's innards out onto the ground. If you do the birds can get at it too quickly and be away with the 'dissected delicacies', leaving a gutted and less attractive bait. The eyes seem to be a particular favourite and once taken, a dead rabbit can soon become 'spent' and the bait rendered quite ineffective. There also seems to be a pecking order amongst a group of magpies. A few birds may dig into the rabbit but often one will stand nearby as if waiting its turn. As the other bird or birds will be moving and ripping at the bait the static bird is the one to target.

You can also use decoys to make the scene look more natural but I feel rather than setting a scene what you're actually doing is creating a pack mentality. A situation where the birds arriving want to join in before everything has gone. Whatever it is, a few sensibly placed magpie deeks can work wonders.

When I use a magpie 'deek', I place it right next to the bait with its beak in the open slit. This can have others flying straight onto the bait to join in for the easy meal as their greed seemingly overtakes the usual cautious nature. Alternatively position one in a nearby tree.

Now the crow is a different matter altogether. The crow will more often than not just appear silently as if from nowhere to land upon the bait filling your scope with a black flurry of wings. At others it's deafening as you hear them calling from around the shooting position but none in plain view. Then again, you might experience what I term 'the long walk' approach. This is where you'll see the birds land out in the field and walk slowly forward pecking at nothing in particular then walking back on themselves in a very strange display of behaviour. Whether this is because they're not that hungry or are suspicious – which can be the case if the bait is positioned too close to heavy cover such as a thick hedge or treeline – is debatable. In this and other similar scenarios the hunter needs to be patient and wait.

Just as infuriatingly they might circle overhead, incessantly making that distinctive 'kaarr' call with eyes scanning the area for anything untoward down below. If you're experiencing these situations of 'hesitancy' there are ways to give the black stuff a feeling of security. The best by far is to use the 'confidence' deek trick. But anything that seems wrong with the decoy, usually the fact it doesn't quite look 'realistic' enough will put the birds off. In the past I'd 'weather' my traditional plastic deeks so they lost the shine but now we have deeks including magpies and of course woodies covered in a soft fibre that makes them look remarkably realistic. As previously outlined, these are known as 'flocked' decoys, but even then, when specifically targeting the crow, unlike the magpie, positioning can have a marked effect on how other crows react. Some advocate putting the deek right next to the bait, others say it works better put well to one side. Both ways work on their day. Maybe the crow's not in the mood for a scrap so it won't go near the bait until the other leaves or if hungry enough isn't fussed so decides it wants to dive straight in. Whatever you're experiencing, wherever you place the decoy stick with it as there's no way you can leave the hide and expect any more action in a hurry – not from crows that's for sure. But, when it works, the extra attraction obviously installs false security in the crow flying over – proof that the crow is even seen by other crows as the cautious creature it is. If you really take to crow shooting you can even put out a pattern of crow deeks. But note unlike woodies crows don't give each other much room to feed as if one has found food, the others want to get to it as well. Some have success using this trick using a 'smattering' of crow deeks, and also placing a rabbit or even using dead pigeon as bait near the pattern. Again, all are methods that are worth trying. And as with decoying woodies, there are pecking decoys and flappers available for the dedicated 'crowman'. And lets not forget there's no better deek than a 'dead natural' so if you shoot a crow, set it out using a chin stick.

Incidentally I've already mentioned the use of calls for squirrels and some shooters swear by crow and magpie calls. If used correctly in conjunction with a deek they'll even be answered and they do work. Over used and used incorrectly and the corvids soon know that the 'sound' wasn't right. Calls are designed to either reassure quarry that it's safe to land or annoy by imitating the territorial challenge call of the species the call is intended for. Some imitate distress calls of the quarry's prey such as a young rabbit or mouse could possibly lure a crow or magpie into range. They're not only for fox shooters and are another accessory to consider for the kit bag but also until you're sure you've got the knack of using them – stick to the deeks and bait.

Another trick if you have one on your shoot is to position yourself under an old tractor-trailer; farmers often leave them out on the side of tracks. The bonus of this is it's something already accepted by the birds on the shoot. No problems from being seen from above but obviously you'll need to build a screen of camo to totally conceal you hidden beneath. In this scenario I use another trick, which is to put out the 'main' bait as usual but also put a few, and I mean a few scraps of pet food, bacon rind, chum mixer – anything that only acts as an appetiser on top of the trailer. Then I can hear birds landing above me. They will then more often than not move onto the bait. While magpies can make their familiar noisy arrival, a thud above usually signals a crow has arrived. Fast galloping 'footsteps' (or should that be claw steps) mean magpies have arrived quietly yet are clattering quickly around as they compete for the scraps you've left out above.

As mentioned, one of the bonuses of this method is you can position the bait at the exact same zero of your combo. And over this distance of 30 – 40yds I choose a precharged .177 with a low light scope for the early morning work as in winter it seems to take an age for the light levels to rise.

Now all this is fine on arable land but what of airgunners who have land devoid of much cover such as moorlands. Here don't be deterred as I've found baiting down to be just if not more effective. Here magpies and especially crows can be found in great abundance, living off the 'dead' of the land so to speak as they're used to finding stillborn lambs, dead sheep etc.

When shooting on barren landscapes such as moors cover for the hide can be difficult to find but a few hide poles with one of the darker autumnal pattern camo netting leant against a dry stonewall or even around fencing will usually conceal you well enough to make the effort worth your while.

Needless to say I'm sure you can appreciate that baiting an area for suitable quarry can reap rich rewards for the patient hunter.

So there you have it – Hunting Techniques. In this chapter I've outlined more methods than most hunters will ever get to try and in some cases depending on the type of land you're allowed to shoot over – some methods aren't going to be viable to use. In fact, it's fair to say most airgun hunters shoot over pastureland, and if lucky enough you might get the chance of a shoot through a large mature wood. Some are unfortunate in the fact they have mainly moorland at their disposal. Often harsh and bleak areas especially in winter. I've shot all over the UK and due to my geographical position I regularly get up onto the Pennines, down to the lovely lush land of Shropshire, over to the rolling and wonderful country of Wales and back to the relatively flat open mixed countryside or even the industrial wastelands that scar some parts of the North West.

Though I have my obvious preferences, each area sets the airgun hunter a challenge of which it's always up to the individual to accept and make the most of.

Even if you don't get to try all the techniques mentioned you'd surely get a chance to try your hand at most. Hopefully as you become more proficient you'll quite possibly start to develop tactics of your own. And we haven't even looked at shooting 'after hours' yet.

Chapter 13
Shooting at Night

While there was once only one way to hunt at night, now with advancements in technology the 'night hunter' now has a choice. Either to target quarry with an artificial light source (lamping) or using a dedicated Nightvision Riflescope. Firstly the traditional method.

LAMPING

Sport shooters and pest controllers, be they fullbore foxers to the old village rabbit catcher with his trusty old .22 rimmy (and let's not forget 'the less unscrupulous' poachers) have been targeting quarry at night using lights for many a moon – excuse the pun. In the early days these were homemade light sources – from big searchlights mounted on ex-Army Land Rovers, cumbersome torches strapped under barrels for ratting and gun lamps made up of bits acquired from old motor vehicles. Motorbike headlamps and batteries were favoured with wires and other such components all ingeniously cobbled together to have the enterprising shooter emerge triumphant from the garden shed with a contraption to search out scut tails in the dark. And even now, as with the situation in those early days, the night shooter was always striving to find kit that worked more efficiently. But many a hunting apprenticeship was learned from a son carrying the heavy battery pack for father's lamping trips. Teenage friendships were similarly forged, shooting rats with a lamp or torch.

But it must be remembered that to the non-shooting public, a lamp seen 'scanning' over a field at night must be the work of a poacher or ne'r-do-well. I mention that from the beginning of this chapter as even when you intend to hunt over land you have legal permission to shoot over, always inform the landowner or farmer if you are planning a trip at night. And in certain cases, even put a call into the local police station. It's courtesy and prevents a time-wasting trip out for the local bobby to investigate who could be out and about and what they're up to.

The countryside after dark is a completely different world to the one you see in daylight. Sounds are not only magnified but as certain animals and birds go about their nocturnal activities, strange noises can at first be unnerving to the newcomer to night shooting. If so, go with a shooting partner, but if you've served your apprenticeship operating the lamp for experienced night hunters – you'll already be pretty clued up – so no worries. But, never be complacent. Consider this saying – 'always be properly equipped to shoot and hunt effectively, efficiently and safely' – that could never be more appropriate than at night. In fact, for reasons of safety always let someone know where you are going – a family relative, friend, wife or girlfriend – and when you expect to be due back. Unfortunately, accidents can and do happen, and at night if you're not prepared it could have disastrous consequences.

Required Kit

We mainly have Deben Group Industries Ltd to thank for many of today's 'lamping' innovations, as they are a company who've pioneered the design of lamping kits in turn helping the sport become more established, especially amongst airgunners. Lighter lamps and battery packs, lamps of varying intensity, some with optional dimmer switches, stock mountable on/off switches with or without dimmer control, different battery pack options including belt mounted, case with shoulder strap, compact enough for carrying in a jacket pocket or even designed to be 'mountable' on the rifle stock! Then of course there's choice of coloured filters, different type and power of bulbs – the lot.

Then came along other companies such as Cluson Engineering Limited, and a whole industry devoted to night shooting equipment began and one that flourishes to this very day.

And although we'll see later in this section, while in some case using a dedicated Nightvision (NV) Riflescope is a better option for night shooting or to use another term – shooting in a 'lightless' area – the traditional night time walk with lamp and air rifle searching the autumn fields for rabbits is still a very challenging and most rewarding experience.

As we're dealing strictly with air rifles, there are more shooting techniques and opportunities available to the airgunner using the lamp than just shooting at night over fields for rabbits. These amongst others include close range indoor shooting for rats. Due to this, in the following sections I'll deal separately with 'lamping' over fields for rabbits, and using a gun lamp for rat shooting in and around farm buildings. Also due to the fact lamping is done outdoors for rabbits, and often indoors for rats – I'm segmenting this section so it fully details lamping technique for each species – including methods specific to both outdoor and indoor use.

As we progress, you'll come to notice, I often make reference to the use of Nightvision (NV) equipment with traditional lamping kit. The modern day airgun hunter now has the opportunity to take advantage of such useful accessories as a handheld, pocket size NV monocular, and where possible I feel they should. I'm sure even the hardened traditionalist will realise the benefits for observation of an area without disturbing it with light – both indoors and out.

In the Spotlight – Rabbits

A major consideration for using a lamp with an air rifle is range and this alone being the major reason, choosing a suitable lamping kit isn't all about candlepower. Remember, more often than not, you only need to 'spot' quarry at 80–100 yards at the most, not dazzle everything out to 200! For the airgun

hunter, gun mounted lamping kits are plentiful as there are a reasonable amount of companies now making this equipment and though all have various models, they're basically very similar. Their job simply being to illuminate the target thereby enabling the shooter to take an effective shot.

The lamp needs to have a tight, controllable beam, not overly intense – even without a filter. If gun mounted, you want the lamp to be light, unobtrusive as possible so as not to affect the handling of the rifle and of course be easy to use. The last thing you need to be doing is fumbling around searching for switches, or controls at a critical moment. Similarly of concern is loose fitting filter that may fall off

Taking on the rabbit at night is very challenging

Gun mounted lamping kits have come a long way since the early days of cobbled together motorcycle headlights and heavy battery packs

at the least opportune moment and lead attachment points that can easily become disconnected.

Incidentally, lamps classed as 'gun mounted' are more often than not affixed onto the scope via a scope mount adaptor that quickly clips, or clamps, onto the body tube of the scope.

In relation to lamping kit – buy from the reputable brand leaders and you won't go far wrong. As part of any hunter's standard 'lamping kit', I'd always recommend you take along a spare bulb or two, spare battery fuses, couple of different coloured lamp filters for diffusing the light down if rabbits are twitchy or difficult to spot on a 'dimmed' un-filtered white beam.

Incidentally, there's also another very good reason to use a red filter on a lamp but not so often written about so I'll take the opportunity here to explain. While 'white' light to some extent shines back off the rabbit's eyes, you'll see a much more pronounced red glow from the animal's retina when using a light with red filter. This makes rabbits far easier to spot amongst scrub and when within range, aids you as a useful reference point to put the pellet into the headshot kill-zone. So filters – very much essentials for spotting as they are for diffusing a harsh white light.

Now to the powerhouse – always ensure the battery's had a full charge before setting out. And remember a 6volt battery pack and lamping kit gives less 'run time' than a 12V – but the larger battery does of course tend to be heavier.

Whichever you use, if your budget stretches, take a spare battery pack and leave it in the car should it be needed. If your lamping kit can be boosted with one, take the vehicle charger out as well. Apart from that, there are other pieces of kit you'll find useful for all manner of night shooting. A small torch such as a mini-maglite or better still a compact headlight. In fact I highly recommend you keep a LED torch in a pocket or on a lanyard (tucked into your shirt) around your neck so it's close to hand at all times. Great for little jobs you don't need to use the main lamp for. Small button size LED lights or compact LED torches mentioned previously are very handy for changing/re-filling magazines or reloading a single-shot in the dark. But here I must say a multi-shot air rifle at night is a big bonus. Carry a few pre-filled spare magazines and you'll be sorted for all but the longest of forays. A small roll of camo or insulation tape is useful for securing 'trailing' leads out of the way and if you get a troublesome connection on your kit, it'll be handy to bind it together. Here again, your Multi-Tool will come in handy, not only because a sharp blade and scissors are always useful, but also the pliers can help you sort electrical connections.

For the rabbits you bag, then you'll need a knife, string, Para-cord or game carrier to aid carrying. That is if you haven't mastered the art of 'hocking'. This is threading a back leg through a slit carefully cut in the lower part of the other back leg, this allows the rabbit to be 'hung' on a branch to cool. If you can't or haven't mastered this 'trick' in daylight – tie the back legs up with string or Para cord and similarly hang the rabbits to cool on a gate or fencepost until you pass back that way.

And of course, once you've done your 'rounds' and collected them up, a rucksack (with plastic bin bag liner) is very useful to carry them away in. Some recommend you paunch (gut) them in the field as this is less weight to carry off the shoot. But if you don't shoot everything that hops within range, and only take a 'few' for the pot, taking a 'rucky' specifically for this purpose isn't strictly necessary.

Keep some wet wipes in a jacket pocket to keep your hands, knife and gun clean. These are useful for removing fresh blood splashes off metal – but once home, use a suitable silicon oil wipe. Talking of which, never forget cleanliness when dealing with any situation where an accidental cut or spilt blood is involved, and yes, here's when you also might welcome the antiseptic spray and plasters in your first aid kit. And remember – a mobile phone can be a life saver. As I always say, you can switch it off when actively hunting, but it's your contact for help should it be needed. It might be because the vehicle you arrived in has broken down or got caught in mud. Never presume anything and that's why an emergency whistle is another back up safety and contact device to have with you. So there's the kit, but before we look at its use a quick word on something that many shooters tend to forget.

As the traditional lamping season passes through autumn into winter, the temperatures at night can drop suddenly and surprisingly low – so dress accordingly. Whether you wear a facemask and gloves is up to the individual. At night, during the colder months, there is reason to use them for keeping warm as wind can soon chill the face and numb the hands. As for concealment, on a dark relatively moonless night they're not essential. I may or may not wear them depending on situation but I do tend to find they help 'focus me' into 'hunter mode' and in turn help me shoot with more confidence. However, and I know I'm getting ahead of myself, if using a Nightvision scope on a night with moonlight I would recommend you do. Thermal black balaclava and black fingerless gloves will suffice, it doesn't need to be camo, but certainly dark enough to hide the white face and hands. I know many may scoff at this but you'll soon realise a rabbit can often react to seeing a white face approaching – if there's any light, even from a slight moon, it'll reflect off the face and hands. But again, it's up to personal choice.

As sound carries much further at night even more care must be taken with your movement. Zips and buckles you hardly notice in the day can sound like metal gates rattling in the wind in the still of the night. Another no-no is clothing that rustles.

Also, the only sure way of walking more quietly at night is to lift the feet higher than normal and place the feet down slowly and carefully. Reason being you can't see to be sure of the terrain as you can during the day. Place them down cautiously, there's no need to rush and you want to know the ground's still flat not find yourself going down in a rabbit hole, furrow or ditch. Walking over terrain as unobtrusively as possible really is an art form in itself. But one that can and should be mastered!

231

Note this has been dealt with in-depth in the relevant sections elsewhere in this book pertaining to the correct way to move across land. What should be addressed here is not to overly exert yourself in the process of your night hunt. If you do, by the time you reach any quarry, your pulse will be racing, you'll be breathing heavy, resulting in a very unsteady, shaky aim. Always be prepared to rest when needed before carrying on, and certainly know when to call an end to a hunting foray. Also, don't try to cover too much ground. Better to cover a reasonable amount well, while shooting on top form than cover a lot but shooting and generally performing well below par due to tiredness and over exertion. You might think you're fit, but be sensible and know your limits.

Now a note on practising with the lamp: as familiar as you are with your combo, it will at first feel strange shooting at night with the light illuminating the target. First problem will be head position to look through scope and the next will definitely be rangefinding. I don't recommend you shoot on your back garden range after dark as neighbours won't take kindly to this even if they tolerate some daytime zeroing and practice sessions. Preferably get out on a quiet part of the shoot, one usually barren of rabbit activity and practice at night on a few knockdown targets. Set out a small course, three or four put out at staggered intervals. And don't give yourself the added bonus of knowing ranges from set positions or range markers. This defeats the object. Once set, start from approximately 100 yards from the first target, walking up and actually practice your lamping routine. Once you feel you're within range try a shot. Don't take forever in taking it as few bunnies just sit there as if dazed by light. Shoulder the rifle, put the lamp on, take aim and shoot. This will soon get you up to the required skill required. You may think this a waste of time but believe me not half as much as going out night after night only to miss every opportunity that presents itself. As you practise and familiarise yourself with the lamp and shooting in these 'simulated real-life' conditions, you'll really begin to appreciate judging range can be very deceptive with artificial light. This is because light is being directed at the target from your shooting position and not coming from all around, as in daylight. This tunnel of light can make targets look further than they actually are. Some experience the opposite – that targets seem closer than they actually are. Obviously lamping conditions can affect different people's senses and perceptions of distance in different ways. And practice is the only way to master this visual distortion. Another 'trick' is to use a laser in the set-up as detailed earlier in the book as a reference for quick range estimation. I must admit I use these in certain indoor shooting situations and especially with NV scopes I find them a godsend. But for the traditional art of lamping rabbits – dedicated practice should soon have you acquire the skill to judge without one. And before leaving the subject of range, a big no-no is to try long-range shots at night, it's irresponsible and unsporting. If you can't 'stalk' closer – leave 'em until another night.

Here a reminder on safety and safe shooting practice. All that holds true in the day must be strictly and possibly scrutinised more closely when shooting at night. Though you are using a relatively low powered rifle, always ensure the backstop is safe behind the target. Though tempting, don't pot a rabbit on the brow of a hill if you aren't 100% sure there can't be any person or for that matter a domestic or farm animal over that hill. Know your shooting ground, paths thoroughfares, anywhere someone might 'just appear' don't go there at night. Remember, safe shooting at all times.

So now – the method: firstly, I'm presuming you know your shoot well and have a good idea of where the rabbits feed. Even so go at dusk without the rifle and observe the area. Watch from a distance and you'll see the rabbits and which fields they venture into. If you want to really reconnoitre the area at night, then invest in a pair of Nightvision (NV) binoculars. The knowledge you'll learn observing various areas of the shoot with NV is priceless. A small monocular is handy to have with you while out shooting, but a pair of good quality Gen 1+ NV binos is far better for this type of dedicated observation.

Compact headlights and torches – accessories you'll find invaluable for night shooting

First major no-no is never overuse the lamp or to go clumping straight into a field you 'presume' will contain rabbits. For this reason I now always recommend the airgun hunter use a NV observation aid such as a compact monocular to examine the area he's planning on operating over. At risk of sounding like an 'NV sales rep', believe me when I say, in the time I've incorporated one into my lamping kit and routine it's revolutionised my night hunting.

Not all areas will be overrun with nocturnal feeders, and after a few days checking the fields, warrens, feeding spots, runs and hedgerows, a few hours at various times of the night (if you can spare the time) will show if you should be out an hour after last light or the wee early hours of the morning. Then, once all is established, it's kit together, and off into the area you've assessed rabbits most likely to be feeding.

Everything you've previously read about stalking holds true when lamping – if anything doubly so. Be especially mindful of wind direction because at night the rabbit will be relying heavily on its sense of smell and hearing. Before you use the lamp you should have one major bonus on your side. They most likely haven't seen your approach. This is where stopping at regularly intervals for a quick shufty through the NV monocular can be a great bonus. Granted, before these came along shooters 'lamped' rabbits very successfully at night but they do give you an edge. When you spot the feeding rabbits, your approach should begin with even greater care. Incidentally, when looking through a NV device quarry can look a lot closer or further than it actually is. So don't overly rely on it. Let the observation unit aid you in two things. Spotting the rabbits that appear to be 'stalkable', and to plot your route across the area between you and a suitable shooting position. Never try to get too close without quickly scanning the area with the lamp. This may seem strange as you have the opportunity to watch 'undetected' but this first quick sweep 'light on, light off' will allow you to determine how twitchy the rabbits are and where they will now be in relation to the distance you've travelled. Whether using an NV device or not, the optimum way to use the lamp for detecting rabbits is the same. Don't as some advise continually bring the rifle up to the shoulder, switching the lamp on, scanning around looking through the scope to observe. Not only will this quickly become tiring on the arms, but you'll also miss spotting a lot of rabbits – even if using a scope with a good width of view.

The way I've found suits me is to hold the right arm at 90 degrees with the rifle cradled in your arm and against your body pointed forward. It should be resting along the inside of the right forearm with the right hand holding the underside of the stock just forward of the trigger guard.

The left should be holding the rifle at the forend in a position to bring the rifle to bear when required, with the thumb over the stock mounted on/off switch. This allows you to easily operate the lamp switch and 'sweep' the light from left to right without bringing the rifle up to your shoulder. This allows you to direct the beam in the exact places you want it to shine and keeps the strain off your arm muscles. Rabbits within reach of the light beam will be detected by the light reflecting back showing red in the animal's eyes – remember the importance of the red filter. If they're out in more open ground with their backs to you or heads down feeding you might however only spot them in part profile. But once spotted switch the lamp off immediately, and stalk slowly towards the target.

In the dark you might think you're heading in the right direction, but unless you've also picked out a landmark on the horizon, clearly silhouetted in front of you, it can be surprisingly easy to stray 'off' the line of approach. So, on first pass of the light, look for four major things – closest target to set zero, other potential targets close by, the state of alertness of all the rabbits in the bunch and of course check the terrain.

This is a most crucial moment. I always recommend the hunter quickly switch off the lamp and stop to gather composure and calm nerves as adrenalin will be pumping. If you've approximated 60, 70 yards or beyond to the target, when ready to move on, count your steps until you've counted off enough to approximately bring you within 25 yards of the target. Then, move forward a tad further depending on the initial range judged. When you flick on the light you'll more often than not still be at the range you thought you would be before you moved forward the extra. Because you're moving slowly, the distance of your pace is less, so you cover less ground than when walking in the daylight. Also, rabbits, even if not overly twitchy have a habit of shuffling around and moving away from anything detected in the field. I'd recommend you steady yourself, adopt the standing or preferably if the terrain allows the more stable kneeling position, bring the rifle up to your shoulder, flick on the lamp, choose your target through the scope and without too much dithering take the shot. OK, you missed or hopefully you've knocked your first rabbit over, but as soon as you see miss or hit as long as it isn't a wounding turn the lamp off immediately. This is where an NV monocular comes in handy

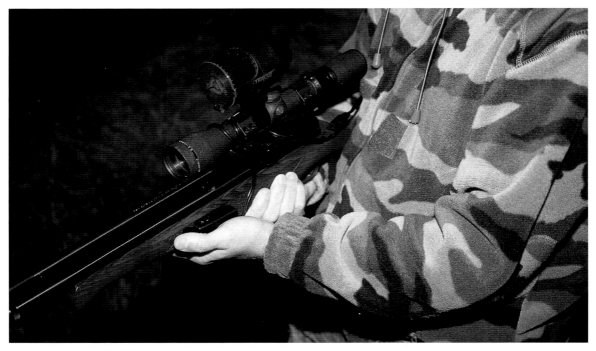

This 'relaxed' way of holding the rifle for searching with the lamp keeps the strain off the arm muscles

again as you can use the unit to assess the situation with other quarry. If other rabbits were in the proximity, they can either have fled for cover, whilst some might even hang around bolt upright, ears pricked up, wondering what happened. Your actions at this moment could give you another chance of a shot or a short stalk for a shot. Experience will show whether that's on the cards or you need to retrieve the prize and hang or hock it for collection later. Don't wander off aimlessly in another direction in search of any other rabbits before retrieval, as you'll not find the first rabbit you've shot. Not without much searching and disturbing the area with light.

So a quick recap. Never overuse the lamp, to prevent spooking quarry and save your nightvision. A tip on regaining the latter if you inadvertently catch a flash of the light is to look at the sky, look at the floor and then look at the horizon. Try it – it works!

When rabbits are running and twitchy don't follow, it's more often than not a pointless exercise. Try another area or tactic. One is to cut off the rabbits' escape route. This may sound strange but rabbits really are creatures of habit. Why do you think they make such well-worn runs out into the fields. If really late, the rabbits could well be a long way from the main warrens or boltholes. If the wind is in your favour approach from the warren along the rabbit runs. Incidentally, the direction of the flattened grass in the run will often help indicate which way the rabbit headed and experience will even help you determine how fresh a rabbit run is. So, when you find the 'far feeders' this method of approach and the light hitting them from your position will cause confusion. Often, rather than risk bolting past you for the cover (which you are cutting them off from) at seeing the light they'll often squat down low and as flat to the ground as possible.

Another factor that will have bearing on results are the weather conditions. If there's the risk of fog or even a light mist coming down that night – at ground level this can cause infuriating bounce back from the lamp making spotting very difficult. Most say ideal conditions are a cloudy, moonless night with some wind and a light drizzle! Well, as for the latter, living and lamping in the North of England, drizzle can often be the norm at night, especially during the latter part of the year. Whether it does help mask the sound of your approach is debatable, but you shouldn't need to rely on anything overpowering the sound you 'shouldn't' be making anyway. But, on nights with drizzle, rabbits aren't troubled and go about their nightly routine – they're used to the elements anyway. As for cloud cover, I'm not one convinced a sky heavy with cloud is off such high importance. For a start ambient light from a partial moon and a few stars can be a bonus, especially for using the NV monocular. Obviously you don't want a crystal clear, cloudless, still night with a full moon but you certainly don't always need a total blackout. And consider this. Years ago there weren't as many streetlights, factory and workplace security floodlights or even house lights to light up a night sky. Also, in some country areas, streetlights used to be switched off very late on to conserve power. Now with rising crime, lights are everywhere and for people's security and safety that's a good thing. However, when the cloudbase is really low all those lights actually reflect down making the ground lighter – creating an orange tinted glow. Unless you're in the Outer Hebrides you're then faced with being seen quite easily from a rabbit's 'ground view' as your silhouette is visible in the 'glow' no matter how well you conceal yourself. Food for thought on weather conditions eh?

Other variables to consider are which fields hold sheep or cattle. A lone horse can be a nightmare. Livestock such as cows will come and see what you're up to and sheep being sheep will either charge round or sit around just getting in the way. No use shooting fields with long grass or over land with too many ridges to cross either. Also know what the farmer has planned, no use walking carefully over to a far field to discover the tractors out late with the roller flattening grass or he's working late cutting or trimming hedge side foliage!

Favourite areas are freshly cut grass fields, a lovely scent in the air and the rabbits relatively easy to spot at medium range even without the lamp. Stubble fields are hard to walk over silently but do attract the rabbits. If you can, walk around the perimeter of the stubble field you might well spot a few and be able to keep a hedge or some such cover behind you therefore helping conceal appearing in silhouette.

Always be prepared to put in a lot of effort and don't be put off by the times you'll come home empty handed. Don't presume you're going to live out the 'fantasies' you've probably so often read about in some 'armchair' articles. Unfortunately, they're largely written to entertain – not inform. Suffice to say lamping with an air rifle isn't as simple or easy as many would have you believe. And always alternate shooting areas; never go to the same place repeatedly – rabbits survive because they wise up quickly to an area they soon come to know holds potential danger.

Now to other ways with lamps: The airgunner can even use a simple headlamp, either powered with batteries in a head mounted pack or for longer duration attached up to a belt mounted battery pack. If you're fortunate enough to be driven around the shoot in a 4 × 4, there are remote operated vehicle mounted lamps, or simply use the gun mounted lamp to scour the area within range, out from the sides of the track or fields you're travelling over.

A ride around a suitable field at the right time of year can bring easy pickings until they learn to scarper at the rumble of the vehicle.

As mentioned earlier – if unsure about going it alone, then shooting with a partner is an option. One operating a handheld lamp while the other shoots. Pairing up in this way you can take it in turns to take the shots. If you try your hand at this method, then establish a set working routine with your shooting partner. Lamp man spots – shooter shoots. The lamp man should keep the main beam off any rabbit spotted until within range so the shooter has a clear and hopefully straightforward shot when they arrive. He should never walk behind the shooter as this can cause the lamp to produce glare in the eyepiece of the scope making targeting nigh on impossible. Slightly to the front, but obviously out of the line of fire, and keeping to one side, usually the left is the name of the lamp man's game. Also, as you're not dealing in mega-searchlights, why take a big light with a long duration cumbersome battery pack. Most cordless re-chargeable hand held lamps will have enough power for the duration of a usual session. If not, take two or at least a spare fully charged battery, and leave one at a convenient pick up point to swap over if one runs low. It's also useful to communicate with hand signals to cut down the need to verbally tell each other of opportunities spotted, time to stop, or change a line of approach. If verbal communication is needed, do so in whispers.

Incidentally, although scopes have been dealt with in previous chapters it's worth looking at a few factors pertaining to optics best suited to lamping. You've probably read that you need a scope with a large objective lens. This isn't strictly true because any quality scope will afford you enough light transmission to target your quarry when using a gun lamp. Of more importance is you have a scope with a wide field of view and one that doesn't have overly thin cross hairs that can get lost in the sight picture. If using a general specification 3 – 9 × 40 scope, winding the magnification down to 3 or 4 × will give a reasonably wide field of view enabling you to quickly find the target in the sight picture.

Now to a subject of some contention: personally I'd say never take a shot at a rabbit on the move. I cringe when I hear people 'brag' they can 'regularly' shoot rabbits running using an air rifle. Always go for the headshot, a clean kill is imperative as you'll never find a wounded 'runner' at night without a dog. Don't get frustrated as you will find rabbits that hold in the lamp. So why educate ones into putting the equation together that 'you + light + sound of pellet whistling past = danger'. They'll be much more twitchy the next time you go out. Talking of which, if the rabbits do seem overly twitchy or there's few around where your observation has told you otherwise. It could well be that a fox has been out that night already. As I mentioned in a previous chapter, foxes at times can leave an extremely distinguishable aroma. Much worse than 'cat wee', and trust me you'll know when you smell it.

Unfortunately, on occasions such as this rabbits can be very unpredictable. They could re-emerge from their burrows sooner than expected or stay hidden for a good few hours. When faced with this situation, depending on how much time you have, I'd recommend the hunter try a totally different area or maybe better to return another night.

And don't get too complacent or lackadaisical, know your hunting area and watch how you go. Stumbling into a ditch or tripping on rough ground isn't recommended with a loaded rifle. One very experienced airgun hunter of my acquaintance did this and got away with snapping the lovely walnut stock of his favourite hunting rifle. I say lucky, as it could have been his leg or worse!

Well, that's it for outdoor bunny bashing with the lamp but of all hunting methods when you get it right it can be one of the most rewarding. Equally though one of the most frustrating. But like most things, patience and practice will go a long way towards helping you achieve the ultimate goal – wild rabbit stew. Now to lamping of the inedible – rats.

In the Spotlight – Rats

Shooting rats with a gun lamp is even less about 'candlepower' than lamping rabbits, usually because it's done at much closer range. But before altering your rifle's zero, it's advisable to have a recce of the shooting location to assess the ranges you'll more likely encounter targets. In some cases it can be as close as 10 yards or even less, others 20yds or if the barn is a high 'hangar' type you might well be best leaving your zero set as normal.

Also invest in one of the gun mounted lamping kits with a variable power control to dim the lamp. If you want to use the lamp you use for bunnies, then certainly get a coloured filter that really does diffuse the brightness of the lamp – red or amber filters being the preferred colours of most hunters and again it'll help you 'spot' those beady eyes.

Also worth a mention are the small low power 'tactical torches'. These can be mounted to the scope

You'll often have to target rats on their well-established 'overhead' routes

body tube like a gun lamp and most have a stock mountable pressure pad on/off switch. Ideal for close range ratting when using baiting out tactics or alternatively even – when permitted – for indoors feral pigeon shooting.

As for a NV monocular – whilst for rabbit shooting you don't strictly need one, neither do you for rat shooting but once they've become very skittish to the lamp – for giving you an edge, I reckon you do. And as they've dramatically come down in price since they first came available to the civilian market, you won't need to pay a fortune for a good compact Gen 1 model. A basic handheld compact device will suffice for ratting but you do require it to have an infrared (IR) illuminator which allows you to see in total darkness and the IR light projected reflects back off the rats eyes, this time seen 'glowing' whitish/green when viewed through the NV device so you have no problem spotting them in the furthest, darkest recess.

Again, a multi-shot PCP air rifle is the ideal choice coupled with a scope with good light gathering properties and of course a wide field of view. Also, a standard red laser sight with rear mounted push button on/off switch or the more versatile stock mountable pressure pad design switch can be useful. Before we get into the pros and cons of the laser in the set up – firstly a look at the method with traditional gun mounted lamp.

As always, location is the key to success. Even a quick look around will show where the rats have been visiting – the signs of rat infestation are droppings, scratchings, teeth marks, chewed sacks or materials and other such damage.

As you are shooting rats 'indoors' in the farm barn you need to be mindful of your personal safety. A farmer knows his own barn and outbuildings like the back of his hand and could easily run around inside in the pitch black. You don't, so check the place over during daylight or with the lights on before you settle in for the night. It's all too easy to walk into a piece of angle iron or trip over a wooden pallet or a welding torch hose.

If actively searching around the inside or outside of the barn, have the rifle half mounted with the butt in your shoulder and the leading hand in a position to hold and both operate the lamp switch and direct the beam. Holding the rifle in this manner means you're able to react more quickly once you spot a rat or just catch the red glint off those beady eyes. Then you can fully mount the rifle and shoot. Rats rarely give you time to think, so quick range estimation and careful aim are needed – quick smart! Now that can be as difficult as it sounds or easy depending on how much activity the rats tolerate, the population present and if they've been shot at before. If searching inside, scan all the beams, girders, nooks and crannies. Rats love overhead structure that can provide 'off the floor' routes to and from areas of interest to them.

To establish which beams or girders rats use to get to and from a food supply is to simply get into a position that allows a good view of the barn interior and just quietly stand or sit, carefully watching and listening. Yes listen, as more often than not you'll hear their sharp claws scratching around in the grain silos, storage bins and the odd scrabbling or squeaks as they pass overhead on a run along a beam. You might actually only see them at the points they enter (drop) into the grain bins or make out the unmistakable silhouette when they travel along the top of beams and girders in the gloomy roof space. And whilst you can target them searching with the gun lamp, a more productive method is to employ an NV device into the technique.

Using the NV monocular you can spot scaly tails without disturbing them with the light. At first you'll get 'sitters'. Sat up aloft on their little perches they'll either be nibbling something or just hunched up watching. Once a 'static' rat is spotted through the NV monocular, carefully put the hi-tech sighting device to one side, bring the rifle up to the shoulder but angle the rifle higher than the rat's position so when you switch the lamp on, the beam doesn't hit the rat full on. Ideally you want the light to point above not shine directly at the rodent as it may immediately run for cover. The optimum way is to slowly bring the beam down to the point your cross hairs reach the rat's kill-zone, then fire.

When you get into the swing of lightless sighting – and this particular 'lamping and gun handling technique', you'll soon have scaly tails thudding down onto the barn floor. But they'll not hold in the light for long and the shooting will become even more demanding as you eventually need to tackle them on the move.

In fact when shooting, take regular breaks to lull the rodents into a false sense of security so they might come out once they've settled again after the initial disturbance. Remember few barns are overly large so you're effectively continually shooting the same area.

If trying your hand at rats on the move, you need to get into a position that allows you the best view of the rat as it travels the beam or girder. Usually the main beam in a roof space will be crossed and met with other beams, or angle iron strengtheners. At these points the rat will slow down to negotiate them and often – if wary – will pause momentarily here before moving on. These are the areas to take the shot but you often only get a split second to take a 'snap shot' of the target. Shooting them in this manner requires pinpoint accuracy, coupled with the discipline of knowing when not to shoot.

If they're not pausing, then shooting really is demanding. As long as they're not moving too quickly, you can 'track' the rat in your sights and actually shoot the rat as it's moving along the beam or alternatively at ground level along the base of a wall. You need to establish the backdrop is safe and you have to be skilled enough to give the rat just enough 'lead'. As once you slip the trigger, like the shotgun shooter you need to keep your rifle moving with the target so the pellet keeps on line to go into the kill-zone on impact. As you can imagine this isn't easy but once mastered it is very rewarding. Similarly establish a point the rat enters another area or climbs up or down an adjoining beam. The rat 'may' also pause at this junction and if you can time your shot as the rat passes through the area you're in business. Again this takes skill and until it is acquired be prepared to waste a fair amount of ammo. But, once you get the 'timing' right, it's very rewarding. Eventually tracking the rats this way with a beam of light from a gun mounted lamp will have them run more quickly and the rat really can shift when it needs to. If they're running this fast then it's even unsporting on the rat to try to shoot them in this fashion but there are still a few tricks you can employ.

The obvious one is to diffuse the light even further with a filter and if your lamping kit has one which I advise – bring the brightness of the light down with the dimmer switch as low as you possibly can but still see to target the quarry.

When shooting in pairs a trick at stopping a rat in its tracks is for one hunter to track the rat with the gun lamp then the other shooter using a gun lamp or handheld, suddenly illuminates the area the rat is heading for. This can often cause the rat to pause for a second or two, deciding whether or not to dash through the light to safety. This hesitancy can be just enough for the first shooter to take a shot. But, when they're becoming overly 'lamp shy' and scurrying for cover at the slightest disturbance, it's time to target them using dedicated Nightvision riflescopes – a particular specialised form of shooting and one we're now ready to look at for both rabbits and rats. Just before we do a few word as promised on lasers. If the situation has had you set the scope zero at 20 yards, the laser can be set either as an aid for quickly assessing range or as a 'secondary' sighting system for the rats that really do appear too close for comfort. Often while you're scouring the beams or sitting quietly watching an area one will cross the barn floor, even appear from a grain funnel or from under cover no more than 5 or 6 yards away. Often there can be enough ambient light in the building for you to see the rat in the gloom, especially if positioned close to a large open entrance. Even with your scope on lowest magnification you'll have no chance in even seeing it through the lenses let alone assessing the holdover very close range shots require. With the laser set for a range of 8 yards or so – without using the scope you can put the dot on the front third of the cheeky devil's body, resulting in a smack of a solid hit or the 'zing' of a clean miss. But I must quantify this technique by saying I only use this set up shooting .22 calibre and I only set up the laser in this manner when experience of an area has indicated rats are often coming in this close. Also, the laser in these cases isn't scope mounted but rather fixed in a special mount on the barrel or silencer so as to be as close to the axis of the barrel bore as possible. As you can see, lasers are very versatile and there's even more on these devices to come in the next section.

NIGHTVISION

When Nightvision equipment first came available to the UK sport shooter it caused great interest but didn't have immediate mass appeal due to the comparatively poor performance in relation to cost. Also the early models had very basic reticles and in many cases the devices were heavy and gave a poor or 'grainy' sight picture. But for those like myself fortunate enough to test this gear at the outset, despite this we realised that here was a new type of technology, with a few modifications and improvements that could totally revolutionise the way we hunt at night.

However as this equipment was originally designed by the military for detecting and ultimately 'shooting' man size targets at night (later the export models were designed for sport shooters targeting large animals such as bears, wild boar, elk etc.), this is one of the reasons reticles weren't very subtle, usually being little more than a thick lined inverted Chevron. Also, the 'grainy' green image produced inside by the image intensifier was not really up to the standard required and 95% of units were poor quality Gen 1 scopes with pitifully weak infrared illuminators. Some factories were producing new Second Generation intensifiers, these offered more range and better performance but it wasn't of high build quality. The internal 'noise' of the picture was poor – slightly fuzzy – a bit like a television set not tuned in properly.

Now I know there have been other military references in this book but this really is an area that can only be clarified by charting the development of NV technology for the Armed Forces before we can appreciate how it began to become accepted into our sport. And ultimately where this exciting product can be of great benefit and its future development realistically lead.

Nightvision – The Full Story

Since the 1960s, military officials predicted battles would be fought at night. No surprises then that both superpowers – the USSR as it was then known and the USA and NATO pact countries had a program dedicated to the development of observation devices and Riflescopes that could be used in the dark.

The early devices, using technology that dates back to the end of the Second World War, which to some extent can be termed Gen 0 and operated by bathing the target in infrared light. Something that is important in NV usage for sport shooting and one that I'll return to in much more detail later. The fact being, the observation aid or scope had an IR projector and IR detector that picked up this light and produced a sight picture.

Though usable and effective, they had one major drawback for the military. That was if you sent out an IR beam of light, the enemy watching using a device with an IR detector could spot your position. This was because these devices were 'active' (emitting a beam) and not passive as with the more advanced equipment that doesn't use IR.

Immediately the boffins got tinkering and moved up to what is classed as Generation 1 equipment

Using a NV monocular to spot, then the gun mounted lamp to target and shoot

which is basically where it now becomes of interest to the sport shooter. This was the first passive system that could actually use natural ambient light provided by the moon and stars to produce a sight picture, negating the need for the IR giveaway. Even so, some had an IR facility to boost viewing range when needed and gave the benefit of being able to see into areas of total darkness. One of the most important facets of these early Gen 1 devices was they were cascade devices. In their construction they had three Gen 1 intensifier tubes 'butted' one up against the other to create a cascade effect. Each tube had a gain of approximately 50 times the outside nighttime screen so this gave $50 \times 50 \times 50 = 125,000$. This brings us to the downsides, one of which being these units – especially NV Riflescopes – tended to be big, heavy and often cumbersome because they required a large body to house the three intensifiers and a large objective lens – both helping to overcome the primary need for the IR booster. By the late 60s the development of even more hi-tech gadgetry meant image intensifier tubes could be made smaller but with higher gain and therefore offering a much better sight picture. Now as I'm sure you've now noticed, the heart of any NV unit is the 'intensifier tube', and it's the quality of the 'tube' or the grade or 'Generation' classification that both gives a better sight image but also often will be the reason the unit is much more expensive than lower Generation equipment. As technology moved forward, the devices then progressed to Gen 2, 2+ and then Supergen. It was the advent of the Micro Channel Plate MCP that gave the breakthrough, the MCP gave the necessary high gain; this did away with the need for three Gen 1 cascade tubes, which in turn allowed the construction of one single small intensifier tube and the construction of small effective 'man portable' night vision devices.

Gen 2 devices have a fibre optic window where the nighttime scene is focused, in Gen 2+ technology

Covert mission? No, kitted out for a session hunting with Nightvision

it was replaced by anti-reflective glass giving more resolution and gain. SuperGen® technology made even more improvements to the intensifier tube and increased the lifespan to 7,500 hours. When the 'inventors' moved up from Gen 1 to Gen 2 we also saw the introduction of fibre optic input windows. Anything butted up to the fibre optic window is in focus – such as the reticle. The later improvement in the form of Gen 2+ was the use of a glass input window instead of the fibre optic 'bundles' which affords greater resolution and higher sensitivity. Most agree this gives 20% better performance up from Gen 2 because the image is literally being projected straight into the intensifier tube through the glass input window. But I think that's enough technical data for us to be concerned with and amply illustrates how these units have developed.

The military have now produced Gen III, Gen IIII units and possibly beyond (official secrets and all that – y'know?) so we can only guess at the quality of construction and surmise the amazing quality of sight picture, and stealth of operation these units afford. Not forgetting when those currently on the prohibited sales list do eventually become available on the civilian market – the cost!

In brief, that's how Nightvision Equipment came into being and how it developed. As you'd expect, certain military powers of the world still do work on the technology to 'see at night'.

And so, back to the introduction of these 'scopes' into the civilian market for the use in sport shooting.

After the 'Cold War' and the demise of the Berlin Wall in 1989 quite unexpectedly a quantity of what was in effect ex-Military Night vision equipment came available to the Western commercial market in the early 90s. But to recap on what was detailed earlier, those early devices still had limited use in a civilian sporting market. In particular, the lack of precision as the windage and elevation adjustment of the Riflescopes was very crude. Whereas the sport shooter is used to one click on a scope turret for ¼ inch movement at 100yds, military nightvision was imparting movement of approximately 4 inches per click at 100yds.

However, certain forward thinking importers of optics in our industry realised the benefits of the equipment and began to develop and also modify existing equipment so it would be of use to the hunter. Unfortunately though, expectations were initially high, but quality wasn't as initially we were still seeing ex-military equipment coming from the Eastern Bloc. Feedback from the public had companies address the problems. These were to install better quality intensifier tubes; more precise windage and elevation adjustment and some even changed the reticle for a more traditional cross hair. The latter usually being a more precise and acceptable red illuminating cross hair that would show up in the ghostly green glowing sight picture familiar to all NV equipment. So whilst we now have 'usable' scopes, in lower 'Gen' classification they still do have certain limitations. But be aware of those and you have usable equipment for specialist situations.

How Does it Work?

Whilst a conventional telescopic sight or as we know them 'scope' uses light from the sun during daylight hours to produce a sight picture, Nightvision equipment – be it sighting device or observation aid – uses the invisible photons of light both inside and outside the usual spectrum. The intensifier tube 'amplifies' and changes these into electrons and finally back to light when they hit a phosphor screen at the back of the intensifier tube, thus a window of green light is 'magically' formed inside the tube and miraculously the dark is pierced and we can in effect see through and into the night. Check out the cross section diagram of a typical internal set up of a Gen 2 NV Riflescope. Incidentally, Gen 2 has been used for this due to the fact there's a less complicated internal structure but it also amply illustrates the major components of a NV Riflescope.

ANATOMY OF A NIGHTVISION RIFLESCOPE

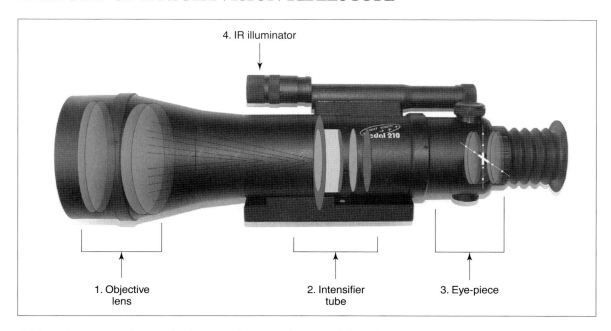

4. IR illuminator

1. Objective lens

2. Intensifier tube

3. Eye-piece

With reference to the Nightvision Riflescope diagram: The objective lens (1) used in a nightvision device has a very high light transmission factor, much higher than a normal daytime scope. This allows more light to be gathered for amplification by the intensifier tube. Also, special coatings allow better transmission of the infrared (IR) spectrum which is something greatly utilised by the 'tube'.

The intensifier tube (2) is situated at the heart of the nightvision riflescope. It has a thick anti-reflection coated input window composed of either glass or fibre optic. The highly 'light sensitive' coatings of the photo-cathode are situated here. This converts rays of light to the particles known as electrons.

The image intensifier tube – the heart and soul of any NV device

These electrons then stream into a thin glass plate full of lead lined microscopic pores – approximately 75 million of them. This is where the 'amplification' of light takes place by a cascade process resulting in even more electrons being knocked off the surface of the pores causing a chain reaction – this is known as the 'gain' of the tube. The intensified electrons leave the micro channel plate and strike a phosphor screen completing the intensification process. This results in the eerie green glow sight picture familiar to all night vision devices – be it riflescope, monocular or binocular.

The sight picture sent back through the small screen of the intensifier tube is magnified by the eyepiece (3) of the nightvision riflescope which is positioned just behind the intensifier tube and before the ocular eyepiece. The illuminated reticle – or as it is termed 'lit' is usually situated at this area.

The IR illuminator (4) is a very powerful torch that shines 'invisible' light in the infrared spectrum. The torch doesn't use bulbs, rather IR diodes that are many times more powerful than conventional light bulbs. The IR beam is invisible to the naked eye but visible through the night scope and also reflects back from the eyes of animals making detection of quarry much easier. It is this that makes the IR illuminator invaluable in very dark conditions supplying the intensifier tube with a light source to amplify. Even in zero light conditions, utilising the IR, the intensifier is able to create a sight picture allowing the shooter to effectively see in the dark.

Time now to look at the devices in relation to our sport and why the airgun hunter doesn't have to have the highest Generation grade device to hunt effectively.

Its Relevance to the Night Hunter

As the airgun hunter generally operates at ranges well within 30yds – then the equipment doesn't have to be of such high grade or 'Generation.' Granted, a sharper clearer sight picture is always useful but Gen 1 and certainly Gen 1+ units are more than capable of giving a sight picture of sufficient quality to target quarry accurately at sensible airgun hunting ranges. The need for better and more precise adjustment of the aim point in these devices was soon realised. This means the problem has now been remedied with both reticles and turret adjusters being modified and re-designed to suit sport shooting.

That nicely brings us back to the reason airgun hunters can use these units more readily than any other shooter. Firstly, the limited effective range of the air rifle leant itself to the fact early Gen 1 and even Gen 1+ had a similar targeting range. Using the IR intensifier that was fitted to these devices also helped target quarry as it actually made the sight picture brighter and clearer. Not forgetting the 'infrared' light would 'bounce off' the eyes of quarry showing up as white-ish/light green dots. Even under the gloomiest hedge or in the black of a barn, shine an IR torch into the area and the shapes may, at first, be hard to pick out but the eyes will always give the quarry away. From that initial 'sighting' you can concentrate your vision and soon fully see the quarry. In fact, as with early lamping equipment, night hunters continually hankered for better kit. They soon realised a stronger IR illuminator would 'boost' the unit's performance. Remember, the sport shooter isn't worried about being detected by another IR user. As the units on early Riflescopes were either not fitted with or had poor and low power IR units, we overcame this by fitting our own. In the early days we did this by incorporating a conventional lamp in the set up but fitted with an IR filter. The most popular was the Deben Tracer Compact, an early model as it was light in weight, and the plastic clip mount could be adapted to fit under the rifle air reservoir or on the eyepiece of the NV Riflescope. Granted, it looked unsightly but it worked well. Yes, those of us 'tinkering' knew that IR was the key to helping us target quarry with basic NV Scopes. The companies importing equipment realised this as well and that's why extra IR illuminators such as IR torches are now readily available. However by and large, of all the extra IR units you can incorporate into the set-up, I've no hesitation in saying the best by far is still a conventional gun lamp with IR filter.

Even with extra 'detection ability', the actual shooting range always has to be kept within the sensible realms of the ability of the shooter – and more hunters such as myself 'experimenting' but having success with these units soon realised the .177 calibre was the better choice due to its flatter trajectory and therefore more forgiving of errors in range finding. So those really were the pitfalls – poor image quality and the nightmare of using these units to successfully and precisely determine range. The reason for the latter is due to the fact most units were only 2X magnification, coupled with the narrow field of view resulting in a sight that tended to give an image akin to looking through a 'toilet roll tube'. This made estimating distance very difficult. And, you think rangefinding is hard enough at night with a lamp. But consider this, couple that with the fact certain early NV Riflescopes had large objective lenses meant there was a notably increased distance between the axis of the rifle bore and the axis of the sight. Try judging holdover or holdunder at varying ranges and those new to these devices soon become frustrated at the regular misses. Thankfully, the major NV manufacturers, or that should be importers into the UK knew this was a problem that needed addressing and first reduced the size of the objective lens so it could be mounted lower. So now with NV hopefully explained, onto type, and proper usage.

Observation Devices

These can range from a compact hand held monocular to a more substantial pair of binoculars. All quality units have IR facility. As with other NV devices, the IR is invaluable as it extends viewing range and also reflects back off quarry's eyes to up your detection rate. Not much else to say on these except they're an invaluable aid to scanning the area in front and around you. If you want to be hands free, there are models of monocular that fit onto a head harness. These are designed so the monocular can be 'flicked' down to look through or when not needed, 'flicked' up out off the way so you can sight through a scope. More advanced higher 'Gen' equipment is available as head mounted goggles that cover both eyes when in the deployed position. I've used both types successfully. Spot the target using the NV and stealthily get within range, then quietly 'flick' them into the upward position out of the way and then either use a traditional lamping set-up to target the quarry or an NV scope. More on head mounted NV when we come to lasers.

Nightvision Riflescopes

These are the 'bread and butter' to the night hunter looking for ultimate stealth and ability to be undetected in the pursuit of nighttime rabbits and rats. Classification and specification 'Generation' of equipment has already been explained in full. If looking to enter this exciting branch of the sport, a Gen 1 or better still Gen 1+ unit is more than suitable for air rifle use. However, as with virtually all equipment, you do get what you pay for and if possible I'd recommend you do go for the slightly higher Gen 1+ and if finances can stretch – you might think you're spoiling yourself using Gen 2 but you'll come to appreciate it. Most at this level will have powerful IR integrated into the unit, some with two-stage power settings. Worth their weight in gold and it means no need to have to find a place to mount an additional IR device as outlined previously.

But firstly – how to properly mount and zero the NV Riflescope itself.

Most NV scopes are designed to fit a weaver style of mounting rail so for airgun fitting you need the appropriate adaptor to fit it to dovetails or scope rails of an air rifle. The mount specialists B-Square makes these mounts to suit virtually all air rifles, even for mounting to multi-shot rifles which have magazines that 'protrude' quite high from the action. Other specialist companies can supply adaptor rails for mounting to rifles with fixed scope mounts such as on popular PCP Theobens.

So, once this is sorted and the scope is mounted securely, like a conventional optic you need to set zero. Due to the sensitivity of the internal circuitry, the NV scope can only be used in daylight with the front lens cover cap left in place. The lens cap will either be a camera screw on type or more often a push fit heavy-duty rubber cover. This will have a small pinhole through the centre that allows just enough light in for you to use it in daylight safely allowing you to switch on the unit and initially set zero and test your shooting in daylight. However, once set up in this way, always double check and if necessary 're-set zero' in the night as this prevents image shift problems and ensures zero is set accurately for the 'lightless' conditions you'll be hunting in.

Incidentally, the mount adaptor elevates the NV scope higher than a more conventional optic, but now the devices themselves are of a more reasonable build – rangefinding, although an art that needs 'fine-tuning' for using these units, isn't the almost impossible task it was with early equipment. In fact, certain manufacturers have seen the popularity of Gen 1 with air rifle hunters and are building them with conventional dovetail mounting instead of Weaver bases. And this also brings back into the equation of these devices and facilities the 'need' for an IR facility/projector or additional IR torch.

This does apply to some extent on range, but in many hunters' experienced opinions they will agree the use of IR may well help give more range observation, it should mainly be used to sight and identify quarry. Also this 'extra' light is especially useful for looking into really 'blacked out' areas such as barns when targeting rats but more as we come to the technique for NV ratting.

As mentioned previously, if you aren't able to afford a 'high' Generation, then it must be noted that generally many Gen 1 Riflescopes only have relatively low power onboard IR illuminators. If this is the case then as explained previously, it's certainly worth investing in an additional IR unit. Incidentally, the extra IR unit can be mounted on the barrel, the silencer, onto the side or underside of the stock, and there are even NV scopes that are 'rigged' with tactical rails to take such extras. All types and mounts are readily available from the specialist NV companies and don't cost the earth.

Incidentally before looking at how to use the equipment, it's worth noting there are now a few day/night scopes on the market. These units can be used as a normal optic in the day and at night, with the flick of a switch, or addition of a NV complex to the eye-bell, they transform into a NV Riflescope. Whilst they do solve a problem of not having to take out two rifles if hunting from day into night, or vice versa, not forgetting negating the need to keep chopping and changing scopes on a favourite rifle. They also hold the same zero and are in my opinion worth investigating if this form of versatility appeals.

Of more general appeal but not as commonplace, are red dot sights with NV monocular attachments that allow the user to see the red dot in the front sight screen in the dark. I've had particular success with these in barns and outbuildings taking rats at sensible ranges.

So with kit explained let's look at how to use it.

NV Stalking

Just because you 'think' you're not going to be 'seen' due to you not using a light doesn't mean you

Hunting with Nightvision is an exciting branch of the sport

can let your fieldcraft lapse. Using NV means you can hunt in the dark with more stealth, and indeed when practised you'll be surprised at how close you can get to your quarry. But the major issues such as, keeping sound to a minimum, feeling your way with your feet across the ground, taking care to prevent showing as a silhouette and of course walking up to quarry from downwind all need to be considered. Also, take the time to familiarise yourself with the control layout of the NV Riflescope. It will have a few 'whistles and bells' that need switching on or adjusting depending on usage. You don't want to be fiddling around trying to 'brighten' the reticle when you've sighted a rabbit or switch onto the next power setting IR. It should all be second nature. Consider this simile: you wouldn't consider driving a car at night not knowing how to switch the headlights on now would you? I think that illustrates my point.

There are two ways to 'stalk' quarry with NV. Either walking forward scanning the area continuously with the rifle up to your shoulder or alternatively, only bringing the NV scope up to the eye to scan for potential targets, then moving forward and stopping and scanning again. Once within range – you compose yourself, choose a shooting position, put the scope up to your eye and take the shot. The latter method is less strenuous on the arms as you're not continuously holding the rifle up, but if using a very lightweight carbine, the former can be a better option for short 'search' periods. Especially if actively looking for rats around the side of outbuildings. Ratting will be dealt with further in this piece, but I will say, this method tends to strain the eye and play havoc with your own night vision.

Also, when using this method, it's all too easy to get totally absorbed scanning for targets as you move and while moving all too easy to stumble over rough ground or something lying on the farmyard floor. Much better is to sweep the ground ahead with the NV riflescope and IR illuminator switched on, looking to first locate quarry with the tell tale reflection from the eyes. Once spotted, slowly move forward, ideally approaching from downwind until within range. The inexperienced will usually chance longer-range shots but be patient as you can and with practice will be able to stalk to a position well within your set zero. Once in position, take careful aim, slip the trigger and the rabbit should roll over dead. Using a silenced air rifle, the sound of the lead impacting the skull will seem very loud in the darkness, even louder than when lamping – or so it seems! Other rabbits in the vicinity will prick up their ears, but many times hold position wondering what's happened. In these cases you'll be able to get in another shot or possibly two! Needless to say a multi-shot PCP is the optimum tool for the job. The lighter the better and one that handles well with the NV rig on board. When using NV scopes in this way, it's also a time I prefer to use one of the specialist slings to hold the rifle in the optimum position. The sling I prefer is the Cheater Sling, but some specialist mail order military equipment stores have 'tactical slings' suited to the job. The 'Cheater' doesn't attach as normal to conventional sling swivel studs but due to the design uses elasticated 'loops' that can be fixed virtually anywhere on the rifle. I attach the loops around the butt, usually behind the pistol grip of the stock, and around the forend, thus allowing the rifle to 'sit' side on across the front of the body. I adjust the height of the sling so the rifle sits approximately mid-way up the chest. This means little movement and effort is needed to bring the gun to bear to scan through the scope and when bringing the gun up to take the shot. Whilst I often recommend an NV monocular for observation, for this particular stalking technique I don't find it necessary. However, if planning on stalking but waiting up in ambush during the hunting foray, a compact NV device slipped in the jacket pocket is always handy. I take what I need in a bum bag or tactical belt with pouches. Whilst on the subject of accessories there are other bits 'n bobs that are useful and necessary. As always, safety first so pack the mobile and as with any form of night shooting let the appropriate people know where you're going and when you'll be back. And although you're hunting without a conventional light source (gun lamp) to illuminate the target, as with other night shooting techniques, you will still need a light source for other necessary tasks in the field. I recommend a small head torch, especially one with a multi-LED facility. Use the lowest LED setting for reloads or hocking rabbits, then use multi-LED facility or main beam for locating and retrieving shot rabbits before moving position.

Now to one of the most overlooked essentials for any nighthunter – a good pair of shooting gloves. At night your hands have a nasty habit of finding every nettle on the ground, every rusty nail sticking from a wooden post or discarded piece of barbed wire. I often wear a pair of SOLAG fingerless mitts by Blackhawk. These are strong but flexible, they offer a tactile feel and as they're fingerless there are no problems loading pellets, changing magazines or 'twiddling' dials. In fact, they're ideal for lamping as well as 'lightless' NV hunting.

Indeed, virtually all accessories that have been mentioned for lamping apply – but definitely don't forget the spare batteries for the Nightvision Riflescope and extra still if using other devices such as laser or IR torch.

Now I've made stalking rabbits with NV sound ridiculously easy haven't I? Well, you guessed it, it isn't but once you become experienced you'll find this a very exhilarating branch of the sport. But whilst I've outlined the plus points of shooting with NV let's accept and address the downsides.

Basically, assessing range is without doubt the major obstacle to overcome. Whilst you can quite easily visually pick out the targets with the sight, as your view through the scope is very 'tunnelled', the view of much of the ground from your position to the target is virtually non-existent. Granted, this is the same for using a conventional scope in the daylight but consider how many times you 'weigh up' the target with the naked eye before putting the scope to your eye to shoot. Basically, you've assessed range well before you begin placing the cross hairs on the kill-zone. With NV your first sight of the target is through the sighting device. The only and best way of determining range to the target is by one of two means. Using the reticle as a guide and bracketing, as you would with a conventional scope or to use a laser in your NV rig. This can either be a conventional red dot laser or an IR laser. The latter only visible when viewed through an NV device.

Whichever you use, I first recommend you practise in the following way. Draw and cut out the profile of an average sized rabbit from a thick piece of cardboard and place it upright on the ground. Walk 25 yards from the target and using the NV scope reticle assess a reference point as you would if using the reticle of a standard daylight scope to bracket the target. Some reticles will help you to some extent bracket the head others the body. As the scope will be fixed magnification you can then use this as a starting point for ranging. However, accurately judging the size of a rabbit through NV equipment is almost impossible so I'd say use this as a very rough guide and more so use a laser in the set up as will be outlined in full later.

But you're still practising in daylight with the protective cap covering the objective lens. Now, as we've covered before on setting a 'field course' for lamping, do the same but now attempt it with the NV. On your first practice runs in the dark you'll probably be quite dismayed at your results. There's no peeking over the scope as in daylight hours or using a lamp to illuminate the way. Don't get too disheartened, it will come and you'll eventually become adept at rangefinding in what must surely be

Retrieve shot rabbits immediately – you'll easily lose their position if you wander off

the most difficult hunting scenario of all. Now with a laser in the set up you obviously need to set the laser to coincide with the set zero of the scope reticle. More on my personal preferences for this later but the basics for proper usage still apply which are: depending on how it's mounted, either above scope or under the barrel will like any laser set up give you the reference you need to assess range. But, as you're stalking in a very stealthy manner, whenever possible, and it will be practical more often than not. Stalk carefully up to the target until the laser does coincide exactly with the reticle cross hair aim point (that is if set conventionally) and take the shot, safe in the knowledge you can aim 'bang on' as you're at your set zero from the quarry. Incidentally, as I use both IR laser and traditional red dot laser I don't have a preference to lasers for NV shooting. But one thing I certainly now do is to set the dot mark of the laser to one side of the centre of the cross hairs at the set range my scope zero is set for.

Let me explain why.

The image intensifier will 'magnify' the dot of either IR or conventional daylight red dot and I've found the dot when set to coincide with the centre of the cross hairs can obscure precise aiming.

Although I use a pressure pad switch to just 'dab' the laser on to determine range, granted it isn't always 'shining' there to obscure the cross hair. But, I've found setting the laser dot to hit the horizontal cross hair, slightly off to the right of centre helps me determine range much more efficiently. Of course it hits the horizontal line of the reticle at the set zero point. Now while this suits me it may not you but try it – I think you might just find this set up more precise for you also.

Now to the practicalities and my recommended method of actively pursuing and seeking out quarry when stalking with NV. And presuming it's on a specialist sling the way is as follows.

The rifle combo should be hanging in front of you as previously outlined but only with your neck through the sling – not including a shoulder. The sling supports the weight of the 'rig' and the rifle steadied and angled slightly away from the body with the right hand cupped under the forend, the majority of the stock just resting on the underside of your right arm. (Opposite applies for left handed shooters.)

The reason for this is if the eyepiece is allowed to rest against clothing, or to direct back in the direction of your body, the intensified light image that's created (the green glow) will be reflected off your clothing or face. If this is allowed to happen, you might as well be walking around holding a green torch. The rubber eyecup shields the glow from the side but not when put slightly askew at the side of a solid object. It's equally important not to pass your hand or part of the arm over the eyepiece if reaching for something as this gives a solid surface for the green light to reflect from and show forward of your position. Because of this 'problem' you should also adopt a set routine for bringing the rifle up to your eye for scanning and aiming. When bringing the rifle to bear, whilst moving the rifle upwards, also push it out to your right (opposite applies for lefties), and then bring the gun fully up until the butt is in the shoulder ensuring the eyepiece is facing over the shoulder. When ready to scan or take the shot, bring your aiming eye into the eyecup from the side, carefully but purposely without too much delay. You'll get the knack of this through practice, and it is worth the effort as especially when relatively close to the target as you are at airgun range, that reflected sight picture can and will spook your quarry. Incidentally, while on the subject of eyepieces you'll notice the NV Riflescope has a habit of catching condensation more easily. This can be annoying as you need to wipe the rear lens, and depending on conditions, this can be infuriatingly all too frequent. You can use the pad of your forefinger or better have an easily accessed pad of tissue for this purpose. And don't forget; if anything goes near the eyepiece the green light will reflect so take this into account when clearing the lens.

Now if you thought magpies a pain in the day spoiling a stalk, or calling out to all and sundry when they catch sight of a lamp you should hear them when they spot you skulking near the hedges at night – and you think NV makes you undetectable? Magpies aren't the only problem as trust me – a covey of partridges suddenly 'flushing up' as you stalk towards a target can bring on minor heart palpitations! Also, if you 'surprise' a rabbit and are too close for a shot, don't use the 'backing away' technique as is more useful with rats. Stand stock-still and the rabbit will in most cases shuffle around, or hop away, but often stop and sit within range. Now you can target the quarry. Now as you're operating with much more stealth, you usually won't be crawling within range as per a daytime stalk. You will have to stoop at times, but this is usually so you don't appear as a silhouette.

The bonus of hunting in this way is you're more relaxed and can adopt a more stable kneeling shooting position. This allows you to steady the rifle and the forward knee supports the weight of the combo for the shot. If you do take the shot standing, tuck the elbow of the leading arm into the hip for support. These rigs can be hefty but the extra weight does have a benefit in that it can at times help steady aim.

It must be noted that hunting with NV can be very tiring both physically and mentally. As with lamping, rest when needed, no need to rush as in effect you have all night!

Now to the subject of the clothing you wear. Granted foliage patterns aren't needed but dark non-reflective, rustle free clothing is a must and in my experience so too is a facemask and gloves. The latter not only for concealment but also for reasons given earlier in this chapter.

Incidentally, many experienced pest controllers operate at night in black boiler suits and black gloves and masks. Granted, not very 'PC' but it does show it can sometimes be the appropriate form of clothing to wear. Another potential problem to address is the fact that at night sound is seemingly amplified. The sound you make will be heard at a much greater distance and stepping on a twig can sound like a pistol shot.

Incidentally, it's often said animals can't detect infrared light. Debatable whether a rat or rabbit can detect infrared but I reckon to some extent, especially close, it possibly can. If you continuously switch a powerful IR illuminator on and off the animal does seem to notice it and will eventually get wise to it. Leave it on or use a low power IR sparingly is the better option.

As a matter of safety – never look directly at any laser be it conventional red dot or IR. Your eyes are very precious!

NV Ambushing

The method is exactly the same as for daylight ambushing but with the added advantage you're able to target them in darkness with the highest level of stealth. But you must adhere to a few strict guidelines to have the best results. Firstly, you need to position yourself within range of a well used entrance point to a warren or a place they sit out near a warren before they move out further into adjacent fields to feed. As rangefinding is the biggest pitfall of NV use, I recommend you choose the 'main' entrance hole and pace 25 yards from that to a position downwind to use as the shooting point. I'll more often than not put two stones either side of this entrance point, setting these at 5yds beyond the entrance and 5yds closer to my position. This gives two clear range markers at 20 and 30 yards. In effect you've chosen a 10-yard long killing-zone. If you've chosen well, there's a lot of traffic that can pass through in that corridor. Items you'll find useful for ambushing in this way are a pair of NV binos or NV monocular and to use a multi-shot PCP on a bipod. Incidentally, using a pair of NV binoculars is preferable as they give less strain on the aiming eye as you diligently watch the area for activity. But, don't be tempted to use them too often as you ruin your night vision and of course the bounce back of the green sight picture could possibly 'bathe' your face when you bring them up or take them away from the eyes. When you do use the binos, only switch them on when you're looking through them, and when you take them away from your face do so in a swift fluid movement preventing the 'green sight picture' in the eyepieces finding anything solid to reflect off.

Also, while lying in wait, use your ears as much as your eyes. You'll hear rabbits plucking at the grass, scratching and generally moving around in cover. If your eyes have become accustomed to the dark, not 'spoiled' by overly using the NV, then you'll possibly see their shapes move out into the designated shooting area. This is the ideal scenario, as once spotted you can put the rifle in your shoulder, eye in the rubber eyepiece and switch on the NV scope. As the ghostly green image develops there should be rabbits in your sights and if all has gone according to plan one within range and soon in your bag. No need to rush the shot as ideally you're operating totally undetected. Take careful aim, and shoot. Once you've shot one, don't rush to pick up as long as it's a clean kill. At night, and shooting in this 'stealthy' manner, more rabbits soon appear and are certainly not troubled by the fallen ones you've felled.

Incidentally, while watching and ambushing rabbits in this manner, I've discovered an unusual trait of rabbit behaviour that you too can put to good use. That's to actually use a fox call – one that mimics the distress call of a small rabbit or vole to actually entice rabbits out into the open. Even towards your shooting position. For some reason the rabbits are drawn to the sound rather than repelled. I've had rabbits come running in to a 'squeaker' and standing like knockdowns well within range. It also can make them move further out from cover presumably so nothing can pounce on them – strange behaviour but a trick to use if they're keeping out of range or too close to tall cover.

NV Rat Shooting

All the above information and tips for NV use apply to ratting except you'll be shooting indoors and around barns and outbuildings. Therefore, the safety aspects remain the same for indoor shooting and targets will more often than not be closer. As you can get close to your quarry anyway using NV then this is an area I'd advise you reset zero down to 20yds maximum, maybe even less at 15 yards. Stalking around the farmyard at night can be particularly productive. If circuiting the perimeter of buildings, were possible walk the same distance as your set zero from the walls, continually scanning the base of walls and along the top of any materials stacked near it for scaly tails. Once you spot one, position yourself as near as possible to the set zero and shoot. If you come across one much closer than your set zero – don't attempt to adjust your aim for the range, rather physically back away until you're at the required distance (close as possible to your set zero) and then take the shot.

Indoors you can patrol in much the same way scanning the interior, especially the beams and girders, anywhere above that can provide the rat with a walkway. Alternatively, use baiting down tactics without a light and shoot them with the NV Riflescope when they come to feed. Also if you know an area that has a lot of rat activity, make yourself comfortable on a chair or bale of hay and sit and wait. This is when using an extra aid such as an NV monocular for spotting is very advantageous. This negates the need for you to continually hold the rifle up to use the riflescope to survey the roof space. Using an observation aid keeps the strain down to a minimum, but be mindful, that when you spot a potential target, you make the least disturbance swapping over from observation aid to riflescope.

As mentioned in the section on lamping, using these devices gives you the edge on the quarry. With the IR illuminator switched on, work along the areas the rats are known to frequent. You'll soon spot the animal, even if it only pops its head out of a hidey-hole by the infrared light reflecting off its eyes to be picked up in the NV observation device. Once you spot a rat within range, put the observation aid down and carefully sight in using the NV Riflescope.

IR and Conventional Laser Sights

The introduction of IR lasers that emit an invisible beam and a 'dot' (aim point) on the target are fascinating. Even the projected 'dot' is invisible to the human eye until viewed through a device incorporating an image intensifier. These can be either a head mounted monocular, NV goggles or by looking through the NV Riflescope. The supposed benefits aren't as cut and dried as you might think though. You can, albeit in a limited manner use the IR laser as a 'primary' sighting device but it must be remembered that this has very limited accuracy potential. Some use them by setting the 'dot' to a set range of 20 or 25yds and shoot rats 'from the hip' as they spot and sight targets through head mounted NV equipment and literally place the dot on the kill-zone and shoot. In theory all's well and good but the reality isn't nearly as good as it sounds.

Depending on how the laser is mounted also has bearing on the accuracy. If you're intending on using a IR laser in this manner the laser should ideally be positioned as close to the bore line of the barrel as possible so it follows more closely the pellet path until trajectory drop takes over. Also, the range the laser's set for needs to be strictly adhered to, I recommend 20yds maximum. Even at this range you'll only have a few yards either way of set zero until the dot (set aim-point) is inaccurate. So if you use an IR or conventional laser in this manner, use a special mount to attach the device to barrel or silencer and be very disciplined in your shooting and well practised in estimating range.

As I've previously outlined, I personally feel lasers of both types better serve the shooter when used as rangefinding aids. The way it works with a NV Riflescope being the same for how a conventional laser is used with a conventional riflescope. Incidentally, when viewed through NV equipment the aim point of both IR laser and conventional red light laser appear as a very light green almost white dot.

As I've mentioned previously, rangefinding is very difficult with NV Riflescopes and this is the area most shooters will find lasers to be of most benefit.

So that's it for Shooting At Night. Due to the fact rabbits are once again a major agricultural pest and rat numbers are reaching ever-higher dangerous levels night shooting is a part of airgun hunting that will always thrive as long as we're legally allowed to do it. One reason being creatures can, especially the latter become very nocturnal in their habits and due to the areas they inhabit the air rifle is more often the optimum tool for cleanly dispatching them. And yes, that includes rats as even with so-called 'designer' poisons and clever traps the rat can build up immunity and can easily learn to avoid a trap after a near miss. And, due to the uncanny communication of these creatures, they can pass on the experience so others don't fall – literally into the same trap. With lamping kit at an all time 'quality' high, NV devices becoming more affordable, the opportunities for the night hunter are many. Indeed where NV goes from here is anybody's guess. Certainly better quality equipment will come available as long as its sale to the civilian market isn't restricted by sanctions. Upon the writing of this book I've had my first look through some of the first Thermal Imagers to come into the UK. Currently at a price far exceeding the majority of airgun hunter's pocket, these are yet another device that will detect animals at night but pick up the heat given off by the animals. But that's equipment we'll possibly see more of in the future. Getting back to basics of the matter, that being the fact an airgun hunter is far better equipped to hunt small vermin at night, we should remember one important factor pertaining to this branch of our sport.

If there's one thing guaranteed to get an air rifle hunter granted permission to shoot on a farm it's the initial offer to sort rats causing destruction in the barns and grain stores and rabbits destroying the fields. We really do have a lot to thank these pesky pests for.

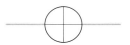

Chapter 14
FAC Air Rifles, Advanced Shooting Techniques, 4 x 4s and More

Throughout this book I've made mention of FAC rated air rifles, usually with the slant on the fact they give more kill-zone options on quarry encountered. But this is only one benefit.

Others include a flatter trajectory and they can be used in many situations where a live round bullet gun such as a rimfire is either too powerful or unsuitable due to other factors – and as you'll read further in this piece, they nicely bridge a gap in the all-round shooters armoury.

However, most airgunners may never want to own or use an FAC rated hi-power air rifle but it's a tool in the armoury for the all-round airgunner that at certain times can be and is very useful – albeit in reality it's still a very specialised piece of kit.

But first you obviously need to go through the process of applying for a Firearms Certificate (FAC) or as it's known getting your 'ticket'. This is usually what puts most off but don't be deterred because after filling in the relevant application forms (Form 101), as long as you can satisfy your local Police Firearm Department you are a fit and suitable person to own a firearm, it's just a matter of going through 'due process' and you have your FAC. And of course the fact, which will be addressed after your initial application and visit by your Firearms Liaison Officer (FLO) you need secure storage for said 'firearm'. And that means a gun cabinet is more often needed because yes that's what an FAC air rifle is – a firearm. A factor that should always be remembered when and where you use it. And before and after using it – it stays where it belongs – inside the gun cabinet, locked secure and safe. Now even after that very brief overview to obtaining an FAC, you'll probably now be asking yourself is it worth all the hassle of applying and satisfying the responsibility of ownership criteria to have an air rifle with a bit more 'puff'. Quite frankly, if you are content to hunt at 12ft lbs then no – but a resounding yes if you want to broaden your shooting horizons and experience air rifle hunting to the absolute 'max' and eventually maybe even move into other shooting disciplines. Notice I've refrained from saying 'if you're serious about shooting you'll get one' which is something I've heard many times from FAC holders in relation to non-FAC shooters.

That's baloney as a hunter using a 12ft lb air rifle can be just as much if not more serious about his sport than a 'fully certified' (ticket waving) power blessed one.

The Power Game
In previous chapters of the book we've mainly dealt with hunting with a rifle of legal limit. That's why a good phrase to use for air rifle hunting is 'precision over power', but what about when you can have precision with power. That brings us to immediately address one of the most popular misconceptions surrounding FAC powered air rifles – that being that 'extra' power gives you some sort of super long-range ability. It doesn't but they do hit far harder at ranges right out to 70yds and beyond – but it still needs to be fired accurately. But I must quantify this statement in the sense conditions need to be suited for longer range shots and in reality the FAC air rifle allows a harder hit, a flatter trajectory and even then, shots should generally be at furthest be taken out to 50 – 60 yards depending on shooter's ability and prevailing weather conditions. However there'll be much more on longer-range work in the relevant section later in this chapter.

Indeed, mention hi-power rifles and it does seem to bring out the dreamers. Shooters with ridiculous claims that 'such and such' rifle 'running at 'such and such' ft lb puts pellets straight as a die out to 'X' many yards. This is codswallop as if anything the FAC air rifle is too specialised for most shooters' requirements. Let me explain that statement. Overkill, especially at close to medium range can easily come into the shooting equation with a bullet gun – that's why the hunter using a 12ft lb air rifle fills a niche in the fact he can operate where other types of guns are unsuitable – for instance inside barns, around out-buildings, land with footpaths on or around, smallholding with little land, dense woodland etc. Now carrying this statement of fact forward, the FAC air rifle shooter has a firearm that to some extent and to coin a phrase 'bridges the gap' between legal limit air rifle and live round rimfire. At 40ft lbs of muzzle energy, an FAC power rated .22 calibre air rifle might only be starting to nudge up to a .22 rimfire short in terms of power level, but even so, the hi-power pellet is certainly not as potentially dangerous as a bullet fired from a rimfire. But even so at close and even medium range, a hi-power FAC air rifle can be too powerful for the job in hand. Incidentally, despite popular misconception, ricochets aren't as near dangerous

The FAC power rated air rifle is a very specialised piece of hardware

on open land as some suppose. Reason being a deflected pellet soon runs out of steam even if fired at hi-velocity. More so you should be mindful of what lies behind the target – the major consideration for any shot taken with any sporting gun.

So, that brings us back to the fact, in effect it's only out to a certain range the 'big power' air rifle delivers the 'big power' punch. And even if this is an air rifle with a muzzle velocity of 30 or 40ft lb – that distance being at most 70yds. After that set distance – as you'll read further in this piece – even a pellet fired at hi-power is already dropping like a stone whereas a rimfire bullet continues for up to a mile if unobstructed. See how the FAC air rifle can be most useful and in the situations it caters for a much safer type of firearm to use?

Now to a major feature of a FAC air rifle – that being the flatter trajectory it offers. And as I'm sure many can accept, a .177 calibre rifle at FAC power level has the flattest trajectory of any of the calibres along a given distance.

But let's get the downsides out of the way before we look to the true benefits.

Firstly, the FAC is the first hurdle but acquiring a 'ticket' for FAC air rifle is usually easier than for 'live round' cartridge firing rifle such as a rimfire. Reason being more land will be deemed suitable for FAC air rifle than bullet gun. This can be due to the land being too close to highways or public rights of way. Whatever, getting your 'ticket' for the FAC air rifle isn't that daunting.

Next up, mechanically operated rifles such as springers or gas-rams capable of hi-power are few and far between. Granted, most springers can be 'tuned up' to run at higher power above the legal limit 12ft lbs but by and large it's best the rifle is built to achieve those power levels from the outset. Also, higher power in a springer often means more recoil, thus accuracy can be affected. So that brings us to the PCP power source and this is where you'll really appreciate the hi-power capabilities with no recoil. The major downside is a hi-power PCP gives less shots per charge than its 12ft lb counterpart. So that small bottle you used to use for home fills is best now taken into the field for 'top ups' and an even larger diver's bottle kept at home. If you don't have access to your own filling gear or a diving centre close by for filling the larger bottles, you could opt to acquire a rifle that uses buddy bottles, but always remember to take enough pre-filled spare buddy bottles into the field.

Another point pertaining to hi-power FAC rifles is that most are full length. Not only due to the capacity of the air reservoir being 'limited' in a carbine, but also a short barrel of a carbine doesn't impart enough spin to the pellet due to lack of rifling. For a 12ft lb air rifle, all carbines are suited to impart enough spin on the pellet for optimum accuracy but for a hi-power heavyweight slug it benefits from having more barrel to travel along. Some FAC rifles even have longer barrels than their standard length legal limit counterparts. The Theoben Rapid Series being a prime example of this. And now to a very important aspect of hi-power and indeed for legal limit air rifles is the need for a top quality, highly efficient sound moderator.

As you've seen mentioned much earlier in this book, the muzzle crack (report) from a PCP is loud when unsilenced – well it stands to reason this is more pronounced from a hi-power rifle. Here you really need to obtain the best silencer for the rifle you've chosen. But, follow the guidelines offered in the section on silencers a while back and you'll be heading in the right direction. But don't forget you need to have provision to own one and it needs to be included on your licence when you purchase one.

Choosing the rifle itself can become an issue because you don't want to make a costly mistake. Most FAC rated air rifles won't hold value bought from new as the resale market for them is relatively small. Good for those looking to pick up a used bargain, but if you're

Powerful air rifles require heavy weight, quality pellets and in turn pack quite a punch

set on a new rifle, be warned that as with buying a new car, leave the 'showroom' and your luxury new 'boy's toy' becomes a very expensive loss.

I'd advise most shooters new to FAC, after getting the relevant paperwork sorted (if they have one in their armoury), to have a rifle 'tuned up' to a suitable hi-power level by a reputable gunsmith. Alternatively buy a good quality used PCP air rifle suited to tuning and have that powered up. Just remember to get it put on your ticket. This is the least expensive route into the FAC power game and will help you assess if your hunting requires a hi-power air rifle.

As for choice of sights: Any of your favourite hunting scopes will suffice but the more you shoot FAC then many will realise scopes that have a reticle that offers multi-aim points are very useful. I prefer the mil-dot reticle and now use this scope type almost exclusively on my hi-power air rifles.

As we're dealing with choosing hardware, we now definitely do come to the major bone of contention – that being what calibre to choose and at what power? If you thought airgun hunters were divided on calibre choice then add another variable such as 'power level' in relation to calibre and you really do open up another 'can 'o' worms'. While some swear by .22 calibre at 40ft lbs others are equally smitten with the same calibre fired at 22, 24, 28 or 30 ft lbs. To throw even more controversy into the pot, some would say you cannot beat .20 calibre at 24ft lb or even .177 at the same or at 18 or 22ft lbs. Truth of the matter is, once again, not only is it very much up to personal choice. But there is a simple 'equation' of what I term 'balance of power'. This we are coming to but it basically is the relationship between the weight of projectile fired to the power it is fired at. Now as you'll soon discover there follow a fair few examples that illustrate the .177 calibre FAC rifle being the better option in many hunting situations, the .22 again being a good general-purpose calibre whilst others can very much be an acquired taste.

Incidentally, before going further, let's again dispel the myth that an FAC rifle will give you a magic pass to long-range instant kill shots. It doesn't. Fact is they do give you a better edge on certain longer-range hunting situations (which will be dealt with later), but accuracy is still of paramount importance for success. Also, ultra-hi-power air rifles are available up to 80ft lbs and beyond. These bazookas, even silenced, go off with an almighty crack and give ridiculously few shots per charge. Neither useful nor practical, more so novelty rifles that are manufactured to prove that this power does exist. And by and large they actually fire pellets so heavy they're fashioned and in general termed 'air bullets'. Interestingly though a new pellet of bullet shape design has now entered the scene – designed and weighted to suit more reasonable FAC power levels. More on these as we come to look at ammo in more detail.

Balance of Power

A hi-power air rifle in any calibre affords the shooter a flatter trajectory over a sensible given range and the confidence that if the pellet has been placed with sufficient accuracy it transfers a mighty 'whack' at the target. Now power as I said at the very beginning of the book is somewhat of a misnomer and definitely in the case of the FAC air rifle, all too easily misunderstood. Yet again consider that many very experienced FAC air rifle shooters recommend power levels of 18–24ft lb. Some might feel it not worth the trouble getting an FAC for this but remember this is approximately double the power of a 12ft lb 'off ticket' air rifle. Also, the trajectory of a .22 calibre air rifle fired at FAC power levels is much flatter – in fact behaving more or less similar to a .177 fired at 12ft lbs and of course due to the heavier weight of the .22 pellet, many will be glad to note it delivers a big punch at the target. However, this is only if you're keeping your range to within 50 yards and using suitable ammo.

This is where the term 'balance of power' becomes very apt. In respect of power in (ft lbs) in relation to pellet weight (grains), to gain optimum performance it becomes somewhat of a balancing act. Matching the weight of pellet to the power that projects it to achieve the optimum performance from that particular weight of ammo and power of air rifle. As selection and choice of pellets in .22 calibre is greater, then this is probably the best calibre to use as an example to illustrate this phenomenon.

If shooting an air rifle with a power level up to and including the mid-20ft lb bracket, you have a far greater choice of pellets that will withstand these power levels. And though not primarily designed for hi-power rifles, due to their weight and construction, quite a few lend themselves to being good performers at specific power levels and even in certain rifles. Crosman Accupells, Air Arms Field and Webley Lazadome are a few that are of sufficient weight and robust design to stand up to the rigours of the FAC. But step beyond the 26ft lb power mark and these become more and more unstable in flight. It's here we need to look to the heavy weight champion of the pellet world – that being the Bisley Magnum. At 21.4g this is the heavy slug that will withstand being ejected from the air rifle at 40ft+ pounds of power.

Personally, in .22 calibre I favour 30ft lbs and I've not found myself underpowered and the 'balance of power' I feel being nicely met with the pellet not being 'over-stressed' in its function to do its duty at that power level.

These observations aren't grabbed from thin air but born from personal experience. In fact, some shooters think an FAC air rifle the choice of the 'lazy shooter'. Granted, if you're set on .22 calibre and you are never fully confident in your rangefinding, keep the distances reasonable and you really can enjoy the benefits a flatter trajectory hi-power rifle affords. Also, the need to allow or take into consideration the effect wind has on the pellet is less. Obviously this only applies to sensible ranges, and you can be more confident in the flatter trajectory for taking awkward upward angle shots. A reason if roost shooting I sometimes prefer to use an FAC air rifle. Also I'm sure you can see the benefits for using a hi-power air rifle for both lamping and when using NV Riflescopes. More on this at the very end of this section and one that really will give you food for thought!

Indeed, a 30 or 40ft lb air rifle in the right hands can be pushed to take effective shots right out to 70-80yds along the horizontal. But, and I can't stress this enough, this power is only of use at range if you know the trajectory drop for the calibre and you're certain of the range. As I've already stated, I personally feel 30ft lbs is the optimum power level in .22 calibre and 22-24ft lbs in .177 calibre. The reasons also explained, those being you're already getting limited to choice of ammo and beyond the mid-20ft lb power level in .177 and 30ft lb level in .22 calibre you're certainly pushing even the heavy ammo to the limit – not forgetting testing the quality of the barrel. Let me explain: The force of the sudden blast of air from an FAC rifle acting on the skirt of the pellet on firing is quite savage. Skirts can quite literally get 'blown out' on unsuitable weight pellets and even though you're using a suitable pellet, when it rockets out of the barrel at hi-velocity it will lose stability faster than a pellet fired from a 12ft lb air rifle. These are reasons pellet choice is so critical and barrels need to be of sufficient high grade.

Indeed, remember in chapter 4 on Ammo we looked at checking pellets? Well, while it's important to use quality un-damaged pellets in 12ft lbs, when using a FAC air rifle, the slightest deformity or damage will render it very unpredictable and should be discounted. Whilst pellet choice is always important, correct pellet choice and scrutiny of the quality is vital for using a pellet in a hi-power air rifle.

I'm sure you're now appreciating the fact the higher the power level of the rifle, then the fewer brands of pellet you're able to use. This is because they're the only pellets of a sturdy enough build, weight and design to withstand the forces acting on them. The downside is pellets suited to very hi-power FAC are much heavier than normal and so trajectory is more pronounced the further the pellet travels. In fact if FAC air rifles were more popular, I'm certain we'd have a wider selection of pellets to choose from that suited these rifles and weighted to match up to being fired at a specific power setting.

At present, if you choose to shoot at higher power, especially .22 calibre at 28-30ft lbs then you're looking at very few pellets – those being the Bisley Magnum, or the H&N Barracuda Match. But, by and large even these pellets are one and the same.

Another heavyweight pellet worth considering is the Logun Penetrator. At 20.5g in .22 calibre and 9.5g in .177 calibre this 'bullet shape' pellet has proved very efficient in certain rifles. But as with selection of ammo for any power of air rifle, try the ones available and find the one best suited to your rifle and power setting.

Interestingly, many hunters using a .177 calibre rifle running at 18-24ft lb recommend the Bisley Magnum pellet and at 10.6g it does seem to be the optimum choice for the small calibre FAC fan. As proof of the popularity of the Bisley Magnum for FAC, it's available in a few slightly different head sizes in the popular calibres, so you really can 'tailor' those heavyweights to suit your particular gun. And as I'm sure you're now aware, taking the trouble to find exactly the right one that suits your rifle barrel will certainly show itself in the accuracy you're able to achieve.

Though I'm using the popular calibres as examples, obviously as mentioned in the Ammo section .20 has its devotees and in FAC format those shooters can be even more fanatical of the calibre. But, to give it its due, the .20 performs admirably at legal limit and at FAC is certainly one to consider but as for the power setting – as I'm sure you can now agree it's a case of getting the balance right.

And as for .25 calibre, well, personally I feel the big slug is too 'cumbersome' and 'troublesome' a

If you're going to push the air rifle to the limit you need to put in dedicated practice under field conditions

Kit required for long range sniping – note the laser rangefinder, binos and shooting mat – bunnies an optional bonus

brute, especially when fired at 50ft lbs. Granted, it certainly does transfer a mighty whack at 50-60 yards but quite frankly for the downside of that fast looping trajectory I'd recommend for the size and distances that are generally realistic for these rifles .20 and certainly .22 calibre are going to be more 'usable' and beneficial for most FAC hunters. Talking of bigger calibres nicely brings me to the next factor to address in relation to FAC rifles and calibre size is the misconception of power or 'hitting force' at the target being the main requisite for effective hunting. Once again, dive back into the Ammo chapter and you'll see this particular misconception is more than dismissed for a pellet fired from a 12ft lb air rifle and so it equally applies for FAC rifles. It's accurate shooting that puts the pellet into the kill-zone not power, though power does offer better accuracy potential under certain conditions. But consider this fact – a .177 calibre 22-24ft lb air rifle still delivers approximately 12ft lb of muzzle energy at the target at 60yds – that's some clout!

You can of course with practice get to a level where you can consistently hit the target at this range with a 12ft lb rifle but due to the flat trajectory it's 'easier' to do with a hi-power rifle that has an even flatter trajectory. And that does indeed again bring us back to the fact the FAC rifle is much more forgiving of inaccuracies in range estimation.

I usually zero my .177 BSA Superten MkII Custom FAC at 35 or 40yds, and with 10.6g Bisley Magnums this allows me to virtually aim bang on for rabbits from 25yds out to approximately 60yds without having to worry too much on change in aim point. Now that's a flat, very useful trajectory wouldn't you agree? And again, at the very end of this section, you'll see a firearm such as this can lend itself to very specialised forms of hunting.

So with calibre size and weight in relation to power out of the equation, what other reason is there to specifically use an FAC powered air rifle?

Some areas of land might be certified fit for an FAC air rifle but not necessarily suitable for rimfire. As the law is continually becoming more stringent there are no grey areas pertaining to responsibility of gun ownership. In other words land is either passed for rimfire or it isn't. If it isn't then more likely it will pass for FAC air rifle and in these cases if you feel the need of the extra oomph, the FAC air rifle is the tool for the job.

A typical example that regularly and periodically faces me is wary crows sit just outside 'comfortable' range of 12ft lb but are foolish enough to hang on the 60-65 yard mark. Now this is on land not passed suitable for rimfire, if it was I'd reach for the rimmy. I swear sometimes it's as if the crows know the area is safe and free from bullets. So the tool here is my .177 'bruising Beeza' running at 22ft lb punching out 10.6g Bisley Magnums at well over 900 f.p.s. In a 'non allowed' rimfire scenario that's my ultimate crow culling tool.

I'm sure you can now realise, it's all too easy once you get your 'ticket' to get carried away and go for the most powerful rifle you can find. Many shooters who've a lot of experience hunting with FAC lever air rifles will surprisingly tell you a rifle of 22-24ft lb is probably the best compromise. You need to weigh up your needs and abilities. The ranges you're likely to encounter quarry and the reason you needed or wanted the extra power in the first place. And to return to the subject of kill-zones, more areas of vulnerability on quarry targeted is also now open to be made use of.

To steal a rifleman's phrase of 'putting one in the boiler room', which is possible with FAC air rifle as it means the centre target mass. That will usually be the heart lung area. Heart lung shots not dared possible with 12ft lb are acceptable with a hi-power rifle. So too are the side on 'smash-through' hits on the chest area of corvids and pigeon. For the latter though you do risk bruising at least one side of the breast meat. But if this is the only way to tackle them, if you own an FAC the tool is at your disposal. Consider this example of the opportunities having a FAC air rifle can open up for you. If shooting from a reasonable size hide I often take in both a standard 12ft lb air rifle and a hi-power rifle. For quarry that presents at medium range, the FAC can often be 'too much gun' for the job so the 12ft lb does the duty there. For woodies or crows that sit further out or higher up at longer range in trees, the FAC rifle is the one to pick up for that shot. With my Theoben Rapid MkII allowing me to have 30ft lbs at my disposal 50yd woodies in sitty-trees drop out like stones when bashed with 21.4g of lead. And the bonus is I don't need to worry about the small leaf or twig as that heavyweight pellet will brush those aside and still crash with deadly duty into the carefully targeted and selected kill-zone. Another reason I'd pick up the FAC is for roost shooting and other birds found high in trees. Bunnies that frequent an area with no cover to snipe from at 30 yards but stray within range of a covered shooting position at 60yds – if there's no time or allowance to build a hide to get closer – then again the FAC PCP air rifle shot off a bipod being my first choice of gun if the land isn't passed for rimfire.

So there you have it, the FAC air rifle may well be a specialised tool, and have specialised uses but should the situation be encountered, the rifle fulfils its roll admirably well.

In actuality there's much more to say on the subject, but I'll end on this very telling example of the FAC air rifle and its specialised use.

Relatively recently using a hi-quality Gen 2+ Nightvision Riflescope on my .177 calibre BSA Superten MkII Custom running at 22ft lb, zero set at 35 yards and shooting off a bipod, I was confidently sniping rabbits in total darkness out to 50 yards. I must stress that I was using range markers on the floor near the killing area (a ranging technique outlined in previous chapters), and this was a very specialised pest control situation where the rimfire wasn't allowed. That's food for thought what the right equipment in practised hands can do. And more than illustrates that FAC air rifles are indeed very specialised tools that in the right hands fulfil a vitally important roll in shooting for pest control as well as being another iron in the fire of the dedicated all-round airgun hunter.

Further and Further

Though your fieldcraft should now be of such a degree that you more often than not can get well within sensible hunting range to employ the techniques outlined in previous sections. There are times you'll find shots only present at range. This can be because quarry is very twitchy and you have no choice but to take them at longer range or 'sniping'.

I would never recommend anybody except the very experienced, and very practised shooter, try the following technique. But there are times the quarry is so wary you have to resort to allowing it a little extra distance where it feels comfortable to sit or feed. And before any feel this irresponsible consider this – FT shooters can comfortably knock over targets at 70yds and that's with a 12 ft lb air rifle. These shots are within the capabilities of those who put the effort into honing up their shooting skills. But, no matter what power of rifle you use if your accuracy isn't of a high enough standard or even if it is, weather conditions still have to be on your side as well. Personally, I'll never take a very long shot up into the trees – too many variables to contend with – variables that have been dealt with in a previous section. Now, using the correct hardware shooting along the horizontal is a different matter altogether.

Firstly you need to really ask yourself – 'can you not get within range?' No cover to use, full camo not working, can't even build a hide? If the answer is no then the only way is to try the longer shots but only after much practice on the target range at inanimate targets. Now I don't much like continually punching paper or hearing the 'ting' of a knockover but it has to be done if you're ever going to achieve success with this technique and be sure you'll either make a clean miss or a clean kill.

As for hardware, a 12ft lb rifle will get you out to 70yds. These words might seem ridiculous but put in the practice and it can be done and done with consistency. However, I've purposely followed on from the subject of FAC rifles with this technique because when longer range sniping, I'd opt for an FAC rifle every time. Now I know that might immediately sound like I'm contradicting myself about FAC rifles not giving you extra distance – I'm not – as primarily they don't. But as you've previously read they do give you less to contend with in terms of trajectory drop and still deliver more heft at the target. Personal choice has me reach for a .177. Again, a flatter trajectory and still enough heft once the pellet gets there, but even though .177 is more forgiving on rangefinding, it doesn't mean you've not got to know the impact points beyond the set zero. Setting zero for longer range shooting is yet another one for personal preference. What suits one, won't another. Practice and you'll know what suits you, the set-up you're using and here's a very important factor – the range you're intending on reaching. Also, for obvious reasons when adopting this technique I'll use a scope with a mil-dot reticle – just one of the reasons my FAC rifles are fitted with them. When I know the distance that each lower dot from centre corresponds to then I have confidence I can hit the mark as long as weather (wind) permits. After assessing all aim points there is another important piece of kit I'd never think of not using when using this technique – the laser rangefinder. Ok, I could twiddle parallax rings and trust my judgement but personally I'm not 100% confident that's the distance. Remember, it's a live target you're aiming at not a metal knockdown. I'd rather know the distance by certainty and to me that's by using a laser device. A handheld monocular doesn't cost the earth and will be accurate to within +/– 1yd. If you remember way back in Accessories I mentioned it might be one to add to the list. You can even get laser rangefinder binos, which mean a steadier target lock but if you use the monocular correctly and take two or three 'steady' readings you'll get the distance correct. I also use a top quality multi-shot PCP for lack of recoil and 'shot' back up. Then there's the all-important bipod, not forgetting quality 'checked', washed and lubed ammo. I've already dealt in detail with the correct

A compact carbine is the order of the day when shooting from the confines of a cab

technique of using the bipod but I will say for this type of shooting you 'must' set zero for this position. Also, to totally eliminate the possibility of cant, this is a time I would consider using a scope mount spirit level. I need to know everything is as it should be and as I'm operating at range it often means you've got more time to use these devices and accessories. And as for comfort, a shooting mat is beneficial as you'll likely be hold up at the same point for some time. One of the 'specialist' gunbags that opens out to form a full length padded shooting mat is ideal.

So now the method: you'll still need to be concealed, usually I'll shoot from under camo netting or just wearing full camo wear – possibly a ghillie suit. Once your quarry is spotted you then need to assess range.

If it really is too far don't try to move forward, that defeats the object of allowing the quarry – which will usually be rabbits – to feel the area is safe. The last thing you want is movement on your part having them scampering to safety disturbing the area – possibly moving further away! Wait and eventually another rabbit will appear and more often than not it'll be closer. Now check range on that with the laser rangefinder, if it's within reach, then this is the shot to take.

I'll interject here to say you must give yourself a self-imposed 'cut off' point as to the range. Be it 70yds or 75yds – don't be tempted to shoot if the rangefinder says the quarry is even only 2 or 3yds further. Remember, even fired from a hi-power air rifle at that range the pellet is now dropping like a stone. Long range shooting requires a very high level of shooting discipline, as it does skill.

When quarry is within your set 'cut off' zone, sight through the scope and watch the grass near the target for any breeze. Flat calm days are often few and far between. There'll usually be some breeze to contend with. And whilst a slight cross breeze doesn't affect the pellet one jot at medium range, go further and it will drift to one side or another depending on prevailing wind direction. If you're lucky there'll likely be a lull. If there is – take the shot.

But, in most cases you need to know how much allowance to make for a crosswind. I say wind but I do only recommend trying this technique when any wind is so light that it can be classed as a light breeze. You must first set zero, say at 35 or 40yds on a flat calm day or preferably on an indoor 50yd target range. When set, go out and shoot in various wind conditions and watch how that breeze affects the aim point at your set zero and your self-imposed 'cut off' range. It can at times be quite alarming especially after 60 yards. For days where the breeze is constant, your practice on targets at these ranges and in all conditions, which you should have undertaken will allow you to aim off to allow for drift. The multi-aim point of a mil-dot reticle scope really comes into its own in this situation. But consider the more sensible option – if there is a stronger breeze, lessen your 'cut off' range. Only experience against inanimate targets will give you the skill to assess how much aim off to give a shot for any given condition.

Now back to the technique in the hunting field: if the rabbit is comfortably within your self-imposed 'long range' shooting distance aim where the corresponding mil-dot to laser range finder tells you. If it's somewhere in between ranges assessed with laser to the corresponding mil-dot, always aim a little higher. If you miss the pellet will at least go zinging over your quarry's head. Hit low and you might wound it. If you do hit the mark – what a buzz, but if you do go over its head a quick reload can allow you the chance to drop your aim slightly and get it second time around. That might sound unbelievable. Believe me, it's not – in my experience because the rabbit is at such a distance it will often sit tight wondering what flew over its head. Again remember why we use silencers – it heard nothing from your position but did hear something strike the ground near it. Granted some scarper, sit bolt upright or shuffle around agitated but I've actually had rabbits duck down wondering what had happened but sit tight. Again, I can't stress the importance of checking your pellets. This is a situation they get tested to the limit!

Indeed, this is a very advanced shooting technique but if you practise long and hard enough on the range, you'll be able to achieve those long-range 'sniper' shots with precision and consistency given the right circumstances.

'Drive by' Shooting

Long established and accepted as the workhorse of the gamekeeper and farmer, four wheel drive vehicles or 4 × 4s are now the affordable mode of transportation of many sport shooters and of all disciplines. Be it the battered ex-army Land Rover or top of the range Discovery, Trooper or Shogun most shooters have access to a vehicle, whether that's to be a potential owner or to hitch the occasional ride from a shooting acquaintance. Now this isn't a guide to buying a motor for your shooting but there are many good 4 × 4 guides on the newsagent shelves. Have a clear perspective of what you want from the vehicle, engine power, load and carrying capacity and then it's down to finance and of course if you can justify the cost of running one. Personally, since owning 4 × 4s I've not looked back and I feel they've helped me not only achieve more enjoyment from my shooting but brought more success and certainly have opened up different avenues and certainly allowed me to use some unique hunting techniques.

In fact, let's be honest – few things can be more self indulgent or 'cushy' than being able to drive around a shoot potting a few bunnies from the cab of a 4 × 4. In the past I've used all types of ATVs such as quad bikes, mules – even hitched a ride on the farmer's tractor, but to be able to drive yourself along a hedge line dropping a bunny every so often is a real luxury. Obviously you need a 4 × 4, but just as importantly you need a suitable rifle/scope combo and the knowledge of how to use it properly and safely from the confines of the cab. Here I'll stress that of all rifle types available to the sport shooter, this is a situation the 12ft lb air rifle once again is often the optimum tool for the job. And a ruggedly built compact carbine size rifle that will stand up to the knocks is another major requirement. So, presuming you own, are considering buying or do get the chance to shoot from an 'off-roader' here are the salient points of shooting from a vehicle.

Like many other 4 × 4 owners I prefer to drive myself around a shoot. This allows me to react as soon as I spot quarry so I can act accordingly. Also you need to adhere to a few basic safety guidelines, as you have to be aware of the terrain you're driving over, visually search around for quarry and still maintain the same high level of safe shooting practice when you reach for the rifle.

Rabbits can be surprisingly tolerant of an off road vehicle. They're used to seeing a tractor or some such farm machinery or mode of transportation almost every day. Most farmers don't have time to keep stopping to 'pot' rabbits so the vehicle is accepted as a 'something' that just trundles unthreateningly around and past them as they go about their business. This is where the airgun hunter really can make inroads – pardon the pun – into the rabbit population before they wise up that it isn't always safe to stick around to watch the traffic. But the technique shouldn't be overused. It's easy enough to overshoot an area on foot – using a vehicle it's all too easy! Also, if you regularly ride too close to quarry it will make rabbits twitchy and they'll scarper at the first sight of the bonnet or sound of the engine. Incidentally always drive around a field anti-clockwise as you're already facing towards the hedge line. Generally, this is the best way to work a field.

Where practical, as long as the field hasn't been ploughed, isn't sown and is bereft of growing crops,

Sheer luxury – drive up, take the shot – one in the bag – or should that be the boot?

I drive adjacent to a hedge line approximately 40-50yds out. When I spot a bunny, I slowly drive closer, to a position, comfortably within effective 'killing range' of the air rifle and stop. The beauty of shooting from a vehicle is you can rest the rifle on the side of the car door or front wing mirror for a rock steady aim. Even better is to use one of the many specialist shooting bags; you can buy models that rest on the door lip on the open window.

Alternatively, use a double 'V' camera beanbag as a rest as I often do. They stay firmly in place while driving and are great for resting the rifle. There'll be more on moving position and resting the rifle as you drive further in this piece.

Alternatively use the 4 x 4 as a mobile hide. Often before rabbits wise up they can be surprisingly tolerant as you park up within range of a warren. I'm now of the opinion the rabbit initially tolerates the vehicle because it doesn't see the unmistakable human form. The image it sees, I presume is blurred or confusing, and until the vehicle is classed as a danger signal you'll have some easy shooting at your disposal. Even just parking up alongside a hedge you know to be infested with rabbits, shooting from the 4 x 4 is a form of 'comfortable' ambushing. 'Vehicular Rabbit Slaughter' you could say.

As for the single seater off-roaders such as quad bikes where the human form is recognisable as you're not largely surrounded and obscured by bodywork. There are even hides that break down for transportation on the quad and when in position and needed they are simply erected into a hide to enclose and engulf the quad. Ideal if you're getting over to an area pigeon are feeding and you need to be hidden quickly – these are all very advanced pieces of kit but available if you're lucky enough to be in a position to have use of them and of course afford them. In fact, you can even have the bodywork of your 4 x 4 camo covered! Is that too extreme, tres cool or what?

But back to the basics of the matter and there's nothing finer than being chauffeured around a shoot on a summer's evening potting bunnies from the passenger seat of a 4 x 4 or for the more adventurous – lamping at night shooting off the back of an open pickup. Going solo in your own vehicle, riding a quad bike – they all have advantages and it's not only because you don't need to walk. In many cases you'll get the chance of shots otherwise you wouldn't have a hope in hell of taking.

Also the all-terrain benefits mean you can not only reach areas more quickly than on foot, but cover more ground in a given time and even get to some areas impractical to reach by any other means.

Incidentally, as you drive onto the land scouring the area around for rabbits – as that will be your major quarry to target in this manner. Many times you'll see the white of the rabbit's scut disappear into the hedge or bob up and down as the rabbit hops further up the field. Don't be tempted to chase after bunnies spotted like this or carry on driving towards a rabbit behaving in this way. It's already showing a reluctance to hang around so leave it until a better opportunity presents itself. More often rabbits that are sat under or next to hedges will sit motionless and can be very difficult to spot in these dark background conditions. But keep those eyes peeled and you'll eventually spot a few too confident for their own good. It's also advisable to keep those eyes peeled on the rough tracks, often rabbits sit out in the open a long way from cover. This is when two shooters operating in a 4 x 4 can be deadly effective. One drives, the other spots and shoots. Get really good at it and both can spot and shoot and cover all angles around the vehicle.

In some cases where I've been asked to help, a 4 x 4 also makes the job of checking live catch traps and snares less time consuming. And, when moving from area to area – having a rifle within reach allows you to take advantage of opportunities that might otherwise be missed while on this type of pest control duty.

The 4 x 4 can also become a home from home housing all manner of shooting goodies and creature comforts. If I was to reel off a list of 'stuff' that's often in permanent residence in mine it'd take pages. A few I always have are a portable hide, a few hide poles, a choice of pattern of camo netting, decoys, lamping kit, brewing kit, water etc. As you can see, it can become a useful base. And as I've mentioned elsewhere I do often use mine as a base camp to return to for a change of rifle, an 'in-field' top up for the PCP if things are going 'very well' or very badly depending on the good shots and missed shots! Even just to sort myself out for another type of hunting or even a well-earned brew and a rest.

Before leaving the subject here are my views on the types of rifle to use from a vehicle.

Firstly, never ever consider using any rifle not only air rifle that hasn't got a reliable trigger safety. Granted, you should only cock the gun when ready to take a shot, but you'll appreciate the ability to slip the gun back at the side of you, with safety applied if quarry disappears from range and you need to shift position or are just sitting tight waiting. But never rely on the safety alone – the safest gun is an unloaded or un-cocked one. That's why for many years my favourite rifle for 4 x 4 work was a Falcon Lighthunter. Having a separate cocking bolt and loading probe makes this one of the safest of PCPs. The BSA Hornet multi-shot carbine is another handy 'mobile' tool. There are many others, use them right and you won't come unstuck.

Incidentally, as it's preferable you use a compact, easy to cock and preferably multi-shot air rifle then it follows basic traditional break barrels and under-lever action spring powered rifles are just not suited to this type of shooting. This certainly is the domain of the carbine size PCPs and little wonder at one time and even now, shooters had special made to order PCP bullpup air rifles for this type of work. In fact, you could say bullpups were very much precursors to carbines before the latter became more commercially available and popular for sport shooting – and we all know how useful they are in cramped spaces such as shooting in this manner or from a hide.

A multi-shot might be seen as a luxury but if driving yourself around, the fact you're not having to load for each shot as well is a big bonus. As you won't or most likely won't need to be shooting at excessive range, a compact scope or even small fixed magnification spec is ideal. This allows quick target acquisition once you stop and sight in – the last thing you want when you've carefully 'rolled up' within range is to pick up the rifle and be messing around trying to find the rabbit in your sights. In fact, there is a way of 'carrying' the rifle as you drive that is better suited than continually reaching over for it from where it's wedged pointing down into the seat well of the passenger seat.

I prefer to have the rifle across my lap with the rifle muzzle pointed out of the window. Ideally you should be driving in a direction that allows you to have the area you intend to target on your right. As briefly mentioned earlier, that means working the field in an anti-clockwise direction.

As you slowly drive along a track or the edge of a field you should keep your eyes peeled.

This is even more difficult than when walking an area as you're driving as well. You'll likely see some movement ahead or near a hedge. Stop frequently to assess the area. Rather as you would if opportunist shooting but this time on wheels! Once a rabbit is spotted you shouldn't drive straight towards it rather turn away so you'll run in a slight diagonal direction but eventually get within range before passing the animal. Then slowly put the handbrake on.

I know this will sound obvious but depress the button so the ratchet doesn't sound. Then carefully move the rifle to the shooting position taking care not to bang metal or wood on the top of the door of the open window because in my experience 'noise' at this stage is likely to spook the bunny rather than a small amount of movement. If it's still looking at you it's more likely only registering a stopped vehicle that it has seen many times before. So as long as you aren't leaning too far out or madly waving the barrel around the rabbit will often tolerate the vehicle's presence.

A factor here to address when shooting from any vehicle is vibration from the engine causing your cross hairs to waver on the target. It can be a pain to keep switching off the engine to shoot but on some vehicles such as 4 x 4 'mules', golf cart type and some quads you'll have to switch off the engine to prevent 'shudder'.

Another pays the price for watching the traffic

Now to another very important factor to be mindful of when shooting out of the cab of a vehicle – that being closed windows. If shooting alone always get into the habit of having both passenger seat and driver's side window fully open. If not, you guessed it, there'll come a time you sight across to shoot a rabbit spotted out at the passenger side and the window isn't open. I know of more than one shooter – not only using air rifle – who's done this and not only is the shattering glass costly but there can be even more potentially dangerous consequences. You have been warned as they say. In fact, an example here that reinforces my views on sound being more troublesome than worrying over slight movement. Once I waited until on the shoot until opening the window. Spotting a bunny, without budging a visible muscle I operated the electric window and the rabbit clearly spooked at the sound.

Now to the benefits of being a passenger: if being driven, the driver needs to work a field clockwise so you face the hedge line. A major benefit of being driven is unlike when driving you now have much easier access to a wider arc of fire. Almost a full 180 degrees from front to back. If driving, and you're a right-handed shooter, which most are you'll struggle to reach around back much over 90 degrees from the forward facing driving seat position. Then again, a passenger who's a left-handed shooter has the same problem. Even a left-handed shooter who's driving will be limited to some extent from the forward area. In fact, the best by far is to be a right handed shooter in the passenger seat or sitting in the back of an open top pick up. Then again, I've found the sunroof has given me a full all-round shooting view when stationary. And I do take advantage of it!

Talking of stationary shooting, if using the vehicle in this way and quarry really is getting wary, try draping camo netting over the door's open window. First open the door, and then placing a suitable length of camo screen across the top, shut the door to trap the camo in place. Cut a few holes if needed to shoot through. I've only found this necessary in extreme cases but it does work when parked side-on to a warren or similarly parked alongside a hedge with the driver's side facing into the field the rabbits frequent. And again – don't forget that those windows should always be open.

But in many cases when the rabbits are wising up to even a parked vehicle in their vicinity you'll find you've got quite a long wait until there's any activity – in these cases there are usually better hunting methods to employ – most that entail getting off your bum!

But it's not only the fact you can shoot from a 4 × 4 that makes them so useful to the hunter. They can be used to 'drop' baits such as slit open rabbit for corvids into inaccessible or the far reaching areas of a shoot. This means less time in doing your rounds when baiting out which can be time consuming but also it negates the need to show the human form. Also, if you have a shooting partner one of the best methods after this is to use the quad or off-road vehicle to be driven to a hidden shooting position that has been regularly baited. Leave the 4 × 4 as quickly and unobtrusively as possible and get yourself into the hide or the allotted chosen shooting position. Once the vehicle has left – the area settles down more quickly than when you've arrived on foot. Quarry will come to the bait presuming the danger has passed as the vehicle disappears into the distance. Another bonus of using this trick is you don't have to arrive at the usual ungodly hour before dawn to be in position. However, quarry soon wises up and again this isn't a magic trick just another technique to employ to fool wary quarry – in particular – corvids.

So as you can see, having a suitable off-roader can bring many opportunities for the shooter and make life all the easier for carting all that kit you'll accumulate onto the shoot. In fact, I've taken this concept to the point of driving using NV goggles to drive without headlights. I've had varied success with this method but for getting into a field and sitting in comfort with a rifle equipped with a NV Riflescope. It has given me bonus opportunities.

In fact, I suppose there are occasions a 4 × 4 can really make you lazy.

Getting High

Here in the UK, the high seat is the norm for the deer hunter and in many parts of Europe they are similarly used for 'ambushing' wild boar, foxes and other large vermin. Similarly the American hunters use all manner of high seats and elevated shooting positions for many different quarry species – mainly prized whitetail deer. In fact, some ingenious devices are now coming into the UK which I'll briefly outline shortly. Firstly though why does the 'high seat' work?

In this country both deer hunters and some fox shooters take advantage of high seats, be they fixed or portable models, leant or freestanding and of various heights off the ground. Now the 'theory of use' of a high seat is it elevates the shooter to a position that gives him a clear shot at the target. Being above ground level means little chance of him being scented by the animal and it affords a commanding view of the surroundings. Not forgetting of course as he's using a high velocity rifle – the ground is a very safe backstop.

They will work just as well for the airgun hunter – but the problem we face is like the deer hunter it needs to be built where the animals feed, frequent or move past. As we work at closer range the disadvantage being it's all too easy to site in a bad position and waste a lot of time 'up in the air' so to speak. Being stuck up a tree as it were and rabbits appearing at 15 yards further than the effective range of your air rifle is unbelievably frustrating. However, being in a position above land borne quarry such as the rabbit can sometimes give the hunter an advantage. I first came across the usefulness of being 'above' quarry as a lad climbing trees, the views great and it's amazing what will 'trot past' down below, and even land in the same tree. Now transferring this theory to a sensible applied airgun hunting technique doesn't take that much modification. But, as the airgun hunter's shooting position is more dictated by range constraints, the area has to be chosen with thought and care.

Most permanent sited hide seats on a shoot are of little or no use to the airgun hunter. Not only are few airgun hunters likely to be on a shoot were high seats are used, but they're usually a good distance from a clearing or animal thoroughfare. Best we can manage from these is a cocky squirrel sat in an adjacent tree. However, portable hide seats have been on the market for some time and are reasonably priced and do offer a solution to certain hunting problems. But consider the fact if a land built hide will do the job rather than lugging and erecting a high seat – no matter how portable.

Alternatively, a comfortable position sat up in a tree can be of more use. Find a tree near the quarry and snipe from this, using the tree's foliage as cover and wearing suitable 'season' camo wear.

Incidentally, I'm sure you've often heard the supposition that rabbits rarely look up but I'm not sure a rabbit is ever so dense. A twitchy rabbit will bolt if a bird swoops low, or clatters out of or into a tree near its position. It certainly hears or sees that disturbance. Young naïve rabbits are taken by virtually any flying raptor strong enough to carry them off. But as for the adults rarely looking up, I'd say to some extent this holds true unless the animal's attention is attracted by some other disturbance from the area. So it goes without saying – once again keeping motionless and quiet are requisites for successful hunting – even above ground.

Over the years I've tried the more traditional portable high seats, sniped rabbits from out of an upper window of a run down country house, looking down from barn lofts shooting ferals and collared doves landing amongst the grain in feed pens – all types of scenarios where I was in a elevated shooting position. The most unusual but very effective while it lasted was shooting down into a flat spot at the edge of a cornfield at woodies that had found this secret safe haven. The only way to target them once in this rapidly increasing strimmed flat spot was to shoot from a nearby mature sycamore.

There are ingenious, self-climbing high seats and even freestanding hides cum high seats. And yes, they all work, but I'd say always consider the alternative of a hidden ground level shooting position. If you do go aloft – stay safe and don't risk your neck for the sake of a few bunnies. If you use a ladder to get to the lower branches, secure it to the tree so it doesn't slip on climbing or fall away leaving you stranded once up in the foliage. Consider using a safety harness to secure your upper torso to the tree limb you're leaning against or lying on.

Also, the downward angle is again a shot where compensation needs to be allowed for. This has been dealt with in a previous chapter but suffice to say I'll remind hunters to take a few shots at selected targets at various ranges on the deck before attempting the same on live quarry. There is an upside to this position as it affords the back of the napper shots on rabbits and birds. The most effective as the angle of fire offers few other kill-zone options, with the exception of a downward angle into the side on head shot. But, if I'm using this technique I don't climb very high up into the tree or use the highest setting on the hide seat.

Apart from that, if you've a head for heights give any of the methods a try – they work and as I've mentioned can sometimes solve the problem of getting within range of the quarry.

And now we really are coming to the end of the book. You might think all methods of bagging quarry are here and hopefully in the main they are. But if you think about your hunting, work out solutions to problems there are techniques that you'll develop yourself – especially the more experience you gain. And quite frankly if you do, pass them back onto me – and on that note I can't think of a better way to end this part of the book.

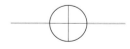

Chapter 15
General and Routine Maintenance

Many moons ago when I got my first air rifle, kids such as myself borrowed a tin of WD40 and 3 in 1 oil from our dads and some furniture polish from our ma's and that was how we looked after our slug guns. Of course it isn't the best way to do it but strangely enough – as basic and in many ways as un-subtle as it was – it was at least an attempt at keeping the rifle clean and corrosion free. Amazingly it didn't do half bad a job either. WD40 isn't the best but is good at preventing rust, and while furniture polish did clean the stock it left it 'slippy', but at least it did smell nice!

But even so, had we known then, what we know now that those lubes and oils can actually have an adverse affect on the finish of chemically blackened parts, I'm sure we wouldn't have been so enthusiastic in their use.

Obviously, as we grew older and learned by way of magazines and books we took more time and effort in looking after our guns. Even now though you'll see it written – 'wipe over with a oily rag, put it away in a gun case and place in a safe dry place.' To a certain extent, I feel that's better than nothing but advice that's of little more use than what we did way back when we first shot springers on the 'cut' for rats.

Most shooters have their own views on what are the requisites for gun maintenance – some, most or all being done on a regular basis. For reasons of thoroughness in this chapter I'll not only give my recommendations but I've managed to persuade a well-respected gunsmith to contribute some sound advice – that being Tony Wall who you've heard mention of way back at the start of this book. He's somebody I not only rate highly for his knowledge on the subject and hunting prowess in the field, but also someone I owe a great debt of gratitude to for advice and other such help in the sport of ours.

Firstly though, my thoughts on Gun Maintenance and the very basic dos and don'ts of DIY 'Gunsmithery.'

The Basics

Firstly a word or two of caution: If you buy your air rifle new, consult the manual and associated literature – the rifle more likely than not will have a recommended lube list with guidelines.

Follow these to the letter as if you don't, and the rifle needs major repair it will need to go back under warranty. If the manufacturer sees you've ignored the guidelines and used inappropriate lubes or have just 'tinkered' then the warranty will be void and you'll probably end up having to fork out much more than expected for what could be a very simple fault – even one you've maybe unwittingly had a hand in causing.

A basic set of tools is needed, a more substantial set being all the better. In the least you should have a reasonable size tool box containing various sizes of slot and cross head screwdrivers, a selection of standard size Allen keys – both imperial and metric, long nose pliers, scissors (for cutting cleaning patches and swages), small mole grips, small adjustable spanner, multi-tool, a ratchet multi-bit head set, barrel pull through, barrel cleaning rods with brushes and jags, scope lens cloth – and of course the correct oils and lubes are definitely needed. In fact, a good selection of the lubes in suitable dispensers will enable you to have a full service and maintenance kit for the air rifle you might say.

Portable workstations make rifle maintenance easy and allow the storage of essential tools, lubes and oils

There's a wide selection of lubes and oils on the market but you really do need to know which to use for what part of the rifle or else you can end up doing more harm than good. Incidentally, whilst a simple plastic tool box for keeping everything together will suffice – one of the portable rifle maintenance centres – incorporating a cradle rest to secure the gun while you're working – including storage areas on a box or tray is a much better option. These workstations don't cost the earth and make working on your rifle much easier and they can even be used for setting up the scope and zeroing. I use one manufactured by MTM with an accompanying shooters' accessory box. This allows me to store everything in the same place. Small items that are needed frequently store at the top section and larger cans of oils and tools in the accessory box. Invaluable if you take your sport seriously and care about the rifle you shoot.

Now a look at what lubes your maintenance box should ideally contain and where the various 'types' can be used.

As we now know, it's definitely not wise as we did in the past to spray the whole rifle liberally with any aerosol lubricant or cleaning spray. In fact, when applying anything (and that means anything), spray it onto a clean cloth, then apply to the rifle. So with that in mind, here's what you should have at the ready.

A silicone cloth for wiping down metalwork and the stock, Have one for metalwork and a lint free cloth will suffice for the stock wood. Incidentally, always carry a cloth in the field and should blood drip onto or splash onto the metalwork – wipe it off immediately and clean properly and oil when home. Nothing attacks the metalwork as viciously as blood, moisture or rust.

This wiping 'maintenance routine' should be the first and last thing you do to the rifle, before use and certainly after use in the field. Talking of which, if the rifle is wet after a hunting trip, initially wipe over with disposable absorbent kitchen towel, then leave it to dry fully and naturally in room temperature in an 'airy' place before lubing and storing away.

If your rifle has a non-lacquered stock, be it walnut or other such wood, then make sure you have the appropriate stock wood oil and use it regularly to keep the stock wood 'replenished' of the natural oils the weather and your hands will remove.

Now as I've already mentioned silicone, I must follow that immediately with the warning that silicone is fine for protection and the initial wipe over but any oil or grease that uses silicone as a base substance should never be applied to a load bearing surface such as breech jaws or pivot pins. You'll find it's available as silicone spray and silicone grease. But of all the lubes this is probably the most specialised. It was wrongly, and more so in the past, thought by some to be a wonder lube for lubricating any metal surface – it's not! It has no uses except to protect external metalwork from moisture, including the acid in perspiration from your hands and fingers so therefore helps stop the onset of rust. That is its primary job – to dispel moisture and it does it well. As for silicone grease – this is even more specialised and should only be used for lubricating plastic surfaces.

Grease that can be associated with silicone is Molykote 33. This is silicone with lithium base and its function when used sparingly and properly is to lubricate O-ring seals such as the breech seal, buddy bottle O-ring seal and on the seals of pellet probes. But words of caution – use very sparingly and wipe off any excess.

Grease that is the most useful is Molygrease. This is usually a thick dark grey paste and is the one to apply to the large load bearing surfaces such as breech jaws and springs. For the pivot pins and linkages best to use a lighter lube such as Molyoil. If you are wondering 'Moly' is the airgun's friend as when you see the name it's the shortened reference term for the substance known as Molybdenum Disulphide.

Now you may think it strange I leave it until last to mention one of the most useful and usable but I once again want to stress all lubes, even and including molybdenum should always be used sparingly. Another magic lube is good quality 'light' machine oil. Remember that good old 3-1 oil we've used for years? Well forget it because there are special light gun oils that are more suited. Light oil in itself does no damage wherever it is applied but always remember nothing, repeat nothing should be put either in front of the piston and in a PCP never put anything in the air reservoir. And do not put grease on or near the inlet valve – keep it clean but do not have anything near it that could have cause to be transferred into the reservoir on filling.

Talking of which I'm sure you'll have noticed most of the maintenance advice pertains to spring powered air rifles, rather than PCPs. As you'll read further even the experienced advise you have a PCP serviced by an expert. Of course barrel cleaning can be done as can exterior work but for the valving and other such mechanics of the PCP – leave it to the experts. Incidentally, for more in-depth info there are books on the subject but we're fortunate here to get a few 'tricks of the trade' from a professional. I now hand the platform over or maybe that should be the 'oily rag' to Tony Wall of Sandwell Field Sports.

From the Man who Can

Tony Wall – Gunsmith: After many years in the trade I know all too well how the elements can soon affect a lovely new rifle. Even as soon as it leaves the shop, and after you've put your hands on the metalwork, it's already under attack from corrosive elements. Even the moisture from your touch will start to eat away at that lovely lustre of the metalwork. And after saving the 'hard earned' cash and after many weeks of deliberation over which to choose it's only fitting you look after what is in effect a precision instrument.

So, like many others who enter the sport, you've been keenly shooting it, on and off for about three months with no problems and everything is rosy, or is it? Now you've done your bit to keep the nasty rust monster at bay by wiping the gun over with an 'oily rag' as Mr Wadeson so succinctly puts it, and putting it back in its bag to protect it from bumps and scratches that will inevitably occur over its coming lifetime but have you thought with all that vibration and recoil (bi-products of the internal operation of a spring powered or gas-ram air rifle) that maybe the stock screws have come a little loose? Now then, that may explain the inaccuracy of the gun all of a sudden! How do we cure the problem of loose screws? Simple, degrease the threads with a quality degreasing agent or methylated spirits and apply a very weak thread lock if no thread lock can be found then a small dab of nail varnish will suffice, failing that because not every bloke has nail varnish in his gun maintenance kit (I'd be worried if he had!), a bit of cotton thread wrapped around the screw threads will do the job equally as well. Loose screws not only cause inaccuracy in a gun but in the case of a recoiling gun can potentially cause split woodwork as well.

While we're checking over the gun for loose screws it's always worth checking the tightness of the scope mounting screws as well, although on a recoilless PCP air rifle, if you've mounted the scope correctly, this is rarely a problem. Just a gentle 'tweak' is all that's needed, don't go like a bull at a gate and tighten it so that you need a length of scaffold pole for leverage to undo it again but just enough to hold the clamps securely in the dovetails without them being damaged. If you do re-tighten, always re-check zero.

If you own a break-barrel recoiling gun then pay close attention to the area of the breech jaws as all sorts of problems can occur if left to its own devices. First of all, check for the biggest killers of all airguns – dirt and grit.

Grit has the annoying habit of actually shaving metal away when compressed and making what was once a wonderfully smooth gun into an old clapped out banger. So what do we do about it when we see a fair amount of dirt and the like accumulated in thus said area? Well I'm afraid there's no way around it really apart from a full strip down but if there is only a small amount to be seen then there is an easier method to apply. If you know someone with a compressor then give it a quick low-pressure blast around the area, pointing away from your person. (NOTE: YOU SHOULD ONLY ATTEMPT THIS METHOD WHILST WEARING APPROPRIATE SAFETY GOGGLES – ALSO DO THIS UNDER THE GUIDANCE OF SOMEONE WHO HAS INTIMATE KNOWLEDGE OF HOW PRESSURE EQUIPMENT WORKS.)

You'll now be feeling pleased with that job but when you 'jetted' away the unwanted grit and dirt – unfortunately you also unintentionally disposed of the oil and grease that the manufacturer put there to lube the area. You guessed it, now we have to put it back again. So, what lube is best? Well, I wish I had a penny for how many times I've been asked that question! There are many lubes out there and I could write reams alone on the subject, but I'll condense it to specify a few lubes that I use and recommend. Around the breech area if stripped down I'll use a thick synthetic Molybdenum paste as made by a company called Lurbo Teknik. If you don't feel competent enough to strip your gun down then pop along to a good motor accessory shop and ask for a can of non-silicone motorbike chain spray oil. This can be termed oil or grease as it comes in aerosol form and leaves the can as a liquid spray to dry as a viscous greasing and protecting agent. Use it very sparingly on the inside of the breech jaws, pivot pins, at the barrel detent and just about any area where there is a high load factor. Also check your breech seal for signs of wear, if there is the slightest of 'nicks' in it then replace it as it will only get worse with use and as sod's law dictates, will fail you as you were on that long weekend hunting trip or squeezing the trigger on what could have been a shot of a lifetime. Breech jaws and shims need checking for wear as does the breech axis pin for working loose. That's the big screw bolt that holds the barrel onto the breech jaws.

If you feel confident enough to take the action out of the stock then do so and wipe away all the debris that has accumulated underneath the action and in the recess of the stock. Then using the chain spray oil, spray a little onto the coils and spring guide if your gun sounds particularly 'boingy'. But for more dedicated 'spring dampening', change lubes and use a cotton bud to smear some thick Molygrease into the cocking slot and between the coils. And when all is complete and nicely 'oiled' be it pneumatic or a springer,

The spring and piston powerplant will periodically need care and attention, eventually even replacing

before putting the action back into the stock, sparingly spray the motorcycle chain oil onto the underside of the action to protect against the elements.

Probably the most important part of an air rifle is the trigger unit, not only has this component the laborious task of releasing the piston or valve spring hammer – time and time again. But it has to do it with the consistency of a Swiss clock over a good many years of use. If any foreign object or debris finds its way into a trigger unit, a multitude of problems can arise. This is an area I personally pay great attention to, cleaning it meticulously when I service or tune a gun. A word of caution though – if you're stripping down to clean a trigger unit you really need to know what you're doing. One small misalignment of the components upon reassembly and you've got a dangerous gun on your hands. The golden rule is 'if you don't have a mechanical mind, then leave well alone'. Take it to a reputable gunsmith who for a very modest fee will only be too glad to do the job for you. If a trigger is to be lubed (which is very rarely needed), then use a very small amount of the lightest oil you can find. But I must stress the importance of careless hands and fiddly fingers in relation to trigger units. Over the years I've had cause to put right many DIY bodged up tampered with trigger mechanisms. The air rifles' owners thinking they were doing the right thing and adjusting the trigger to suit them as well as cleaning it. In fact I'd always say for safety's sake and the peace of mind it will give – do leave this area to the experts.

So, though I've warned against tampering with triggers, I'm presuming you've followed my advice and taken the action out of the stock and carried out all the other routine lubing. If so, when you put the stock back onto the action again you will see a slight gap all around where the action seats into the woodwork.

This is an area where rain can and does run to the underside of the metalwork and in extreme cases can cause the woodwork to swell and split so smear a good 'dollop' of Petroleum jelly into the gap all around and wipe away any excess with an oily rag. Oops, nicked that one from Pete. Anyway, pay particular attention to the butt pad where it joins the woodwork, again smearing Petroleum jelly into any gaps where rain can get and in time do its worst.

If any dents or bruises have occurred to the stock, any competent gunsmith can sometimes repair them if it is an oiled finish but on a lacquered one I'm afraid then you'll just have to live with them. For cosmetic repair of an un-lacquered stock, I use an electric kettle with a narrow spout that emits a small jet of steam which I hold the dent over until it has 'raised' then I 'cut it' back with very fine wire wool and oil it again so that it looks like new. On some lacquered stocks, which have scratches, I've successfully used boot polish to hide the unsightly marks but this is more of a temporary measure rather than a long term one.

We've now 'covered' the protection of the external metalwork and woodwork but what about the insides of the gun? Well here comes the controversial part, do we clean the barrel or not? There are many trains of thought on this matter and I'm afraid I live in the camp of clean it, be it with a Phosphor bronze brush and rod or a pull through. A barrel can never give its full potential if it is dirty and I always clean mine every 200-250 shots whatever the gun, while FT shooters on average swear by cleaning theirs every 80-100 shots. Then again – some just swear!

Though modern pellets are a lot better made than they were in grandpa's day and even though they may look clean in a tin believe me they are in fact very dirty with minute lumps of swarf and oils on them. OK, we can wash and lube them in many of the pellet lubes that have become fashionable these days, but the truth is lead is a very dirty material (you only have to look at your loading fingers at the end of a long practice session to see that) coupled with the speed of the pellet travelling up a choked bore you can see why a barrel becomes dirty quite quickly. So how do we clean a barrel then? I favour two methods, the first is to scrub the bore with a good quality phosphor bronze brush and rod to loosen up any lead fragments – I promise you it won't damage anything. Then I pull the bore through with a lint cloth with a few drops of airgun barrel cleaning fluid on it (NOTE: Don't use the solvents intended for the cleaning of fullbore rifles; these solvents are very corrosive and if allowed to trickle inside a pneumatic air rifle valve or come into contact with any synthetic material, over a period of time it will dissolve them. Only use cleaners intended for airgun barrels; if in doubt contact your local gunsmith or manufacturer of the gun.)

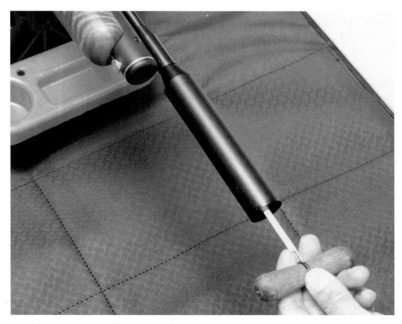

Tony's straw and pull thru' trick for cleaning a barrel with silencer fitted

I then proceed to use the barrel pull through, replacing the patches until they appear clean. When you are satisfied it's clean, fire a few shots through the gun to 'settle' the barrel down again.

If you have a silencer fitted – which most hunters should have – then it can be very frustrating trying to get a pull-through wire into the front of a barrel through a long silencer. If it's a screw on silencer, no problem, just unscrew to remove, clean the barrel, then after refitting the silencer check the zero. But if it's a push fit silencer held in place with a grub screw, it can be time consuming and quite a struggle to remove – nigh on impossible if it has been bonded in place! So how do we overcome this problem? Well, a simple little trick I use is to insert an ordinary plastic drinking straw into the silencer until you feel it 'bottom out' (come up against resistance), as it touches the muzzle or crown of the barrel itself. Then place the pull-through wire into the protruding straw's hole and feed it in until it shows at the breech loading area. Then fit with a clean patch and pull through as per usual. On exiting the barrel the patch catches on the drinking straw and hey presto - all come out of the silencer together.

Taking of silencers, unlike on powder burning guns (live round bullet guns), airgun silencers don't really need cleaning inside as there's no real residue discharged by the airgun to get rid of so on this matter I'd say leave well alone. If it ain't broke, don't fix it and as the internal baffles are precisely set for the airgun silencer to work at its best – no point risking upsetting this harmony.

Pellets

As for pellet care – do we lube the pellets or not? If you've washed them then I say a resounding yes. The reason being is after 'washing', pellets have nothing on them to protect them from oxidisation and so if left to the elements they turn white and 'scabby' and don't shoot at all well. If you shoot unwashed pellets in a pneumatic then I would also say again lube them because quality lubes cut down the need to clean the barrel as often, while I find spring guns don't really like a lubed pellet at all. I have a theory about that because when a springer shoots it disperses a tiny amount of its own lube up the barrel therefore adding any more oil to the equation seems to upset the equilibrium causing the odd flier to occur therefore spoiling an otherwise good group. To help prevent this, for my springers, I use a wax based lube very, very sparingly on the washed pellets so as not to cause any dieseling. As many hunters like Mr Wadeson now prefer to use a multi-shot PCP air rifle a word or two on the maintenance and care of pellet magazines. These little ingenious but relatively simple 'units' can be an area where all sorts of muck and grime can accumulate so a good cleaning session wouldn't go amiss here as well. Cleaning some magazines such as the removable 8-shot drum magazines can be done with relative ease whilst others such as those with an outer casing and inner drum 'sprung or free moving' have to be stripped down/disassembled. You'll either see through the Perspex cover if dirt is accumulating or for closed face types you'll actually feel the grit as you rotate the inner drum of the magazine while filling with pellets. And yes, this isn't an uncommon occurrence; especially if you've dropped your magazine in the mud a few times, or keep them in dirty jacket pockets, even pay scant attention to the ammo you load into them. I clean these types of magazines with a product called 'Gunk-Out' made by Kleanbore. This is a quick evaporating degreaser and cleaner. If you can't get this excellent product, then once again pop down to the local motorist spares shop and get a good quality brake and clutch-cleaning agent. Spray the magazine liberally inside to get rid of all the nasty debris and place on one side for this inner pellet carrier to dry naturally. Then lube lightly with a good pellet lube or Teflon based lube and never use a gooey thick grease otherwise you'll find after assembly the internal carrier soon gums up catching more dirt than it did before. (Note: The above is a base guideline and will suit most removable rotary feed magazines currently in use, however, check with the rifle manufacturer for advice on 'lubing' their particular magazine, not all magazines work well with lubricant.)

As for specific maintenance of a PCP – I'd recommend you always take it to a reputable gunsmith. Most work done is commonsense and not difficult but can be very dangerous for 'Fred In The Shed' to go willy nilly at.

Before I hand back to Pete, I'd like to stress the point that as responsible airgun hunters it's our duty to ensure the air rifle in our possession is running within the UK legal limit currently set at 12ft lb. As I do much custom tune work on rifles, the most common request is to make the rifle as powerful as possible up to the limit. I won't and don't do this for a specific reason. If an air rifle is set 'dead-on' 12ft lb with one pellet brand, use a different, say lighter pellet and then the rifle will stray over the limit – rendering it in effect a firearm and if you haven't got an FAC with this on your ticket – you're breaking the law. I always recommend and set the rifles up at approximately 11.4-11.6ft lb depending on rifle. Small, basic chronographs aren't costly, and if you can't get to a specialist dealer who has one – though in my mind all gunshops should have one – it's no great task to keep a check of the rifle power output at home. This helps you ensure you're legal and importantly for your hunting, that the rifle isn't dropping in power for any reason.

I'm sure Pete's pointed this out, but I still feel it needs clarifying from a gunsmith's point of view. Everybody is an ambassador for the sport and we want all who take part to do so safely and within the law.

So that's about it – all I've outlined is within the capabilities of the most 'DIY-Phobic', but there are times when the rifle, be it spring-powered, gas-ram or PCP will inevitably have to go to a reputable gunsmith for repair or service. But beware. Not all gunsmiths have the knowledge of the intricacies of modern air rifles. They may be expert at repairing shotguns and superb at servicing fullbore rifles but airguns are a totally different matter. If you are unsure where and to whom to entrust your prized possession, look in the adverts in one of the many airgun magazines and you'll find certain companies who advertise are experts in the field of airguns. They'll know how to 'breathe new life' into your pride and joy. Failing that, you can in most cases send it back to the manufacturer themselves, after all they built the darn thing in the first place didn't they.

Tony Wall (2004)

Gun Storage

We've had some very wise words from Tony on Gun Maintenance so time now to look at a subject that is equally important – the safe storage of the air rifle.

Like myself, Tony and many others of my acquaintance believe that storing your gun should be as important as cleaning it. What's the use of spending all that time meticulously oiling and cleaning your pride and joy only to put it in your bag and stand it in the corner of a damp room or garage.

Do this and leave it in there for any amount of time and you'll come back to a brown and black coloured gun that resembles a patchwork quilt with moss growing on it! OK, maybe I'm over dramatising that a little – but how do we stop the dreaded rust from attacking the gunmetal in the beginning? Well, this is where we come back to the oily rag. Yes, wiping the metalwork over is a help but there are now numerous lubes on the market these days and they all claim wonders and miracles for keeping a gun 'rust free' but depending on how the rifle is stored – oil often isn't by itself good enough to protect a rifle. Reason being it is easily absorbed into some gun bag linings and so the rifle is soon rendered dry. If the rifle is not going to be used for a while then more protection is needed. A popular one with collectors is to smear a thin lining of grease or petroleum jelly onto the metalwork. Also, guns that are not being used very often should preferably be stored lying horizontally. This mainly applies to springers as internal oils will only run one way – and that's downwards!

Now as for storing rifles that are used with some regularity, without doubt the best place to store a gun is in a gun cabinet or enclosed gun rack. Not only does this protect the rifle from the bumps and bruises that can occur in a soft gun bag but also it allows it to 'breathe' and equally importantly – it's away from prying eyes. If young children are in the house then it certainly should be in more substantial storage than just being put away in a bag at the back of a wardrobe. If you can afford it

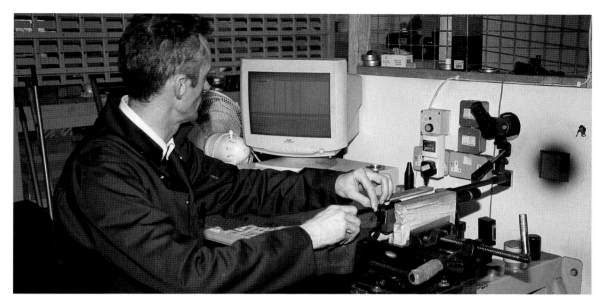

All air rifles are meticulously checked over a computer chronograph before leaving the gun manufacturer – it's every shooter's responsibility to ensure the rifle's power level stays within the legal limit

then go for a lockable cabinet, not only can you store your gun in it but you can put small personal valuables in there as well. As a shooter a sounder investment you will never buy – and remember if you do decide to apply for your FAC, and the cabinet is secured and sited properly in the house then gun security is already taken care of.

Personally I have two storage areas. One is for the 12 ft lb air rifles and is in actuality a purpose built floor to ceiling cupboard. In this I have a gun rack that holds up to 12 rifles and has storage space and drawer units for various accessories. Here the rifles are safe and secure, ready rigged with scopes, zeroed and ready to be picked up and slipped into the appropriate gun bag for use when needed. My other storage facility is a locking gun cabinet. This houses my FAC air rifles nestling alongside live-round firearms.

And before leaving the whole subject I'll end on this thought.

While we think nothing of having our cars regularly serviced why is it so different to put our springers, gassers or PCPs in for servicing by trained personnel? Personally, I say a yearly 'tune-up' or service should be considered for your most used hunting rifle. At the very least, now armed with the information in this chapter you have no excuse for not giving it the 'close scrutiny' every four to six months or so. But certainly, in the case of a PCP – read the manual to see what the manufacturer recommends. Many have their own in-house service departments and do in fact recommend either a yearly or 18-month service. Don't think they're just after more money – they're not, as no service is overly expensive and surely it's worth the cost to have the rifle back up and running at peak performance.

As they say – Stay Clean!

Chapter 16
The Airgun Hunter's Larder –
Preparation of Game

Although hunting with an air rifle is done primarily for pest control of vermin there are obvious benefits besides it being an absorbing, challenging and enjoyable sport. A major plus being the fact certain quarry species is very tasty to eat.

I've now come to a point in my shooting career that I feel if quarry that is edible isn't taken for the table, it's a waste of good food. Even if it's not to your taste or maybe you've no room left in the freezer – then you'll likely not need look far to find somebody who will welcome the nutritious meat on offer. And if you really 'get into' cooking your own game, then it's wise to invest in a small fridge freezer – a large chest-freezer stored in the garage being even better. That way it stops the arguments with the missus that you've taken up valuable freezer space and you can store a lot more game at any given time in various forms of dress. By that I mean there are times you might only gut a rabbit but want to freeze it – leaving the fur coat on means the rabbit meat is protected from freezer burn and tastes just as fresh once you defrost it to fully skin and prepare for cooking. Also, if you really take to the technique of baiting down crows and magpies, save the rabbit heads and the carcass with guts. Freeze in strong freezer bags to use as bait at a later date. Corvids aren't fussy and 'off-cuts' and dissected heads work just as well at bringing them in as a whole rabbit. And in the long run who wants to waste too many good rabbits?

Now, unfortunately though, in this age of processed, pre-packaged, ready prepared 'food' there are many who wouldn't know 'one end of rappit from 't'uther', as they say in old Lancashire.

If I have the time, which I rarely seem to have, I gladly prepare fresh game for the pot for friends. And I feel all who can prepare for the table should show those willing to learn how. If not then that's yet another traditional country way of life lost.

Of course it can be messy because fresh game preparation requires gutting, paunching and jointing. The cutting of flesh and cleaning out of a carcass to some is unpleasant but many hunters will find some dissection educational. Just check out the crop of a wood pigeon and discover what it had been feeding on. It'll indicate where to look for more at that time. Also, I'm of the opinion depending on foodstuff especially as I've noticed the difference in woodie by the season – these different foodstuffs can slightly affect the flavour. When gutting a rabbit – as a hunter check out where those vital organs in the body are. Yes, they are small and as I've mentioned in the section devoted to the rabbit in Quarry Files, the heart and lungs are very high up in the chest. As you slip the sharp blade of the knife up, notice how easily that rabbit comes 'unzipped'. Not much protection at the top end where the ribs are either. You're now discovering these critters' vulnerable areas for yourself and you might well be surprised at just where they actually are in relation to their 'outward' profile.

But, enough biology and animal skeletal make up as of all meat available the game we shoot is amongst the most nutritious you can find being both low in saturated fats and cholesterol.

And this is true untainted wild protein because all wild meat has an unrivalled quality as during that animal's existence it lived as nature intended, in most cases eating a natural diet. Not being fattened up and pumped full of growth hormones or fed hi-boost animal feed. Yes, no dangerous chemical additives to worry about, no excessive salt or the dreaded E-numbers. Once prepared you're left with good flavoursome, wholesome fresh meat.

Game from the airgun hunter's larder is amongst the most nutritious you can find

Before leaving the subject of 'taking for the pot', as I have mentioned elsewhere in the book, though I rarely shoot jays, if I'm shooting where they are in large numbers I will take one if the shot presents itself. Reason being I know of several people more than grateful of the feathers for fly tying. And that in turn will result in a friend catching a sea trout and again the basis for a fresh healthy meal. The 'edible' game we shoot is rabbit, wood pigeon, collared dove and squirrel – yes even the grey bushy tailed ones cook up to make a tasty meal. Rook pie – sorry, not for me, so here follows how to prepare my favoured quarry for cooking with a recommended recipe or two thrown in for good measure. Game cookery books are widely available and you might be surprised how interested you become in the subject. Even to the extent you obtain reference works to help you identify edible wild mushrooms and natural vegetables and herbs.

Also, you can easily adapt most recipes that use game to utilise the meat from the airgun-hunting larder. You can even use a few types of meat in the same dish to make stews, casseroles or even pies – my 'Airgun Hunter's Game Pie' recipe at the end of this chapter being a prime example. And let's not forget the fact any meat here can be used in a curry, kebab and even cut in strips for a stir-fry. The adventurous amongst you can have a field day.

But, whichever way you prefer to cook the meat, you'll first need a few essential tools to prepare it. The knife is the most versatile tool in the hunter's accessory kit and shows itself to be very useful even in game preparation. Most hunters should have at least one good quality compact folding lock knife. You can skin and paunch and even fully joint up a rabbit with such a knife as long as the blade is strong and sharp. Nothing's more useless or potentially dangerous than a blunt knife. So always keep those knives sharp.

However, a few more specific utensils are required if you want to prepare the game more easily and efficiently. A small skinner, a sharp fixed blade preparing knife, a meat cleaver and or heavy serrated edge boning knife is handy as are a strong pair of game shears. Chopping boards are a must as is a sharpening tool for keeping a keen edge on the knives you use for preparation.

Now, to our staple quarry species and the candidate for many a culinary delight – the rabbit.

Rabbit – Preparation

While traditional to let some game 'hang' for a time, no need to do this with the game airgun hunters will bag. Even rabbits need only be allowed to fully cool before being prepared for the pot.

There are two ways to deal with the rabbit, paunch in the field or wait until you get home. Now I'll usually take rabbits home whole, and 'gut' the rabbit prior to skinning but only as mentioned after it's cooled for up to 24 hours. I prefer to do it this way as long as I've not got a lot to carry around before leaving the shoot. A word of caution though – don't allow them to 'stay' intact too long before gutting as the insides can start to go off and possibly taint the flavour of the meat. While on this subject while it's not very appetising they say you'll come to no harm eating a rabbit that has Myxy. Personally, it doesn't appeal and a way to spot the disease if signs aren't too obvious externally are by white spots on the animal's liver and occasionally you'll find them on the other internal organs. These can go to the dogs, ferrets or people who fly hawks –- so even these needn't be wasted.

First job is to empty the animal's bladder. This is done by holding the rabbit with stomach facing away from you, the hind legs pointed towards the floor while running the thumbs down either side of the animal's lower abdomen towards the lower thigh joint. Do it this way to avoid getting an eye-full of rabbit pee when skinning!

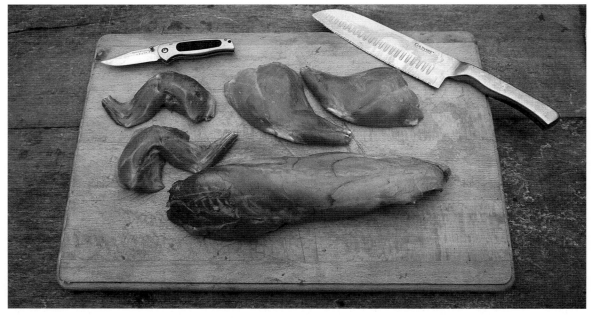

A jointed rabbit – ready for the pot!

Most shooters who regularly prepare their own rabbits for the table have a set way of doing it and though all are similar here's the way that suits me.

Once I've purged the rabbit of its last 'widdle' (and of course gutted it), I'll then pinch the fur of the rabbit across the middle of the back with the thumb and forefinger of my left hand and using a sharp pointed blade held in the right hand, push this through the pinched fur to pierce between fur and rabbit body – taking care not to go into the animal's flesh. In effect, what you are doing is slitting the fur across the back to facilitate the skinning process. To make the next step even easier, using the same sharp blade and cutting away from you, cut the fur downwards towards the animal's belly

Flash frying any meat sears in the taste

on one side then turn the rabbit over and repeat the procedure. This now will have created a long slit right across the rabbit's coat. At this stage you can if you wish, as I often do, cut the head off at the base of the nape of the neck. It's now time to pull the fur off the rabbit. Take hold of one side of the open slit across the back in one hand and the other side in the other. Then pull in opposing directions to pull apart whereupon the fur coat will quite literally and relatively easily 'peel' off the carcass. It's at the hind and front quarters that you'll need to manoeuvre the legs out of the rabbit's coat, and if you haven't first cut the legs off, once you do this you'll be left with a skinned rabbit still wearing furry little boots. I leave it until now to cut the feet off as this shows the natural point to cut keeping as much meat as possible on the bone. Jointing is done by cutting off both hind legs and thighs from the body and then removing the front forelegs and shoulders. The body can be left whole but most cut in two or into a section of three for ease of cooking. Also you can now at this stage, carefully pare and cut away the sinewy clear tissue – this is a layer of white sinew or clear skin – use a very sharp filleting knife or dedicated fixed blade skinner.

And after removing the tail, and all excess skin and any remnants of fur the meat needs a thorough rinse. You now have one rabbit, ready for the pot. Should you wish to freeze it at this point, dry it off with kitchen roll, then wrap in cling film or use freezer bags to prevent freezer burn on the exposed flesh and always date the bags so you know which to use first.

Some say the meat of young rabbits is very tender and succulent, but obviously there's little meat on a small rabbit. Only the hind legs are worth jointing and I'm not one for taking such young unsporting game unless specifically working to a strict pest control directive. I am told though that glazed and dipped in flour and then pan-fried the legs are delicious! That's for you to find out if you happen to have call to deal with a very large rabbit cull operation.

Here's a couple of my favourite ways with rabbit. And though I might call them casseroles, soups or pies – the recipe differs for various tastes and all can be modified to suit. Look upon them as guidelines. That includes how much you add in terms of seasonings such as garlic or black pepper. They are certainly adjustable to suit your own particular taste including the amount of ingredients. But the recipes as stated are more than enough to serve two generous hunter-size portions.

Recommended Recipe – Rabbit Stew

Ingredients:

2 large onions, diced
2 tbsp olive oil
2 cloves of garlic, chopped
1 large rabbit – cut the meat 'off the bone' into manageable but chunky pieces
3 large carrots, sliced
½lb mushrooms, sliced
2 vegetable stock cubes
Worcestershire sauce
black pepper
gravy granules, for thickening

How To Cook

Using a large stew pot, fry the onion in the oil until starting to soften, add garlic and further fry for no more than a few minutes. Then place vegetables and meat into the pot.

Mix the stock cubes in a pint of boiling water and pour over the contents into the pot. If you need more water to cover the ingredients, add now. If you like garlic – add another clove on top at this stage. Add a dash of the Worcestershire sauce and sprinkling of black pepper.

Bring to the boil, place lid on stew pot and turn down to simmer stirring occasionally. Cooking time may vary but should be approximately 3 hours. Towards the end of the cooking time add gravy granules to thicken the dish and test meat to check if it is tender and fully cooked.

Once cooked – serve with mashed potato and winter vegetables such as broccoli, cauliflower and cabbage.

Incidentally, if you fancy a rabbit and pigeon stew – you simply add some woodpigeon meat. Simple isn't it?

Recommended Recipe – Simple Rabbit Soup

Ingredients:

1 rabbit, jointed
1 potato, diced
1 tin of sliced carrots
2 tins of Heinz chicken and leek big soup
dried mixed herbs
black pepper

How to Cook

This is the easiest to prepare and one that's surprisingly tasty due to the tang of the leeks in the soup – not forgetting the mixed herbs.

Firstly, the rabbit should be pre-cooked by roasting or boiling and the meat allowed to cook until it falls easily off the bone. Strain off the liquid and juices from the cooked rabbit and put into a dish to cool. This can be frozen for use at a later date as stock in other dishes.

Now remove all bones from the cooked rabbit and chop meat into chunky pieces.

The potato should be boiled in a separate pan until just beginning to fall. Then drain off the water from the pan the potatoes were boiled in and add the tins of soup, drained tin of carrots and the rabbit cubes. Add a liberal sprinkling of mixed herbs and black pepper and simmer for 4-5 minutes stirring regularly.

Serve with crusty bread of choice.

Recommended Recipe – Rabbit and Onions
Ingredients:
6 rabbit leg and thigh pieces, whole
2 large onions, sliced
2 vegetable stock cubes
celery, diced
salt and pepper to taste
gravy granules, for thickening

How To Cook
Put the onion in the casserole dish and place the rabbit thighs on top. Mix the stock cubes in a pint of boiling water and pour over the contents in the dish. Place lid on dish and pop in a pre-heated oven at 180°C/350°F/gas mark 4 for 2 hours. After this reduce the oven heat to 160°C/325°F/gas mark 3 adding celery and cook for a further 3 hours. The casserole should be removed from the oven every hour or so for stirring and to check water content. Towards the end of the cooking time, add gravy granules to thicken the dish and test meat to check if it is tender and fully cooked.
Serve with mash potatoes and seasonal vegetables.

Woodpigeon – Preparation
This really is a simple job and requires little or no plucking if you are only using the breast meat.

A tip before commencing 'breasting' the pigeon is to cut off the wings as close to the breast as possible with game shears. This makes the task of breasting much easier not having to contend with 'floppy' wings getting in the way as you carefully cut the skin away and peel back before cutting the breast meat from the 'keel' of the breastbone itself.

Breasting woodies is a simple matter – but use a sharp knife

Firstly place the pigeon on a worktop such as a chopping board, facing breast up, then starting from the top just below the crop, pierce the skin and carefully slice down the centre with the blade following the top of the breastbone. A tip is to pluck a few downy feathers off to find the skin for the blade. Once you've made the cut, carefully tease the skin back from the flesh and cut away to the side if necessary, peeling this back with your fingers to expose the dark breast meat found on either side of the large solid breastbone.

As a hunter – marvel at the size and strength of that 'keel' and consider now why full on chest shots are so easily deflected? Once you've exposed the breast meat carefully slice down the side and against the keel, and then follow the natural guideline of the breast meat around and under the wings. Repeat for the other side of the breast.

You should now have two large chunky teardrop shape pieces of meat. If not using immediately, rinse, dry and wrap in cling film or a freezer bag and freeze for future use.

Incidentally, same process applies to breasting a collared dove. And don't discount this dove as the meat, though a tad tougher is considered by some to be even tastier than woodie. It does require a longer slower cooking time and to 'moisten' and soften the breast meat it benefits from being marinated in olive oil and herbs for 24 hours.

Recommended Recipe – Wonderful Woodpigeon

Woodpigeon makes a fine addition to stews, casseroles and game pies but if you like to taste the pigeon as it should be tasted – I recommend you prepare it as a starter as it makes a lovely dish on its own. It has a strong distinctive flavour and one that deserves not to be hidden amongst other meat, or 'covered up' with rich sauces or heavy seasoning.

I can't take any credit for this as I only 'discovered it' when fortunate enough to be served it as a starter at a 'posh do'. After tasting the woodie on its own I was hooked and I must admit this is certainly the way I prefer it.

Ingredients:
2 woodpigeon breast
2 tbsp olive oil

How To Cook

The cooking process is a simple one. First heat a heavy-bottom frying pan then add a little amount of oil. When the oil is hot, carefully place both halves of the pigeon breast into the oil to flash fry on either side to seal in the goodness. Cook approximately 3 minutes a side. When done, leave whole or carefully cut into thick slices.

Serve with a light salad of mixed leaf, cherry tomatoes and cucumber with a few mixed herbs. Depending on personal preference – liberally 'drizzle on' a balsamic vinegar dressing or a generous dollop of garlic mayonnaise – wonderful.

Incidentally, even if the woodpigeon is to be put into a stew I still prefer to sear the meat by flash frying to keep in the flavour before fully cooking. If using in a casserole or pie cut the half breasts in two before searing – when done, remove and place in the casserole dish with other meats.

As everybody seems to have a recipe for pan fried pigeon. I'm no exception but if cooking this way, the same applies for most meats and that's don't overcook or else the meat goes rubbery.

But for another succulent way with woodie I recommend the following

Recommended Recipe – Woodpigeon, with roasted peppers and mushroom
Ingredients:

1 Red pepper, sliced
1 Yellow pepper, sliced
1 large onion, thickly diced
4 large grilling mushrooms
2 tbsp olive or vegetable oil
6 pigeon breasts (whole halves)

How To Cook

Place peppers and onion on baking tray and pop into pre-heated oven at 200°C/400°F/gas mark 6. After 20-25 minutes prepare mushrooms, place on a baking tray, brush with oil and pre-heat grill. While grill is heating up – warm oil in frying pan and place pigeon breasts in hot oil. Now put mushrooms under a medium heat grill. Cook mushrooms and pigeon breast for 4-6 minutes depending on taste.

Remove everything from the oven and grill and serve as follows.

Either as a 'mixed dish' on a bed of rice or alternatively as a starter with a mixed crispy leaf salad. Garnish with vinaigrette dressing and serve with rustic wholegrain bread rolls.

Squirrel – Preparation

Though not something you'd expect Jamie Oliver to whip up or indeed find in a supermarket, squirrel is quite tasty and if you've shot a few it's a pity to waste them. In fact I don't know why it's frowned on so much in the UK as our American cousins are very partial to a bit of squirrel. The main problem that deters most people is how to prepare them. Best way is to think of it as a small skinny rabbit. First gut as you would a rabbit, and skin as you would with rabbit but only worry about fully pulling back the fur off the back legs and the skin up to the forelegs. Then cut the body, straight across two thirds up along towards the head. This leaves you with two hind legs and some meat on the lower carcass – the saddle.

Incidentally, before detailing the recipes you'll see recipes with names such as 'Squirrel Fricassee', deep-fried squirrel or just plain and simple pan-fried squirrel – similar to the one I show below. They're all very much of a muchness but with slight changes in ingredients or coatings. As you'll read at the end of the section, with squirrel, I prefer to cut the meat into pieces and add to other off-cuts of game to make a nutritious and mouth watering game pie or casserole. But I will here give a couple of simple 'squirrel' dishes.

Recommended Recipes - Pan Fried Squirrel In Breadcrumbs

Ingredients:
3 squirrels, use only legs and thighs
1 egg, beaten
2 tbsp olive oil
breadcrumbs

How To Cook

Obviously as the squirrel is so small you need at least 3 per person, preferably a half dozen medium size bushy tails and the only meat needed for this recipe are the back legs and thighs.

Coat each leg and thigh in the beaten egg mix and dip to coat in breadcrumbs. Place these in a pan of hot oil turning frequently to avoid burning. After the initial browning, turn the heat down and fry slowly for a good few minutes to ensure the squirrel is thoroughly cooked and crispy.

When done, serve with a salad garnish and add a dip such a garlic mayonnaise or sour cream and chives.

Recommended Recipes – Quick & Easy Squirrel Stew

Ingredients:

2 squirrel saddles, meat cut off the bone into small chunks
2 tbsp of olive oil
1 beef stock cube
1 small tin of stewing steak
1 large onion, chopped
2 cloves of garlic, chopped
1 small tin of garden peas
1 tin of sliced carrots
dried mixed herbs
Worcestershire sauce
black pepper
cornflour

How To Cook

In a deep heavy-bottom pan, fry the squirrel 'chunks' in the hot oil to seal in the taste until brown. Then add onion and garlic – cook until soft. Add the beef stock mix and simmer for approximately an hour.

When meat is tender, add the tin of stewing steak, tin of garden peas (drained), tin of sliced carrots (drained), Worcestershire sauce, dried mixed herbs, and liberally sprinkle with black pepper. Now simmer adding corn flour to thicken the stew. If you've cooked correctly there shouldn't be too much liquid left so it should thicken easily.

Serve piping hot in a dish with rustic rolls or crusty fresh bread.

With all that game at our disposal, when you've prepared other dishes what to do with those frozen off-cuts you've saved – or should have. Simple – make the ultimate airgun hunter's game pie.

And believe me, once you've tasted this it'll make you more determined to fill that game bag!

Airgun Hunter's Game Pie

Ingredients:

One rabbit – jointed, and cut off the bone into chunks
4 woodpigeon – breast halves cut across into chunks
4 collared dove – breast left in halves
2 jointed squirrel, off the bone cut into chunks
2 large carrots, sliced
2 large onions, sliced (in fact add any root vegetables you prefer) I sometimes add some thick cubed
    potato for good measure.
½lb mushrooms, sliced
2 cloves of garlic, chopped
Worcestershire Sauce
gravy granules
frozen puff pastry (saves hassle and I'm no Hugh Fearnley-Whittingstall!)

How To Cook

Mix together the raw vegetables and put these with the mixed meat pieces in separate layers into a large casserole dish. One layer of mixed vegetables, then a layer of mixed meat, then a layer of vegetables,

Airgun Hunter's Game Pie – now who wouldn't want some of that?

then a layer of meat, then a layer of vegetables etc. until all ingredients are layered in this manner in the dish. In between 'layers' add a dash of the Worcestershire sauce and sprinkling of black pepper, not forgetting the garlic.

Mix the stock cubes in a pint of boiling water and pour over the contents into the dish. If you need more water to cover the ingredients, add now.

Place the lid on casserole dish and pop into a pre-heated oven at 180°C/350°F/gas mark 4 for 1 hour. After the first hour reduce the oven heat to 160°C/325°F/gas mark 3 for a further 3–4 hours. The casserole dish should be removed from the oven every hour or so for stirring and to check water content.

During the cooking period, take out a portion of the frozen pastry for defrosting.

Towards the end of the cooking time, add gravy granules to thicken the dish and test meat to check if it is tender and fully cooked. If it is, turn up the oven to 220°C/425°F/gas mark 7. Now it's time to roll out the pastry following guidelines on packet then place pastry onto casserole. Return to oven and cook for a further 25-30 minutes, whereupon the pastry should have risen to form a crispy golden brown crust.

Serve with mashed potato and extra vegetables of choice.

So there you have it, my recipes might only be basic but they're a good basis for you to try what you've harvested from the land yourself with the air rifle. In fact nothing tastes better than a rabbit taken after a long nerve racking stalk or a hard tricky shot on a woodie in the trees.
Bon Apetite!

Chapter 17
The Law, Safety and You!

I originally envisaged this section of the book would be relatively straightforward. Combine what I've known and adhered to myself for many years on the legalities of airgun use, with information gleaned from 'the legal eagles' who 'police' our sport, ask a few pertinent questions of the shooting associations, consult relevant literature – ha, what literature – then give you the facts.

Well, I'm sad and surprised to say there's very little information that's 'easily accessible' or for that matter 'seemingly speaks plain English' on the law pertaining to airguns. Of course leaflets are provided, but in many cases you get the same tale trotted out of 'don't point a gun at anybody, don't carry one in a public place', etc, etc, etc.

Don't get me wrong – they're all very important points which I will detail fully in this section but you need to grasp the fact any person who partakes in any discipline of the shooting sports is in actuality governed by more than one law – the hunter even more so is under scrutiny to 'behave correctly' and broadly speaking – that is how it should be.

In that respect I'm going to outline the salient and important points of a selection of laws that govern the use of air rifles. But by and large, misuse an air rifle, or firearm for that matter and you are governed by the same rules of conduct. These are found in the Firearms Acts of 1968 – 1997 and the Wildlife and Countryside Act 1981. Add to that the penalties that can be imposed on you for breaking the law under the Criminal Damage Act 1971, Public Nuisance Act or Anti-Social Behaviour Bill *et al* – then you're going to suffer the consequences.

Let's try to sift through what outwardly and inwardly seems to be a very mixed up subject.

So here as they stand are the laws. Whilst all shooters need adhere to them, I leave it up to the individual to decide if the Law is indeed an Ass!

First up we need to recap on something briefly touched upon at the beginning of the book, that being the Wildlife and Countryside Act of 1981 – here is the full extent in respect of how it concerns our sport and its bearing on what we can and cannot legally do with the airgun.

The Wildlife and Countryside Act 1981 – Its meaning and relevance to the airgun hunter

The quarry we are allowed to shoot with an air rifle of a suitable power has remained unchanged for many a moon – longer than the Act itself but the Countryside Act at least spells it out clearly what are deemed legal quarry for the airgun hunter using a rifle with a power – not exceeding 12 ft lbs.

Incidentally, according to the act, all species of bird, their eggs and nests are protected. But every year, the Government issues what is known as the 'Open General Licence' that allows certain species of bird – deemed pests – to be killed. It also makes reference to animals on the unprotected list due to the fact their population is in need of management and/or the animal is classed as vermin.

All have been listed at the beginning of the book but I mention them in entirety here with pertinent notes to their culling.

The corvids (crow family) including magpie, rook, jackdaw, crow and jay – the latter however currently protected in Northern Ireland. I'll add here that it was only after much investigation I finally got a tentative answer on a pertinent fact. Does the mention and use of the term 'crow' encompass both species of carrion and hooded crow? You'd think this a straightforward question – it isn't. Whilst carrion crow is definitely on the airgun hunter's hit list, seems the hooded crow should only be culled in Scotland with a suitable firearm – that being the shotgun. Scotland is its natural boundary as it is rarely if ever found south of Hadrian's Wall. In other words, shoot as many carrion crows as you are able – as for hooded, I'm still not convinced I have been given a satisfactory answer for the airgun hunter.

The humble house sparrow and starling are on the list but of little relevance for the sport shooter. However, use your discretion and commonsense and don't go taking pot shots at these birds just because you can. As mentioned in Quarry Files, the house sparrow isn't nearly as common as it once was. I'd always now let this little bird pass.

As to the starling, a recent test case had a person prosecuted for shooting starlings without it seems a 'good and proper' reason. Seems to err on the side of caution we should let these go unmolested unless they truly are causing damage and threatening health – and only then with correct permission.

Now to a genus of bird much more straightforward to deal with in terms of our rights – this being pigeons and dove family. In the W&C Act this makes mention of woodpigeon, feral pigeon and the collared dove – the latter like the jay being a protected species in Northern Ireland.

Of the gull family there is herring gull, lesser and greater black back gull. But, if you do live in a particularly 'gully' area – I certainly advice that you get to know your seabirds. Juvenile seabirds can be deceptively similar to protected species – but as with all animals and birds the hunter must ensure he can clearly identify all species and it's very useful in fact important to be able to recognise protected species as it is the unprotected ones you target.

Before we leave feathered felons, the law doesn't say the airgun hunter isn't allowed to shoot certain 'game birds' but the practice is deemed by many to be unsporting.

Personally, I say if the landowner or gamekeeper allows you to take the odd one or two for the pot, if shot cleanly, then it's acceptable albeit a little out of the norm. However you must hold a game licence and the following species can only be shot within the 'season' allotted to them. They are pheasant, partridge, grouse (red and black), ptarmigan, common snipe, woodcock and golden plover.

In respect of wildfowl, while these don't require a game licence, they can

Armed trespass carries a hefty penalty

only be shot during their allotted season. These are ducks including mallard, tufted duck, teal, wigeon, shoveler, pochard, pintail, goldeneye and gadwall.

We are also allowed to shoot geese – including Canada goose, greylag and pink-footed goose – I bet that surprised a good few readers!

And let's not forget those troublesome two-some dealt with in Quarry Files the coot and moorhen. Incidentally, I feel that some comment should be made on areas of the country where local restrictions apply, such as the Norfolk Broads, where it is illegal to use airguns on areas of water and land controlled by the Broads Commissioners. So if in any doubt, as always – check your local byelaws.

Now, whilst I will refer over to shooting organisations at the end of this section it's worth noting the B.A.S.C does actually recommend that wildfowl only be shot with shotgun. My views are, certainly any legal quarry species when in flight should only be tackled with shotgun, but as for a 'one shot, head shot, clean kill' on a stationary bird – why only let the 'scatter blasters' have duck or pheasant on the menu?

Now to the 'furry' animals on the list and whilst the fox is included but only for suitable calibre and power firearm, I'll not comment other than to say this crafty predator certainly needs a bullet or buck shot so onto the vermin we can cleanly dispatch with a pellet fired from a 12 ft lb air rifle.

These are rat, rabbit, most species of mouse (not including the dormouse family) the grey squirrel, weasel, stoat, mink, feral cat (not including the Scottish wild cat) and the hare. Now we've come to a few species that often cause some controversy. These being feral cat and the hare as though legally deemed quarry species these aren't encountered that often or particularly in the case of the hare, not as widespread or as plentiful as it once was in many parts of the UK. However, specifically in relation to the hare, if the 'odd' one crosses your path let it go on its way as it adds to the variety of wildlife and is a noble animal that has a tough enough time living all its life above ground. However, if they're plentiful and encountered by the airgun hunter using a hi-power FAC air rifle – that's certainly a powerful enough firearm to capably dispatch it at sensible range. As for stoats and weasels – as they hardly ever keep still, they're certainly better served by the shotgun. As for the mink – I've mentioned previously I've had cause to shoot them but mainly when dispatching them when caught in live catch traps.

Now to the legalities of the actual shooting of all quarry species deemed as pests.

Pests can only be shot if you have the landowner's permission to shoot on the land he actually owns or has precedent over. If you don't you can be charged with armed trespass and if you shoot any quarry charged and prosecuted with poaching. Both carry hefty penalties – especially armed trespass!

Add to this the fact that even if you have the landowner's permission to shoot you can only do so if the species is actually a pest – this is what the powers that be say on the matter.
The species is classed a pest if:

- It's threatening other 'protected' wild bird populations.
- Endangering public health and/or spreading disease.
- Causing damage to crops, livestock, fisheries, young trees or waterways.

Sift through those outlined above and you can be in no doubt why we can target rabbits, rats, wood pigeon, feral pigeon, magpies and crows to name but six now can you?

But a very important point is there are laws not in the W&C Act that govern cruelty to animals and the purposeful wounding of any animal – even those classed as pests. And again prosecution can carry heavy penalties. I'll outline a hypothetical scenario to illustrate this point.

Say you 'legally' shoot a woodpigeon or magpie in your garden or on your shoot and it flies off and lies wounded in a neighbouring garden or on private land you have no permission to be on. Should it be found, and the 'finder' takes it to the authorities – such as the police or R.S.P.C.A – with an accusation you shot it wilfully. You could, if found guilty, be charged for a crime.

In fact it's a very contentious subject to shoot birds in your own garden as being able to prove they are a pest species causing damage in the garden is very difficult. Also few if any neighbours would accept someone shooting birds in gardens – remember, the majority of the non-shooting public don't know what is considered, by law, to be 'a pest' – except maybe the feral pigeon that is.

And consider the following – shoot a rabbit and it goes under a fence onto private land you have no right to shoot over. Say it is injured to the point it can run no further but needs a *coup de grace* for merciful dispatch and you nip over the fence to administer the final shot and retrieve it. If you do go over with your air rifle, you can be charged with armed trespass. Go over and just retrieve the animal – legally it's still trespass and you could be called to prove you weren't poaching! And what of the rabbit that kicks its last on a public footpath after legging away from a wounding due to an unfortunately misjudged shot. Woe betide you should you be the one accused of shooting it and it has been found by an 'animal lover'. You might think these scenarios mentioned very unlikely or judge them 'grey areas.' In some ways, maybe – but in reality these are situations that can so easily happen. To avoid straying into these minefields I feel it is advisable here to remind hunters never, no matter how tempting it may seem at the time, to venture onto land you don't have a right to be on.

Certainly the airgun hunter who leans over another farmer's gate to 'nab' an early morning rabbit with a 'naughty shot' as it sits on a dirt track on another's land – you poached that rabbit – no grey area there and in the process you committed several offences in the shooting and retrieving of it.

Even when on land you have right to shoot on, never, repeat never shoot any species of legally deemed vermin unless you have a clear, safe shot and one that 'should' to the best of your knowledge cleanly dispatch the intended target.

As always – if in doubt – then don't shoot!

So that covers the W&C Act as it stands at present, but remember it's possible that these laws could be amended. Certain quarry species may be added but certainly more likely taken off the list governed by the 'Open General Licence.' So consult the relevant literature, organisations, authorities and web-sites. If you can find them.

Age restrictions and laws pertaining to ownership, transportation and other use.
These are quite clear-cut and need little if indeed any comment from myself.

- If you are under 14 years old you cannot buy, hire, be given or own an airgun or airgun ammunition – that's right – even pellets. However an under 14 can use an airgun but only if supervised by someone 21 years or older. And you must only shoot on land you have permission to shoot on or are shooting at an approved shooting club and the rifle is only used for target shooting at that club.

Now I did say I wouldn't comment but here I must have a say on what I feel is a great loss to the sport. This law is quite frankly not only unfair (what's new) but doesn't work! Few under 14s unless they have older brothers will be able to shoot. And, let's be realistic, those older lads have little time to help little Johnny when they're at an age they could well be more interested in cars, girls and having a drink than family matters. To be totally realistic, that 'older' sibling will have a life of his or her own and quite frankly have zero interest in air rifles or shooting. Also we now unfortunately live in a social climate of part time parents, particularly fathers – that's if they're on the scene at all. In that respect, quite frankly, some under 14s will never get the chance to try shooting with an air rifle and that comradeship of youthful shooting we enjoyed is also effectively removed. But then again, this law is supposedly designed to stop 'kids' getting up to no good with an air rifle. Pity it won't stop them sitting around a street corner scaring elderly people and smashing something out of boredom. And to think a large part of the reason we were given our first air rifles was because our parents knew what we'd be up to and it gave us something to be interested in, have pride of ownership in having and something to respect using. Hell, we got air rifles to keep us out of mischief!

When we were kids, getting our first air rifle was part of growing up. You got a fishing rod, an airgun then you discovered girls and the first two go out the window. OK, only half joking but what I'm trying to illustrate is a large part of the culture of growing up is lost. When people such as myself were kids we could go anywhere (with some exception but not anything like the Draconian rules that govern freedom of movement now) with our air rifles and shoot – usually rats and small birds such as 'spadgers' (house sparrows) and 'sheppies' (starlings). Lancashire lads will know what I mean on that but to the broader picture. We did no harm. Obviously there was always the idiot who did something daft with his airgun but by and large he grew out of it or if not just grew up and did other stupid things often resulting in them committing further crime. In other words that person would have done something stupid or malicious no matter what he had his hands on or was involved in.

But back to the law as it now stands and the reasoning being to 'keep guns out of the hands of youngsters!' The knock on effect of this 'law' pertaining to youngsters may seem to have little importance to 'long term' shooting adults, but think on this. The law effectively prevents a whole new generation of youngsters being able to naturally 'grow' into shooting as we did. If it was 'your thing', you carried on shooting, if not you looked to another sport, hobby or pastime. It's that simple. But, robbing generations to come of experiencing shooting in their formative years is a terrible pity. They won't go on to discover it at a later age – quite frankly, even back then we grew up too quickly. And as you approach 17 shooting air rifles is probably going to be the last thing on your mind. Don't be misled; they're chipping away at our sport from the ground up. Sorry that turned into such an issue but I think we should all be aware what is happening. Back to the law.

- No person under 17 can be given an airgun as a gift. On the outset that seems sensible enough but consider this. Parents or relatives, who give their under 17 an air rifle, are themselves breaking the law. But reach the magic age and between 14 and 17 you can be given, or loaned an airgun and ammunition but you can't buy or hire one yourself. Now doesn't all that make sense. Right from now on I won't comment because I'm getting far too opinionated and importantly if I carry on we'll never reach the end!

- If an air rifle or pistol is used on private land including the garden of a private dwelling the pellets mustn't stray outside the boundaries of that land. This is the reason we need solid backstops for the home target 'plinking' range. If it does go 'zinging' out of bounds, this is now also an offence under the Anti-Social Behaviour Act, carrying a maximum £1000 fine as a penalty.

- An air rifle can only be carried or transported by someone of the appropriate age, or one who is properly supervised in a public place when covered with a securely fastened gun cover – this means a gunbag - which should be zipped closed at all times. Commonsense, and no excuse for not adhering to this. But a law that 'slipped' in to yet again undermine the sport is you can't take a gunbag on public transport. Then again a youngster cannot carry a gun bag until 17 in a public place anyhow.

- Never carry a cocked or loaded gun in a public place out of or inside a gunbag. Now this is one to be very cautious of as a rifle is deemed loaded if it has a pellet or even a cleaning felt in the barrel and for a multi-shot if it has a magazine – even an empty one – in the action. Always remove the magazine from a multi-shot and store separately while travelling to and from the land you are legally

Always know the exact location of footpaths, bridleways and any public thoroughfare on the land you shoot over

allowed to shoot over. As for the former, you should never have cause to carry a 'cocked' rifle and/or a single-shot rifle with a pellet in the breech. A simple rule of safety. And further consider that the magazine of a multi-shot should be empty even when not with the gun as this in itself is deemed a loaded weapon!

There are more but they come under a broader rule of gun law that we will now try to decipher. But to recap – generally speaking for the under 14s, very strict rules apply to airgun use, between 14 – 17 years of age for all practical purposes you must be supervised by a person over 21. However, you can when 17 purchase an air rifle and ammo – the air rifle not having a power exceeding the 12 ft lb UK legal limit. But it must, and can only be used on land you have written permission from the owner to shoot. And don't take it for granted the person who signs your written permission is the owner. Double check, I'm not saying go behind anybody's back snooping, but do take the trouble to ensure that written permission is as it should be – correct and legal!

Now to something that doesn't affect hunters as they're virtually all too low powered to use for hunting but should be borne in mind if you happen across one. The law has now deemed airguns that use the self-contained air cartridges such as Brocock, Saxby & Palmer etc. need to be on an FAC. If you own one and didn't get an FAC for the time limit stipulated in April 2004 or hand it in – well, you're now breaking the law and can be sentenced under the Criminal Justice Act 2003.

The next set of guidelines are taken from the Firearms Act and are relatively straightforward as they pertain to responsible usage of an airgun or firearm.

- It's against the law for anyone to have an airgun in a public place unless they have some proper reason for doing so. Public places are any areas the general public have legal access. These are roads, footpaths, canal towpaths, public parks – any such area. And in relation to this never presume a bridle path or footpath is not used just because you rarely see anyone on it. The time you do could be the time a costly and dangerous mistake is made!

- It is an offence to fire an airgun or any firearm within 50 feet of the centre of any roadway or 'public thoroughfare' – which includes the pavement. This is seemingly straightforward but there is one exception. If you shoot in your back garden on a plinking range you will likely be within this distance. This being the case you should be out of view from the public, behind tall screen of hedge or fence. You should also be shooting away from the road. If in doubt to your plinking area consult your local police force – they can advise on your rights. While on the subject of shooting of plinking, never presume your neighbour is accepting your participation in the sport. Some will, but more likely just as many don't. Shoot at reasonable hours and don't shoot for hours on end.

This may seem like an infringement on your rights, which in some ways it is, but have consideration for others as to uphold neighbourly relations. The continuous sound of a pellet striking a backstop can become unnerving and irritating and is as annoying as any loud music. Think on that carefully in relation to the times you practise.

That's how the law stands at the moment. Whether it will change is up to the governing bodies and unfortunately these changes are usually driven by public acts of stupidity.

Hopefully commonsense will prevail and Whitehall will realise that the general shooting public go about a satisfying and challenging sport and airgun hunters and sport shooters alike perform a helpful and necessary service to the country community helping to uphold and protect the natural balance of the great outdoors.

And although a few basic rules of safety have been outlined elsewhere – here are the important one's we all must adhere to for safe gun use.

- Always treat an airgun as if it is loaded and cocked. Never presume it isn't.
- Always store an airgun securely in a safe place, always storing it un-cocked and unloaded.
- Never load or cock an airgun until it is safe to fire it.
- Never point an airgun at anyone – even if unloaded.
- Never touch, pick up or attempt to use someone else's air rifle without their permission.
- As a matter of course, whether you are hunting or getting 'kit' together, make a point of always checking a rifle is safe and unloaded before putting it in a gunbag. Also check again immediately that you remove it from its case.
- Keep airguns out of sight from prying eyes. And never let young children near them – they're not toys.
- Never shoot beyond your 'seeing distance' – for example past the end of a building, wall and if in open country, past the end of solid hedgerow.

And so at last that does bring this section to a close. I will however mention you should always carry your written permission with you whenever you go shooting on the land it relates to.

Also, remember that though the statute laws previously stated apply to you, you also have to bear in mind that should the unexpected or unimaginable happen – you could due to mishap or accident find yourself facing a civil action for damage to property or worst still unintentional injury to persons or livestock. In my opinion, every shooter should have Third Party Public Liability Insurance. You can obtain this privately but upon joining one of the associations that represent shooters' interests you can gain insurance as well as being part of a public voice on the sport. These are the British Airgun Shooters Association (B.A.S.A) or the British Association for Shooting & Conservation (B.A.S.C)

These are currently the main two, representing Airgun Shooters within their ranks along with other sport shooters.

I'd also like to mention and give credit to the Airgun Education and Training Organisation (A.E.T.O) for the good work they do in educating and training people as to safe shooting practice in relation to the use of all airguns.

Farewell and Thanks

So there you have it – *Total Airguns*. I hope you've enjoyed it, and I'm sure – well, I most certainly hope – that you've found something here to enhance your shooting, allow you to try a new hunting technique, or just encourage you to go out and enjoy the sport. Incidentally, you'll notice that although I've made reference to the demanding sport of F.T (Field Target) shooting, there's been no section here devoted specifically to that discipline, because this book is primarily concerned with the use of air rifles for hunting and control of small pests. That's certainly not to imply that F.T. isn't worthy of very serious consideration, and for those who participate they now have the opportunity to shoot in H.F.T (Hunter Field Target) events. These are competitions that challenge the shooter to complete a set course in simulated hunting conditions, at targets of appropriate size and shape. These H.F.T. events may or may not be the way forward for target shooting, but anything that attracts people into the correct and skilled use of air rifles is beneficial. In particular, H.F.T. has a hunting 'slant', which is very useful to those who will go on from there to the pursuit of live quarry in the field. I have great respect for dedicated and skilled F.T. shooters, because many techniques, especially pertaining to gun handling, have been adapted from target shooting to be of great use in the hunting field.

On reflection, after writing this book, I've come to realise just how far I've progressed in my own shooting career, and also how much more there is to learn, and how much further there may be to go. Indeed, you really never stop learning, and that's particularly true of sport shooting, especially the hunting of wild quarry that lives by its wits.

I'd like to say that the writing of this book was a total pleasure, and in part it has been. But it's also been one of the most difficult projects I've ever undertaken. It's been very stressful, time-consuming, and felt at times like a journey I'd never complete. So I'd like to thank all those who have encouraged and helped me along the way.

Now this book really is at an end, so I'll sign off by saying this: respect the countryside, respect the people you shoot with, the land you shoot on and especially those kind enough to let you do so. And no matter what the situation – indoors or outdoors, 4 x 4-ing, ambush shooting or stalking – shoot well, shoot wisely and most of all shoot safely!

Before I express my thanks to all those who have helped and encouraged me in so many ways, I'd first like to offer an extra special 'No Thanks' to certain elements of The System, and those who tried to pull me down, hassle, stress, annoy or hinder me in any way. You know who you are. But it hasn't worked, has it?

More positively, I'd like to thank the following, whose names appear in no particular order (besides bribery!):

Personal thanks to Pat Farey, Colin McKelvie, Andrew Johnston and all at Quiller Publishing, Tony Wall, Peter Moore, Glynn, Chris, Richard A, Howard, Terry Almond and Dave Mills (AETO).

My gratitude to James Marchington, for that first ever acceptance slip for a magazine article.

To Richard North, Tim and all at T & J. J McAvoy Gunsmiths, Target Sports of Bolton, Sandwell Field Sports, Jan and all at AirgunSport, John Bowkett, Paul and Donna at Realtree Outdoors Europe

Ltd; and to all magazines and their editors, who not only have time for my scribblings and witterings but also give support to the sport and trade. If I've forgotten to list anyone who deserves a mention, all I can do is apologise most sincerely. Blame it on too much – er, Rock 'n' Roll.

Acknowledgements:
Photos by Pete Wadeson and Glynn Eatock. Additional photography by Chris Aldred.
Basic Graphics – Julian Marsh, Debbie Harley.

Gun Companies:
Air Arms, BSA Guns (UK), Daystate, Falcon, Logun, Theoben Ltd, Webley & Scott Ltd, Venom, Weihrauch (Hull Cartridge Co).

Shooting Accessories & Clothing:
AirgunSport, Attleborough Accessories, Cluson Engineering Limited, Deben Group Industries Ltd, Edgar Brothers, Garlands, Gerber, HydroGraphics, John Rothery (Bisley Shooting Products), Napier of London, Soviet Bazaar, Starlight NV Ltd, The Shark Group

Index